SHAKESPEARE SURVEY

ADVISORY BOARD

SHAKESPEARE SURVEY

AN ANNUAL SURVEY OF

SHAKESPEARE STUDIES AND PRODUCTION

43

EDITED BY

STANLEY WELLS

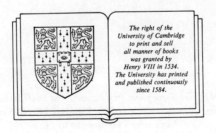

*The right of the
University of Cambridge
to print and sell
all manner of books
was granted by
Henry VIII in 1534.
The University has printed
and published continuously
since 1584.*

CAMBRIDGE UNIVERSITY PRESS

CAMBRIDGE

NEW YORK   PORT CHESTER   MELBOURNE   SYDNEY

Published by the Press Syndicate of the University of Cambridge
The Pitt Building, Trumpington Street, Cambridge CB2 1RP
40 West 20th Street, New York, NY 10011, USA
10 Stamford Road, Oakleigh, Melbourne 3166, Australia

First published 1991

Printed in Great Britain at the University Press, Cambridge

British Library cataloguing in publication data

Shakespeare survey: an annual survey of
Shakespeare studies and production. – 43:
[*The Tempest* and after].
1. Drama in English. Shakespeare, William –
Critical studies – Serials
822'.3'3

Library of Congress catalogue card number: 49–1639

ISBN 0 521 39529 1 hardback

Shakespeare Survey was first published in 1948. Its first
eighteen volumes were edited by Allardyce Nicoll. Kenneth
Muir edited volumes 19 to 33.

EDITOR'S NOTE

Volume 44 of *Shakespeare Survey*, which will be at press by the time this volume appears, will focus on 'Politics and Shakespeare' and will include papers from the 1990 International Shakespeare Conference; Volume 45 will have as its theme '*Hamlet* and Its Afterlife'. Topics for Volume 45 may include the afterlife of *Hamlet* in production, adaptation, and influence up to our own time.

Submissions should be addressed to the Editor at The Shakespeare Institute, Church Street, Stratford-upon-Avon, Warwickshire CV37 6HP, to arrive at the latest by 1 September 1991 for Volume 45. Pressures on space are heavy; many articles are considered before the deadline, so those that arrive earlier stand a better chance of acceptance. Please either enclose return postage (overseas, in International Reply coupons) or send a copy you do not wish to have returned. A style sheet is available on request. All articles submitted are read by the Editor and at least one member of the Editorial Board, whose indispensable assistance the Editor gratefully acknowledges.

Unless otherwise indicated, Shakespeare quotations and references are keyed to the modern-spelling Complete Oxford Shakespeare (1986).

With this volume Peter Holland succeeds the Editor as reviewer of theatre productions, and Henry Woudhuysen takes over as reviewer of Editions and Textual Studies from MacDonald P. Jackson, to whom we are grateful for a long period of service.

In attempting to survey the ever-increasing bulk of Shakespeare publications our reviewers inevitably have to exercise some selection. Review copies of books should be addressed to the Editor, as above. We are pleased to receive offprints of articles which help to draw our reviewers' attention to relevant material.

S.W.W.

CONTRIBUTORS

John H. Astington, *University of Toronto*
James Black, *University of Calgary*
Michael Dobson, *Indiana University*
Richard Dutton, *University of Lancaster*
Inga-Stina Ewbank, *University of Leeds*
R. A. Foakes, *University of California, Los Angeles*
Elena Glazov-Corrigan, *University of Saskatchewan*
Richard Hillman, *York University, New York*
Macdonald P. Jackson, *University of Auckland*
Stephan Kukowski, *London*
Russ McDonald, *University of Rochester*
Lois Potter, *University of Leicester*
N. Rathbone, *Birmingham Shakespeare Library*
Peter L. Rudnytsky, *Janus Pannonius University, Hungary*
Martin Scofield, *University of Kent*
Camille Wells Slights, *University of Saskatchewan*
Kurt Tetzeli Von Rosador, *University of Münster*
Stanley Wells, *The Shakespeare Institute, University of Birmingham*
Matthew H. Wikander, *University of Toledo*
R. S. White, *University of Western Australia*

CONTENTS

vii

ILLUSTRATIONS

ILLUSTRATIONS

THE POWER OF MAGIC: FROM *ENDIMION* TO *THE TEMPEST*

KURT TETZELI VON ROSADOR

With almost Pinteresque insistence *The Tempest* dramatizes conflicts of dominance and subservience. 'Where's the master?' (1.1.9–10)[1] – this is the question the first scene raises. With Prospero's decision to present himself as he was, 'sometime Milan' (5.1.86), the last act seems to provide an answer. These conflicts *The Tempest* embodies variedly and invariably in the relationships of father and child, master and servant, ruler and subject. Even young love is discussed in terms of freedom and bondage (3.1.88–9) and is objectively, if playfully, correlated with the checkings and matings of rival kings and queens. Small wonder that recent criticism has considered *The Tempest* first and foremost as a political play, emphasizing its patriarchal structures[2] or lodging it within ever-widening contexts of colonial discourses.[3] That the play deals with problems of power, of authority, and their representation, these studies have made abundantly and convincingly clear. They have laid bare many of the material and ideological assumptions and contexts within which the play's meanings unfold.

One of these contexts, however, has so far been strangely neglected: the power of magic. Reasons for this neglect may be sought among the numerous essentialist and functionalist (mis)readings the play's magic has been accorded in the past.[4] Being axiomatically aware that the pursuit of essences and inner-textual functions is, to put it politely, an unprofitable one, the cultural materialist, new historicist or deconstructionist critic searches –

[1] All quotations from Shakespeare's works are taken from *The Riverside Shakespeare*, ed. G. Blakemore Evans (Boston, 1974).

[2] See, for instance, David Sundelson, 'So Rare a Wonder'd Father: Prospero's *Tempest*', in *Representing Shakespeare: New Psychoanalytic Essays*, ed. Murray M. Schwartz and Coppélia Kahn (Baltimore, 1980), pp. 33–53; Marilyn L. Williamson, *The Patriarchy of Shakespeare's Comedies* (Detroit, 1986), chap. III.

[3] For a listing of the more important older studies see Charles Frey, '*The Tempest* and the New World', *Shakespeare Quarterly*, 30 (1979), 31, n. 10. Among the more recent essays Trevor R. Griffiths's may be singled out for its detailed history of images of Caliban on the nineteenth- and twentieth-century stages: '"This Island's mine": Caliban and Colonialism', *Yearbook of English Studies*, 13 (1983), 159–80. See also the stimulating discussions by Francis Barker and Peter Hulme, 'Nymphs and Reapers Heavily Vanish: the Discursive Con-texts of *The Tempest*', in *Alternative Shakespeares*, ed. John Drakakis (London, 1985), pp. 191–205, 235–7, and Paul Brown, '"This thing of darkness I acknowledge mine": *The Tempest* and the Discourse of Colonialism', in *Political Shakespeare: New Essays in Cultural Materialism*, ed. Jonathan Dollimore and Alan Sinfield (Manchester, 1985), pp. 48–71.

[4] This is an approach I have myself been – unashamedly – guilty of in *Magie im elisabethanischen Drama* (Braunschweig, 1970). Perceptive and logically stringent recent accounts of the dubiousness of Prospero's art have been provided by D'Orsay W. Pearson, '"Unless I Be Reliev'd by Prayer": *The Tempest* in Perspective', *Shakespeare Studies*, 7 (1974), 253–82, and Margreta de Grazia, '*The Tempest*: Gratuitous Movement or Action Without Kibes and Pinches', *Shakespeare Studies*, 14 (1981), 249–65. The whitewashing of Prospero has been taken furthest by Barbara Howard Traister, *Heavenly Necromancers: The Magician in English Renaissance Drama* (Columbia, 1984), pp. 125–49. Barbara A. Mowat has splendidly summarized and extended the gallery of

not without success – among subjects promising a richer and surer return: the other, the body, gender, class, race. He or she may have turned aside too soon. For the study of magic repays attention beyond the subtle distinctions of its essence. It is the contention of this paper that magic occupies a prominent place within the most momentous post-Reformation struggle, centring, in Stephen Greenblatt's words, on 'the definition of the sacred, a definition that directly involved secular as well as religious institutions';[5] that the Elizabethan plays on magic of the late eighties and early nineties reflect, and intervene in, this struggle; and that *The Tempest*, especially the uneasy cohabitation and sequence of Prospero's magical and ducal powers, the donning and doffing of the magical robe, and the abjuration of magic, must be placed within this context.

The fundamental questions informing this post-Reformation struggle have been succinctly formulated by Greenblatt: 'What is the sacred? Who defines and polices its boundaries? How can society distinguish between legitimate and illegitimate claims to sacred authority?'[6] Answers are variously provided by the main parties engaged in this struggle, which is a three-cornered affair between the institutions and ideologies of religion, magic, and the monarchy (with science making ready to enter the lists[7]). Given the ideological and political conditions of the sixteenth century – above all the schism of the Reformation – it is obvious that no consensual solution was envisaged. Nor was such a solution to be left to the evolutionary processes of history. The extreme violence of the struggle, however, was no doubt due to the fact that all parties engaged saw their authority as derived from the same source: religion, magic, and the monarchy all claim charismatic investiture. What characterizes charismatic authority is, according to Max Weber's important analysis, its extraordinariness, its transcendental legitimation. Hence it can demand the unconditional subordination of its followers and the strictest adherence to its doctrines. It is thus absolutist in character, suffering no rival. It is, however, not granted once and for all but is under permanent obligation to prove itself. This it must do by continuously trailing clouds of glory, that is, by sustaining its followers both materially and ideologically. The failure to do so, be it because of the ruler's weakening or his neglect of government, results inevitably in the fading and vanishing of charismatic authority.[8]

It is within such a general context that the half-latent, half-overt rivalry between the royal magic of the monarchy and the magician's art and its representation in Elizabethan times and drama must be seen.[9] This was a conflict which rarely flared into the open, as it did in the case of the North Berwick witches, who in 1591, as the

---

Prospero's literary and historical prototypes in 'Prospero, Agrippa, and Hocus Pocus', *English Literary Renaissance*, 11 (1981), 281–303.

[5] 'Shakespeare and the Exorcists', in its most recent revision in *Shakespearean Negotiations: The Circulation of Social Energy in Renaissance England* (Oxford, 1988), p. 95.

[6] Ibid., p. 96.

[7] For the relation between magic and science and the nature of scientific thinking in the sixteenth century, see *Occult and Scientific Mentalities in the Renaissance*, ed. Brian Vickers (Cambridge, 1984).

[8] *Wirtschaft und Gesellschaft: Grundriss der verstehenden Soziologie*, ed. Johannes Winckelmann (Tübingen, 1972), pp. 654–87. For a brief account and discussion of Weber's ideas see Wolfgang Schluchter, *Die Entwicklung des okzidentalen Rationalismus: Eine Analyse von Max Webers Gesellschaftsgeschichte* (Tübingen, 1979).

[9] The discussion of the representation of the conflict between religion and magic in Elizabethan drama must be left to some future date. Some of the ideological and social implications have been studied usefully and from widely differing angles by D. P. Walker, *Spiritual and Demonic Magic from Ficino to Campanella* (London, 1958), *passim*; Keith Thomas, *Religion and the Decline of Magic: Studies in Popular Beliefs in Sixteenth and Seventeenth Century England* (London, 1971), pp. 258–78 *et passim*; Stephen Greenblatt, 'Invisible Bullets', most recently in *Shakespearean Negotiations*, pp. 21–65. See also the wide-ranging survey by Michael MacDonald, 'Science, Magic, and Folklore', in *William Shakespeare: His World. His Work. His Influence*, ed. John F. Andrews (New York, 1985), I, 175–94.

title-page of the account of their evil doings has it, 'pretended to bewitch and drowne his Maiestie in the Sea comming from Denmarke'.[10] Quite understandably, James paid considerable personal attention to the matter, attending and guiding the judicial proceedings. But even in this case, or the similar instances of sticking pins into royal images known to have occurred in Elizabeth's time, it is never the witch or the magician who thinks worldly power within reach.[11] Quite the contrary: to whichever of the numerous varieties of the species the adepts of the occult may belong, whether their art can be described as ceremonial, natural or demonic, as white or black or rough, their aspirations stop far short of desiring office or rule. Agrippa's definition of his art may serve as an example:

Magick is a faculty of wonderfull vertue, full of most high mysteries, containing the most profound Contemplation of most secret things, together with the nature, power, quality, substance, and vertues thereof, as also the knowledge of whole nature, and it doth instruct us concerning the differing, and agreement of things amongst themselves, whence it produceth its wonderfull effects . . .[12]

Agrippa is quite obviously at pains to keep within the bounds of a Neoplatonic bettering of the spirit through contemplation and not to encroach on the realm of the active political life. Similar restrictions can be found in the works of all other practitioners of the occult arts. The mastery of nature and of the world of spirit(s) or the small-scale power over one's fellows by hurting or healing is deemed sufficient by all of them.

Still, if, in George Eliot's words, 'the rude mind with difficulty associates the ideas of power and benignity', more difficulties necessarily arise even for sophisticated minds from the simultaneous existence and attractions of two charismatic powers. For the monarchy did not, could not, refrain from invading magic's proper realm. How could it, resting at least partially on the same ground? One of its central tenets, the myth of the king's or the queen's

two bodies, is quite obviously closely allied to magical thinking.[13] The similarity of claims is furthermore strikingly illustrated by that glorious piece of royal magic, touching for the evil, which both Elizabeth and James used signally to boost their somewhat doubtful legitimacy. This is indeed what the title of William Tooker's defence of Elizabeth's royal healing power of 1597 calls it, *Charisma Sive Donum Sanationis*. And it is both magical and royal charisma.[14] The process of appropriating magical authority in order to prop and extend the crown's power accelerated dramatically with James's accession to the throne.[15] Francis Bacon, in his dedication to *The Advancement of Learning*, could then apply the name of the arch-magician to the king himself: 'your Majesty standeth invested of that triplicity which in great veneration was ascribed to the ancient Hermes',[16] a triplicity comprising ruler, priest, and magician. And in his masque *Oberon*,

---

10 *Newes from Scotland* (London, 1591).

11 The only such claim known to me comes from a severe critic of magical practices and pretensions. In *The French Academie* (London, 1586), Pierre de La Primaudaye writes: '(as histories teach vs) some haue been so wretched and miserable, as to giue themselues to the Art of Necromancie, and to contract with the deuill, that they might come to soueraigne power and authoritie' (p. 230, misnumbered 239).

12 *Three Books of Occult Philosophy* (London, 1651), pp. 2–3.

13 See the classical study of Ernst H. Kantorowicz, *The King's Two Bodies: A Study in Mediaeval Political Theology* (Princeton, 1957), and Marie Axton, *The Queen's Two Bodies: Drama and the Elizabethan Succession* (London, 1977).

14 For the political use of touching, see Thomas, *Religion and the Decline of Magic*, pp. 192–8; for its status within occult thinking Stuart Clark, 'The Scientific Status of Demonology', in *Occult and Scientific Mentalities*, ed. Vickers, p. 358.

15 The problem is very speculatively treated by Douglas Brooks-Davies, *The Mercurian Monarch: Magical Politics from Spenser to Pope* (Manchester, 1983); for a general view of James's literary politics see Jonathan Goldberg, *James I and the Politics of Literature: Jonson, Shakespeare, Donne, and Their Contemporaries* (Baltimore, 1983).

16 Ed. William A. Armstrong (London, 1975), p. 51.

Ben Jonson invested James's 'True maiestie' with 'sole power, and magick'.[17]

That the author of the *Daemonologie* was pleased by such identifications with royal magicians or the ascriptions of magical power to himself may seem strange. It becomes less strange if one realizes that James's attitude towards magic and witchcraft cannot be summed up under the heading of inquisitorial anxiety. He himself chose Solomon as the model of the perfect ruler and identified with him, Solomon, whose reputation rested not only on his wisdom but also on his magical skill and who was known to be the author of *Claviculae Salomonis*, a textbook for magicians.[18] Moreover, the process of appropriating magical authority by the monarchy was based on, and had been preceded by, strategies for containing the magician's power within fairly narrow limits. These limits were set and policed by the secular powers. For their two main strategies we can turn to king's evidence. The devil, writes James,

will make his schollers to creepe in credite with Princes, by fore-telling them manie great thinges; parte true, parte false: ... And he will also make them to please Princes, by faire banquets and daintie dishes, carryed in short space fra the farthest part of the worlde.[19]

This is, on the surface, a warning against the slyness of the devil in tempting and corrupting the ruler with the help of his followers, who try to insinuate themselves into the prince's confidence. But the description of the devil's and magician's power is also one of its severe limitations. Just as in real life Elizabeth made use of John Dee, but kept him at more than arm's length, so James very efficiently reduced the powers of the occult practitioners to those of courtly careerists and masters of revels serving the prince and never aspiring to the royal office themselves. The question of power was transformed into and contained within one of courtly behaviour and moral pragmatics.

The second strategy is even more drastic and efficient. It not only limits magical power to

certain functions, it annihilates it altogether. If, writes James, formulating a commonplace of demonological literature, magicians are apprehended

by the lawfull Magistrate, vpon the iust respectes of their guiltinesse in that craft, their power is then no greater then before that euer they medled with their master. For where God beginnes iustlie to strike by his lawfull Lieutennentes, it is not in the Deuilles power to defraude or bereaue him of the office, or effect of his powerfull and reuenging Scepter.[20]

In other words: the king and the magistrate, being God's representatives on earth, the possessors of royal charisma, cannot be touched by devilish or magical power. Royalty is thus enabled to appropriate whatever prestige attaches to its rival. Most important: by overcoming the powers of magic or by not being touched by them, the monarch proves him- or herself legitimate and truly charismatic.

From the viewpoint of the monarchy, the drama of royal versus magical magic is thus virtually one of foregone conclusion – with one important reservation: magical power vanishes only, as James repeatedly insists, in the presence of the lawful king, that is, if confronted with and seized by an unstained royal charisma. Yet neither Elizabeth nor James was the unquestioned possessor thereof, neither of them having a claim to the throne based on the single unquestionable charismatic legitimation, blood –

[17] In *Ben Jonson*, ed. Percy and Evelyn Simpson (Oxford, 1941), VII, lines 330–1.

[18] For a wide-ranging survey of Renaissance images of Solomon see Michael Hattaway, 'Paradoxes of Solomon: Learning in the English Renaissance', *Journal of the History of Ideas*, 29 (1968), 499–530.

[19] *Daemonologie in Forme of a Dialogue* (Edinburgh, 1597), p. 22. For an excellent account of James's changing views on witchcraft and the highly political dialectics of demonism and kingship see Stuart Clark, 'King James's *Daemonologie*: Witchcraft and Kingship', in *The Damned Art: Essays in the Literature of Witchcraft*, ed. Sydney Anglo (London, 1977), pp. 156–81, esp. pp. 166–7.

[20] *Daemonologie*, p. 51.

that is, on direct lineal descent. The rise and popularity of plays on magic and witchcraft just before 1590 may thus be of some political significance. These are the years of the papal Bull of Excommunication, of Mary Stuart's bid for power, of the Babington Plot, of the Armada – all of them founded on the denial of Elizabeth's legitimacy, all of them inspired by the rival charisma of papal magic, by 'Poperie the nurse of Witch-craft'.[21] It would be a matter of some surprise if Elizabethan drama, always ready to seize on such topicalities, if Shakespeare, no despiser of well-considered literary trifles, were not to deal with a problem so obviously and inherently dramatic. The dramatic presentation of such general topicality of theme or problem is, however, never attempted by unilinear identification of real persons with the *dramatis personae*. It works by means of displacement, of allegorizing, of refraction – all of them techniques which tempt the latter-day reader into totalizing allegorical interpretations.[22]

John Lyly's *Endimion* is a case in point. Written and produced in the second half of the 1580s, it is in all likelihood the first Elizabethan play to stage magic locked in a struggle with monarchical power.[23] To do so, it employs those strategies James and the literature of demonology also use, strategies of displacement, containment, and annihilation. First, for purposes of distancing, the ground of the conflict is shifted to the realm of the dramatically traditional: the play is, in G. K. Hunter's words, 'a fairly obvious case of adapting the feelings of love to shadow forth the complex of fear, ambition, admiration that real courtiers felt about their real sovereign'.[24] Within the traditional love-theme the plotting and the structural arrangement in *Endimion* guarantee the subordination of Dipsas's magic to Cynthia's authority. For Dipsas is brought into the play by, and as the instrument of, Tellus, the figure intended to represent Cynthia's rival. Hence, right from the beginning Dipsas's merely instrumental character

and subordinate position in the play's hierarchy are assured.

To the inferiority of her position Dipsas herself points with her boasts of power, grandiose as these may sound:

I can darken the Sunne by my skil, and remooue the Moone out of her course; I can restore youth to the aged, and make hils without bottoms; there is nothing that I can not doe... (1.4.20–3)[25]

World-encompassing aspiration is what seems to characterize Dipsas's magical powers. Their potential threat is thrown into relief by the myth underlying them, by the model quoted: Ovid's Medea. But Dipsas's boast is also at once much reduced and limited by her admission that 'there is nothing that I can not doe, but that onely which you would haue me doe; and therin I differ from the Gods' (22–4). The strategy is exemplary: hubristic, boastful speeches become stock-features of all Elizabethan plays on magic. But the limitless aspirations, the clamorous protestations of power by the practitioners of the occult, are always ironically negatived either by the magician's own admission of limitation and failure (as in *Endimion*) or by the acting out of the discrepancy between the vastness of the design and the

---

21 Thomas Cooper, *The Mystery of Witchcraft* (London, 1617), p. 120. The identification of the Pope and the Catholic religion with magical evil is a commonplace in Elizabethan literature, Sylvester II, Gregor VI and VII, and Alexander VI figuring as the most prominent examples; see, for instance, Thomas Beard, *The Theatre of Gods Iudgements* (London, 1597), pp. 122–3.

22 See the circumspect investigation of David Bevington, *Tudor Drama and Politics: A Critical Approach to Topical Meaning* (Cambridge, Mass., 1968).

23 Earlier representations, such as those in *Clyomon and Clamydes* or *The Rare Triumphs of Love and Fortune*, belong to the romance tradition which deals with the problem of rival authorities, if at all, at some further removes.

24 *John Lyly. The Humanist as Courtier* (London, 1962), p. 184.

25 All quotations from *Endimion* are taken from *The Complete Works of John Lyly*, ed. R. Warwick Bond (Oxford, 1902), III.

pettiness of its realization (as in *Doctor Faustus* or, indeed, *The Tempest*).

However, such seems to have been the threat of magic that Lyly does not stop short here. By richly facetting his theme and antithetically structuring the whole play, Lyly creates Cynthia and Dipsas as polar opposites in their attitudes to love, their functions in the play, and the powers they wield. To the restricted power of Dipsas, Cynthia is able to oppose a 'Maiestie ... al the world knoweth and wondereth at' (2.3.16–17) and a government nothing short of the 'miraculous' (2.1.38). For Cynthia's power is the true charismatic one. It is transcendentally legitimized and under heaven's protection. In Cynthia's own words addressed to Dipsas in the scene of judgement at the end of the play:

Thou hast threatned to turne my course awry, and alter by thy damnable Arte the gouernment that I now possesse by the eternall Gods. But knowe thou *Dipsas*, and let all the Enchaunters knowe, that *Cynthia*, beeing placed for light on earth, is also protected by the powers of heauen.   (5.3.24–8)

Through the lady's overmuch protestings and sudden shift into obtrusive preaching ('and let all the Enchaunters knowe') Elizabeth's own voice insisting on her legitimacy and the charismatic nature of her authority may be heard. By defeating Dipsas's magic, Cynthia-Elizabeth triumphantly vindicates her own authority and right of position. Under such circumstances the annihilation of the rival charisma becomes a necessity and a matter of course. It is an annihilation managed by reformation, not by punishment or destruction – the latter are but the ungentle means of persuasion (5.3.258–61). In the prestabilized harmony of Lyly's courtly view, dramatic antithesis, the presentation of alternatives, initially so richly set out, has after all no place in the play. It is dissolved into the unfolding of the sovereign's power.[26] The questioning dramatist has ceded his place and task to the complimenting courtier.[27]

This is certainly not a part which any reader ever ascribed to Christopher Marlowe. Yet despite the common emphases on the rebel-

liousness of Marlowe's protagonists, their blaspheming or 'masochistic transgression',[28] Una Ellis-Fermor's apolitical view of *Doctor Faustus* still prevails today. For her, 'the scene is set in no spot upon the physical earth, but in the limitless regions of the mind, and the battle is fought, not for kingdoms or crowns, but upon the questions of man's ultimate fate'.[29] Consequently, Acts 3 and 4, Faustus's confrontation with Pope, Emperor and Duke, are relegated to the realm of crude popular entertainment or just tolerated within a scheme of ironic reversals. Hence, the political dimension of these scenes has gone unnoticed, a dimension in which magic is deeply implicated.

The aggressive potential of Faustus's aims becomes apparent if one realizes that he is the only magician in Elizabethan drama who reaches for the sweet fruition of an earthly crown. Having dismissed all academic disciplines as stale, flat, and unprofitable, Faustus at once formulates a vision of power:

O what a world of profite and delight,
Of power, of honour, and omnipotence,
Is promised to the Studious Artizan?
All things that moue betweene the quiet Poles
Shall be at my command: Emperors and Kings,
Are but obey'd in their seuerall Prouinces:
But his dominion that exceeds in this,
Stretcheth as farre as doth the mind of man:
                                        (80–7)[30]

---

[26] See also Peter Saccio, 'The Oddity of Lyly's *Endimion*', in *The Elizabethan Theatre V*, ed. G. R. Hibbard (London, 1975), pp. 92–111, esp. p. 94.

[27] Thus *Endimion* is indeed in Joel B. Altman's fine phrase for all of Lyly's plays an 'emasculated "problem play"'; see his *The Tudor Play of Mind: Rhetorical Inquiry and the Development of Elizabethan Drama* (Berkeley, 1978), p. 197.

[28] The phrase is Jonathan Dollimore's in *Radical Tragedy: Religion, Ideology and Power in the Drama of Shakespeare and his Contemporaries* (Brighton, 1984), p. 114.

[29] *Christopher Marlowe* (London, 1927), p. 87.

[30] All quotations from the play are taken from *Doctor Faustus 1604–1616. Parallel Texts*, ed. W. W. Greg (Oxford, 1950). It is the B-version which is interpreted here.

Read exclusively within the psychomachia tradition or against Pico's oration on the dignity of man, this speech can be taken – as it frequently has been – to express nothing but Faustus's spiritual aspiration, the glorification of the limitless reach of man's mind. The insistent use of the vocabulary of power, however, undercuts such a reading: 'power', 'omnipotence', 'command', 'dominion' define Faustus's aspiration in terms of a barely disguised will to power, an absolute power at that. For when Faustus repeats his claim a little later he specifies it beyond the possibility of a spiritualizing misinterpretation:

I'le be great Emperour of the world,
And make a bridge, through the mouing Aire,
To passe the Ocean: with a band of men
I'le ioyne the Hils that bind the *Affrick* shore,
And make that Country, continent to *Spaine*,
And both contributary to my Crowne.
The Emperour shall not liue, but by my leaue,
Nor any Potentate of *Germany*.   (329–36)

Nowhere in Elizabethan drama does any magician advance larger claims or is the threat to royal authority more decidedly expressed. Such a threat must, if at all possible, be unambiguously and rigorously countered. Marlowe sets out to do so by suggesting that the claims advanced by his hero are nothing but the products of a diabolically corrupted imagination. Since all of Faustus's visions of power, riches and voluptuousness follow immediately upon devilish temptations, they must be understood to be their results. They are thus emptied of reality and appear as fantasizings, inordinate in their scope, deeply ambivalent in their exhilarating upward thrust.[31] Elizabethan spectators acquainted with the methods of diabolical suggestion would be aware that such visions are totally divorced from any grounding in reality. The imaginatively imaginary nature of such claims is ocularly demonstrated by Faustus's encounters with the worldly powers, the Emperor and the Duke of Vanholt. During these scenes we hear nothing of Faustus's ruling ambition. Faced with established power, the

threat of magic vanishes just as James postulates. What we see is a Faustus eagerly swallowing morsels of royal flattery and abjectly prostrating himself and his vaunted powers before the superiority of royalty:

These gracious words, most royall *Carolus*,
Shall make poore *Faustus* to his vtmost power,
Both loue and serue the Germane Emperour,

(1250–2)

By emptying out magic's reality, that is, by turning it into merely verbal magic, and by subordinating it to the only true magic, royal charisma, Faustus's licentious fantasizings of absolute power are contained. Faustus's behaviour at the papal court, his abduction of Bruno, is no proof to the contrary. For the encounter of Faustus and the Pope is not one of two charismas, magic and religion, but of two different versions of the same, magic. The doctrine of transubstantiation and the workings of exorcisms are sufficient proof to the Protestant mind of the magical character of Roman-Catholicism. For William Perkins, listing the abominations of popery, the

fourth sinne is Magicke, sorcerie, or witchcraft, in the consecration of the host in which they make their Breadengod: in exorcismes ouer holy bread, holy water, and salt; in the casting out or driuing away of deuills, by the signe of the crosse, by solemne coniurations, by holy water, by the ringing of bells, by lighting tapers, by reliques, and such like. For these things haue not their supposed force, either by creation, or by any institution of God in his holy word: and therefore if any thing be done by them, it is from the secret operation of the deuill himselfe.

In short, 'if a man will but take a view of all poperie, he shall easily see, that the most part is meere Magique'.[32] The attempted exorcism of

---

[31] See my '"Supernatural soliciting": Temptation and Imagination in *Doctor Faustus* and *Macbeth*', in *Shakespeare and his Contemporaries*, ed. E. A. J. Honigmann (Manchester, 1986), pp. 42–59.

[32] *The Works* (Cambridge, 1603), pp. 744, 36.

Faustus by the priests with the help of 'Bell, Booke, and Candle' (1111) clearly defines papal power as superstitiously magical. The confrontation at the papal court must therefore be regarded as one of those contests of rival magicians so popular in the drama of the 1590s. In this contest Faustus comes out best. And since his power is effectively contained by royal authority, royal authority comes out even better. In Marlowe's grim vision, the stretching out of the mind of man is mere fantasizing, fit for the enclosed spaces of the scholar's study or the magician's circle (or the artist's little room),[33] while the reality principle, embodied by the wielders of worldly power, bears absolute sway over the rest of the world.

In Shakespeare's histories, the power of magic is similarly restricted. Two of the three plays which treat magic, *2 Henry VI* and *1 Henry IV*, virtually limit its presentation to one scene. Faint praise, condescension or total neglect has consequently been the critical fate of these scenes.[34] But there are better reasons than those of popular entertainment and ornamental function for the episodic treatment of magic in these histories, if magic is once again placed within the post-Reformation conflict of rival charismas. In a play about English history, the possessor of magical power is likely to confront the rival pretender to charismatic authority more or less directly. Displacement by theme (*Endimion*) or space (*Doctor Faustus*) is thus not available to the dramatist as a strategy to contain the claims of magic. They must be marginalized and delimited by different means. Episodic treatment, a way of formally and quantitatively containing magic, is one of them, necessitated by the choice of genre.

In *1 Henry VI*, however, the question of the power of magic is raised right in the first scene, never to be totally dropped throughout the play.[35] Exeter seems to interrupt the formal lament for the dead Henry V with a question tonally somewhat out of place, an inquiry into the causes of the king's death:

Or shall we think the subtile-witted French
Conjurers and sorcerers, that, afraid of him,
By magic verses have contriv'd his end? (1.1.25–7)

This is no merely rhetorical question.[36] To be killed by magical art would plainly and posthumously negate both the king's legitimacy and authority, since it is of the essence of royal charisma that magic cannot touch it. Exeter's question raises a highly problematic issue: the legitimacy of Lancastrian rule in general and of Henry V – and by indirection Henry VI – in particular. It is not a question ever completely lost sight of in either of the tetralogies, insinuating itself into such a seemingly harmless compliment as the one about the 'witchcraft' in the French Princess's lips in *Henry V* (5.2.275–6) or emerging in Henry's troubled ruminations on the eve of the battle of Agincourt: 'Not to-day, O Lord...' (4.1.292–305). Yet in *1 Henry VI* Exeter's question seems to be quickly answered by what amounts to a quintessential definition of the legitimacy of royal rule: 'He was a king blest of the King of kings.' (1.1.28)

It is not only the form of the answer, the insistent repetition of one word, turning on itself and becoming self-legitimating, which conjures up ghosts of special pleading. Though verbally answered, Exeter's question is

---

[33] For a discussion of the play in terms of closure see Marjorie Garber, '"Infinite Riches in a Little Room": Closure and Enclosure in Marlowe', in *Two Renaissance Mythmakers: Christopher Marlowe and Ben Jonson*, ed. Alvin Kernan (Baltimore, 1977), pp. 3–21.

[34] For a perceptive essay see S. P. Zitner, 'Staging the Occult in *1 Henry IV*', in *Mirror up to Shakespeare: Essays in Honour of G. R. Hibbard*, ed. J. C. Gray (Toronto, 1984), pp. 138–48.

[35] The theme of witchcraft in *1 Henry VI* has been influentially treated by E. M. W. Tillyard, *Shakespeare's History Plays* (London, 1944), esp. pp. 163–8. Within Tillyard's problematic view of the providential course of English history, the play demonstrates 'the testing of England ... by French witchcraft' (p. 163). The political dimension of witchcraft or of authority is not taken into account.

[36] For such a view see A. L. French, 'Joan of Arc and *Henry VI*', *English Studies*, 49 (1968), 425–9.

variously embodied and thus posed again in the course of the first two acts. Henry V being dead, there is no one to take his place authoritatively. The heir is conspicuous both for his youth, evoking the Preacher's woeful warning (x, 16), and his absence: he makes his entry only in Act 3, Scene 1. During his absence almost every scene parades a different claim to power: that of the Church in the person of Winchester, that of the Dauphin and the French, that of Richard Plantagenet, who augments his own with that of the Earl of Mortimer and, most important and most threatening, that of Joan la Pucelle.

Joan is introduced as a truly charismatic figure, a 'holy maid', the conveyor of 'a vision sent to her from heaven' (1.2.51–2), whose 'profession's sacred from above' (1.2.114). This is the French view. She is also seen as 'a witch' (1.5.6,21), the embodiment of the forces of hell (1.5.9). This is the English view. The double vision is not used by Shakespeare to dramatize the mutual exclusiveness of partisan views of history or to point ironically to the delusive forces of the process of name-calling. Instead, with all his positive and positively chauvinistic capability, Shakespeare loads the dice against Joan and the French. The essence of Joan's mission and the basis of French rule are unambiguously, if half-retrospectively, identified, when the fiends desert Joan (5.3). In a sense, magic is thus once again episodically contained, the witch's power being only affirmed in departing. It is more efficiently contained by the portrayal of Joan as both Pucelle and pussel, Maid and whore, and the many ironies directed at her.[37] The potentially charismatic figure is reduced to the human, all-too-human by the *double entendres* of the French courtiers (1.2.119–23; 2.1.67–9) and finally exiled into the realm of the despicable by her frantic attempts to save her life (5.4).

Still, there is a lure about the presentation of magic in *1 Henry VI* beyond the crudity of Joan's portrayal. It is a lure deriving from a pervasive and nostalgic desire for charismatic

authority. This desire, however, the play demonstrates in a 'pattern of decay',[38] is tending towards the anachronistic. Royal charisma is dead and gone, it's with King Harry in the grave at the beginning of the play. Talbot, the ideal martial hero, dies in the course of it, and Joan, the possessor of demonic power, is executed at the end. The historical world is left to the intrigues of the factions, to the ambitious schemers, such as Winchester, Suffolk, and York.

What *1 Henry VI* crudely indicates, *Macbeth* richly dramatizes. Like *1 Henry VI*, *Macbeth* opens with authority and power suspended: a battle is being lost and won, in which rival kings and rebels are engaged and of which a bleeding soldier reports 'The newest state' (1.2.3); the crown is prophetically promised to a brave, gore-bespattered army-leader; to his comrade-in-arms it is prophesied that he will father kings; a successor to the crown is nominated. Thus the 'imperial theme' (1.3.129) is fully sounded at the beginning of *Macbeth*, proving the crown and royal power very volatile articles indeed, apparently only to be seized and held by force. Why this is so, the play does not present. Something may be inferred from the age of the present incumbent of the office or from the fact that he has to rely on others to fight his battles and rests his power on the

---

37 See Leo Kirschbaum, 'The Authorship of *1 Henry VI*', *Publications of the Modern Language Association*, 67 (1952), 809–22; David M. Bevington, 'The Domineering Female in *1 Henry VI*', *Shakespeare Studies*, 2 (1966), 51–8. Since the writing of this paper two articles have been published, persuasively widening our conception of Joan: Gabriele Bernhard Jackson, 'Topical Ideology: Witches, Amazons, and Shakespeare's Joan of Arc', *English Literary Renaissance*, 18 (1988), 40–65, has placed the rôles Joan acts out within the context of Elizabethan ideologies of gender, and Richard F. Hardin, 'Chronicles and Myth-making in Shakespeare's Joan of Arc', *Shakespeare Survey 42* (1990), pp. 32–5, has described her as a Girardian scapegoat.

38 The phrase is Edward I. Berry's: *Patterns of Decay: Shakespeare's Early Histories* (Charlottesville, 1975).

unsure foundation of 'absolute trust' (1.4.14).[39] Yet nothing conclusive can be drawn from such dispersed hints: *Macbeth* does not stage the conflict of powers in the socio-political terms of the tetralogies. Nor is it staged in terms of a mere conflict of conscience, of an interiorized battle of good and evil.

The power vacuum at the beginning is the thematic *donnée* of *Macbeth*. It is created and fully dramatized to allow contending powers to appear and to invade the world of the play. If royal charisma is in doubt, magical charisma may stake its claim. It does so with all the ceremonial pomp and circumstance due to magic's darkly majestic realm. This is not to say that Terry Eagleton's ingenious reading of the weird sisters as 'the heroines of the piece', 'inhabiting their own sisterly community', is totally convincing.[40] It fails to be so since such an inversion of the critical tradition is as one-dimensional in its premature finality as what it sets out to combat. Still, Eagleton's reading loosens the bonds of functionality which tie the weird sisters to Macbeth, subordinating them as catalysts to his process of corruption. It clears the way for a fresh look at the four scenes in which they appear (and which, I take it, have to be looked at as they stand, Hecate and all). Thus viewed, a world with its own language, manners, and atmosphere becomes visible. It is a world pervaded by a distinctive verbal music,[41] setting it metrically apart from blank-verse or prosaic humanity. It is a world of sense impressions, of sensuality and corporeality. And it is a world of ritualistic ceremony, possessed of its own hierarchy, structured by the potent number three and expressing itself through incantation, dance, and spectacle. Although not a vision of complete otherness, this is truly one of a rival mode of existence. Hence the display of magical power by the weird sisters quite naturally leads to that of magical authority in the person of Hecate. Whatever her textual status, Hecate's dramatic and thematic place in *Macbeth* is an assured one as the embodiment of magical charisma.

Staged thus powerfully, the threat of magic is a considerable one. It invades the world of (political) man by means of suggestion, corrupting the imagination and reason and giving rise to 'cursed thoughts' (2.1.8). To contain it efficiently, the strategies of containment must correspond to its power. Yet there is no displacement of magic through theme or space in *Macbeth*, nor is magic formally and quantitatively restricted to a single episode. The demonstration of the limits of magical power by the help of a contrasting and resisting figure such as Banquo – a technique Marlowe had employed in the Old Man scenes in *Doctor Faustus* – is singularly weak in *Macbeth*. Banquo's temptation is dramatized in a highly indirect, allusive manner, turning the contrast into one of mere implication. At the same time we watch Macbeth and his lady writhing in the grip of night's black agents and feel engulfed by an atmosphere suffused by a witchcraft celebrating 'Pale Hecat's off'rings' (2.1.52). Stronger forces must be marshalled to delimit magic's power and Shakespeare summons the strongest: royal charisma, pure and absolute. It is personified in the English king. Edward's divine kingship is strongly emphasized by the 'sanctity' that 'heaven hath given his hand' (4.3.144), by his 'heavenly gift of prophecy' and the 'sundry blessings [that] hang about his throne', all of which 'speak him full of grace' (4.3.157–9). Small wonder that the power of Hecate's magic vanishes with the appearance of Edward's royal one. The fifth act knows nothing of it.

But the fifth act knows nothing of Edward and his royal charismatic authority either. Even

---

[39] See Wilbur Sanders and Howard Jacobson, *Shakespeare's Magnanimity: Four Tragic Heroes, Their Friends and Families* (London, 1978), pp. 72–3.

[40] *William Shakespeare* (Oxford, 1986), p. 2.

[41] The weird sisters' music has been analysed by Robin Grove, 'Multiplying Villainies of Nature', in *Focus on Macbeth*, ed. John Russell Brown (London, 1982), pp. 113–39, esp. pp. 115–19.

his presentation in the fourth has been a mediated one: royal charismatic authority is never present on stage. There is, as it were, no ocular proof for it. A divinely instituted, yet unrepresented power is thus contrasted with a magically authorized one which has been exiled beyond the pale of the play's action. A strong dichotomy between magic and the monarchy is thus established, producing all those antitheses and contrasts which clearly mark *Macbeth* as a 'play of opposites'.[42] Since, however, both the representatives of magical and royal charisma, Hecate and Edward, are not direct participants in the ensuing action, since both of them are identical in being absent, an equally strong dichotomy is set up between the charismatic powers on the one side and the agents of the mundane conflict on the other. All transcending visions and alternative modes of existence belong to the charismatic powers. Consequently, the world left to Macbeth and Malcolm is emptied out. Not only Macbeth must needs feel 'cabin'd, cribb'd, confin'd' (3.4.23) and 'fall'n into the sear, the yellow leaf' (5.3.23). The whole play shrinks; a sense of claustrophobia, not of tragic catharsis, sets in.[43]

This shrinkage is most depressingly demonstrated by the transfer of power at the end of the play. In the play's last speech, Macbeth is not granted that tribute, both generous and saddening, that the waste of human potentiality in all other Shakespearian tragedies rightly elicits. Instead, Malcolm scripts what has happened as the crude melodrama of the extermination of a 'butcher and his fiend-like queen' (5.9.35) by the bearer of a self-awarded 'grace of Grace' (5.9.38). This is the scripting of politic calculation, exactly in accord with Malcolm's mean sounding of Macduff earlier on (4.3). But nothing else is to be expected in a world deserted by charismatic authority. In such a world there remains nothing to do but to wait for the messianic return of the magically promised and divinely legitimized ruler – whom court performances of *Macbeth* may have announced by holding a mirror up to him.

Doctor Faustus formulates the magician's fantastic desires for worldly power; *1 Henry VI* introduces the conflict of rival charismas into a historical setting; *Macbeth* dramatizes this conflict starkly as one of the polar opposition of representatives of charismatic authority: *The Tempest* stages a further turn of the screw by presenting what the literature of demonology had pronounced incompatible and therefore non-existent, the ruler as magician, the magician as ruler.[44] Once again, the play's opening shows authority suspended. On board ship even royal authority is in abeyance, but, in addition, the master's is as unavailing as that of the absent king. If neither the roarers nor the mariners care for the name of king (1.1.16–17), the question 'Where's the master?' (1.1.9–10) is indeed an urgent one. It is answered in a way which turns *The Tempest* into an anatomy of rule and authority. Scene by scene the question is implicitly or explicitly posed and dramatized on different levels, such as those of service, the family, and the state. That the theme of legitimate sovereignty and that of usurpation run through and structure the whole play has therefore quite rightly become a commonplace of criticism since the early seventies.[45]

That this is the necessary concomitant of the rivalry of magic and kingship is, however, less

---

[42] This has often been remarked. The phrase is Terence Hawkes's in *Shakespeare and the Reason: A Study of the Tragedies and the Problem Plays* (London, 1964), p. 124.

[43] For a similar diagnosis see Wilbur Sanders, *The Dramatist and the Received Idea: Studies in the Plays of Marlowe and Shakespeare* (Cambridge, 1968), p. 258.

[44] This has frequently been commented on in moral and structural terms. For a brief discussion of the politics of the relationship see Stephen Orgel's introduction to his edition of the play in the Oxford Shakespeare series (Oxford, 1987), pp. 20–3, 36–9.

[45] One of the earliest essays to state this view as against the previous ahistorical interpretation of *The Tempest* as an 'eternal conflict between order and chaos' (Rose A. Zimbardo, 'Form and Disorder in *The Tempest*', *Shakespeare Quarterly*, 14 (1963), 50) is Philip Brockbank's '*The Tempest*: Conventions of Art and Empire', Stratford-upon-Avon Studies, 8 (1966), 183–201.

'widely acknowledged.[46] Theoretically, there is no way for a sixteenth or seventeenth-century ruler to achieve what Prospero attempts to do, namely to appropriate both charismas. Consequently, ascribing both powers to one person, *The Tempest* very carefully and quite rigidly separates them again sequentially. Neither the retrospect nor the play's action ever grants Prospero the virtue of both powers simultaneously. When Prospero turns, during his Milan past, to what he euphemistically calls 'the liberal arts' (1.2.73) and to 'closeness and the bettering of [his] mind' (1.2.90), he can only do so by virtually abdicating, making his brother 'out o' th' substitution, / And executing th' outward face of royalty / With all prerogative' 'indeed the Duke' (1.2.103–5). Prospero repeats in a different key Lear's fatal error, that of separating being and doing. (That this is shown in retrospect within the mode of romance – the literature of second chances – assures us that the mistake can and will be remedied.) His loss of power and subsequent exile are the results and the objective correlatives of the fact that magic and monarchy do not go together.

The power Prospero wields on the island, a geographical version of the magician's circle, is based on and authorized by nothing but magic – the play's attempts to insinuate such legitimations as cultural and moral superiority notwithstanding. Prospero's peremptory treatment of both his servants, Ariel and Caliban, right at the beginning of the play leaves no doubt about the source of his authority. It enables him to act as the grandmaster of 'surveiller et punir', producing some of the moral and social ambivalences such a process of civilizing necessarily involves. Anticipating the course of Foucaultite history, Prospero locks his subjects into prisons, real ones, such as caves and magic circles, or mental ones, such as the one Ferdinand speaks of (1.2.491, 494), by means of which desire is repressed and, as in Alonso's case, guilt interiorized. Brute physical subjection – 'For this, be sure, to-night thou shalt have cramps' (1.2.325) and 'Go, charge my goblins

that they grind their joints / With dry convulsions...' (4.1.258–9) – alternates with and is joined to psychological transformation directed towards 'heart's sorrow, / And a clear life' (3.3.81–2).

Thus, on the face of it, Prospero's magic power seems to be unbounded, his rule absolute. Yet not only the sequential separation of ducal and magical government, visualized by Prospero's doffing of the magic robe when recounting his ducal past (1.2.24) and donning it again when returning to magic's business (1.2.187, according to Stephen Orgel's Oxford edition) in the second scene, undercuts magic's claims to unlimited authority. They are also delimited by the very indifferent results of Prospero's educational efforts – a thing of darkness which he must acknowledge, his failure to transform the counterfeit resentment of two brothers and to change the moral obduracy of a brace of lords. Yet magic's charisma is even more effectively subverted by being parodistically tested. By their relationship, Stephano and Caliban enact and bring to the fore the basis and mechanisms of charismatic leadership and its consequences. Stephano, like any charismatic ruler, is transcendentally authorized, he is a 'wondrous man' (2.2.164), 'a brave god' (2.2.117), 'dropp'd from heaven' (2.2.137). The sign and means of his authority is 'celestial liquor' (2.2.117). What it produces is intoxication, a state in which any hold on the real is replaced by fantasies of freedom and omnipotence: Stephano envisions 'a brave kingdom' (3.2.144) where he and Miranda 'will be king and queen' (3.2.107). His inhibitions weakened by alcoholic excess, Stephano's vision turns into one of overreaching self-delusion. The parallels with Prospero's magic are plain enough. In exact correspondence with Stephano's liquor Prospero's magic is the basis of charismatic rule. It engenders visions of omnipotence – 'At this hour / Lies at my mercy

---

[46] But see, e.g., Karol Berger, 'Prospero's Art', *Shakespeare Studies*, 10 (1977), 211–39, esp. pp. 218–20.

all mine enemies' (4.1.262–3) – which prove to be as hubristic as they are self-deluding.

The Tempest insists on the illusionary nature of magical power. Magic may uphold authority and rule under the laboratory conditions of a secluded island setting, contained in time and space and strictly segregated from secular, divinely legitimized power. It may have its brief hour during the theatrical present, but is shut off from both past and future reality. It follows that Prospero's reassumption of ducal power must be preceded by his relinquishing all magical activities. For whatever moral reasons Prospero may have to abjure his magic, the politics of power cannot tolerate the fusion of magic's and the monarchy's charisma. Only when Prospero doffs his magic robe once and for all and presents himself as he was, 'sometime Milan' (5.1.86), is the sequence complete.

Various as the strategies to contain magic in *The Tempest* enumerated so far have been – they range from strict sequential segregation of ducal and magical rule, the limitation of magic's realm to the island, the discrepancy between magical claims and their results, the demonstration of the illusionistic nature of all magical doings, to the parodistic subversion of magic's basis and mechanisms – Shakespeare has saved his subtlest stroke for the end. For the epilogue of *The Tempest* radically relodges power and authority: on the supernatural level not within magic's dominion but in that of a transcendental beyond, in 'Mercy itself' (Epil. 18); on the theatrical level not in the illusionist's two hours' traffic of the stage but in the audience's perception which may provide 'release' (Epil. 9); on the political level not in the hands of some remote Duke of Milan or King of Naples but in those of the clapping and paying audience.[47] And it cannot have done the dramatist much harm, if the centre of that audience was the King himself.

---

[47] Whether theatrical representation serves the interests of royal power or subverts them is a much debated question. For a recent and stimulating discussion, arguing the latter, see David Scott Kastan, 'Proud Majesty Made a Subject: Shakespeare and the Spectacle of Rule', *Shakespeare Quarterly*, 37 (1986), 459–75.

READING *THE TEMPEST*

RUSS McDONALD

My subject is *The Tempest* – how it has been read recently and how it might be read otherwise. My vehicle for approaching this subject is the poetic style, its most minute formal details. My immediate purpose is to read *The Tempest* in a way that offers an alternative to, and an implicit critique of, certain readings produced by American New Historicism and British Cultural Materialism. My larger aim is to discover uses for stylistic criticism that will reassert the value of textuality in a nontextual phase of criticism and that may contribute to the reconciliation of text and context, the aesthetic and the political.

I

It will come as no surprise to anyone who has followed developments in Renaissance studies that treatments of *The Tempest* seldom concern themselves with the verse. Recent criticism looks beyond textual details and formal properties to concentrate on cultural surroundings, addressing the play almost solely in terms of social and political contexts, particularly its relation to colonial discourse. The essay by Francis Barker and Peter Hulme in John Drakakis' *Alternative Shakespeares* is typical: 'The ensemble of fictional and lived practices, which for convenience we will simply refer to here as "English colonialism", provides *The Tempest*'s dominant discursive "contexts". We have chosen here to concentrate specifically on the figure of usurpation as the nodal point of

the play's imbrication into this discourse of colonialism.'[1] If American New Historicists seem slightly less virulent than British Cultural Materialists, their concerns are scarcely less political and their methods similarly contextual.[2] The Virginia pamphlets, Shakespeare's personal association with contemporary colonial projects, Montaigne on cannibals, twentieth-century racism and political oppression and their relation to Caliban – these are the contexts that have dominated recent treatments of this text.[3]

---

1 '"Nymphs and reapers heavily vanish": The Discursive Con-texts of *The Tempest*', *Alternative Shakespeares*, ed. John Drakakis (London and New York: Methuen, 1985), pp. 191–205.

2 Recent British readers seem especially unsympathetic to the play, perhaps because, as Walter Cohen suggests, their response to its colonial associations undermines an otherwise unified vision of Shakespeare's political progressivism. See 'Political Criticism of Shakespeare', in *Shakespeare Reproduced: The Text in History and Ideology*, ed. Jean E. Howard and Marion F. O'Connor (London: Methuen, 1987), p. 37.

3 Some of the essays that make the topic of colonialism their central theme are the following: Paul E. Brown, '"This thing of darkness I acknowledge mine": *The Tempest* and the Discourse of Colonialism', in *Political Shakespeare*, ed. Jonathan Dollimore and Alan Sinfield (Ithaca: Cornell University Press, 1985); Paul N. Siegel, 'Historical Ironies in *The Tempest*', *Shakespeare Jahrbuch*, 119 (1983), 104–11; Thomas Cartelli, 'Prospero in Africa: *The Tempest* as Colonialist Text and Pretext', in Howard and O'Connor, *Shakespeare Reproduced*, pp. 99–115; Terence Hawkes, 'Swisser-Swatter: Making a Man of English Letters', in Drakakis's *Alternative Shakespeares*, pp. 26–46; Stephen Orgel,

Many of the readings that regard *The Tempest* primarily as what Paul Brown calls an 'intervention' in European colonial history are tendentious in conception and narrow in scope. In disputing them, however, I do not wish to neglect their nuances nor to suppress the differences among them: Greenblatt's 1976 essay, 'Learning to Curse: Aspects of Linguistic Colonialism in the Sixteenth Century', for example, contextualizes *The Tempest* in a way that is balanced and sensitive to ambiguity,[4] but recent readers have become increasingly single-minded and reductive, often adopting a censorious and shrill tone in delineating the text's relation to the problems of cultural tyranny, political freedom, and exploitation. One of the most notable of these discussions, Paul Brown's '"This thing of darkness I acknowledge mine": *The Tempest* and the discourse of colonialism', printed in Dollimore and Sinfield's *Political Shakespeare*, states its purpose in a way that fairly represents the revisionist reading. 'This chapter seeks to demonstrate that *The Tempest* is not simply a reflection of colonialist practices but an intervention in an ambivalent and even contradictory discourse. This intervention takes the form of a powerful and pleasurable narrative which seeks at once to harmonise disjunction, to transcend irreconcilable contradictions and to mystify the political conditions which demand colonialist discourse. Yet the narrative ultimately fails to deliver that containment and instead may be seen to foreground precisely those problems which it works to efface or overcome.'[5] Something like this point of view is expressed more succinctly by Walter Cohen: '*The Tempest* uncovers, perhaps despite itself, the racist and imperialist bases of English nationalism.'[6] And some critics decline to treat the work at all. Richard Strier, for example, considers *The Tempest* 'more conservative than the plays, from *Hamlet* on, which precede it,'[7] and the adjective is not intended as a compliment.

As these remarks show, a basic argumentative move on the part of many poststructuralist critics has been to attack the play's sophistication. This gambit follows an earlier one, a critical usurpation of the dramatic sovereignty of Prospero and a concomitant attack on the idealist reading set forth in Frank Kermode's Introduction to the Arden edition.[8] Having cast the benevolent Prospero out to sea, New Historicists and Cultural Materialists have

---

'Prospero's Wife', *Representations*, 8 (1985), 1–13, and 'Shakespeare and the Cannibals', in *Witches, Cannibals, Divorce: Estranging the Renaissance*, Selected Papers from the English Institute, NS 11, ed. Marjorie Garber (Baltimore: Johns Hopkins University Press, 1986), pp. 40–66; Stephen Greenblatt, 'Martial Law in the Land of Cockaigne', in *Shakespearean Negotiations: The Circulation of Social Energy in Renaissance England* (Berkeley: University of California Press, 1988), pp. 129–63.

[4] The essay is printed in *First Images of America: The Impact of the New World on the Old*, ed. Fredi Chiappelli, 2 vols. (Berkeley: University of California Press, 1976), pp. 561–80.

[5] (Ithaca: Cornell University Press, 1985), p. 48.

[6] *Drama of a Nation: Public Theater in Renaissance England and Spain* (Ithaca: Cornell University Press, 1985), p. 401.

[7] 'Faithful Servants: Shakespeare's Praise of Disobedience', in *The Historical Renaissance: New Essays on Tudor and Stuart Literature and Culture*, ed. Heather Dubrow and Richard Strier (Chicago: University of Chicago Press, 1988), p. 133 n. 81.

[8] *The Tempest*, ed. Frank Kermode (London: Methuen, 1954). Other studies now considered limited for their neglect of political issues would include those of G. Wilson Knight, *The Crown of Life* (Oxford: Clarendon Press, 1947), pp. 203–55; Reuben A. Brower, 'The Mirror of Analogy: *The Tempest*', in *The Fields of Light: An Experiment in Critical Reading* (New York: Oxford, 1951), pp. 95–122; Northrop Frye, Introduction to *The Tempest* in *The Complete Pelican Shakespeare*, gen. ed. Alfred Harbage (Baltimore: Penguin, 1969); D. G. James, *The Dream of Prospero* (Oxford: Clarendon Press, 1967); Harry Levin, 'Two Magian Comedies: *The Alchemist* and *The Tempest*', *Shakespeare Survey 22* (1969), 47–58; Derek Traversi, *Shakespeare: The Last Phase* (London: Hollis and Carter, 1954); Harry Berger, 'Miraculous Harp: A Reading of Shakespeare's *Tempest*', *Shakespeare Studies*, 5 (1969), 253–83; Howard Felperin, *Shakespearean Romance* (Princeton: Princeton University Press, 1972); Joseph H. Summers, 'The Anger of Prospero', in *Dreams of Love and Power: On Shakespeare's Plays* (Oxford: Clarendon, 1984).

sought to exert their hegemony over the text (and interpretation of it) by urging the claims of discourse, usually asserting that *The Tempest* cannot be aware of its own participation in the language of oppression and colonial power.[9] Such readings are not simply uninterested in the contribution of poetic texture; in fact, much criticism of *The Tempest*, like much political reading in general, is deliberately anti-aesthetic. The verbal harmonics can too easily be considered a means of textual mystification, a tool in Prospero's magic trunk contributing to the 'enchantment' that has made this play especially appealing and thus especially dangerous, made it 'a powerful and pleasurable narrative'. Some voices have been raised against the tendentious and monochromatic quality of much interpretation of *The Tempest*: Meredith Anne Skura, for example, in a persuasive psychological essay, argues that 'recent criticism not only flattens the text into the mold of colonialist discourse and eliminates what is characteristically "Shakespearean" in order to foreground what is "colonialist", but it is also – paradoxically – in danger of taking the play further from the particular historical situation in England in 1611 even as it brings it closer to what we mean by "colonialism" today'.[10] Despite this and a few other protests, the colonialist reading in the past decade has demonized Prospero, sentimentalized Caliban, and tyrannized conferences and journals with a new orthodoxy as one-sided as that which it has sought to replace.

Sensitivity to the verse offers an alternative to both of these restrictive interpretations. In the first place, awareness of the poetic complexity of *The Tempest* suggests that the play is considerably more self-conscious than the recent demystifiers will allow. Repetition – of vowels and consonants, words, phrases, syntactical forms, and other verbal effects – is a fundamental stylistic turn in *The Tempest*; these aurally reiterative patterns serve to tantalize the listener, generating expectations of illumination and fixity but refusing to satisfy those desires.

Such poetic echoes function in concert with the open-endedness of the romance form and with the reappearance of a host of familiar Shakespearian topoi: verbal and ideational patterns entice the audience by promising and withholding illumination, demonstrating the impossibility of significational certainty and creating an atmosphere of hermeneutic instability.

Moreover, the style and form of *The Tempest* engage the audience textually with the same issues of control and mastery – the problem of power – that are brought into sharp focus by considerations of historical context. The tendency of words and phrases to repeat themselves may be linked to the play's profound concern with reproduction, in various senses from the biological to the political. Versions of this very broad topic appear especially in those episodes that have appealed to recent critics: the story of the deceased Sycorax, the absent wife of Prospero, Antonio's usurpation, Prospero's taking the island from Caliban, the attempt of the 'savage' to rape Miranda, the enslavement of Ariel, the political ambitions of Stephano and Trinculo, the arranged marriages of Clari-

---

[9] For a fascinating commentary on this kind of critical power struggle, see Anthony B. Dawson, '*Tempest* in a Teapot: Critics, Evaluation, Ideology', in *Bad Shakespeare: Revaluations of the Shakespeare Canon*, ed. Maurice Charney (Rutherford, NJ: Fairleigh Dickinson University Press, 1988), pp. 61–73. Dawson is especially eloquent on 'the way "materialist" critics expose the hidden biases of traditional criticism ... but fall into some of the same traps, particularly in the vexed area of evaluation and the ideological assumptions that the act of evaluating often makes plain' (71).

[10] 'Discourse and the Individual: The Case of Colonialism in *The Tempest*', *Shakespeare Quarterly*, 40 (1989), 47. One of the earliest complaints about the excesses of recent political criticism was Edward Pechter's 'The New Historicism and its Discontents: Politicizing Renaissance Drama', *PMLA*, 102 (1987), 292–303. On the other hand, Carolyn Porter has attacked New Historicists for being insufficiently historical and insufficiently political: see 'Are We Being Historical Yet?', *South Atlantic Quarterly*, 87 (1988), 743–86.

bel and Miranda, the masque's concern with fertility and succession, the problem of dynasty, the effort to reproduce the self through art. I shall argue that the stylistic implications of repetition offer a way of treating these political topics that is considerably more nuanced than most recent discussions of the play, more responsive to its balances and contradictions. The repetitions of the dramatic poetry help to expose the problems inherent in the act of cultural re-creation and to magnify their complexity, not to supply answers. Virgil Thomson described 'structural elements' in music as 'expressive vocabularies, ... repertories of devices for provoking feelings without defining them'.[11] In *The Tempest*, as in late Shakespeare generally, the effect of the poetry is to promote *un*certainty and to insist upon ambiguity, and attention to the verse makes one increasingly dubious about the bluntness of most political interpretation.

II

Repetition becomes a prominent figure in Shakespeare's late style generally, and *The Tempest* in particular derives much of its poetic power from phonetic, lexical, and syntactical reiteration.[12] From the confused echoes of the first scene ('We split, we split!') through Prospero's re-creation of the past ('Twelve year since, Miranda, twelve year since') to the pleasing assonantal chiming of the Epilogue, aural patterns impart a distinctive texture to this text. And yet *The Tempest* is something of a stylistic paradox, being simultaneously one of the most pleonastic and one of the briefest plays in the canon. The incantatory tone is in turn reinforced by the ellipses that represent a complementary and equally prominent feature of the late verse. But the repetition of sounds and words is only one type of larger and more frequently discussed modes of iteration, to which Jan Kott in particular has directed our notice: the replicated actions of usurpation and assassination, the structural mirroring of the

aristocratic and the servant plots, the allusion to and reproduction of major motifs from *The Aeneid*, the creation of a masque within the play, and Shakespeare's representation of some of his own most familiar dramatic actions and topics.[13] Likewise, omission makes itself felt narratively as well as stylistically. By this stage of his career Shakespeare has told the story of, say, regicide so many times that he now presents it in its most abbreviated and indicative fashion. Such a mimetic approach might be called abstract: the artist is sufficiently confident of his ability to tell a story and of his audience's capacity to receive it that he is able to signal an action rather than develop it in detail.[14] We are in the realm of the comedian performing at a convention of comedians: since everybody knows the jokes, he need only refer to a gag by number, and the house breaks into laughter.

Presence being easier to demonstrate than absence, I shall concentrate on figures of repetition, but a few words are in order about

---

[11] 'Music Does Not Flow', *New York Review of Books*, 17 December 1981, p. 49.

[12] Although everyone agrees that the poetry of the last plays is difficult and different from the earlier verse, surprisingly little has been written about it. See F. E. Halliday, *The Poetry of Shakespeare's Plays* (London: Duckworth, 1954); J. M. Nosworthy's Introduction to the Arden edition of *Cymbeline* (London: Methuen, 1955), lxii–lxxiii; N. F. Blake, *Shakespeare's Language: An Introduction* (London: Methuen, 1983); John Porter Houston, *Shakespearean Sentences: A Study in Style and Syntax* (Baton Rouge: Louisiana State University Press, 1987); and George T. Wright, *Shakespeare's Metrical Art* (Berkeley: University of California Press, 1988). In preparing this essay I have also profited from Cyrus Hoy's 'The Language of Fletcherian Tragicomedy', in *Mirror up to Shakespeare: Essays in Honour of G. R. Hibbard*, ed. J. C. Gray (Toronto: University of Toronto Press, 1984), pp. 99–113.

[13] '*The Tempest*, or Repetition', in *The Bottom Translation: Marlowe and Shakespeare and the Carnival Tradition*, tr. Daniela Miedzyrzecka and Lillian Vallee (Evanston: Northwestern University Press, 1987).

[14] For an intelligent discussion of the 'abstract' qualities of Shakespeare's late work, see Marion Trousdale, 'Style in *The Winter's Tale*', *Critical Quarterly*, 18 (1976), 25–32.

Shakespeare's impulse to omit. The gestural approach to storytelling corresponds to the poet's attempt at concentration and density throughout the last plays: Shakespeare strives for power of expression not only by contracting words and skipping over non-essential syllables, but also by discarding participles, pronouns (especially relative pronouns), conjunctions, and even nouns and verbs. Asyndeton appears about as frequently as in *King Lear* and *Antony and Cleopatra*, two plays of much greater length.[15] And the play is replete with verbless constructions: 'Most sure the goddess / On whom these airs attend' (1.2.425–6); 'No wonder, sir, / But certainly a maid' (1.2.431–2). Participles often do the work of longer noun/verb phrases, thus accelerating the tempo: 'I, not rememb'ring how I cried out then, / Will cry it o'er again' (1.2.133–4). Anne Barton, in a brilliant discussion of this stripping away of nonessentials, points out that the vocabulary of *The Tempest* is spiked with spontaneous compounds ('sea-change', 'cloud-capped', 'hag-seed', 'man-monster'), proposing that such phrases 'seem to be driving towards some ultimate reduction of language, a mode of expression more meaningful in its very bareness than anything a more elaborate and conventional rhetoric could devise'. She groups Shakespeare's urge towards linguistic compression with his disjunctive approach to characterization, observation of the unities, and reluctance to supply apparently pertinent details, all strategies by which *The Tempest* 'continually gives the impression of being much bigger than it is'.[16]

For all its compression and abbreviation, however, it is also pleonastic and reiterative – phonetically, rhythmically, lexically, syntactically, and architectonically. Although the structural and narrative replications are more likely to be the subject of critical interest than the aural, most listeners find themselves beguiled by the musical repetition of vowels and consonants, reduplication of words, echoing of metrical forms, and incantatory effect of this musical design. Even enthusiasts of prosody, however, are apt to weary of the repetitions of my close analysis, and so I beg the reader's indulgence as I lay the groundwork for the demonstration, in the second half of this essay, of how these effects function ideologically.

One of the play's most distinctive stylistic properties is the interlocking of aural effects in a way that recalls the etymology of *text* in weaving. Instances of consonance and assonance call attention to themselves in virtually every line: in a phrase such as 'There's nothing ill can dwell in such a temple', 'ill' is glanced at in 'dwell', then both are altered with the repetition of the *e* and *l* in 'temple', and these harmonies are augmented by the reiteration of the *th* and *n* sounds. Such interweavings are audible in lines that seem merely declarative ('For thou must now know farther') as well as in the obviously musical ('Wound the loud winds, or with bemocked-at stabs / Kill the still-closing waters'). They dominate Prospero's recitation of Ariel's history:

> within which rift
> Imprisoned thou didst painfully remain
> A dozen years, within which space she died
> And left thee there, where thou didst vent thy groans
> As fast as mill-wheels strike. Then was this island –
> Save for the son that she did litter here,
> A freckled whelp, hag-born – not honoured with
> A human shape. (1.2.279–86)

To begin with the smallest units, a series of vowel sounds spin themselves out to almost absurd lengths ('within which rift / Imprisoned thou didst painfully remain'); pairs of long vowels alternate with short ('she did litter here'); consonants can be repeated indepen-

---

[15] On this and many points of stylistic criticism, I have been aided by the analysis of John Porter Houston in *Shakespearean Sentences*.

[16] Introduction to *The Tempest* (Harmondsworth: Penguin, 1968), pp. 13–14.

dently and then combined and split apart (in 'put thyself / Upon this island as a spy', the *p*, *s*, and *i* sounds establish themselves separately and then coalesce in 'spy'). This practice of joining and splitting phonemes creates what Stephen Booth has called 'pulsating alliteration', a sensation of expansion and contraction that implies density and activity, making the text effectively 'poetic' even when it may not sound conventionally so.[17]

Lexical repetition is largely responsible for the incantatory appeal of *The Tempest*, and thus for some of the most memorable passages in the play. Even in the prose of the opening shipwreck – 'All lost! To prayers, to prayers! All lost!'; '"We split, we split, we split!"' – the confused shouts of desperation take a reiterative form that functions poetically in the early speeches of Prospero and then throughout the work. Here, for instance, is a seven-line passage from the beginning of the play.

PROSPERO   ... Tell your piteous heart
  There's no *harm done*.
MIRANDA   O woe the day!
PROSPERO   *No harm*.
  I have done nothing but in care *of thee*,
  Of thee, *my* dear one, *thee*, *my* daughter, who
  Art ignorant of what thou *art*, naught knowing
  Of whence *I am*, nor that *I am* more better
  Than Prospero, master of a full poor cell
  And thy no greater father.   (1.2.14–21)[18]

In addition to the italicized repetitions, the passage echoes with phonetic duplication: 'heart ... harm', 'O, woe', 'my dear ... my daughter', 'naught ... daughter', 'naught knowing', 'full ... cell', and 'greater father'. (Our uncertainty about Elizabethan pronunciation may limit but surely does not invalidate speculation about such phonetic echoes.) The regularity of certain metrical patterns and the isocolonic arrangement of clauses intensify the effect of the repeated words, notably 'thee, my dear one, thee, my daughter' and 'Of whence I am, nor that I am'. And then there are all the negatives: 'No', 'no', 'nothing', 'naught', 'knowing', 'nor', 'no'.

To catch the repetitive flavour of Prospero's narrative to Miranda is to learn how to hear the language of the text as a whole; the following examples are taken from the first two hundred lines of the long second scene:

Which thou heard'st cry, which thou saw'st
    sink. Sit down,
For thou must now know farther.

If thou rememb'rest aught ere thou cam'st here,
How thou cam'st here thou mayst.

Twelve year since, Miranda, twelve year since

What foul play had we that we came from
    thence?
Or blessed was't we did?
                    Both, both, my girl.
By foul play, as thou sayst, were we heaved
    thence,
But blessedly holp hither.

                    how to grant suits,
How to deny them, *who t*'advance and *who*
To trash for over-topping, new *created*
The *creatures* that were mine, I say – *or* changed
    'em
Or else new *formed* 'em; having both the key
Of *officer* and *office*, ...

                    no screen between this part
    he played
And him he played it for

Which now's upon's, without the which this
    story

To cry to th'sea that roared to us, to sigh
To th'winds, whose pity, sighing back again

---

[17] *An Essay on Shakespeare's Sonnets* (New Haven: Yale University Press, 1969), pp. 87–8. Booth's comments on how poetic effects function in individual sonnets are extremely stimulating and applicable beyond their immediate subject. See also the essay by Kenneth Burke, 'On Musicality in Verse', in which he demonstrates the complex effects of assonance and consonance in some poems of Coleridge: *The Philosophy of Literary Form* (Berkeley: University of California Press, rpt. 1973), pp. 369–79.

[18] Here, as in a few other passages, I have added emphasis to illustrate certain poetic effects.

Sit still, and hear the last of our sea-sorrow.
Here in this island we arrived, and here
Have I, thy schoolmaster . . .

Since stylistic criticism often founders in an elaborate summation of what its examples have already disclosed, I leave it to the reader to note the poetic and rhetorical details, the instances of assonance, alliteration, epanalepsis, isocolon, several species of paronomasia (polyptoton, syllepsis, antanaclasis), not to mention the fundamental pleasures of the repeated sounds. The various kinds of verbal play impart energy and motion to what is dramatically a notoriously static scene.

That such echoing patterns are not confined to the protasis or to the protagonist but resound throughout the work is apparent by a glance at the episode in which Antonio seeks to inveigle Sebastian into fratricide, the temptation scene (2.1.204–311). The villain begins his scheme by priming his partner with anaphoric and rhythmic restatement: 'They fell together all, as by consent; / They dropped as by a thunder-stroke' (2.1.208–9). He continues by arguing that Ferdinand's disappearance is Sebastian's good fortune, demonstrating the transformation linguistically:

SEBASTIAN I have *no hope*
  That he's undrowned.
ANTONIO   O, out of that *'no hope'*
  What *great hope* have you! *No hope* that way is
  Another way *so high a hope* that even
  Ambition cannot pierce a wink beyond,
  But doubt discovery there.   (2.1.243–8)

Apart from the obvious echoes, the passage rings with assonance and consonance; in addition to the aural repetition, we also catch the relentless negatives characteristic of Shakespeare's villains; the glance at sleep imagery ('wink') to which the dramatic atmosphere of the scene and the island has acclimated us; and the self-conscious worrying of words that extends the game begun earlier, when the conspirators toy with the metaphor of 'standing water' (226). As is often the case in *The*

Tempest, language emerges as a subject itself, as speakers play with it, take pleasure in it, test its capacities, and misuse it consciously and unconsciously, sometimes, as here, at the same time.[19]

Antonio's principal trick is structural recapitulation, the stringing together of formally similar clauses. Consider his appositional elaboration of Sebastian's one-word speech, 'Claribel':

  She that is Queen of Tunis; she that dwells
  Ten leagues beyond man's life; she that from
      Naples
  Can have no note – unless the sun were post –
  The man i'th'moon's too slow – till newborn
      chins
  Be rough and razorable; she that from whom
  We all were sea-swallowed, though some cast
      again –
  And by that destiny, to perform an act
  Whereof what's past is prologue, what to come
  In yours and my discharge.   (2.1.251–9)

This string of clauses – the reader will have noticed that it is not even a sentence – is calculated to inveigle the auditor into rhythmic sympathy with and, finally, assent to the speaker's claims. It depends for its seductive power on the reiterative disposition of phrases, specifically on the pattern known as *conduplicatio*, the repetition of words in succeeding clauses. Antonio/Shakespeare strives for a kind of hypnosis with simplicity of diction, at least in the first half, where until 'razorable' no word is longer than two syllables and most are monosyllabic; with regular disruption of the normal metrical structure, each of the 'she that' phrases being a trochee substituted for an iamb;[20] and with syntactical recapitulation. Even those qualifying clauses that violate the pattern of 'she that' develop their own rhythmic echo: 'unless

---

[19] See Anne Barton, 'Shakespeare and the Limits of Language', *Shakespeare Survey 24* (1971), 19–30.

[20] On the expressive possibilities of this tactic, see Wright's *Shakespeare's Metrical Art*, especially chapter 13, 'Trochees'.

the sun were post' and 'The man i'th'moon's too slow' are identical in length and regularity, similar in the importance of consonance and assonance, and completed with the repeated 'o' sound. In these dramatic circumstances, Antonio's periphrastic style amounts to verbal overkill, as even the dim Sebastian seems to perceive in his response to the 'Claribel' speech: 'What stuff is this?' But the local effect is less important than the overriding dramatic goal: Antonio and Sebastian are merely the agents of a playwright seeking to seduce his audience with words.[21]

So it goes through other scenes and with other speakers. Some of the richest passages in the text depend upon such lexical and sonic echo. One of the play's axiological cruces, for example, the complex relation between biology and culture, is set forth in an aurally pleasing and complex frame:

> A devil, a born devil, on whose nature
> Nurture can never stick; on whom my pains,
> Humanely taken, all, all lost, quite lost.

(4.1.188–90)

'Full fathom five thy father lies', 'Where the bee sucks, there suck I' – the power of the play's songs is at least partly attributable to various kinds of echo. Finally, the notorious mystery surrounding Gonzalo's 'Widow Dido' has been examined in almost every conceivable context except, I think, that of aural identity, simple rhyme. Is it perhaps just another case of internal rhyme that sounds as if it ought to mean more than it does? Such density and concentration are essential to the sense of pregnancy upon which *The Tempest* depends.

III

Verbal patterns are congruent with and supported by larger networks of reiteration, most of them narrative and structural. Internal repetition of action has been a staple of Shakespearian dramatic structure since the early 1590s, the double wooing of Katherine and Bianca in *The Taming of the Shrew* being

perhaps the most illustrative case. But rarely are the symmetries and parodic constructions made so obvious – or so obviously the subject of comment – as in *The Tempest*. The play is famous for the density and congruity of its mirrored actions.[22] To mention only those events associated with the celebrated example of usurpation, 'the nodal point' of colonialist readings: Antonio's prompting Sebastian to regicide and fratricide seeks to repeat in Naples his own theft of power in Milan and re-enacts Prospero's seizure of the island and enslavement of Caliban, and all are burlesqued in 'that foul conspiracy / Of the beast Caliban and his confederates / Against [Prospero's] life' (4.1.139–41). This reticulum of stories contributes to a dramatic design that seems both familiar and wonderful.

But the pattern of narrative and thematic recapitulation goes far beyond this text. *The Tempest* is flagrantly intertextual, and the cluster of echoes is especially audible, again, in the temptation scene. As commentators since Coleridge have noticed, both in general structure and particular details – Antonio's hectoring Sebastian about 'What thou shouldst be', the image of the crown, the sleep imagery implying failure to understand or to act, the suppression of conscience, even the image of the hungry cat (although it is used differently) – the episode restages the scene between the Macbeths before the killing of Duncan.[23] Every-

---

[21] On the relative importance of specific and general effects in the last plays, see Anne Barton, 'Leontes and the Spider: Language and Speaker in the Last Plays', *Shakespeare's Styles: Essays in honour of Kenneth Muir*, ed. Philip Edwards, G. K. Hunter, and Inga-Stina Ewbank (Cambridge: Cambridge University Press, 1980), pp. 131–50.

[22] See, for example, Joan Hartwig, *Shakespeare's Analogical Scene: Parody as Structural Syntax* (Lincoln: University of Nebraska Press, 1983), chapter 8; Brower's *The Fields of Light*; and Knight's *The Crown of Life*.

[23] For an excellent discussion of the densely allusive quality of this scene, see Paul A. Cantor, 'Shakespeare's *The Tempest*: The Wise Man as Hero', *Shakespeare Quarterly*, 31 (1980), 64–75.

where in the scene Shakespeare is repeating himself, unashamedly gazing back over his entire *oeuvre* and summoning up scenes, persons, themes, metaphors, bits of vocabulary, and other minor theatrical strategies, so much so that the personal allegorists can hardly be blamed for the vigour with which they have approached this text. The recreated actions and speeches function as all allusions do, giving pleasure by exercising the mind and flattering veteran spectators on their perspicacity; and this audacious kind of authorial self-cannibalism contributes another layer of complexity, another apparently meaningful pattern of familiar and yet rearranged material. The duplication which constitutes the original source of meaning and pleasure, and which contains all the other patterns I have mentioned, is the troping by the play of the actual world: reality is (re)presented on the stage.[24] This act of repetition is the most general instance of the process I have been describing in little, in that the relationship of play to life would seem to amount to a meaningful pattern, and yet it is immensely difficult to articulate that meaning. As Stanley Wells puts it, 'The enchanted island reverberates with sounds hinting at tunes that never appear fully formed.'[25]

IV

The prominence of the figure of repetition in both the verbal style and dramatic structure of *The Tempest* leads perforce to the question of its importance – what does the figure import through the text to the audience? what is its function? how does it mean? Although for the most part I would decline to assign specific stylistic functions to particular sounds, certain aural configurations do undeniably accomplish certain small tasks of characterization and tone.[26] The hieratic style suggested by Prospero's repetitions is clearly appropriate to his vatic persona and elegiac frame of mind, it is a commonplace that some of his poetically knotted reiterations attest to his agitation at

[24] See Ruth Nevo's comments on this metatheatrical device: 'The embedding of play within play dissolves representational boundaries so that the audience is required to suspend its attention, to negotiate a constant interchange between fictional reality and fictional illusion.' *Shakespeare's Other Language* (London: Methuen, 1987), p. 136. This point of view is consistent with Shakespeare's late attitude toward a device that had served him well from the beginning, as Anne Barton points out: 'On the whole, efforts to distinguish the fictional from the "real", art from life, tales from truth, come in the Romances to replace the older, moral concern with identifying hypocrisy and deceit.' 'Leontes and the Spider', p. 147.

[25] 'Shakespeare and Romance', in *Later Shakespeare*, ed. John Russell Brown and Bernard Harris, Stratford-upon-Avon Studies, 8 (London: Edward Arnold, 1966), p. 75.

[26] From time to time aural echoes function as images do, pointing up crucial words and the ideas they raise. Consider the effect of 'be' in the following exchange:

> ALONSO   Whe'er thou beest he or no,
> Or some enchanted trifle to abuse me,
> As late I have been, I not know: Thy pulse
> Beats, as of flesh and blood; and, since I saw thee
> Th'affliction of my mind amends, with which
> I fear a madness held me. This must crave –
> An if this be at all – a most strange story.
> Thy dukedom I resign, and do entreat
> Thou pardon me my wrongs. But how should Prospero
> Be living and be here?
> PROSPERO (*to Gonzalo*) First, noble friend,
> Let me embrace thine age, whose honour cannot
> Be measured or confined.
> *He embraces Gonzalo*
> GONZALO   Whether this be,
> Or be not, I'll not swear. (5.1.113–24)

The hammering of the verb underscores the problem that Alonso and finally the audience must confront, the ontological status of what we are witnessing.

Stanley Fish has written brilliantly on the logical dangers of such interpretation, specifically on the circularity of thematic stylistics: 'formal patterns are themselves the products of interpretation and ... therefore there is no such thing as a formal pattern, at least in the sense necessary for the practice of stylistics: that is, no pattern that one can observe before interpretation is hazarded and which therefore can be used to prefer one interpretation to another'. *Is There a Text in This Class?: The Authority of Textual Communities* (Cambridge, Mass.: Harvard University Press, 1980), p. 267. See also John Hollander, 'The Metrical Frame', in *The Structure*

narratively recreating his deposition, and Caliban's exultant 'Freedom, high-day! High-day, freedom! Freedom, high-day, freedom!' ironically establishes his personal entrapment, his exchange of one master for another. But for the most part these and other such instances of functional echo constitute special cases. There is small profit in seeking 'meaning' in Miranda's antanaclastic quibble on 'your reason / For raising this sea-storm', in the vowels and consonants of Gonzalo's 'If I should say I saw such islanders', or in most other lines.

I would argue that the operation of these acoustic and lexical echoes is musical, and that this music is only indirectly functional. The mutual effect of concentration and repetition creates a poetic counterpoint that challenges and exhilarates the auditor – Jan Kott describes *The Tempest* as a fugue[27] – and this contrapuntal effect induces aurally a sense of wonder corresponding to the aims and effects of the romantic or tragicomic mode. The operation of these verbal patterns is thus paradoxical, their greatest significance being precisely their ostensible significance combined with their refusal to signify. The effect is dream-like.[28] The verbal music is related to the oneiric and unreal atmosphere that attends and complicates the action of Shakespeare's late romantic forms; it promises much and delivers little, and I propose that it is just this dynamic that makes *The Tempest* uncommonly meaningful.

The insistent poetic reiterations interact with the elliptical verse style to mystify the audience about a function that never manifests itself. The play encourages its audience to scrutinize the linguistic and structural patterns for meaning, but it stoutly refuses to yield those meanings easily or fully. Eager to satisfy the desire for comprehension, we find ourselves both stimulated and frustrated. On the one hand, the repeated sounds or phrases in a brief and complicated text offer a kind of aural comfort: specifically, they create a richness of texture that seems to promise profundity. On the other, the text never fulfils the expectations of clarity which the discovery of such patterns engenders: in the rapid flow of the dialogue the repetitions themselves are succeeded by more repetitions which seem equally promising and equally unyielding. Such a strategy tantalizes the audience with the hope of clarification and fixity that art seems to promise, but it also demonstrates the difficulty and perhaps, finally, the impossibility of attaining them. Since order and comprehension seem always available but never thoroughly realized, the audience participates directly in the atmosphere of evanescence vital to this play.

The Tempest thus addresses itself directly to the problem of language and meaning, about which it registers extremely serious doubts. Denied or delayed communication becomes a minor but explicit motif as the action proceeds: numerous acts of communication (a speech, a song, a banquet, a masque) are broken off or delayed or redirected. Our position is something like that described by Caliban in his most memorable speech:

> Be not afeard. The isle is full of noises,
> Sounds, and sweet airs, that give delight and
>   hurt not.
> Sometimes a thousand twangling instruments
> Will hum about mine ears, and sometimes
>   voices
> That if I then had waked after long sleep
> Will make me sleep again; and then in dreaming
> The clouds methought would open and show
>   riches
> Ready to drop upon me, that when I waked
> I cried to dream again.   (3.2.138–46)

Often cited as evidence of natural sensitivity or of the magical atmosphere of the setting, these lines are most helpful as a statement of how the music of *The Tempest* impresses an audience. Robert Graves has shown that the confusion of

---

of Verse: Modern Essays on Prosody, ed. Harvey Gross, rev. ed. (New York: Ecco Press, 1979), pp. 77–101.

[27] *The Bottom Translation*, p. 97.

[28] Of the many studies of the oneiric qualities of *The Tempest*, the most recent is found in Ruth Nevo's *Shakespeare's Other Language*, especially pp. 136–43.

tenses contributes to a feeling of arrested time;[29] lovely sounds 'hum' about our ears; we seem to be about to receive the riches of meaning which remain forever elusive. The desired unity and gratification are contradicted by the brevity and compression of the text, and thus we find ourselves in what A. D. Nuttall has called an 'atmosphere of ontological suspension' that pervades *The Tempest*, a region midway between promise and fulfilment.[30] And lest this seem too solemn let me add that this state of expectancy is also the source of immense pleasure. At this point one of my old teachers would have said, 'You know. The Keats thing.'

v

Tantalization is also one of the principal effects of the new mode of romance or tragicomedy that Shakespeare adopted in the late phase of his career, and the structure of the drama reinforces the fundamental erotic appeal of the verse by protracting but never seeming to supply the imminent resolution. Peter Brooks, commenting on an essay of Freud's, 'Creative Writers and Day-Dreaming', writes about the aesthetic values of literary form, specifically what Freud calls 'forepleasure'.

The equation of the effects of literary form with forepleasure in this well-known passage is perhaps less trivial than it at first appears. If *Lust* and *Unlust* don't take us very far in the analysis of literary texture, *Vorlust* – forepleasure – tropes on pleasure and thus seems more promising. Forepleasure is indeed a curious concept, suggesting a whole rhetoric of advance toward and retreat from the goal or the end, a formal zone of play (I take it that forepleasure somehow implicates foreplay) that is both harnessed to the end and yet autonomous, capable of deviations and recursive movements. When we begin to unpack the components of forepleasure, we may find a whole erotics of form, which is perhaps what we most need if we are to make formalism serve an understanding of the human functions of literature. Forepleasure would include the notion of both delay and advance in the textual dynamic, the creation of that 'dilatory space' which Roland

Barthes, in *S/Z*, claimed to be the essence of the textual middle. We seek to advance through this space toward the discharge of the end, yet all the while we are perversely delaying, returning backward in order to put off the promised end and perhaps to assure its greater significance.[31]

This suggestive paragraph is relevant to the way that Shakespeare's late style functions in, and in concert with, the voguish new dramatic mode. A more or less contemporary description of the process of narrative teasing is found in William Cartwright's prefatory verses in the 1647 Beaumont and Fletcher Folio:

> None can prevent the fancy, and see through
> At the first opening; all stand wondering how
> The thing will be, until it is; which hence
> With fresh delight still cheats, still takes the
>   sense;
> The whole design, the shadow, the lights such
> That none can say he shews or hides too much.

The titillating diction of Cartwright's description is given special meaning in light of Brooks's plea for a textual erotics, for both capture the gamesome or sportive quality of romance or tragicomedy.[32]

Narrative progress towards the satisfactions of complete understanding, or closure, is indirect and irregular, and the chief pleasure rests in the delay and the circuitousness of the journey. Romance depends upon suspense, secrets, surprises, discoveries, peripeties, awakenings, revelations. Thus it automatically raises questions of epistemology but almost invariably leaves them open. It is a knowing form, a self-conscious mode reliant upon the audience's familiarity

---

[29] *The White Goddess* (London: Farrar, 1948), p. 425.

[30] *Two Concepts of Allegory: A Study of Shakespeare's 'The Tempest' and the Logic of Allegorical Expression* (New York: Barnes and Noble, 1967), p. 158.

[31] Peter Brooks, 'The Idea of a Psychoanalytic Literary Criticism', *Critical Inquiry*, 13 (1987), 339.

[32] Although I am sensitive to the various differences between the two kinds known as 'romance' and 'tragicomedy', it will be agreed that the forms share a number of fundamental features, and it is those similarities on which I am concentrating here.

with conventions of tragic and comic story-telling and its willingness to be teased by the playwright's manipulation of generic signals. For similar reasons it is an ironic form in flattering the audience with privileged information; yet it deals in double ironies when it betrays this cosy relationship by a sudden reversal or surprise. Suspense and irony constitute only one pair of several antitheses inherent in tragicomic form (and implicit in its name); these have been described by Philip Edwards as 'the pleasure of being kept out of the secret and the pleasure of being let into the secret'.[33] Brooks's account of formal erotics is especially pertinent to the gestural narrative style of *The Tempest* and of the mode of romance generally.[34] Although the formal divagations are perhaps not as easy to discern in a compact work such as *The Tempest* as they are in *Cymbeline*, they are present none the less, and they recapitulate on a larger scale the sense of promise and profundity fostered by the texture of the verse.

VI

The sophisticated effects of form and style bespeak a degree of self-consciousness considerably greater than most recent political readings can admit, a self-awareness that comprehends the issues of politics and power central to the colonialist argument. The poetic and structural figures of repetition become directly pertinent to the critical debate over the European colonial impulse when that will to power is regarded as an effort to recreate the self in a new environment. Therefore the episodes and topics political critics have chosen to stress – the proprietary claims of the deceased Sycorax and her legacy to Caliban, Prospero's usurpation of the island from him, the enslavement of Ariel, the dynastic marriages of Claribel and Miranda – all these attest to the play's profound concern with reproduction, in various senses from the biological to the political to the aesthetic. Throughout its narrative *The Tempest* raises

disturbing questions about the act of reproduction, not only the genetic possibilities ('Good wombs have borne bad sons') but also the difficulties of recreating society, beginning afresh, repairing in the new world the errors of the old, and it does so in a style that refuses to cease recreating itself.

The opening scene introduces the problem of sovereignty ('What cares these roarers for the name of king?'); Prospero's epilogue begs for remission and release ('let your indulgence set me free'): from beginning to end the playwright gives prominence to the problems of dominion, freedom, political failure, and the repetition of the past. Prospero's expository recital of how he lost control of himself and his dukedom is inflected with multiple variations on political failure and the repetition of past errors. He begins with a consideration of Miranda's memory, her ability to recreate the past imaginatively – 'Of anything the image tell me that / Hath kept with thy remembrance' (1.2.43–4) – and the dimness of that memory prompts his rehearsal of the usurpation. Moreover, the daughter's piteous reaction to the tale reproduces emotionally the ordeal of banishment: she 'will cry it o'er again' (1.2.134). His lecture reviews Antonio's seizure of power and renovation of the court, and, as Stephen Orgel points out, 'this monologue is

---

[33] 'The Danger not the Death: The Art of John Fletcher', in *Jacobean Theatre*, edited John Russell Brown and Bernard Harris (London: Edward Arnold, 1960), p. 164.

[34] Patricia A. Parker brilliantly develops some of the same ideas as Brooks: 'The suspensions which for Barthes become part of an erotics of the text recall not only the constant divagations of romance and its resistance to the demands of closure, but also the frustration in Ariosto of what Barthes calls the teleological form of vulgar readerly pleasure – the desire to penetrate the veil of meaning or to hasten the narrative's gradual striptease – by a continual postponement of revelation which leaves the reader suspended, or even erotically "hung up".' *Inescapable Romance: Studies in the Poetics of a Mode* (Princeton: Princeton University Press, 1979), pp. 220–1.

only the first of a series of repetitions'.[35] Antonio encourages Sebastian to repeat the crime of deposing his brother; Prospero seeks to repair political division by arranging the dynastic marriage of Miranda and Ferdinand; Alonso is desperate at the loss of his son, which is the end of the biological line and the forfeiture of his future, Claribel being 'lost' to him as well; Stephano, Trinculo, and Caliban seek to establish their own kingdom, taking power from Prospero who has himself seized the island from Caliban; Caliban has tried to reproduce himself by raping Miranda ('I had peopled else / This isle with Calibans'); the masque of Ceres dramatizes the importance of fertility, agriculture, and orderly succession; Prospero has sought by his magical art to remake his kingdom; and Shakespeare has sought by his theatrical art to reconstruct the material world. Looked at from one point of view, colonialism becomes a form of political and cultural reproduction congruent with the effort to transcend time through art, and both of these represent versions of the defence against death.

Considerations of political and artistic re-creation lead us back to the poetry of *The Tempest*, for the stylistic and structural repetitions engage the audience textually with the same problems of authority and power that dominate political interpretation. The tendency of words and phrases to repeat themselves is a case of stylistic reproduction that creates, as I have shown, an atmosphere in which control of meaning remains necessarily elusive. The effect of the style throughout is to place the auditor in an intermediate state, and that region of indeterminacy is a version of the various other kinds of liminality associated with this text: the island is located midway between Africa and Europe; it apparently partakes of, or is hospitable to, the natural and supernatural realms; Miranda stands between childhood and maturity, Caliban between demon and human, Prospero between vengeance and mercy; even time seems arrested ('what's past is prologue'). The poetry seduces the audience into a state of

stylistic suspension, an intuitive zone between sleep and wake, 'a strange repose' like that felt by Sebastian (2.1.218) or that described in Caliban's lyric. It is a marginal condition between expectation and understanding, affirmation and scepticism, comedy and tragedy.

Poetic indeterminacy shows us how to evaluate the appropriation of the play by those who see it as a political act in the colonialist enterprise. It helps to complicate the ideology of *The Tempest*, indicating that the political ideas are more subtle and difficult than recent readings would suggest. Pleas for interpretative caution are often attacked as retrogressive politics, but the recognition that this is one of the most knowing, most self-conscious texts in the canon should warn us about pretensions to ideological certainty. On the very issues that have most deeply concerned materialist critics and their American cousins – power, social and political hierarchy, the theatre as a political instrument, freedom of action, education, and race – *The Tempest* is at its most elusive and complicated. The play valorizes ambiguity and irony, ironizing its own positions and insisting upon the inconclusiveness of its own conclusions. The new orthodoxy, which exalts the colonized, is as narrow as the old, which idealizes and excuses the colonizer.[36]

This stylistic interpretation is not, however, merely another version of New Criticism, a retreat, that is, into the restful shadows of irony and ambiguity. The difference is that this reading of *The Tempest* admits the importance of contextual study and historical location, just as it recognizes the inescapable affiliation of the

---

[35] Introduction to his edition of *The Tempest*, p. 15.

[36] See Skura, 'The Case of Colonialism', in which she argues that new historicism 'is now in danger of fostering blindness of its own. Granted that something was wrong with a commentary that focused on *The Tempest* as a self-contained project of a self-contained individual and that ignored the political situation in 1611. But something seems wrong now also, something more than the rhetorical excesses characteristic of any innovative critical movement' (pp. 46–7).

political and the aesthetic. I acknowledge the capacity of new modes of criticism to identify and promote ideological issues and other points of departure that more traditional forms of criticism have neglected or deliberately suppressed. But I also seek to balance those virtues with a sensitivity to the claims of the text. It needs to be pointed out that as students and teachers of literature we are professionally concerned with political issues not just in themselves but as they are embodied in aesthetic forms. The dismissal of verse is dangerous, especially if the subject of inquiry is verse drama. In reaction to the excesses and orthodoxies of New Criticism, our own critical practice is moving farther and farther away from the text, and in reading this play stylistically I register a mild protest against the implicit cheapening of textuality. The poetry of *The Tempest* alerts us to the delicate relation between literature and ideology.

Which is what, according to Kenneth Burke, art ought to do. In an essay on the fictional uncertainties of Mann and Gide, he identifies the pleasures of the unfixed:

so long as we feel the need of certitude, the state of doubt is discomforting, and by its very prolongation

can make for our hysterical retreat into belief, as Hans Castorp descended from his mountain to the battlefield. But why could one not come to accept his social wilderness without anguish, utilizing for his self-respect either the irony and melancholy of Mann, or the curiosity of Gide? One need not suffer under insecurity any more than an animal suffers from being constantly on the alert for danger. In the unformed there are opportunities which can be invigorating to contemplate. This state of technical apprehension can be a norm, and certainly an athletic norm.[37]

The Tempest promotes in its audience a kind of moral and imaginative athleticism, an intellectual fitness that much recent interpretation, by relaxing – or stiffening – into a single mode of reading, has evaded. The play's epistemological sophistication is inconsistent with the baldness of a single-mindedly ideological interpretation. To listen to its language is to become deeply sceptical about the operation of all kinds of power – poetic, political, and critical too.

---

[37] *Counter-statement* (rpt. Berkeley: University of California Press, 1968), p. 106.

THE LATTER END OF PROSPERO'S COMMONWEALTH

JAMES BLACK

In the first act of *The Tempest*, near the conclusion of Prospero's story of their past, Miranda asks an all-important question: 'I pray you, sir ... your reason / For raising this sea-storm' (1.2.176–8). Prospero's reply is enigmatic:

> Know thus far forth.
> By accident most strange, bountiful Fortune,
> Now my dear lady, hath mine enemies
> Brought to this shore; and by my prescience
> I find my zenith doth depend upon
> A most auspicious star, whose influence
> If now I court not, but omit, my fortunes
> Will ever after droop. Here cease more
>   questions.   (1.2.179–85)

The answer to Miranda's question is left to be inferred from the play's ending, or filled in according to each reader's expectation of how Prospero might deal with his enemies through the power that has enabled him to raise the storm. It is partly this absence of clearly stated intention that often leads commentators to express dissatisfaction at his perceived failure to achieve what they understand him to have set out to do: achieve revenge, for instance, or assure himself of his enemies' full repentance before he forgives, or (in the terms of a recent psychoanalytic approach) complete himself by working through his oedipal past.[1] But although Prospero is evasive about his intentions, he has emphasized that he raised the storm and will court his auspicious star solely in Miranda's interests: 'I have done nothing but in care of thee, / Of thee, ... my daughter' (1.2.16–17). I think that the play here suggests,

without tipping its hand, that a way is to be found through its experience by following closely what Prospero is doing for Miranda as well as to his enemies. When we do so we find a surprisingly practical (though still magical) Shakespearian marriage-plot anchored on realism in *The Tempest*'s sea of mythic possibilities.

In the complex of plots which work together in the play, the love story of Miranda and Ferdinand at first appears to be the one most quickly resolved. At first meeting they 'change eyes' and in their second scene together betroth themselves to one another, in defiance, as they think, of the *senex* who in fact is promoting their romance. Their separate solitudes – she is thundered into submissive silence and he is in wooden slavery – are confinements within the confine of the island. But here, in a turn characteristic of fairytale,[2] the confined princess comes to the aid of her rescuer. Miranda's support of Ferdinand has an added twist, though, for in their benign deception (as they think) of Prospero she uses a means employed by her father's most dangerous enemy.

When Miranda first sees Ferdinand, and

---

[1] Coppélia Kahn, 'The Providential Tempest and the Shakespearean Family', *Representing Shakespeare: New Psychoanalytic Essays*, ed. M. Schwartz and Coppélia Kahn (Baltimore and London, 1980), pp. 217–43.

[2] A discussion of the tale type 'The Girl as Helper in the Hero's Flight' is in Max Lüthi, *The Fairytale as Art Form and Portrait of Man*, trans. Jon Erickson (Bloomington, 1984), p. 5.

again when she helps him with his task and pledges herself to him in 3.1, Ferdinand makes it clear that he is the son of the King of Naples, whose enmity and whose part in the usurpation Prospero has described to her. Ferdinand appears to have no knowledge of the old Naples–Milan enmity or of how the usurping Duke of Milan, Antonio, came to succeed. In Act 5 he will call Prospero 'this famous Duke of Milan, / Of whom so often I have heard renown, / but never saw before' (5.1.195–7), but in Act 1 he appears to know only Antonio as Duke, and mourns for him as one of the lords lost with Alonso in the wreck. Miranda, however, has just been told all about the usurping and exiling plot. She hears Ferdinand mourn the wreck of his father and the Duke of Milan, and even responds to this: 'Alack, for mercy!' Yet never again does she appear to connect Ferdinand with the usurpation or consider that Prospero just might transfer his indignation at Alonso to the lost king's son. Her father's wrath at Ferdinand is a continual puzzle to her: 'My father's of a better nature, sir, / Than he appears by speech', she reassures Ferdinand, 'This is unwonted / Which now came from him' (1.2.500–02). Prospero does not of course directly attack Ferdinand for being his father's son; in fact, he justifies his anger by alleging that Ferdinand has 'usurped' the title of King of Naples and come to the island as a spy. In the midst of all this mock-paranoia Miranda may well be confused, but 'Naples' and 'usurp' jog her memory not at all. There may be a suggestion that the sleep which Prospero induced in Miranda directly after telling her their story is a slumber of benign forgetfulness – he calls it 'a good dullness' – so that having told her (and the audience) of the evil that has gone before he causes that dark backward to slip away from her again, restoring her as it were to prelapsarian innocence. The love-plot certainly glances at the edenic state, and a conscious act of forgetting plays a crucial part in the play's outcome.

Miranda's love for Ferdinand and her intention to help him in his labours provoke her to the stratagem of visiting Ferdinand when Prospero's back is turned. As mentioned, she is of course conforming to archetypes as the daughter who assists her lover to fulfil or escape from the tyrannical conditions set him by her father – Medea, or Jessica who 'Did … steal from the wealthy Jew, / And with an unthrift love did run from Venice' (*The Merchant of Venice* 5.1.15–16). However, Miranda has a model in *The Tempest* itself. She observes and takes exactly the same opportunity which Antonio used against Prospero. 'My trust', Prospero told her, 'like a good parent, did beget of him, / A falsehood…' (1.2.93–5) – a circumstance benignly but firmly echoed in Miranda's assurance to Ferdinand:

> My father
> Is hard at study. Pray now, rest yourself.
> He's safe for these three hours. (3.1.19–21)

It seems quite clear that Prospero's tutoring of Miranda during their years on the island has not included magic in the curriculum. Though she speaks, in her very first line, of his 'Art' and even helps him with his magic garment (1.2.23–4), Prospero's ubiquity and power of invisibility appear to be unknown to her. Thus with Prospero 'safe', as she thinks, Miranda proceeds to break one paternal order after another and to acknowledge she is breaking them (3.1.36–7, 58–9). Ferdinand responds by briefly remembering *his* father, and they plight their troth as independent persons.

Prospero watches all this, of course, has promoted it and created the opportunity by separating Ferdinand from the other castaways. Has Miranda observed how safe these three hours are when Prospero is 'transported / And rapt in secret studies' (1.2.76–7); is her security in stealing from him bred only out of her own observation of his habits, or is there any memory of the recent tale wherein Antonio, her uncle, observed and acted on Prospero's retirement in just the same manner though for a less benign purpose? These questions remain; what probably matters more is that while she believes she is conspiring against Prospero she unwittingly is conspiring with him. In this respect she is like Antonio, who in Act Two moves with Sebastian against Alonso in repetition of the crime in Milan. Anticipated by Prospero and allowed to proceed to just before the last moment of enacted will, Antonio's crime merely demonstrates his incorrigibility and his bent for unoriginal sin. His predictability really needs no Art to foresee.

Thus Miranda's stealing to Ferdinand is an aspect of the larger plot, and of Prospero himself, that various critics have commented on – namely that the conspiracies against Prospero, including Antonio's in Milan, are created or at least fostered by Prospero himself. Stephen Greenblatt says of Caliban's, Stefano's and Trinculo's usurpation plan that 'Prospero's art has in effect created the conspiracy as well as the defence against the conspiracy.'[3] Harry Berger argues that Prospero's language in describing the original usurpation to Miranda encourages us to believe that he is partly responsible for what happened, and further that 'unwittingly [Prospero] did everything he could to cultivate whatever dram of evil his brother may have been heir to.'[4] David Sundelson writes of the psychological payoffs of being usurped:

The departure from Milan is an escape from shame and weakness as much as an expulsion. The Duke flees from the fearful demands of office ... In one sense their exile is an ordeal to be endured, but in more important ways it is a delicious idyll on an island which, to borrow Lear's description, unites them 'like birds i'th' cage'.[5]

It does seem perverse or else astoundingly long-sighted of Prospero to have played with his enemies in Italy a conspiratorial game that placed him and his infant daughter at sea in a leaky boat and marooned them (by chance or providence) on a remote island. Yet from what he tells Miranda, Prospero, even when rapt from the political world, seems to have observed Antonio's rise in that world:

Thy false uncle ...
Being once perfected how to grant suits,

How to deny them, who t'advance and who
To trash for over-topping, new created
The creatures that were mine, I say – or
    changed 'em
Or else new formed 'em; having both the key
Of officer and office, set all hearts i'th' state
To what tune pleased his ear.   (1.2.77–85)

And

            He being thus lorded
Not only with what my revenue yielded
But what my power might else exact, like one
Who having into truth, by telling oft,
Made such a sinner of his memory
To credit his own lie, he did believe
He was indeed the Duke.   (1.2.97–103)

No doubt most of this derives from twelve years' reflection on the events and from knowledge of the human heart, but it comes out as if Prospero in Milan, invisible, had watched every stage of Antonio's self-corruption. Though he tells Miranda many details of the usurpation he does not tell her he was surprised. We are left to speculate on whether the prescience exhibited on the island was already cultivated in Milan – whether the volumes he prized above his dukedom and which were brought along by Gonzalo were not already packed for travel. Every major character in the play is a plotter against received authority, Prospero's use of his powers being in effect a counterplot against the King of Naples and the present Duke of Milan. Victims and victimizers are all, so to speak, in the same boat. The gentle conspiracy of his bird to fly the cage (in parallel with Ariel's murmurings about the term of his contract) is really Prospero's own device: he pretends to retire to the library as he did with Antonio and 'It goes

---

[3] Stephen Greenblatt, *Shakespearean Negotiations: The Circulation of Social Energy in Renaissance England* (Berkeley and Los Angeles, 1988), p. 145.

[4] Harry Berger, Jr, 'Miraculous Harp: A Reading of Shakespeare's *Tempest*', *Shakespeare Studies*, 5 (1969), 254, 261.

[5] David Sundelson, 'So Rare a Wonder'd Father: Prospero's *Tempest*', *Representing Shakespeare*, p. 36.

on ... / As [his] soul prompts it' (1.2.423–4).

Deception, then, is part of Miranda's bid for independence. She may be a paragon, but in marriage comedies lovers have stratagems. Ferdinand has the comparatively easy initiation rite of a physical ordeal, and he performs with grace the labour that Caliban has to be driven to do. By degrees, as she daringly breaks her father's precepts, both unbind themselves from parental authority and move into an agreed relationship that on its romance side is the 'Fair encounter / Of two most rare affections!' (3.1.74–5) and on the practical side of a formal, in fact pointedly legal, contract of betrothal: to refresh an old critical phrase, a marriage of heaven *and* earth. This formal process really began when Ferdinand first saw Miranda. Even in his wonder, he made a declaration of his status and intentions. First he put a question, 'My prime request, ... is – O you wonder – / If you be maid or no?' (1.2.429–31). Even when she assured him that she was certainly a maid, his declaration, when he came to it, was conditional on her eligibility for a royal marriage: 'O, if a virgin, / And your affection not gone forth, I'll make you / The Queen of Naples' (1.2.451–3). In between these two speeches he declared (to the father of his prospective bride as one would in a formal suit), 'Myself am Naples': it is worth remembering that *The Tempest* was thought appropriate to be acted in the festivities at the marriage of King James's daughter. The pattern is set here for what in normal circumstances would be the negotiating of a marriage contract (the bourgeois version of the process can be seen in 2.1 of *The Taming of the Shrew*), but the father seems unwilling, to say the least of it. Hence, meeting resistance, the lovers proceed to steal love's sweet bait from, as they think, fearful hooks, and in 3.1 make a private though no less formal contract with one another. The steps are clearly marked:

FERDINAND   I am in my condition
  A prince, Miranda, I do think a king ...
MIRANDA   Do you love me?

FERDINAND
  O heaven, O earth, bear witness to this sound,
  And crown what I profess with kind event
  If I speak true! ...   I,
  Beyond all limit of what else i'th' world,
  Do love, prize, honour you. ...
MIRANDA
  I am your wife, if you will marry me. ...
MIRANDA
  My husband then?
FERDINAND
  Ay, with a heart as willing
  As bondage e'er of freedom. Here's my hand.
MIRANDA
  And mine, with my heart in't.   (3.1.59–91)

Two aspects of this exchange should be noted. First, Miranda clearly has collected herself since 1.2, so that when Ferdinand resumes his profession of love she guides him firmly to a declaration of intent to marry. Second, a contemporary audience, seeing the joining of hands and hearing the exchange of formal declarations, would have known that, magic island setting or not, it was looking in on a *per verba* ceremony of troth-plight. In connection with the playful marriage ceremony between Orlando and Ganymede-Rosalind in *As You Like It*, Agnes Latham cites Pollock's and Maitland's history of English law on consentual espousal in its two forms. These forms were

sponsalia per verba de futuro, which takes place if man or woman promise each other that they will hereafter become husband and wife; *sponsalia per verba de praesenti*, which takes place if they declare that they take each other as husband and wife now at this very moment.[6]

It being clear to the audience that espousal is being declared by both parties, there remains to be established which form, *de praesenti* or *de futuro*, is intended. The tense in which a promise is spoken is vital, as between 'I do take' and 'I will take', and the grammar here in *The Tempest* is inconsistent: 'I am your wife if you

---

[6] Quoted from F. Pollock and F. W. Maitland, *The History of English Law Before the Time of Edward I* in *As You Like It*, ed. Agnes Latham (London, 1975), p. 134.

will marry me'; 'My husband, then? Ay ...
Here's my hand. And mine.' The 'I am' appears
to counter the 'if you will' and even the 'then'
might be temporal rather than conclusive. This,
as I think, studied confusion of tense leaves
Shakespeare with a card up his sleeve: are they
married now or is this a *de futuro* pledge? The
card is produced only a dozen lines from the
end of the play when Prospero directs:

> And so to Naples,
> Where I have hope to see the nuptial
> Of these our dear-belovèd solemnized.
>
> (5.1.311–13)

Prospero has of course been, in two senses of
the word, a witness to the *per verba* agreement,
even though unseen by the parties. That the
ceremony is thus witnessed and not witnessed is
a comic complication. So is Ferdinand's unwitting (but known to Prospero and the audience) misrepresentation of himself as 'I do think
a king.' He thinks he has the right to marry
without his father's consent, his father being
dead – he will ask Alonso's forgiveness for this
presumption in 5.1. Nor is he even free in
another sense, as he and Miranda well know,
for he is Prospero's bondman. He appears to
remember this fact with some bravado, and
when he says 'Ay, with a heart as willing / As
bondage e'er of freedom', the 'Ay' would have
been sufficient.

The church did not approve of *per verba*
marriages unless its blessing was asked,
especially if consummation took place before a
church ceremony was held. And civil law,
which did not consider that a private espousal
conferred property right or identified heirs
(obviously a crucial matter to noble families),
insisted on a public declaration or ceremony,
such as Prospero looks forward to seeing in
Milan. It is precisely in the terms of both ritual
and property that he lectures Ferdinand when
giving him Miranda's hand in 4.1: 'If I have too
austerely punished you, / Your compensation
makes amends', he begins, and goes on from
'compensation' to other terms of legal applica-

tion: 'I tender to thy hand', 'I ratify this my rich
gift', 'Then, as my gift and thine own acquisition / Worthily purchased, take my daughter',
'this contract'. And on the matter of consummation before blessing there is his fierce exhortation to chastity:

> If thou dost break her virgin knot before
> All sanctimonious ceremonies may
> With full and holy rite be ministered,
> No sweet aspersion shall the heavens let fall
> To make this contract grow; but barren hate,
> Sour-eyed disdain, and discord, shall bestrew
> The union of your bed with weeds so loathly
> That you shall hate it both. Therefore take
> heed. (4.1.15–22)

'Sanctimonious ceremonies with full and holy
rite' has a high-church sound. The masque does
not fulfil this requirement, even though it is
dedicated to 'this man and maid, / Whose vows
are that no bed-right shall be paid / Till
Hymen's torch be lighted' (4.1.95–7). Legal
terms creep into the masque, however, for Iris
asks Ceres to celebrate a contract of true love
and 'Some donation freely to estate' upon the
lovers. In fact, in the masque Ceres seems to be
not so much the goddess of earth's fertility in
general as genius of rich and well-kept baronial
acres reaped by sunburned sickle-men; with all
the romance, pastoral and marital blessings, the
goddesses promise and celebrate a very tidy
holding.

Within the masque there is an aside and an
interruption, both of which intrude on its optimistic vision. The aside concerns whether
Venus and Cupid will attend with Juno. 'Since
they did plot', Ceres says,

> The means that dusky Dis my daughter got,
> Her and her blind boy's scandalled company
> I have forsworn. (4.1.89–91)

I call this an aside or digression because it
appears to be a sort of encoded message from
Ariel, who is playing or introducing Ceres.
When Prospero remembers Caliban's plot he
summons Ariel and tells him 'We must prepare
to meet with Caliban', and Ariel's response is

'When I presented Ceres / I thought to have told thee of it' (4.1.166–8). 'Why does Ariel mention this?', Frank Kermode asks in his commentary note on the line,[7] and the answer may be: to show that he wished, or attempted, to warn Prospero without interrupting the masque. Dis, ruler of the underworld, abducted Ceres' daughter Proserpine; Caliban, an underworld figure if ever there was one, is advancing with Stefano and Trinculo to seize Miranda. Did Ariel alter Prospero's script, and did Prospero notice at the time? Whatever the answers to these questions, this part of the masque of heaven and earth, then, is about earth in a more than symbolic sense ('Thou earth' was Prospero's first address to Caliban, 1.2.317).

The other earthly intrusion on the masque is Ferdinand's interruption near the end, breaking the silence imposed on those permitted to view magical business. He takes it upon himself to enquire 'May I be bold / To think these spirits?' This is a question that Ferdinand has been asking in one form or another since he first appeared in the play distressed, confused, drawn on by Ariel's song and wondering:

> Where should this music be? I'th'air or th'
> earth?
> It sounds no more; and sure it waits upon
> Some god o'th' island.   (1.2.391–3)

His conjecture on first seeing Miranda was 'Most sure the goddess / On whom these airs attend' (1.2.425–6). Before the masque we never see or hear him told of Prospero's magic: even when Ferdinand is spellbound, Prospero is just a threatening man to him (1.2.492). In the masque, Ceres and Juno sing, and the effect on Ferdinand is of 'That strain again' (there is in fact some intertextuality between *The Tempest* 1.2.390–97 and *Twelfth Night* 1.1.4–7), and he reacts:

> This is a most majestic vision, and
> Harmonious charmingly. May I be bold
> To think these spirits?
> PROSPERO   Spirits, which by mine art
> I have from their confines called to enact
> My present fancies.

> FERDINAND   Let me live here ever!
> So rare a wondered father and a wise
> Makes this place paradise.   (4.1.118–24)

Finally understanding something of Prospero's magic art, Ferdinand reacts with an initiate's enthusiasm, just as Miranda will do when she sees the rest of the castaways: 'O brave new world'. 'Let me live here ever!' is not consistent with 'I'll make you / The Queen of Naples': the latter end of Ferdinand's commonwealth is forgetting the beginning. However momentary his wish to settle in what he supposes is the island paradise, it none the less raises a question that the masque does not address: the spirits' promises of propertied abundance do not say *where* it will be enjoyed. In context of the carefully negotiated betrothal which Prospero is promoting, and in the equally important matter of just where (literally) the action is heading, the question of where the principals will live is crucial. Goety drives the vision, but geography must also be considered in Prospero's design: the ordered landscape promised in the masque waits back in Italy.

It appears that this landscape is not offered by the island, except in dreams and fancies. The point has been made in 2.1, where Gonzalo also contemplated living on the island forever. No great discriminator of places, Gonzalo thinks Carthage and Tunis are the same country (it is surprising that detectors of personal allegory in *The Tempest* have not considered Gonzalo's geographical confusion as a touch of Shakespearian self-parody); he convinces himself the island could be better than Italy. In the teeth of reason, for even Prospero himself refers to 'this bare island', Gonzalo's determination to think all for the best colours his view: 'How lush and lusty the grass looks! How green!' It is only a step from here to his utopian meditation, which rests on the dismantling of all the bad old world's systems, including degree, priority and place:

---

[7] *The Tempest*, ed. Frank Kermode (London, 1968), p. 105.

> For no kind of traffic
> Would I admit, no name of magistrate;
> Letters should not be known; riches, poverty,
> And use of service, none; contract, succession,
> Bourn, bound of land, tilth, vineyard, none; . . .
> No occupation, all men idle, all.   (2.1.154–60)

And having begun by fancying himself to be king of this ideal state he of course makes the unfortunate slip of adding 'no sovereignty' to his list of innovations, inspiring the jeers of Sebastian and Antonio: 'Yet he would be king on't. The latter end of his commonwealth forgets the beginning' (2.1.163–5). The confusion detracts not at all from the good nature of Gonzalo, who in his own distress still doggedly tries to divert Alonso, but there is a suggestion that utopian schemes run into illogic, or begin in it, as Caliban's hopes for Stefano's rule do. The play's best commentary on Gonzalo's idyll is the masque, where the terms and values which Gonzalo would reject are in effect re-endorsed. Where Gonzalo's commonwealth would abolish contract, succession, property, riches and work, the masque presents these elements as blessings, celebrating especially the fruits of agricultural labour, which are variegated crops, pruned vineyards, winter forage, controlled rivers and the efforts of sunburned sicklemen. *Otium* does not appear to be included: this paradise, if it is a paradise, is built or rebuilt by adamic labour. As Ferdinand declared during his ordeal, when he was less excited: 'There be some sports are painful, and their labour / Delight in them sets off' (3.1.1–2). Thus Ferdinand's enthusiasm for living on the island ever and enjoying a visionary paradise appears to go against the grain of Prospero's efforts and effects. Considered as in part a response to Ferdinand's outburst, the revels speech is less a set-piece or private meditation than a reassurance and mild rebuke. Prospero tells Ferdinand yet again that the actors in the masque were all spirits and the tableaux illusions; one cannot switch on such shows at will or indulge in them endlessly; the brevity of the scene is a metaphor for the shortness of life – one does not live ever anywhere. He does not tell him that the magic which raised the vision has itself a limited term. Its final work will be the confusion of Caliban's plot and settling with the castaways.

Alonso and his party have come to Prospero's island dressed for a wedding, and present a visual contradiction as they mourn 'not in ashes and sackcloth, but in new silk' (*2 Henry IV* 1.2.197–8). Gonzalo points out to Adrian and then to Alonso that despite being drenched in the sea

Our garments are now as fresh as when we put them on first in Afric, at the marriage of the King's fair daughter Claribel to the King of Tunis.

(2.1.73–6, 101–3)

The audience probably should be given some reason for the matter of the royal households of Naples and Milan sailing together past the island, and Shakespeare appropriately puts the reason into the mouth of the most circumstantial of the characters (in contrast to Prospero's mysteriousness, most of his adversaries explain themselves in detail). Gonzalo's comment on their clothing and the wedding is not left there, for Sebastian takes it up with bitter sarcasm – ''Twas a sweet marriage, and we prosper well in our return' – and Adrian tries to keep peace: 'Tunis was never graced before with such a paragon to their queen.' Reminiscences of Claribel throughout this scene obviously are not mere recapitulations of the Neapolitan Court Calendar. One reason for the recurring references to her is that Gonzalo is sorrowing at losing her as well as Ferdinand:

> Would I had never
> Married my daughter there! For, coming thence,
> My son is lost; and, in my rate, she too,
> Who is so far from Italy removed
> I ne'er again shall see her.   (2.1.113–17)

His grief is real, but his remorse is unfocused; he blames himself for the wreck, as he should do, but not for the real reason behind the wreck. Sebastian's perception of cause and effect is equally limited:

Sir, you may thank yourself for this great loss,
That would not bless our Europe with your
    daughter,
But rather loose her to an African ...
You were kneeled to and importuned otherwise
By all of us, and the fair soul herself
Weighed between loathness and obedience at
Which end o'th' beam should bow. We have lost
    your son,
I fear, for ever ...
              The fault's your own.
                    (2.1.129–40)

The Iago-like recrimination about loosing one's daughter to an African seems just to glance at Proserpine, dusky Dis and his kingdom 'ten leagues beyond man's life', the myth touched in the masque and in Caliban's plot – Claribel and Miranda are sisters in more ways than one. But Sebastian means to rub the sore only on the surface. The fault that lies below Alonso's putting the sea between Italy and Claribel is the fault of having done so to Prospero's daughter. Alonso's present remorse recalls (though not yet to him) past remorselessness. It is his original wrong, not his son, that lies deeply mudded, and he has to dredge up the former before he can recover the latter.

Where Gonzalo puzzles over the miracle of the wedding garments emerging fresh from the sea and Alonso, however superficially, looks for some cause-and-effect explanation for his loss, Antonio and Sebastian are untouched by the shipwreck. Everything is opportunity to them, and opportunity seized brings nothing but reward. Antonio even turns the phenomenon of the clothing to use in urging Sebastian to murder Alonso:

SEBASTIAN   I remember
  You did supplant your brother Prospero.
ANTONIO   True;
  And look how well my garments sit upon me,
  Much feater than before.   (2.1.275–8)

Likewise Ferdinand's drowning and Claribel's exile make only a graph of royal succession on which moves can be charted: 'My brother's daughter's Queen of Tunis; / So is she heir of Naples' and 'There be that can rule Naples / As well as [Alonso]' (2.1.260–61, 267–8). This charting is just as base as Stefano's decision to take Miranda as his queen because 'She will become [his] bed ... / And bring [him] forth brave brood' (3.2.105–6) or Caliban's fantasy of using Miranda to people the isle with Calibans. Antonio's very being is linked to these other obscenities by Miranda's explanation of his natural badness and unwittingly her own danger: 'Good wombs have borne bad sons' (1.2.119). Even Caliban has a sense of succession, 'This island's mine, by Sycorax my mother' (1.2.334). As Antonio pawned his dukedom to Alonso in return for help in deposing Prospero, and plots again to make Sebastian king and have his love (2.1.300) by murdering Alonso, Caliban bargains for an easier rule than Prospero's by showing Stefano how Prospero may be killed. It is Caliban who first gives Stefano the idea of being a king, 'I'll swear myself thy subject' (2.2.151), leading to Stefano's decision that 'The King and all our company else being drowned, we will inherit here' (2.2.173–4). When Caliban further on negotiates the removal of Prospero he cleverly works first on Stefano's vanity – 'I know thou dar'st, / But this thing dare not' (3.2.55–6) – and then on his lust: 'And that most deeply to consider is / The beauty of his daughter' (3.2.99–100). Miranda's beauty and the grotesquely-punning assurance that 'she will become thy bed' convince Stefano to declare that after he kills Prospero 'His daughter and I will be king and queen – save our graces! – and Trinculo and thyself shall be viceroys' (3.2.107–9). The plot would make Miranda a queen only in the sense that in Stefano's proletarian imagination the titles of king, queen and viceroy are magic. Still, there is a dim sense of practical economy, butler's economy, in Stefano's declaration of his commonwealth. With a viceroy monster to show him the best springs, and bring the fruit, nuts, fish and game of the isle (2.2.159–71), and the additional services of Miranda and Trinculo, his occupation of the place is not quite as impractical as Gonzalo's utopia. And in its fantasy about being king *here*, on the island, his *realpolitik* is superior to Antonio's and Sebastian's, who appear not to think at all about how they will get back to Italy with their fancied gains. Thus a parody of royal coupling has been arranged – by Caliban. In fact, at Caliban's request the compact is immediately celebrated by a musical entertainment in which Stefano and Trinculo sing a catch and Ariel plays the tune on a tabor and pipe, a mysterious accompaniment which inspires Caliban's beautiful 'The isle is full of noises . . .' Stefano takes the music and Caliban's speech as endorsements of his decision:

> This will prove a brave kingdom to me, where
> I shall have my music for nothing.
> CALIBAN
> When Prospero is destroyed. (3.2.147–9)

The play now has three negotiated 'marriages'. One of them is this gruesome union-by-conquest, another was possibly enforced: 'I . . . married my daughter there.' The only spontaneously-loving one is still being developed, for Prospero says at the end of 3.1 that he still must 'perform / Much business appertaining' to Miranda's and Ferdinand's betrothal.

This business proceeds to the focusing of Alonso's remorse through the device of the disappearing banquet. Kermode notes that the scene recalls Job 20:23, 27, and he quotes the Authorized Version's reading:[8] 'When [the wicked man] is about to fill his belly, God shall cast the fury of his wrath upon him . . . The heaven shall reveal his iniquity; and the earth shall rise up against him.' As Antonio's plot and Alonso's mourning for Ferdinand are re-emphasized at the beginning of the scene (3.3), the Geneva Bible's marginal notes on the contiguous verses, 22 and 28, also seem descriptive: 'The wicked shall never be in rest: for one wicked man shall seek to destroy another' and 'The children of the wicked shall flow away like rivers and be disposed in divers places.' The action of the scene and Ariel's theophanic

performance, scripted by Prospero, are so impressive as to make this sort of attributed derivation reasonable: reading *The Tempest* is like reading mythologies by flashes of lightning. There are less mythic echoes too. Theatrically, the spectacle of the wedding guests (as they still are) approaching the table weary and faint after treading a maze 'through forthrights and meanders' (3.1.2–3), then being tantalized and rebuked, distantly recalls *The Taming of the Shrew* 4:1, where Petruccio makes Katherine's dinner vanish by a not especially quaint device and afterward preaches her a sermon.

Alonso responds to the more profound echoes of the experience. His description of what he has heard out of this whirlwind may recall the Geneva note to Job 37:2 explaining 'the thunder, whereby he speaketh to men to waken their dullness.' Where Antonio and Sebastian are moved only to hysterical defiance, he is stirred to uncover the action for which he should be remorseful:

> Methought the billows spoke and told me of it,
> The winds did sing it to me, and the thunder,
> That deep and dreadful organ-pipe, pronounced
> The name of Prosper. It did bass my trespass.
> Therfor my son i' th'ooze is bedded, and
> I'll seek him deeper than e'er plummet sounded,
> And with him there lie mudded. (3.3.96–192)

This is true desperation, consisting of a deep sense of sin with no apparent outlet for confession or repentance. By Prospero's devices Alonso has been led to see himself as spiritually empty, the condition of diffidence which drives Gloucester to seek Dover Cliff. The dramatic question that hangs fire between the end of 3.3 and the beginning of the fifth act is whether Prospero has preserved Alonso from the sea and

---

8 *The Tempest*, ed. Frank Kermode, p. 85. It is tempting to see parallel readings and echoes from the Authorized Version of 1611 in *The Tempest*, but the dates of this bible and the play make the exercise tricky. For example, does the play's line 'The latter end of his commonwealth forgets the beginning' owe anything to the Authorized Version's Job 42:12, 'So the Lord blessed the latter end of Job more than his beginning'?

from Antonio only to allow him to destroy himself. Prospero's summations here and at the end of the fourth act are ominous:

> My high charms work,
> And these mine enemies are all knit up
> In their distractions. They are now in my
> power;
> And in these fits I leave them   (3.3.88–91)

And,

> At this hour
> Lies at my mercy all mine enemies.
> Shortly shall all my labours end   (4.1.260–62)

But we learn at the beginning of Act 5 that Prospero has not left Alonso to harm himself, but caused Ariel to impound them all. At the beginning of the final act Prospero enters to complete his 'project', a word that is frequently interpreted as suggesting projection, the last phase of a scientific philosopher's or alchemist's experiment, especially as he goes on to say 'My charms crack not' (5.1.2).[9] However, the only 'alchemy' that might be foreshadowed here is the psychological transmutation of the base metal that his enemies represent, and Prospero either renounces this attempt or admits its impossibility (or its disrespectable associations: Antonio is an evil transmuter who 'New created / The creatures that were [Prospero's], ... or changed 'em / Or else new formed 'em' 1.2.81–3). In choosing to forgive, Prospero has few illusions about profound change: 'They shall be themselves' (5.1.32). Simply the things they are shall make them live. But Alonso is still part of a project or 'business appertaining' which will result in his emptiness being filled and in the completion of the one element lacking in Miranda's and Ferdinand's betrothal agreement: Ferdinand's father's consent.

In what follows, Alonso is by artful degrees moved to this consent. First, Prospero makes his sensational appearance as 'the wrongèd Duke of Milan' (5.1.109). While Alonso, Antonio and Sebastian were still entranced Prospero formally indicted each in turn before forgiving them (5.1.71–9), and now, before publicly requiring his dukedom from Antonio, he accuses him of wickedness and again pronounces forgiveness. Presenting himself as 'the wronged Duke' is his only hint of accusation when speaking to Alonso. Thus Alonso's 'Thy dukedom I resign, and do entreat / Thou pardon me my wrongs' (5.1.120–21) is not enforced remorse, though it should be noticed that Alonso pleads in form, legally, speaking precisely to the fact and words of Prospero's grievance. Antonio and Sebastian are of course incorrigible, but they are no longer Prospero's concern in this scene. He has his dukedom free and clear from Antonio and Alonso, and proceeds to treat with the King as between nobility and also as an equal in 'the like loss' (5.1.145) of his daughter and Alonso's son. Berger sees this exchange as nothing more than a cat-and-mouse prolongation of Alonso's pain, while Clifford Leech says Prospero 'delights to keep Alonso in ignorance of Ferdinand's preservation and in riddling speech mocks his grief by pretending that his own daughter is likewise dead', all the while building up to the effect at the revelation.[10] But this effect will depend in great part on how Alonso, to whom it specifically is directed (5.1.167–73), receives it, and how he receives it depends on how he is prepared in heart and mind. Hearing Prospero's equivocal tale of having lost his daughter, he bursts out:

> A daughter?
> O heavens, that they were living both in
> Naples,
> The king and queen there! That they were,
> I wish
> Myself were mudded in that oozy bed
> Where my son lies.   (5.1.150–54)

He speaks as from the former desperation which drove him to seek Ferdinand's corpse

---

9 In the Epilogue there is a (perhaps tongue-in-cheek) reduction of the 'project ..., / Which was to please'.

10 Berger, p. 276. Clifford Leech, *Shakespeare's Tragedies and Other Studies in Seventeenth Century Drama* (London, 1961), pp. 146–7.

'and with him ... lie mudded', but now he envisions some use for himself as a willing counter in a redeeming substitutive bargain that returns not only his son but also Prospero's daughter. The thought is a kind of grace. It also pronounces what Prospero wants and needs pronounced, endorsement of the betrothal. As blind Gloucester blesses his (as he thinks) lost son Edgar on the edge of the supposed cliff and Lear, 'still far wide' or mentally astray, calls the lady bending over him 'my child, Cordelia' (*King Lear* 4.6.43, 63), so Alonso spontaneously confers his seal on the marriage of Ferdinand and Miranda. The pretence that both children are lost is really a small *commedia* movement wherein the old man is tricked into endorsing the young people's desire; the Shakespearian twist is that here one old man benignly deludes another. When Alonso considers Ferdinand and Miranda together, Prospero formally re-declares himself as Duke. And since Alonso has given him so 'good a thing', he proposes to 'requite' him with another (5.1.171): the terms are those of equal bargaining. It is worth noting that even though Prospero has received only what was his own in the first place, for all Alonso has done is clear the dukedom of the suzerainty obligation to Naples incurred by Antonio in exchange for Alonso's help in the usurpation, he makes the matter a gentle transaction, the giving of a good thing for a good thing. The alternative that loomed earlier in the play was the requiting of evil for evil. In this revelation speech Prospero uses the passive voice, studiously avoiding laying blame: 'I am Prospero, and that very Duke / Which was thrust forth of Milan [and] / Upon this shore ... was landed' (5.1.161–3). Thus Alonso receives pardon without public recrimination, and receives his son. And from his son, not from Prospero, he learns the identity of the young woman whom Alonso, like Ferdinand, first takes to be a goddess, and of the betrothal:

> Sir, she is mortal;
> But by immortal providence she's mine.
> I chose her when I could not ask my father

For his advice, nor thought I had one. She
Is daughter to this famous Duke of Milan, ...
>> Of whom I have
> Received a second life; and second father
> This lady makes him to me.   (5.1.191–9)

'Received a second life' suggests revival from death. Alonso scarcely can do other than renew his blessing – 'I am hers' – and, a few lines further on, proclaim his own renewal in this union:

>> Give me your hands.
> Let grief and sorrow still embrace his heart
> That doth not wish you joy.   (5.1.217–19)

This moment of reconciliation through love is often compared to the harmony at the end of *Romeo and Juliet* – Shakespeare at last letting Romeo and Juliet marry and live because Montague has shaken hands with Capulet.[11] The rhetoric of that earlier 'glooming peace' actually throws light on the process of marital negotiations which I have been tracing in *The Tempest*. When Romeo and Juliet lie dead, their fathers reconcile and agree to commemorate their children's love.

CAPULET
> O brother Montague, give me thy hand.
> This is my daughter's jointure, for no more
> Can I demand.
MONTAGUE   But I can give thee more,
> For I will raise her statue in pure gold,
> That whiles Verona by that name is known
> There shall no figure at such rate be set
> As that of true and faithful Juliet.
CAPULET
> As rich shall Romeo's by his lady's lie,
> Poor sacrifices of our enmity.
>> (*Romeo and Juliet* 5.3.295–303)

The legal word 'jointure' used by Juliet's father refers to that portion of marital property which was kept in trust to provide a living for the wife in the event of her widowhood; this portion is negotiated at the time of entering into the

---

[11] See, for example, John Wain, *The Living World of Shakespeare* (Harmondsworth, 1964), p. 257.

marriage contract. Any part of it remaining after the widow dies may be claimed by her father, if living. As the Friar has just recounted to everyone, Romeo died before Juliet, leaving her a widow (a thought that calls for the rephrasing of a startled question in *The Tempest*, 'How came that "widow" in? Widow Juliet!'), and she died soon after. There of course was no marriage contract or property exchanged, and so Capulet's claim of jointure-reversion is a very rueful jest, as to say 'The law requires that you give me what is mine to claim from my daughter's estate; I claim your hand in friendship.' Montague then in effect says he will endow the bride with (or sadly, as) a gold effigy and Capulet gives one equally rich to the bridegroom. This exchange is grimly in the spirit of *The Tempest*'s masque:

> A contract of true love to celebrate
> And some donation freely to estate
> On the blest lovers.

Montague and Capulet in effect fall into negotiating in formal terms and in the language of valuation (does 'no figure at such rate be set' refer to the value of the statue or to Juliet?). What they are negotiating is a marriage contract; with tragic irony, they are doing it postmortem. In FI and QI Capulet's second last line reads 'As rich shall Romeo by his Lady lie': marriage contracts set the property terms by which a man and woman come to lie together.

Like Montague and Capulet determining that their children's story will be figured in gold, Gonzalo cries out that the events he has witnessed should be 'set ... down / With gold on lasting pillars'. In the conclusion of *The Tempest* three stories are in being. The first of these consists of the prologue-tale Prospero told to Miranda and the events the audience has seen and heard. The second is Gonzalo's summation, the record for the pillars. The third is the account by which Prospero says he will make the night go quick away: 'The story of my life, / And the particular accidents gone by / Since I came to this isle' (5.1.308). Will the third of

these accounts be exactly like the first? Though he says 'I'll deliver all', Prospero can hardly reveal his secret studies or dwell too much on the cause of Alonso's suffering. He cannot tell now, as he could not when Miranda asked, his reason for raising this sea-storm. He cannot reveal Antonio's and Sebastian's murder plot, for to do so would be to shatter Miranda's vision of the brave new world and lose the only control he has over these two: 'At this time I will tell no tales' (5.1.130–1). Besides, he already has begun to suppress remembrance of Alonso's and Gonzalo's rôle as thrusters-out. In short, having forgiven his former enemies Prospero has committed himself to a process of creative forgetting of wrongs. He does not have the total amnesia about the past that he apparently induced in Miranda after telling her about it, but he is editing-out Alonso's culpability. In fact, he counsels Alonso to do the same:

ALONSO   I am [Miranda's]
   But O, how oddly will it sound, that I
   Must ask my child forgiveness!
PROSPERO   There, sir, stop.
   Let us not burden our remembrance with
   A heaviness that's gone.   (5.1.199–203)

Prospero's story to the castaways, then, cannot be the full story. The full story already is melting into thin air. In its place is Gonzalo's relation, the gold-letter version (a purple passage, too, for audiences and readers to ring round in their minds):

> Was Milan thrust from Milan, that his issue
> Should become kings of Naples? O rejoice
> Beyond a common joy! And set it down
> With gold on lasting pillars: in one voyage
> Did Claribel her husband find at Tunis
> And Ferdinand her brother found a wife
> Where he himself was lost; Prospero his dukedom
> In a poor isle; and all of us ourselves,
> When no man was his own.   (5.1.208–16)

Gonzalo borrows Prospero's use of the passive voice: was Milan thrust from Milan? His ability to construct a *felix culpa* is endearing, but

Claribel did not exactly 'find' her husband at Tunis; her marriage was arranged and she went there reluctantly. Now Gonzalo absolves and consoles Alonso on that matter through the parallel with Ferdinand's good fortune. The elliptic 'Prospero his dukedom In a poor isle' suggests Prospero found his dukedom there rather than demanded and got it back from his brother and Naples. 'And all of us ourselves' bespeaks a wonderful tolerance of the vicious Antonio and Sebastian, who are still as Prospero told Ariel they would be: themselves (5.1.32). In a grammar of assent that absolves everyone, the official history has begun to be written: *was* Milan thrust from Milan?

Though Prospero knows what he knows, this golden story is perforce the end for which he raised the storm, negotiated the betrothal, used his power and gave it up. His book is or will be drowned 'deeper than did ever plummet sound' (5.1.56), where Alonso thought Ferdinand to be and frantically rushed to 'seek him deeper than e'er plummet sounded, / And with him there lie mudded' (3.3.101–2). It is as if Prospero has given up the book in exchange for the Neapolitan royal house; Miranda is now part of that house, and of its story. When Prospero determined to abjure magic he addressed his spirit-helpers in an extended echo of Medea's invocation in *Metamorphoses* VII.[12] Medea spoke her invocation as a prelude to asking for aid to gather 'the enchanted herbs / That did renew old Aeson' (*The Merchant of Venice* 5.1.13–14): to accomplish one of the miracles that come back in Shakespearean romance, that of physicing the subject, making old hearts fresh (*The Winter's Tale* 1.1.39–40). But though Prospero quotes Medea's invocation he asks only for 'Some heavenly music ... To work mine end upon their senses' (5.1.52–3), not for a transforming or renewing spell. As his response to Miranda's brave-new-world cry suggests, he is too much the realist to believe in myths of renewal. He knows that inside the still-fresh wedding garments of the people Miranda sees little has changed. As change is unlikely and Miranda's future must be secured, wrongs have to be forgiven and, saving out a little control over Antonio and Sebastian, forgotten. Thus, with his story dissolving into the Neapolitan version and his magic place faded to 'this bare island' (Epilogue 8), Prospero faces the audience and asks leave to return to Italy, willing enough to accept that the latter end of his commonwealth must forget the beginning.

---

[12] Arthur Golding's 1567 translation of the lines in *Metamorphoses* VII, 197–209 is reprinted in Kermode's edition of *The Tempest*, p. 148.

HENRY VIII AND THE DECONSTRUCTION OF HISTORY

PETER L. RUDNYTSKY

Two preliminary problems impose themselves at the outset of any study of *Henry VIII*. In both cases, the issues raised may in a narrow sense be dispatched rather quickly, though their wider ramifications continue to bear on our reading of the play.

The first problem, of course, is that of authorship, which has bedevilled criticism ever since Spedding, in 1850, attempted to substantiate Tennyson's intuition that the play was written by Shakespeare in collaboration with Fletcher. The burden of proof that necessarily rests with those who would follow Spedding is augmented by the fact that this hypothesis is unsupported by any external evidence. Indeed, since the surviving ballad concerning the burning of the Globe theatre in 1613 records that Heminges and Condell were both present at the fateful performance of *Henry VIII*,[1] their inclusion of the play in the First Folio ten years later must have taken place with full knowledge of the circumstances of its composition and hence provides a measure of tangible evidence that it is *not* a collaboration.[2] Strikingly, both *Pericles* and *The Two Noble Kinsmen*, the two other plays in the Shakespearian canon most often thought to have been written by more than one hand (the latter on the incontrovertible basis of the title page of the 1634 quarto and an 8 April 1634 entry in the Stationers' Register, both of which ascribe the play to Shakespeare and Fletcher), do not appear in the Folio,

whereas the Hecate scenes in *Macbeth*, which might be cited as a counterexample, are a case of circumscribed interpolations rather than of an entire play written by Shakespeare jointly with a second playwright.

But, as has often been noted, controversy about the play's authorship tends to function as a corollary to doubts about its artistic merits. As critical interest in *Henry VIII*, beginning with Frank Kermode's article of 1948, has intensified, it has seemed increasingly less profitable to dwell on the problem of authorship or to try to dislodge the play from the Shakespearian

---

[1] The ballad is reprinted in *King Henry VIII*, ed. R. A. Foakes (1957; rpt. London: Methuen, 1968), pp. 181–3. In *William Shakespeare: The Complete Works*, eds. Stanley Wells, Gary Taylor, John Jowett, and William Montgomery (Oxford: Clarendon Press, 1986) the play is renamed *All Is True*. But though attention is drawn in the same editors' *Textual Companion* (Oxford: Clarendon Press, 1987) to four contemporary sources, including the ballad on the fire, in which this title is given (pp. 28–30), the notes (p. 619) disclose that two other contemporary sources (a 30 June 1613 letter by Thomas Lorkin and Edmond Howes's 1614 addition to Stow's *Chronicles*) refer, respectively, to the 'play of Hen:8' and 'the play, *viz.* of Henry the eight'. (Foakes (p. 181) gives the date of Howes's addition as 1618.) Because the testimony of contemporary witnesses is inconclusive, and because the Folio is the sole authority for the text, I will retain the title *The Famous History of the Life of King Henry the Eight* and use the Arden edition for all quotations from the play.

[2] See Marjorie H. Nicolson, 'The Authorship of *Henry the Eight*', *PMLA*, 37 (1922), 484–502; p. 484. Nicolson, however, continues to uphold the hypothesis of double authorship.

canon. Although he continued to entertain the possibility of collaboration on stylistic grounds, Kermode sensibly pointed out that 'joint authorship doesn't inevitably produce discontinuity' and concluded that 'the play is substantially what one man would have written, even if more than one hand contributed to it'.[3]

Despite Kermode's cogent reasoning, however, the thematic (as opposed to stylistic) reasons offered by Spedding for his doubts concerning Shakespeare's authorship seem to me to warrant reappraisal. Kermode cites the following passage from Spedding to illustrate what it is in the latter's account that he cannot accept:

throughout the play the king's cause is not only felt by us, but represented to us, as a bad one. We *hear*, indeed, of conscientious scruples as to the legality of his first marriage; but we are not made, nor indeed asked, to believe that they are sincere, or to recognise in his new marriage either the hand of Providence or the consummation of any worthy object, or the victory of any of those more common frailties of humanity with which we can sympathise. The mere caprice of passion drives the king into the commission of what seems a great iniquity; our compassion for the victim of it is elaborately excited; no attempt is made to awaken any counter-sympathy for *him*; yet his passion has its way, and is crowned with all felicity, present and to come.[4]

To Kermode, for whom (in 1948) the official Tudor and Stuart view of the king as 'God's deputy' and a 'minister of grace' made it seem inevitable that 'Henry VIII is represented in this play as exercising certain God-like functions',[5] Spedding's sceptical reading of 'the king's cause' was *a priori* untenable. But just as it is mistaken to assume that a play written in collaboration must be incoherent, so Spedding's own unwillingness to attribute what he saw in *Henry VIII* entirely to Shakespeare need not invalidate his perceptions about the play. Indeed, it would be the obverse fallacy to that exposed by Kermode to think that a play by a single author must be devoid of unorthodox

elements or of contradictory perspectives – especially when that author is Shakespeare.[6]

The second preliminary problem concerns the genre of *Henry VIII*, that is, whether the play is primarily to be grouped chronologically with the late romances or generically with the earlier histories. Here again, Heminges and Condell provide a valuable clue, since they place *The Famous History of the Life of King Henry the Eight* at the end of the section of history plays in the First Folio. (The use of romance as a generic category, of course, is itself anachronistic.) None the less, a great many scholars have preferred to disregard the guidance offered by both the title and the judgement of its first editors and to treat *Henry VIII* as fundamentally a romance. A notable spokesman for this view is Howard Felperin, who holds that Heminges and Condell are 'partly to blame' for misinterpretations of the play, and assumes that because 'Shakespeare had not written a play on English history for some thirteen years',[7] he could not have intended to do so in *Henry VIII*.

---

[3] Frank Kermode, 'What is Shakespeare's *Henry VIII* About?' *Durham University Journal*, 40 (1948), 48–54; p. 49.

[4] Quoted in ibid., 49–50. For the entire passage, see J. Spedding, 'Who Wrote Shakespeare's *Henry VIII*?', *The Gentleman's Magazine*, NS 34 (August 1850), 115–23; p. 116.

[5] Ibid., 50.

[6] See H. M. Richmond, 'Shakespeare's *Henry VIII*: Romance Redeemed by History', *Shakespeare Studies*, 4 (1968), 334–49; p. 338. Other defenders of Shakespeare's authorship are: G. Wilson Knight, '*Henry VIII* and the Poetry of Conversion', in *The Crown of Life: Essays in Interpretation of Shakespeare's Final Plays* (London: Oxford University Press, 1947), pp. 256–336; and Foakes, ed., *King Henry VIII*, pp. xv–xxviii. In the Oxford *Textual Companion*, however, it is affirmed that 'both stylistic and linguistic evidence ... assign to Fletcher at least a quarter of the play' (p. 133).

[7] Howard Felperin, 'Shakespeare's *Henry VIII*: History as Myth', *Studies in English Literature*, 6 (1966), 225–46; pp. 226–7. Other critics who treat the play primarily as a romance include: Ronald Berman, '*King Henry the Eighth*: History and Romance', *English Studies*, 48 (1967), 112–21; Richmond, 'Romance Redeemed by

In what follows, I shall maintain that *Henry VIII* is indeed to be seen as Shakespeare's final history play and that, although it draws upon the romantic elements of masque and spectacle and shares with other late plays the motif of succession through the female line,[8] its spirit is ultimately sceptical and not hierophantic. Central to this entire debate, of course, is Shakespeare's portrayal of the character of Henry VIII himself. For Kermode, as we have seen, Henry is a divine 'minister of grace', and this verdict is upheld by providentialist critics of the play. According to R. A. Foakes, Henry is 'a kind of high-priest on earth' for God, and the 'most significant aspect' of his character is its 'growth in stature', so that, after he shakes off Wolsey's influence, he becomes, like Prospero, 'a representative of benevolent power acting upon others'.[9] John Cox, similarly, finds that the play's 'informing purpose' is 'a celebration of Jacobean kingship' and that its 'central movement' is 'toward a true manifestation of royal power'; and, for Felperin, the 'claim to truth' of *Henry VIII* resides 'in the eternal relevance of the great Christian myth upon which it rests'.[10]

It will be necessary to show in some detail the untenability of such views, although they have, in my judgement, already been refuted in the two finest essays written on *Henry VIII* – those by Lee Bliss and Frank V. Cespedes.[11] Suffice it to note, by way of introduction, that they are often accompanied by disparagements of the play and even by factual errors. Felperin, for example, affirms that the play contains 'no hint of the bloody fates which are soon to overtake Anne, Cromwell, and Chancellor More' and opines that Shakespeare, 'like so many aging English poets after him, embraces traditional answers to questions which he had spent his career formulating on both sides'.[12] The former statement is untrue on the face of it, and the latter follows from his premise that Shakespeare is dramatizing 'Christian myth'. Cox, likewise, who joins Felperin in detaching *Henry VIII* from the histories and in treating it as 'an

imitation of the masque', acknowledges that his reading accentuates the 'disappointing' features of the play: 'its lack of sensitivity to political ambiguity ... its facile religious orthodoxy'.[13]

In contrast, the effect of reinstating *Henry VIII* in its proper generic context is to discover that it is as ambiguous and unorthodox as any of its predecessors. Indeed, in *Henry VIII* Shakespeare carries the complexities of his previous explorations of English history to new heights and into daringly recent waters. One of the hallmarks of Shakespeare's second tetralogy of history plays is that it permits widely divergent interpretations – from the most patriotic and idealistic to the most subversive and

---

History'; Frances A. Yates, *Shakespeare's Last Plays: A New Approach* (London: Routledge & Kegan Paul, 1975), pp. 65–84; John D. Cox, 'Henry VIII and the Masque', *ELH*, 45 (1978), 390–406; Edward I. Berry, 'Henry VIII and the Dynamics of Spectacle', *Shakespeare Studies*, 12 (1979), 229–46; David Scott Kastan, *Shakespeare and the Shapes of Time* (London: Macmillan, 1982), pp. 133–41; David Bergeron, *Shakespeare's Romances and the Royal Family* (Lawrence: University Press of Kansas, 1985), pp. 203–22; Leonard Tennenhouse, *Power on Display: The Politics of Shakespeare's Genres* (New York and London: Methuen, 1986), pp. 96–9; and Foakes, ed. *King Henry VIII*, pp. xxxix–lxiv.

8 Bergeron, *Shakespeare's Romances and the Royal Family*, p. 206.

9 *King Henry VIII*, ed. Foakes, pp. lxi, lxiii.

10 Cox, 'Henry VIII and the Masque', 395; Felperin, 'History as Myth', 246. See also Kastan, *Shakespeare and the Shapes of Time*, p. 134; Bergeron, *Shakespeare's Romances and the Royal Family*, p. 205; Knight, 'Henry VIII and the Poetry of Conversion': 'This is Shakespeare's one explicitly Christian play' (p. 277); and Peter Saccio, *Shakespeare's English Kings: History, Chronicle, and Drama* (London: Oxford University Press, 1977): 'Shakespeare gives us an embodiment of benevolence, wisdom, virtue, and majesty, a dream of a semidivine king' (p. 210).

11 See Lee Bliss, 'The Wheel of Fortune and the Maiden Phoenix of Shakespeare's *King Henry the Eighth*', *ELH*, 42 (1975), 1–25; and Frank V. Cespedes, '"We are one in fortunes": The Sense of History in *Henry VIII*', *English Literary Renaissance*, 10 (1980), 413–38.

12 Felperin, 'History as Myth', 245–6.

13 Cox, 'Henry VIII and the Masque', 401.

cynical. That one can read the *Henriad* as a celebration of royal power and the 'Tudor myth' is undeniable; but it is no less undeniable that the tetralogy interrogates and demystifies these very ideals; and *the simultaneous presence of conflicting perspectives precludes the plays from being in any simple sense 'orthodox'*.[14] To an even more acute degree, the same interpretative tension pervades *Henry VIII*.

The Prologue provides a litmus test for responses to *Henry VIII* as a whole. The announcement of a theme 'full of state and woe' (3), unlike Rowley's recently revived 'merry bawdy play' (14), *When You See Me, You Know Me* (1605), seems straightforward enough; and, in Kermode's summary, the Prologue 'makes it plain that foolery must be absent from a stage displaying what is "only true"'.[15] But, like the couplet of a Shakespearian sonnet, the final two lines of the Prologue cast what has gone before in an unexpected light: 'And if you can be merry then, I'll say / A man may weep upon his wedding day' (31–2). This juxtaposition of weeping and wedding bears a more than incidental relation to the action of the ensuing drama and suggests that there may indeed be cause for laughter as well as tears in *Henry VIII*. As Alexander Leggatt has perceptively commented, 'The author, having offered to make our eyes flow with tears, allows us to see the twinkle in his'; and, citing the comical reference to dozing spectators 'frighted with our trumpets' (4) in the Epilogue, Leggatt adds: 'we may suspect that behind all the pomp and grandeur, even the tragedy, there is an author playing tricks on us'.[16]

The nature of the 'tricks' perpetrated by Shakespeare in *Henry VIII* is best illustrated by the play's enigmatic subtitle, *All Is True*. The range of meanings the phrase can bear has been well delineated by David Scott Kastan:

Since *All Is True* cannot refer to the play's fidelity to chronicle accounts, the phrase might refer to the necessary relativity of truth in a world of flux and deceptive appearances. Yet the romance structure of the historical action and the fortunate falls of some of its principals reveal a dimension of truth that is unconditional and unchanging. Behind the apparently chaotic world of human history lies a sacred reality shaping and controlling the destiny of man and nations.[17]

I agree with Kastan in discarding the possibility that 'all is true' promises historical veracity or 'fidelity to chronicle accounts' (the meaning assumed by Kermode), but I would reverse his assessment of the latter two choices. Since *Henry VIII* subsumes romance to history, the existence of a timeless 'sacred reality' is merely one hypothesis to be entertained among many, and by no means a conclusion underwritten by the play as a whole. Rather, Shakespeare constructs a dramatic universe dominated by 'deceptive appearances' and the 'relativity of truth', in which, in Pirandellian fashion, 'all is true' means precisely that *any* interpretation of the past may be true if one thinks it so, and no point of view is allowed to contain or control all others.

As I shall argue below, what I have termed Shakespeare's 'deconstruction of history' in *Henry VIII* centres on the 'great matter' of the king's divorce that was the focus of historical and polemical writing concerning Henry's reign throughout the sixteenth century. In this connection, it is surely apposite, as Paul Dean has noted, that 'the two great problems which have dominated modern criticism of the play – its authorship and the exact nature of its genre – are both also, in a sense, problems of divorce'.[18] The relevance of the generic tensions to a

---

[14] See the seminal analyses of Shakespeare's 'complementarity' by Norman Rabkin in *Shakespeare and the Common Understanding* (New York: Free Press, 1967) and in *Shakespeare and the Problem of Meaning* (Chicago and London: University of Chicago Press, 1971).

[15] Kermode, 'What is *Henry VIII* About?', 50.

[16] Alexander Leggatt, '*Henry VIII* and the Ideal England', *Shakespeare Survey 38* (1985), 131–43; pp. 142–3.

[17] Kastan, *Shakespeare and the Shapes of Time*, p. 137.

[18] Paul Dean, 'Dramatic Mode and Historical Vision in *Henry VIII*', *Shakespeare Quarterly*, 37 (1986), 175–89; p. 175.

reading of *Henry VIII* should by now be clear enough. And even though I assign the whole of *Henry VIII* to Shakespeare, the controversy that surrounds its authorship strikingly mirrors the crisis of authority thematized within the play itself.[19] In this respect, *Henry VIII* forms a fitting culmination to Shakespeare's career, since it is not necessary to join the ranks of anti-Stratfordians to agree that their challenge to Shakespeare's title to the plays that bear his name poses serious and enduring questions about who and what is an author.[20]

II

It can no longer be said that *Henry VIII* is suffering from critical neglect, and to approach the play through a review of its scholarly controversies has perhaps more than a conventional justification. For, as Paul Dean has remarked, as readers or spectators of this work 'we apprehend history largely through other people's interpretations of it' and 'we repeatedly eavesdrop on reports of events rather than witnessing the events themselves'.[21] Thus, just as one's own reading is inevitably filtered through the lenses of previous interpretations, so one's task as a critic is largely that of deciphering the conflicting versions of events reported within the play.

The prototype for the dilemmas of interpretation posed by *Henry VIII* as a whole is established in the opening scene.[22] Because an 'untimely ague' (4) kept the Duke of Buckingham from attending the Field of the Cloth of Gold, he must hear of this meeting of the English and French kings from the Duke of Norfolk, and so must we as spectators of Shakespeare's play. At first, Norfolk seems to praise unqualifiedly the 'view of earthly glory' (14) he beheld there, about which 'no discerner / Durst wag his tongue in censure' (31–2). But once Buckingham learns that the ceremonies were arranged by Wolsey, he condemns them as 'fierce vanities' (54), and Norfolk reverses himself and agrees that the peace treaty reached

with the French 'not values / The cost that did conclude it' (88–9). By the end of the scene, even Norfolk's earlier terms of approbation – '*earthly* glory,' '*Durst* wag his tongue' – seem ominously qualified, while it is impossible to overlook that Buckingham's censure is motivated by a personal hostility to Wolsey.

The atmosphere of uncertainty thickens during the depiction of the fall of Buckingham, the first of four such episodes – Katherine's, Wolsey's, and the averted destruction of Cranmer – in the play.[23] Buckingham, who in the course of the opening scene had vowed to 'cry down / This Ipswich fellow's insolence' (137–8), is by its end himself arrested and charged with treason at Wolsey's instigation. At his trial, Buckingham is accused by his surveyor of having vowed to seize the throne of England if the king should die without issue. Queen Katherine, however, appeals to Wolsey, who seconds the charge, to 'Deliver all with charity' (1.2.143), and impugns the credibility of the offered testimony: 'You were the duke's surveyor, and lost your office / On the complaint o'th'tenants' (172–3). Subsequently, the outcome of Buckingham's trial is discussed by the Two Gentlemen. The duke 'alleg'd / Many sharp reasons to defeat the law' (2.1.13–14), the First Gentleman states, and 'fain / Would have

---

19 See F. Schreiber-McGee, '"The View of Earthly Glory": Visual Strategies and the Issue of Royal Prerogative in *Henry VIII*', *Shakespeare Studies*, 20 (1988), 191–200; where, however, 'the question of authority in the play ... especially in its relation to authorship and authority in historical discourse' (p. 191) is not linked to the authorship problem of *Henry VIII*.

20 See Marjorie Garber, 'Shakespeare's Ghost Writers', in *Cannibals, Witches, and Divorce: Estranging the Renaissance*, ed. Garber (Baltimore and London: Johns Hopkins University Press, 1987), pp. 122–46.

21 Dean, 'Dramatic Mode and Historical Vision', 177. See also Pierre Sahel, 'The Strangeness of a Dramatic Style: Rumour in *Henry VIII*', *Shakespeare Survey 38* (1985), 145–51.

22 See Bliss, 'The Wheel of Fortune and the Maiden Phoenix', 3–4.

23 On the *de casibus* patterns in the play, see Kermode, 'What is *Henry VIII* About?'

flung from him' the accusations against him, 'but indeed he could not' (24–5). The Second Gentleman adds that 'Certainly / The cardinal is the end of this' (39–40), but the evil intentions of Wolsey do not diminish the weight of evidence against the seemingly noble and sympathetic Buckingham.

Then Buckingham appears on the stage for the last time. Reasserting his innocence, he forgives his enemies, asks for the prayers of his friends, and blesses the king as he prepares for death. Buckingham proclaims himself 'half in heaven' (2.1.88), renounces the trappings of state, and casts off his noble title, 'now poor Edward Bohun' (103). From his spiritual perspective, he deems himself yet 'richer than my base accusers, / That never knew what truth meant' (104–5). But he cannot refrain from once more venting his bitterness, warning against the treachery of friends who 'fall away / Like water from ye, never found again / But where they mean to sink ye' (129–31).

The Field of the Cloth of Gold, which took place in 1520, was the most spectacular royal pageant of the early sixteenth century, though its actual benefit to the English foreign policy of attempting to play off the competing interests of the greater Imperial Habsburg and French Valois powers was negligible. The contrasting attitudes of Buckingham and Norfolk are embodied in their rhetorical styles, in which the plain-speaking of the former first probes and ultimately punctures the florid hyperbole of the latter. And since, in Cespedes's words, the initially glittering image of the king as 'a figure from medieval romance ... is a miniature version of the depiction of Henry VIII in Shakespeare's chronicle sources', what Shakespeare does in the course of the opening scene is to present a 'disillusioned revision' of this encomiastic tradition.[24]

Whereas the dialogue concerning the Field of the Cloth of Gold at least allows the spectator to judge its insubstantiality, the downfall of Buckingham turns on a series of antithetical perspectives, between which it is both necessary and impossible to choose. Buckingham is either guilty or innocent, his fall is due either to his own treason or to the plotting of Wolsey, and the testimony of his fired surveyor either is or is not perjured. Indeed, the surveyor accuses Buckingham, as Pierre Sahel has pointed out, on the basis of third-hand reports: 'words used by his ex-master quoting his chaplain as the latter was repeating the confidence of a "holy monk"'.[25] Even Buckingham's ostensible conversion to spiritual values, which leads Howard Felperin to impute to him 'higher knowledge',[26] is not so simple. After all, Buckingham himself says that he is still only '*half* in heaven', and his final remarks concerning his '*base* accusers' reveal not only bitterness but also a persistence of the aristocratic pride that motivated his attack on Wolsey and has been a feature of his temperament all along.[27]

This reversal of perspectives and veiling of truth continues in the pivotal characterization of Wolsey. As Shakespeare inverts the received image of Henry, so Wolsey appears at first to be the diabolical agent familiar from Protestant chronicles and from Rowley's *When You See Me, You Know Me*, but after his undoing he becomes a powerfully sympathetic figure. The enemies who attack him with unconcealed venom are cautioned by the Lord Chamberlain, 'Press not a falling man too far' (3.2.333); and, following his disgrace, Wolsey's language becomes charged with eloquence:

> I know myself now, and I feel within me
> A peace above all earthly dignities,
> A still and quiet conscience. (3.2.378–80)

In itself, Wolsey's repentance raises the question of whether any moral distinction can finally be made between him and Buckingham or even

---

24 Cespedes, '"We are one in fortunes"', 421. See also Dean, 'Dramatic Mode and Historical Vision', 181.

25 Sahel, 'The Strangeness of a Dramatic Style', 149.

26 Felperin, 'History as Myth', 237.

27 See Berry, '*Henry VIII* and the Dynamics of Spectacle', 234: and Leggatt, '*Henry VIII* and the Ideal England', 139.

Katherine. But though Wolsey gains in spiritual dignity as he falls on the wheel of fortune, he, too, is still only 'half in heaven' and his renunciation of 'earthly dignities' remains less than complete; for he cannot refrain from asking Cromwell: 'What news abroad?' (391).

Wolsey incurs the enmity of the king through an incident of crossed letters derived by Shakespeare from Holinshed, where it pertains not to Wolsey but to Thomas Ruthall, Bishop of Durham under Henry VII. But whereas Norfolk ascribes Wolsey's unwitting disclosure of his private wealth and efforts to delay the divorce proceedings to 'heaven's will' (3.2.128), Wolsey blames his mistake on some 'cross devil' (214); and the reader has no way to choose between these conflicting explanations.[28] Appropriately, the final judgement passed on Wolsey after his death in a dialogue between Katherine and her usher Griffith is an ambiguous one, for Katherine's indictment of him as 'a man / Of an unbounded stomach' who 'would say untruths, and be ever double / Both in his words and meaning' (4.2.33–8) is balanced and even outweighed by the ensuing recitation of his virtues by the compassionate Griffith.

What Bliss terms the 'pattern of contradiction' in the play, whereby Shakespeare 'capitalizes on the inconsistencies of the chronicles and with them enhances his use of multiple sympathetic perspectives',[29] centres, as I have suggested, on his treatment of the fundamental issues of Henry VIII's divorce from Katherine of Aragon and the Elizabethan succession. Although some critics have questioned whether Shakespeare is concerned with political themes at all in *Henry VIII*,[30] I believe that he gathers up and comments self-consciously on the overriding problems confronting historical writers throughout the sixteenth century.

As *Henry VIII* is a work of literary art and not a treatise, however, Shakespeare presents his commentary not directly but obliquely. Thus, when Buckingham refers to his execution as 'the long divorce of steel' (2.1.76) about

to fall on him, the word 'divorce', in association with death, connects Buckingham's fate with that of both Katherine and Anne Boleyn. One of Spedding's objections to the unity of *Henry VIII* pertains to the fifth act, where, he claimed, the greater part 'is occupied with matters in which we have not been prepared to take any interest by what went before ... for what have we to do with the quarrel between Gardiner and Cranmer?'[31] Like Rymer on *Othello*, Spedding gets to the heart of the matter, even though he misses the point. For, as Cespedes has observed, 'Gardiner was a villain in Foxe's *Acts and Monuments* ... because he was instrumental in procuring the executions of Cranmer and Cromwell ... and his eventual success is the backdrop to his ostensible failure in this act.'[32] Once again, an associative rather than narrative logic discloses the artistic coherence and the breadth of historical vision in Shakespeare's final complete play.

Spedding's strictures concerning the fifth act of *Henry VIII* can be satisfactorily answered, but his protest that 'the king's cause is not only felt by us, but represented to us, as a bad one' remains justified. Indeed, it does not go too far to say that, in fundamental respects, Shakespeare upholds a *Catholic* perspective on the divorce, as this was articulated in sixteenth-century polemics.[33]

---

28 See Berry, '*Henry VIII* and the Dynamics of Spectacle', 235–6, where, however, Norfolk's providential explanation is assumed to be the accurate one.

29 Bliss, 'The Wheel of Fortune and the Maiden Phoenix', 3, 6.

30 See Dean, 'Dramatic Mode and Historical Vision', 178: and Saccio, *Shakespeare's English Kings*: '*Henry VIII* is not about Henry VIII' (p. 209).

31 Spedding, 'Who Wrote Shakespeare's *Henry VIII*?', 116.

32 Cespedes, '"We are one in fortunes"', 432.

33 My argument here is compatible with, though it does not depend on, E. A. J. Honigmann's brief for Shakespeare's Catholic origins in *Shakespeare: The 'Lost Years'* (Manchester: Manchester University Press, 1985). Honigmann himself, however, sees *Henry VIII* as expressing 'an uncompromisingly Protestant attitude' (p. 125).

A crucial weapon in the Catholic attack against Henry VIII was the charge that his divorce from Katherine was not motivated, as he claimed, by a religious 'scruple' concerning the lawfulness of his marriage to Katherine (who had been briefly married to the king's elder brother, Prince Arthur, before his death in 1503), but by his lust for Anne Boleyn. As Nicholas Harpsfield, More's early biographer, writes in the *Pretended Divorce between Henry VIII and Catharine of Aragon*: 'I cannot be induced to believe that the King upon conscience only, and for avoiding God's displeasure (as it was pretended), but rather to satisfy and serve his bodily pleasure and appetite, pursued this divorce.'[34] Cavendish, likewise, in his *Life of Wolsey* shows Henry beginning 'to kindle the brand of amours'[35] for Anne Boleyn prior to his divorce from Katherine. With great literary skill, Cavendish in his account of the trial paraphrases Hall's chronicle by having Henry affirm that he acts 'not for any carnal concupiscence, ne for any displeasure or mislike of the Queen's person or age' (p. 87), but he exposes the king's public profession as hypocritical by the artful plotting of his narrative.[36]

The same ironic subversion of the Protestant chroniclers' interpretation of Henry's conduct is to be found in *Henry VIII*. For, in defiance of historical chronology, Shakespeare transposes the banquet at Wolsey's in Act 1, Scene 4 at which Henry meets and falls in love with Anne Boleyn, from 1527 to before Buckingham's execution in 1521. Because Henry's desire for Anne arises *before* the bruiting of the rumour of his divorce, Shakespeare, like Cavendish, undermines the official version of his motives.[37] In the conversation between the Two Gentlemen that modulates from the fall of Buckingham to the 'buzzing of a separation' between king and queen, the Second Gentleman aptly states, 'that slander, sir, / Is found a truth now' (2.1.153–4).

The implausibility of Henry's 'scruple' is highlighted in Act 2, Scene 2, when the Lord Chamberlain declares that the king is troubled because 'the marriage with his brother's wife / Has crept too near his conscience', to which Suffolk retorts in an aside: 'No, his conscience / Has crept too near another lady' (16–18). (Similarly, following Anne's coronation, the Second Gentleman comments with regard to her beauty: 'I cannot blame his conscience' (4.1.47).) Henry refuses to be disturbed by Suffolk and Norfolk to discuss 'temporal affairs' (72), but immediately grants an audience to Wolsey and Campeius who have come to aid him in the divorce. The scene ends with Henry's expression of regret to Wolsey at the necessity of leaving Katherine, in which, however, his conscience proves indistinguishable from his sexual desire:

> O my lord,
> Would it not grieve an able man to leave
> So sweet a bedfellow? But conscience,
>   conscience;
> O 'tis a tender place, and I must leave her.
>
> (140–3)

Henry's speech echoes Hall's *Chronicle*, which reports that he 'absteined from her bed, till the truth was tried, ... which was to hym no little pain, for surely he loued her as well, as any

---

[34] Nicholas Harpsfield, *A Treatise on the Pretended Divorce between Henry VIII and Catharine of Aragon*, ed. Nicholas Pocock (1878; rpt. New York: Johnson Reprint Corporation, 1965), p. 258. Harpsfield's work, probably written under Queen Mary, was not published until the nineteenth century. I am unable to say whether it might have been known to Shakespeare.

[35] George Cavendish, *The Life and Death of Cardinal Wolsey*, in *Two Early Tudor Lives*, eds. Richard S. Sylvester and Davis P. Harding (1962; rpt. New Haven and London: Yale University Press, 1978), p. 32. The subsequent page reference is given parenthetically.

[36] See Judith H. Anderson, *Biographical Truth: The Representation of Historical Persons in Tudor–Stuart Writing* (New Haven and London: Yale University Press, 1984), p. 37. Anderson demonstrates (pp. 136–42) that Shakespeare derived his knowledge of the *Life of Wolsey* primarily from the extensive portions included in the 1592 edition of Stow's *Annales*.

[37] See Bliss, 'The Wheel of Fortune and the Maiden Phoenix', 7; and Cespedes, '"We are one in fortunes"', 414.

Prince might love his wife',[38] but Shakespeare ironizes the passage by the erotic undertones of Henry's references to himself as an 'able man' and to his conscience as a 'tender place'.[39]

Shakespeare's sexual punning becomes even more relentless in the ensuing scene, a conversation between Anne Boleyn and an Old Lady. In the traditional manner of a Nurse, the Old Lady makes light of Anne's reluctance to lose her virginity and to marry the king. To Anne's 'By my troth and maidenhead, / I would not be a queen', the Old Lady scoffs at this 'spice of your hypocrisy' and assures her that 'the capacity / Of your soft chevril conscience would receive, / If you might please to stretch it' (2.3.23–33). Anne does not join in this banter, but we have already observed her behave wantonly at Wolsey's banquet, and her motives are rendered suspect by the bawdiness of the context. The Old Lady continues: 'a threepence bow'd would hire me / Old as I am, to queen it' (36–7). The 'bow'd' or 'bent' coin that would induce the beldame to sell herself is also a pun on 'bawd', and the word 'queen' has become contaminated by its homonym 'quean'. For Anne, to be a queen is to be a prostitute; and the hypocrisy of her 'mincing' is reinforced if we accept the suggestion that Suffolk's remark that the king's conscience has 'crept too near her' indicates that Anne may already be pregnant.[40] By the end of the scene Anne receives the news that she has been appointed Marchioness of Pembroke, and conspiratorially – if unnecessarily – asks the Old Lady to keep this knowledge secret from Katherine.

The Prologue, it will be recalled, promised to eschew a 'merry bawdy play' such as had been served up by Rowley, where the fool Will Sommers banters with Henry that 'thou hast prest her [Jane Seymour] often: I am sure this two years she has serv'd under thy standard'.[41] But Shakespeare's Prologue slights the didactic Protestant purpose of Rowley's play, which emphasizes Henry's wives Jane Seymour and Katherine Parr and the succession of Edward

VI, and it would be difficult to find a scene to which the epithets 'merry' and 'bawdy' might be better applied than this last from *Henry VIII*. And, in its aftermath, Henry's attempt to justify his conduct during the trial scene becomes even more unconvincing than in Cavendish. Exonerating Wolsey of responsibility for the divorce, Henry pleads that 'My conscience first receiv'd a tenderness, / Scruple and prick' (2.4.168–9) after hearing the legitimacy of his daughter, Mary, questioned by the French ambassador and affirms that his inability to produce a living son with Katherine led him to fear that he 'stood not in the smile of heaven' (185). But, at the end of the trial, Henry reveals his true feelings in an aside: 'These cardinals trifle with me: I abhor / This dilatory sloth and tricks of Rome' (234–5). He awaits the arrival of Cranmer, the dutiful servant who can speedily engineer his divorce.

Integral to Shakespeare's 'Catholic' cynicism about Henry's motives is his exceptionally sympathetic portrayal of Katherine of Aragon.[42] There is no known source for her dream

[38] Edward Hall, *The Vnion of the Two Noble and Illustre Families of Lancastre & Yorke*, ed. Sir Henry Ellis (1809; rpt. New York AMS Press, 1965), p. 756.

[39] See Anderson, *Biographical Truth*: 'The least that "tender place" can mean here is a bed' (p. 129).

[40] See Foakes's note to 2.2.16–17; and the Lord Chamberlain's pun on 'conceit' at 2.3.74–5. Additional *double entendres* in the Old Lady's words include her avowals that she would not be a 'young count [= pudendum?] in your way [virgin]' (2.3.41) and that Anne would 'venture an emballing [investiture, copulation]' for the 'little England' (46–7) of Pembrokeshire.

[41] Samuel Rowley, *When You See Me, You Know Me. Or the Famous Chronicle Historie of King Henrie the Eight* (London, 1632), sig. B¹ verso.

[42] Glynne Wickham, 'The Dramatic Structure of Shakespeare's *King Henry the Eighth*: An Essay in Rehabilitation', *Proceedings of the British Academy*, 70 (1984), 149–66, argues that Shakespeare's purpose in writing the play was 'to redeem *in the national interest* the slanders cast in 1531 upon the name of Katherine of Aragon' (p. 165). Wickham overstates his case, which turns on the conjecture that *Henry VIII* may have been performed in the Blackfriars theatre, where Katherine's divorce trial took place in 1528, but he shows how far it

vision (4.2),[43] in which she imagines herself crowned with garlands after death by angelic figures; but Shakespeare's invention finds a striking precedent in Harpsfield's statement that Katherine

changed her woeful troublesome life with the celestial heavenly life, and, for her terrestrial ingrate husband, found a kinder and better and a celestial spouse, from whom she shall never be sequestered and divorced, but reign with him in eternal glory for ever.[44]

Shakespeare reinforces the contrast between Anne's earthly (4.1) and Katherine's heavenly coronation by having them follow each other in successive scenes of the play. Whereas Anne can only become a 'queen' by being a 'quean', Katherine shows herself to be truly regal in death: 'although unqueen'd, yet like / A queen, and daughter to a king inter me' (4.2.171–2).[45]

Although opposites, Katherine and Anne are 'one in fortunes' (2.1.121) as victims of Henrican power. Buckingham's allusion to 'the long divorce of steel' blurs the distinction between death and divorce, Anne and Katherine. This motif recurs both in Katherine's avowal that 'nothing but death / Shall e'er divorce my dignities' (3.1.141–2) and in Anne's conversation with the Old Lady, when she expresses her pity for Katherine's plight:

O God's will, much better
She ne'er had known pomp; though't be
    temporal,
Yet if that quarrel, fortune, do divorce
It from the bearer, 'tis a suffrance panging
As soul and body's severing.   (2.3.13–16)

Whether for a Jacobean or a modern audience, these lines cannot fail to evoke Anne Boleyn's own fate – the 'soul and body's severing' she suffered when her head was 'divorced' from its 'bearer' three years after she had 'known pomp' as Henry's queen. The tumult of the crowd at Anne's coronation prompts the Third Gentleman to comment: 'No man living / Could say "This is my wife" there, all were woven / So strangely in one piece' (4.1.79–81).

After Henry's divorce, neither he nor his subjects can be sure to whom they are married.

This conflation of Katherine and Anne, divorce and death, is part of the larger 'pattern of contradiction' in the play. But perhaps the deepest confusion in *Henry VIII* is that between the identities of the king and God. In Act 1, Scene 1, when the Lord Abergavenny finds himself arrested together with Buckingham, he resolves: 'The will of Heaven be done, and the king's pleasure / By me obey'd' (215–16). For Kermode and other critics who see the king as 'God's deputy', this equation is unproblematic; but Shakespeare subjects it to remorseless scrutiny. Although she has loyally 'lov'd him next heav'n' (3.1.130), once she sets herself against Henry's desires, Katherine has no difficulty in distinguishing earthly from heavenly authority. She admonishes the cardinals: 'Heaven is above all yet; there sits a judge / That no king can corrupt' (3.1.100–1). Wolsey, on the other hand, closes his 'farewell' speech to Cromwell with the famous lines:

Had I but serv'd my God with half the zeal
I serv'd my king, he would not in mine age
Have left me naked to mine enemies.

                              (3.2.455–7)

Wolsey blames his downfall on his inability to differentiate the king from God, a problem that persists in these lines with their equivocal antecedent of the pronoun 'he'.

---

is possible to press a reading of the play as a defence of Katherine.

[43] See, however, E. E. Duncan-Jones, 'Queen Katherine's Vision and Queen Margaret's Dream', *Notes & Queries*, NS 8 (1961), 142–3, where a possible link to a reported dream of – of being crowned – Queen Margaret of Navarre's shortly before her death is suggested.

[44] Harpsfield, *Pretended Divorce*, p. 199.

[45] Contrast Berry, '*Henry VIII* and the Dynamics of Spectacle', 239. On the two queens in the play, see Linda McJ. Micheli, '"Sit By Us": Visual Imagery and the Two Queens in *Henry VIII*', *Shakespeare Quarterly*, 38 (1987), 452–66; and Kim H. Noling, 'Grubbing Up the Stock: Dramatizing Queens in *Henry VIII*', *Shakespeare Quarterly*, 39 (1988), 291–306.

The confusion of God and king reaches its apogee in the aborted *de casibus* tragedy of Cranmer. Although Cranmer delivers the culminating prophecy of the reigns of Elizabeth and James, he is first mentioned by Henry, as I have noted, as the 'learn'd and well-beloved servant' (2.4.236) who will succeed in obtaining the divorce where Wolsey and Campeius have failed.[46] When, in Act 5, Cranmer is threatened by the conspiratorial machinations of his enemies, Henry tells him not to fear the ensuing trial, for 'Thy truth and thy integrity is rooted / In us thy friend' (5.1.114–15). Unlike Buckingham, Katherine, and Wolsey, Cranmer is saved rather than destroyed by the king's intervention, but his pardon depends as much on Henry's whim as does the ruin of the other characters.[47]

When the Archbishop naïvely vows to meet his accusers with 'truth and honesty' (5.1.122), Henry replies:

> Ween you of better luck,
> I mean in perjur'd witness, than your master,
> Whose minister you are, whiles here he liv'd
> Upon this naughty earth? (135–8)

Cranmer is the 'minister' of Christ, yet it is Henry who protects him from 'perjur'd witness' during his trial. Henry looks down from a window while Cromwell is rudely kept waiting at the door by members of the royal council, and exclaims: 'Is this the honour they do one another? / 'Tis well there's one above 'em yet' (5.2.25–6). Henry, standing with Dr Butts, is literally 'above' the remaining actors in the scene, and the ambiguity in his earlier reference to Cromwell's 'master' here becomes a full-fledged identity of God and king.

But if the 'king's pleasure' is indistinguishable from the 'will of heaven', one of two conclusions must follow: either the idea of divine providence is being mocked by Shakespeare, or the cruel follies of human history somehow contribute to a mysterious higher purpose. Although I have stressed the former hypothesis, which correlates with a 'Catholic' view of the play, it is the plausibility of the latter that explains why *Henry VIII* has also been held to exhibit a 'strongly Protestant bias'.[48] The episode of Henry's rescue of Cranmer from his persecutors' clutches is, after all, borrowed from Foxe's *Book of Martyrs*; and, of all the sixteenth-century controversialists, Foxe is the most ardent champion of Anne Boleyn's reputation and of the belief that 'God's helping hand' guided 'the king's heart' in the divorce from Katherine and marriage to Anne, 'which was the first occasion and beginning of all this public reformation which hath followed since, in this church of England, and to this present day'.[49]

The 'Protestant' reading of the play depends on Cranmer's prophecy at the christening of Elizabeth. The climactic position of this speech at the end of the play, its scriptural language, the actual splendour of Elizabeth's reign, and the inclusion of the tribute to James I all combine to give Cranmer's hymn of praise a compelling authority. Throughout the play, moreover, Elizabeth's birth is foreshadowed in ways that harmonize with Cranmer's tribute. The Lord Chamberlain divines that from Anne Boleyn 'may proceed a gem / To lighten all this isle' (2.3.78–9); and the Duke of Suffolk affirms, 'I persuade me, from her / Will fall some blessing to this land, which shall / In it be memoriz'd' (3.2.50–2). Thus, whatever Henry's motives, and despite the human cost, the 'thousand, thousand blessings' poured by the 'maiden phoenix' (5.4.19, 40) upon the land

---

46 See Cespedes, '"We are one in fortunes"', 428.

47 See Bliss, 'The Wheel of Fortune and the Maiden Phoenix', 14.

48 William W. Baillie, '*Henry VIII*: A Jacobean History', *Shakespeare Studies*, 12 (1979), 247–66; p. 262. Other critics who see the play as avowedly Protestant include: Leggatt, '*Henry VIII* and the Ideal England'; Bergeron, *Shakespeare's Romances and the Royal Family*, p. 212; and Yates, *Shakespeare's Last Plays*.

49 John Foxe, *Acts and Monuments*, ed. Stephen Reed Cattley (London: Seeley and Burnside, 1838), 8 vols., 5:45.

indeed allow one to construe history as a providential design making possible the Protestant Reformation and the reign of the two monarchs under whom Shakespeare wrote his plays.

But even the birth of Elizabeth is not exempted from irony. For when Henry asks the Old Lady, 'Is the queen deliver'd? / Say ay, and of a boy', she replies with a politic equivocation:

> Ay, ay my liege,
> And of a lovely boy: the God of heaven
> Both now and ever bless her: 'tis a girl
> Promises boys hereafter.   (5.1.162–6)

This passage draws attention to the frustration of Henry's hopes for a male heir, which had provided the rationale for his divorce from Katherine in the first place; and when he indicates his dissatisfaction by giving the Old Lady only one hundred marks, she complains: 'Said I for this the girl was like to him? / I'll have more, or else unsay 't' (174–5). In contrast to the Lord Chamberlain's rapt tribute to Anne Boleyn, moreover, the Old Lady brands her 'a very fresh fish' (2.3.86) swiftly advancing in the waters of the court.

In *Richard II*, the complexity of Shakespeare's historical vision is due in large measure to the way that he puts forward and holds in suspense three conflicting perspectives on Richard II and his deposition: a 'Ricardian' view, stemming from the French chroniclers, who saw Richard as a martyred king; a rival 'Lancastrian' tradition, which depicted Richard as a corrupt tyrant and regarded Bolingbroke as a supernaturally sanctioned agent of destiny; and a middle 'Yorkist' position, most concerned with blackening the character of Bolingbroke but also prepared to acknowledge the faults of Richard's reign.[50] More generally, the *Henriad* as a whole is (in I. A. Richards's phrase) 'inexhaustible to meditation' because of the moral, psychological, and political ambiguities whereby Shakespeare both upholds and subverts the 'Tudor myth'. In *Henry VIII*, as I have

contended, Shakespeare stretches this tension to its limits by juxtaposing Catholic and Protestant, cynical and providential, views of the divorce of Henry VIII.

At the outset of the *Life and Raigne of King Henry VIII*, the last and most evenhanded Renaissance treatment of this pivotal epoch in English history (which was dedicated to Charles I in the year of his execution), Lord Herbert of Cherbury writes:

It is not easie to write that Princes History, of whom no one thing may constantly be affirmed . . . Nor is it probable that contradictories should agree to the same Person: so that nothing can shake the credit of a Narrative more, then if it grow unlike it selfe; when yet it may be not the Author, but the Argument that caused the variation. It is impossible to draw his Picture well who hath several countenances.[51]

For Shakespeare, no less than for Herbert, 'no one thing may constantly be affirmed' of Henry VIII, and it is inevitable that 'contradictories should agree' in drawing the portrait of a ruler who has 'several countenances'.

III

Cranmer's prophecy highlights a distinctive feature of the temporal structure of *Henry VIII*: events that lie in the future for the characters of Shakespeare's play exist in the past for Shakespeare and his audience. Indeed, as Alexander Leggatt has finely observed, *Henry VIII* is a play 'haunted by the future'.[52] The eventual executions of Anne Boleyn, Thomas More (3.2.395–9), and Cromwell (446–9) at the hands

---

[50] See Ernest William Talbert, *The Problem of Order: Elizabethan Political Commonplaces and an Example of Shakespeare's Art* (Chapel Hill: University of North Carolina Press, 1962), pp. 159–60, 232–3 n. 14; and Henry Ansgar Kelly, *Divine Providence in the England of Shakespeare's Histories* (Cambridge, MA: Harvard University Press, 1970).

[51] Edward Herbert, *Life and Raigne of King Henry the Eight* (London, 1649), p. 1.

[52] Leggatt, '*Henry VIII* and the Ideal England', 141. See also Cespedes, '"We are one in fortunes"', 436.

of Henry VIII are all evoked by Shakespeare's language, and that of Cranmer is likewise implicit in the confrontation with Gardiner in Act 5. (Felperin, it will be recalled, could find 'no hint' of any of these 'bloody fates' in the play.) This responsiveness to history raises a final question, which – like those of authorship and genre – is at once marginal and central to an understanding of *Henry VIII*: its topicality.

As the political dimension of *Henry VIII* has been disputed by some critics, so there are those who deny that the play has any contemporary relevance. According to Paul Dean, for example, 'attempts to give it topical or allegorical significance' are 'quite misconceived'.[53] It must be conceded that these topical readings, most of which seek to tie the play to the marriage in February 1613 of James's daughter Elizabeth to Prince Frederick, the elector Palatine, have not always been conducted with sufficient discrimination.[54] But it is not necessary to accept the interpretations in every detail to agree that there is some connection between *Henry VIII* and contemporary history, and that an exploration of this relationship may enrich our understanding of the play.

In particular, although Foakes presses too hard his claim that the play was performed at Elizabeth's nuptials, the sense that this event, which took place some four months before the performance at the Globe Theatre, provides a shaping context for the play remains valid.[55] Because Cranmer's prophecy comments explicitly on the transition between the reigns of Elizabeth I and James I, moreover, I believe that it is also legitimate to read the play with reference to the question of succession. A cogent topical reading of *Henry VIII*, accordingly, needs to keep in mind these two historical layers simultaneously.

This intertwining of past and present dimensions of the play is grounded in one of history's uncanny repetitions. For, like the princess whose birth is celebrated at the conclusion of the play, the Jacobean princess Elizabeth was the daughter of a Queen Anne, and in both

Elizabeths was vested the hope for the future. As Foakes has pointed out, 'Princess Elizabeth was following her namesake in her support of the true religion if not in getting married, and a comparison or identification of the two is common in the marriage tracts'.[56] Cranmer's tribute to Queen Elizabeth as a 'maiden phoenix', for example, finds an echo in Donne's 'Epithalamion' on the marriage of Elizabeth and the Elector Frederick, where the spouses are termed 'two Phoenixes', and Elizabeth is hailed as a 'faire Phoenix Bride'.[57]

As Foakes's comment suggests, it is specifically because Elizabeth's marriage to Frederick was regarded as cementing the alliance of England with the forces of European Protestantism that a recollection of the Virgin Queen figured so strongly in the iconography of the festivities. Not surprisingly, therefore, it is chiefly those critics who advocate what I have identified as a 'Protestant' reading of *Henry VIII* who also highlight the topical nuances in the play. Cranmer's comparison of James to a

---

53 Dean, 'Dramatic Mode and Historical Vision', 178.
54 See *King Henry VIII*, ed. Foakes, pp. xxviii–xxxv. Other discussions of the play's topicality are to be found in Frederick O. Waagh, Jr, '*Henry VIII* and the Crisis of the English History Play', *Shakespeare Studies*, 8 (1975), 297–309; Stuart M. Kurland, '*Henry VIII* and James I: Shakespeare and Jacobean Politics', *Shakespeare Studies*, 19 (1987), 203–17; Baillie, 'A Jacobean History'; Bergeron, *Shakespeare's Romances and the Royal Family*; and Yates, *Shakespeare's Last Plays*. Baillie, in particular, strains credulity with his attempt to link the play with the divorce proceedings of Frances Howard against the Earl of Essex and the related arrest and eventual murder of Sir Thomas Overbury.
55 See Baillie, 'A Jacobean History', 260. Both Sir Henry Wotton's reference to the play as 'new' at the time of the Globe fire, on June 29, and the fact that *Henry VIII* is not included among the extant record of plays performed at court by the King's Men in 1612–13 strongly suggest that it must be subsequent to the wedding.
56 *King Henry VIII*, ed. Foakes, p. xxxii.
57 John Donne, 'An Epithalamion, Or Marriage Song on the Lady Elizabeth and Count Palatine being married on St Valentine's day', in *The Poems of John Donne*, ed. Herbert J. C. Grierson (1912; rpt. Oxford: Oxford University Press, 1968), 2 vols., lines 18, 23, 29.

'mountain cedar', for example, who shall 'reach his branches / To all the plains about him' (5.4.52–3), fashions its compliment (directed to both father and daughter) from just the sort of biblical language that the monarch himself favoured.

Once it is granted that the marriage of Elizabeth and Frederick forms part of the context of *Henry VIII*, moreover, it becomes impossible to deny the relevance also of the death in November 1612 of Prince Henry, James and Anne's eldest son and the chief hope of English Protestantism. The concluding lines of the Prologue, 'And if you can be merry then, I'll say / A man may weep upon his wedding day', which I have interpreted as an ironic commentary on the action of the play to follow, take on a tragic aura when it is recalled that Elizabeth's marriage took place in the aftermath of the period of mourning for Prince Henry's death.

The inauspicious timing of Elizabeth's marriage to Frederick proved to be a portent for the utter disappointment of the hopes placed by English Protestants on the Palatinate alliance.[58] In 1619, Frederick accepted an offer to assume the throne of Bohemia by the Bohemian Council; but the Catholic League, led by the Emperor Ferdinand, the deposed King of Bohemia, could not accept this arrangement and struck back militarily. King James, who, unlike Prince Henry, preferred to see himself as a mediator between competing religious forces on the continent rather than as a champion of the Protestant cause, refused to intervene, and in October 1620 Frederick suffered a catastrophic defeat at the hands of the Emperor's forces. The Palatinate reverted to the control of Spain, and Frederick lost his throne and became the pathetically exiled 'Winter King', eventually dying at Mainz in 1632.

All these developments, of course, remained hidden in the future in 1613. But they none the less provide a retrospective commentary on *Henry VIII*. For, as I have intimated, one of the most notable features of the play is its sense of closure, stemming from the fact that Shakespeare – writing in the Jacobean period – could look back with hindsight on the crises of the Tudor era, secure in the knowledge that Elizabeth would ascend to the throne and in turn be followed by James. But since the occasion that informs the contemporary reception of the play in turn became entangled in a net of historical irony, Shakespeare's own appearance of Prospero-like mastery over the contingent flux of events itself proves to be an aesthetic illusion.

How James's military vacillation on the continent was judged by subsequent writers may be gathered from *The Princess Cloria*, an imitation of Sidney's *Arcadia*, first issued in censored form under the Protectorate in 1653 and republished in full in 1661 after the Restoration. As Annabel Patterson has shown, this royalist romance is a political allegory, the essential feature of which is that James's refusal to go to Frederick's assistance and the consequent loss of the Palatinate are 'presented as the first cause of the revolution, the original fall from grace of the Stuarts'.[59] Looking back to the Reformation while being tied to the marriage that is caught up in the march to the Civil War, Shakespeare's *Henry VIII* is deconstructed by history as much as it is a deconstruction of it.

This fateful concatenation of events surrounding *Henry VIII* likewise authorizes some concluding speculations on the bearing of the play on the dynastic passage from Elizabeth to James. As Kim H. Noling has suggested, because of the sexual looseness of his mother, Mary Queen of Scots, James continued to feel a sense of insecurity about his claim to the English throne; and 'In such a context the image of asexual procreation found in the "maiden phoenix" should have appealed not

---

[58] For a summary of the relevant history, see Pauline Gregg, *King Charles I* (1981; rpt. Berkeley and Los Angeles: University of California Press, 1984), pp. 59–71.

[59] Annabel M. Patterson, *Censorship and Interpretation: The Conditions of Writing and Reading in Early Modern England* (Madison: University of Wisconsin Press, 1984), p. 195.

only to the patriarchy within the world of the play, but also to the ... dynastic patriarch, to whom the compliment of the prophecy is made.'[60]

Accordingly, the invocation of the 'maiden phoenix' does double duty in idealizing both the marriage of the Jacobean Princess Elizabeth and the transition from Tudor to Stuart rule. But if, as Hume has written, 'The crown of England was never transferred from father to son with greater tranquillity, than it passed from the family of Tudor to that of Stuart',[61] this calm belies the tow of more tempestuous currents beneath the surface. For as Elizabeth I was the daughter of a father who executed her mother, so James – by a macabre symmetry – was the son of a mother who sanctioned the murder of his father. Although modern scholarship tends to dismiss as unreliable those accounts that suggest that Mary Queen of Scots began her sexual relations with the Earl of Bothwell during the lifetime of Lord Darnley, her previous husband and James's father, her marriage to Bothwell, the man chiefly responsible for Darnley's murder, took place in May 1567, less than three months after Darnley's death.[62] Nor can one doubt the psychological impact on James of these traumas, separated as he was from his mother in infancy and reared by the staunchly Protestant tutor George Buchanan, who devoted himself to the task of blackening Mary's reputation, insisting in several treatises that her adulterous liaison with Bothwell had begun by the time of James's birth, in June 1566, or even earlier. It seems likewise plausible to speculate that Elizabeth's aversion to marriage, in addition to its rational political motives, was animated by an unconscious dread of male sexuality stemming from her early experience of its consequences wreaked by Henry VIII on Anne Boleyn.[63]

In *Henry VIII*, Shakespeare passes over these royal scandals in silence, though the resemblance between James I's familial history and the plot of *Hamlet* has not escaped critical notice.[64] But it is precisely as a reminder of what Cranmer's prophecy does *not* tell us – about Elizabeth's fear of having a successor and about James's avidity for the English throne – that the events I have summarized are deserving of recall. It was only in 1613, the year of Shakespeare's play and long after he had tacitly cooperated in his mother's judicial murder at Elizabeth's hands, that James ordered the exhumation of her body and its reburial in Westminster Abbey.[65] Like James's effort to rehabilitate Mary Queen of Scots's reputation, the panegyric with which *Henry VIII* concludes loses much of its suasive power when the circumstances upon which it depends are brought to light.

---

[60] Noling, 'Grubbing Up the Stock', 305.

[61] David Hume, *The History of Great Britain: The Reigns of James I and Charles I*, ed. Duncan Forbes (Harmondsworth: Penguin Books, 1970), p. 63.

[62] See Antonia Fraser, *Mary Queen of Scots* (1969; rpt. New York: Dell, 1973), pp. 311, 363.

[63] See Lytton Strachey, *Elizabeth and Essex* (1928; rpt. New York: Harcourt Brace Jovanovich, 1956), pp. 263–4; and, for more specific documentation that Elizabeth harboured unconscious anxiety and resentment toward her father, see Anne Lake Prescott, 'The Pearl of the Valois and Elizabeth I: Marguerite de Navarre's *Miroir* and Tudor England', in *Silent But for the Word: Tudor Women as Patrons, Translators, and Writers of Religious Works*, ed. Margaret Patterson Hannay (Kent, OH; Kent State University Press, 1985), pp. 61–76.

[64] See, with appropriate caution, Lilian Winstanley, *Hamlet and the Scottish Succession* (Cambridge: Cambridge University Press, 1921).

[65] See Jonathan Goldberg, *James I and the Politics of Literature: Shakespeare, Jonson, Donne and Their Contemporaries* (Baltimore and London: The Johns Hopkins University Press, 1983), pp. 15–16.

THE POLITICS OF CONSCIENCE IN
ALL IS TRUE (OR *HENRY VIII*)
CAMILLE WELLS SLIGHTS

Most historians today see the religious changes that took place during the reign of Henry VIII as a series of discrete events that only gradually were understood to constitute a Protestant Reformation. The text that was published in the Shakespeare first folio with the title, *The Famous History of the Life of King Henry the Eight*, is part of that process of interpretation.[1] Performed first in 1613, it appeared while rumours of a second Spanish Armada were kindling anti-Catholic feeling and a few months after the marriage of the Princess Elizabeth to the Elector Palatine, an alliance intended to strengthen the Protestant cause in Europe.[2] Produced at a time of widespread nationalistic and Protestant fervour, the play interprets events in the reign of Henry VIII as the legitimating origins of Stuart England.

Despite the folio title, the play dramatizes not the life of Henry VIII but a series of individual changes of fortune that taken together chart Henry's emergence as a powerful king. Henry takes no direct part in the first major episode, the Duke of Buckingham's conviction for treason, which seems to be orchestrated by Cardinal Wolsey. Initially, Wolsey also seems to be the source of Katherine of Aragon's problems, intruding between Henry and Katherine as he intrudes between the King and his subjects. Although Henry later traces his doubts about the legitimacy of his marriage to the French ambassador rather than to the Cardinal, he still seems to rely heavily on the judgement of others and possibly to be an unwitting pawn in games of international intrigue. Clearly, his will is frustrated by the power of the ecclesiastical court. The next episode, Wolsey's fall, is accomplished with more dispatch and more obviously as a direct consequence of Henry's wishes. Henry personally taunts Wolsey with veiled threats. A few lines later messengers 'Bearing the King's will from his mouth expressly' (3.2.236) announce Wolsey's downfall. In each succeeding action, then, Henry's will is increasingly evident and effective, though in no case does he act alone. Buckingham is convicted by a jury of his peers, the marriage eventually is annulled by a court of English bishops, and Wolsey's ruin is accomplished through due legal process. But in the last major episode Henry acts independently, overriding the decision of the Council in order to protect Thomas Cranmer.

As Henry appears progressively more active and responsible, his emergence as the powerful source of truth and justice is represented not just as a young king's achievement of independence

---

[1] For a discussion of the attribution controversy, see David V. Erdman and Ephim G. Fogel, eds., *Evidence for Authorship* (Ithaca, NY: Cornell Univ. Press, 1966), pp. 457–78.
[2] On the political context, see R. A. Foakes, ed., The Arden *King Henry VIII* (London, Methuen, 1968), pp. xxx–xxxiv, George W. Keeton, *Shakespeare's Legal and Political Background* (London: Pitman and Sons, 1967), pp. 336–45, and William M. Baillie, '*Henry VIII*: A Jacobean History,' *Shakespeare Studies*, 12 (1979), 247–66.

from unworthy advisers but as a process of freeing England from foreign influences. While Henry's power is mediated through Wolsey, England is entangled with continental powers. The play opens with a description of the signing of the peace treaty with France at the Field of the Cloth of Gold. The Duke of Norfolk describes festivities so splendid that 'no discerner / Durst wag his tongue in censure' (1.1.32–3). But in retrospect tongues do wag: we hear that this 'view of earthly glory' (line 14) was contrived by Wolsey 'Only to show his pomp as well in France / As here at home' (lines 163–4) and that many noblemen ruined their fortunes irretrievably because Wolsey, without consulting the King or Council, demanded that they accompany the King on this extravagant journey. Furthermore this 'costly treaty' (line 165) has proved valueless: France has already violated it. After Wolsey has fallen, charged primarily with offences stemming from his international diplomacy, the play ends with another royal ceremony – this one in England, not France; performed on stage, not reported – the celebrations following Elizabeth's baptism. While the English and French kings appeared 'Equal in lustre' (line 29) during the ceremonies in France, in the baptismal scene Henry clearly is supreme, and Archbishop Cranmer foresees a time when an English monarch will be 'A pattern to all princes living... / And all that shall succeed' (5.4.22–3). While the glittering pageantry arranged by Wolsey dazzled spectators but in time proved specious, the royal baptism inspires Cranmer with a true vision of the future, the reigns of Elizabeth and James. He prophesies an England blessed with peace and prosperity, when

> every man shall eat in safety
> Under his own vine what he plants, and sing
> The merry songs of peace to all his
> neighbours. (lines 33–5)

Henry's assertion of independence also entails a break with Rome. The text neatly hints at the religious implications of the geopolitical ten-

sions even before Henry's troubles with Rome develop. Gossiping with a group of noblemen about the bad habits the young men who had accompanied Henry picked up in France, Sir Thomas Lovell reports measures intended for the 'reformation of our travelled gallants'. A recent proclamation requires them either to drop their foreign manners, 'renouncing clean / The faith they have in tennis and tall stockings' or else to pack themselves off back to France. Lord Sands approves, declaring himself 'glad they are going, / For sure there's no converting of 'em' (1.3.19, 29–30, 42–3, italics added). Doctrinal considerations are introduced more literally when Wolsey worries that his 'cause' will suffer through the influence of Anne Boleyn, a 'spleeny Lutheran' and of Cranmer, a 'heretic' (3.2.101, 100, 103). The charge of heresy then constitutes the last conflict in the play, when Cranmer is accused of spreading the dangerous new opinions that have created such turbulence in Germany. Although Cranmer protests that he is no disturber of the public peace, he does not deny the new opinions and, in his prophetic vision of Elizabethan and Jacobean England, foresees a time when 'God shall be truly known' (5.4.36).

Thus the play represents Wolsey's defeat, Cranmer's vindication, and the replacement of Katherine by Anne as the founding of a Protestant dynasty. But the emergence of Protestantism is not primarily doctrinal change nor England's resistance to papal interference in domestic politics. Although the play treats such issues as papal jurisdiction and the authority of the clergy and alludes to the use of the vernacular and the doctrine of faith, the central issue is the autonomy of the private conscience.[3] Henry's conscience is the force driving the

---

[3] The only critics I have found who recognize the importance of conscience in the play are Judith H. Anderson, *Biographical Truth: The Representation of Historical Persons in Tudor–Stuart Writing* (New Haven: Yale Univ. Press, 1984), pp. 128–30, and especially Alan R. Young, 'Shakespeare's *Henry VIII* and the Theme of Conscience,' *English Studies in Canada*, 7 (1981), 38–53.

action, propelling Anne and Cranmer to success and Katherine and Wolsey to ruin.

Henry's doubts about the lawfulness of his marriage to Katherine of Aragon constitute what Shakespeare's contemporaries called a case of conscience. The conscience, as defined by William Perkins, is 'a part of the understanding in all reasonable creatures, determining their particular actions, either with them or against them'.[4] A case of conscience, William Ames explains, 'is a practical question concerning which, the conscience may make a doubt'.[5] According to Perkins, Ames, and other English casuists who describe the operations of the conscience and recommend procedures for resolving cases of conscience, to act against one's conscience or to act with a doubting conscience is sinful and brings agonies of fear and guilt.[6] Thus, as Henry explains to the ecclesiastical court, when the French ambassador questioned his daughter's legitimacy, doubts about the lawfulness of his marriage to his brother's widow 'shook / The bosom of [his] conscience' (2.4.178–9). Then 'many mazed considerings did throng / And prest in' (2.4.182–3), and he began to fear that his failure to produce a male heir was God's punishment for his sinful marriage. Full of fear and doubt which 'all the reverend fathers of the land' (line 202) were unable to cure, Henry felt himself drifting helplessly on the 'wild sea of [his] conscience' (line 197).

The resolution of these doubts not only brings Henry the joy and confidence that mark a peaceful conscience but also separates the English church from Rome and manifests the Protestant theory of conscience. Protestants accused Catholic casuists of claiming illegitimate power over the conscience. John Donne, for example, blames them for 'entangling and perplexing ... consciences' and for inciting sedition by posing such cases as 'How Princes have their jurisdiction, How they may become Tyrants, [and] What is lawfull to a private man in such a case.'[7] The primary issue, however, was not political subversion fomented by inter-national Catholicism but the conception of moral authority. Catholic casuists held that the opinions of theological authorities could resolve moral doubts. Their treatments of cases of conscience were designed for the use of clergy in the confessional. Protestant casuists rejected the reliance on any external authority. Presenting themselves as guides or advisers without authority to excuse or condemn, they maintained that the individual conscience is supreme, subject only to God.[8] 'A Man's Conscience', wrote Perkins, 'is known to none besides himself, but to God ... It is ... a little God sitting in the middle of mens hearts.'[9] And because the 'Conscience is immediatly subject to God', Ames explains, '[i]t cannot submit ... unto any other creature without Idolatry ... It is never lawfull to doe against oure own opinion ... for respect to other mens authority.'[10]

Henry's doubts arise while he is relying on the judgement of his clerical advisers. As usual in this play where the audience has no special access to characters' secret thoughts, the source of those doubts remains obscure. The people around him hold Wolsey responsible. The Duke of Norfolk, for example, describes how Wolsey

---

[4] William Perkins, *A Discourse of Conscience* in *The Works of ... William Perkins*, 3 vols. (London, 1612–13), I, p. 517.

[5] William Ames, *Conscience with the Power and Cases thereof* (1639), Bk. II, p. 1.

[6] On the theological and literary tradition of English Protestant casuistry, see my *The Casuistical Tradition in Shakespeare, Donne, Herbert, and Milton* (Princeton: Princeton Univ. Press, 1981).

[7] John Donne, *Pseudo-Martyr* (London, 1610), pp. 128, 144.

[8] From the Calvinists William Perkins and William Ames to the Arminian Jeremy Taylor, from William Baxter, chaplain to parliamentary forces, to Robert Sanderson, royalist bishop, Protestant casuists all agreed on the privacy and supremacy of the individual conscience.

[9] *Works*, I, p. 519.

[10] Ames, Bk. I, pp. 6, 16.

dives into the King's soul and there scatters
Dangers, doubts, wringing of the conscience.

(2.2.26–7)

But it scarcely matters whether Wolsey first
provoked doubt in order to spite Katherine's
nephew, Charles V, and then changed his mind
when he was unable to control Henry's marital
choice or whether the French ambassador first
raised the question. What is clear is that Henry's
conscience is troubled and that he expects it to
be quieted externally. We first hear him
mention the problem when he greets Wolsey as
the 'quiet of my wounded conscience ... a cure
fit for a king' (2.2.75–6). At the trial, Henry
narrates how he first confided his doubts to the
Bishop of Lincoln and the Archbishop of Canterbury, who (understandably) ducked the
problem and suggested appealing to Rome.

But even as Henry explains why he has
summoned the Papal legates 'to rectify [his]
conscience' (2.4.200), he shows signs of losing
faith in the authority of others to resolve his
personal moral doubts. When he absolves
Wolsey of encouraging a divorce out of malice
towards Katherine, for example, he carefully
stipulates, 'I speak ... to this point, / And thus
far clear him' (2.4.163–4), hinting that he might
not so readily clear of other charges the man
who was once the keeper of his conscience.
Henry tells the court that he will contentedly
live out his life with Katherine, if they can
prove the marriage lawful, but he complains in
an aside: 'These cardinals trifle with me. I abhor
/ This dilatory sloth and tricks of Rome' (lines
233–4). And this is the last Henry has to say
about his conscience. The resolution of his case
of conscience is not dramatized; it is the absent
presence at the heart of the play. In subsequent
scenes we hear – in this order – reports that
Henry has secretly married Anne Boleyn and
that her coronation will soon take place, that
Cranmer has 'satisfied the King for his divorce'
(3.2.65), and that Cranmer 'with other /
Learnèd and reverend fathers' held a court in
which 'the late marriage [was] made of none
effect' (4.1.25–6, 33). Clearly, Henry is no

longer submitting his conscience to the authority of anyone – not Wolsey, not the Pope,
and not Cranmer. He acknowledges the authority of the clergy to perform and annul
marriages but has decided the basic moral question himself. Initially Henry submitted his
'scruple to the voice of Christendom' (2.2.88),
but he has acted according to the voice of his
own conscience.

Because Henry does not resolve his doubts
on stage, emphasis falls on the essentially
private nature of the conscience rather than on
the merits of the particular case. When the
external judgement by Cranmer and his colleagues finally comes, it seems largely irrelevant, both because Henry has appeared increasingly independent and because the concept of
the independent individual conscience has been
developed through other characters. Buckingham, Katherine, Wolsey, and Cranmer all meet
adversity by affirming the primacy of their
private consciences.

The Buckingham plot, in fact, constitutes a
warning against entrusting one's conscience to
the clergy. The case against Buckingham consists of testimony that he has aspired to the
throne encouraged by his confessors, a monk
who has prophesied that he will govern
England and a friar who has 'fed him every
minute / With words of sovereignty'
(1.2.150–1). At the trial, Buckingham's confessors testify against him. The facts of the case
remain obscure. Buckingham is convicted on
the evidence in a trial that even he calls 'a noble
one' (2.1.120). But he claims innocence
throughout, and there are hints that the evidence has been engineered by Wolsey. On
either hypothesis, whether the testimony was
perjured or whether the confessional was actually used to incite treason, auricular confession
seems a thoroughly dangerous institution.
Although no character articulates the theological implications, Buckingham is twice
advised to think for himself (1.1.135–6, 146–7).
And after he has been sentenced, Buckingham
explicitly distinguishes the external judgement

of the law from the judgement of his own conscience:

> I have this day received a traitor's judgement,
> And by that name must die. Yet, heaven bear
>   witness,
> And if I have a conscience let it sink me,
> Even as the axe falls, if I be not faithful.
>
> (2.1.59–62)

Katherine's case is different: her virtue is universally acknowledged, and, unlike Buckingham, she rejects the authority of the court judging her case. But she too experiences the disjunction between the judgement of others and the judgement of her conscience. When Wolsey suggests a private consultation, she answers proudly, 'There's nothing I have done yet, o'my conscience, / Deserves a corner' (3.1.30–1). 'I care not', she continues,

> if my actions
> Were tried by ev'ry tongue, ev'ry eye saw 'em,
> Envy and base opinion set against 'em,
> I know my life so even.   (lines 33–7)

Ironically, Katherine's argument – that she cannot be treated justly by an English court – cuts both ways, also supporting Henry's analogous suspicion that he cannot expect impartial judgement from a court at Rome dominated by Charles V.

While Katherine and Buckingham invoke their consciences to affirm their consistent virtue, Wolsey learns to know himself only after he loses power. Then he feels his 'heart new opened' and discovers a 'peace above all earthly dignities, / A still and quiet conscience' (3.2.367, 380–1). Cranmer, like Wolsey, first uses the word 'conscience' when threatened with legal prosecution. Unlike Wolsey, who finds temporal honours incompatible with a peaceful conscience, Cranmer insists on the harmonious integrity of his 'life and office' (5.2.67). But, of course, by asserting the consistency of 'his private conscience and his place' (line 74), he too presupposes a distinguishable private conscience that comprises self-knowledge and moral judgement. Through

Cranmer's courage and Henry's protection, the play celebrates the English Church's respect for the integrity of the conscience.

By presenting Henry VIII's repudiation of his marriage to Katherine of Aragon as a case of conscience, Shakespeare closely followed his historical sources.[11] Henry's speech to the Papal legates, with its image of the conscience tossing on a sea of doubt, echoes Holinshed's language. But Holinshed does not mention conscience in connection with Buckingham, Katherine, Wolsey, or Cranmer. The source material has been shaped to emphasize the personal moral judgement, the conscience, of each character as well as to present Henry VIII's conscience as the motivating force of the English Reformation.

So, at a time of intense patriotic and Protestant sentiment, the King's Men produced a play complimenting the reigning monarch. By the strategy that Paul de Man has called 'metaleptic reversal of cause and effect',[12] James I's political and religious policies are justified by a reading of Henry VIII's reign, which is justified retrospectively as the source for Jacobean Protestantism. The portrayal of Wolsey as an arrogant, worldly, intriguing priest, whose ambitions focus on Rome and who intrudes between the King and his subjects, justifies James I's warning against a Pope presuming to 'meddle between me and my Subjects.'[13] By representing Henry's scruples as the source of his hostility to Rome and by celebrating Protestantism as the freeing of individual moral judgement from external authority, the play

---

[11] Holinshed is the primary source. For a modern view that conscience rather than sex or statecraft motivated Henry VIII's divorce, see Lacey Baldwin Smith, 'A Matter of Conscience' in *Action and Conviction in Early Modern Europe*, ed. Theodore K. Rabb and Jerrold E. Seigel (Princeton: Princeton Univ. Press, 1969), pp. 32–51.

[12] Paul de Man, *Allegories of Reading* (New Haven: Yale Univ. Press, 1979), p. 274.

[13] Charles H. McIlwain, ed. *The Political Works of James I* (Cambridge, Mass.: Harvard University Press, 1918), p. 113.

presents the autonomous private conscience as both cause and consequence of the English Reformation.

But even while the emphasis on conscience celebrates Henry VIII as the progenitor of English Protestantism and James I as the heir of that tradition, it also takes less flattering and more disturbing configurations. Before Henry speaks of his case of conscience, we hear of it from the ironic perspective of court gossip. When the Duke of Norfolk reports that the King is troubled because 'It seems the marriage with his brother's wife / Has crept too near his conscience' (2.2.16–17), the Duke of Suffolk objects: 'No, his conscience / Has crept too near another lady' (lines 17–18). This view of Henry's motives is complemented by a similarly sceptical interpretation of the operation of Anne Boleyn's conscience. In the only scene where she speaks more than a few words, Anne expresses her admiration and pity for Queen Katherine and her disdain for the treacherous glamour of temporal glory, protesting, 'By my troth and maidenhead, / I would not be a queen' (2.3.23–4). Her companion scoffs at Anne as a hypocrite with the usual female desire for 'eminence, wealth, sovereignty,' which

> the capacity
> Of your soft cheveril conscience would receive
> If you might please to stretch it. (lines 29, 31–3)

The 'cheveril conscience,' that stretches with the elasticity of a soft kid glove to accommodate its possessor, was a commonplace. In Richard Bernard's *Isle of Man*, for example, Mr Subtilty combines 'Subtilty of wit with a chiverell conscience' to make 'fowle sinnes pass along as no sinnes'.[14] The accusation that Anne's conscience will function not to direct moral choice but to rationalize and justify her desires obviously applies as aptly to Henry's capacity for hypocrisy and self-deception as to Anne's.

Even more unsettling to the claims of moral supremacy for the inviolable conscience are the unavoidable and irreconcilable clashes among individual consciences. Even if one accepts the sincerity of the King's case of conscience, his treatment of Katherine is still disturbing. The play raises no doubts at all about her sincerity, virtue, and suffering. Strangely enough, in a play apparently designed as Protestant propaganda, the most admirable and universally admired character is the Spanish queen who looks to the Pope for justice. Henry's treatment of Wolsey too is problematic. Although Wolsey certainly is portrayed as ambitious, arrogant, and deceitful, even when he confesses and repents of his pursuit of worldly glory, he maintains that he has served his king faithfully. Just as Katherine remains true to Henry, blessing him in her dying speech, Wolsey in disgrace blesses the King and remains confident that 'spotless shall mine innocence arise / When the King know my truth' (3.2.302–3). The point, I think, is not merely that there is good in everyone but that individual truths are incompatible, so that by following the dictates of his conscience, Henry persecutes his 'true and humble wife' (2.4.21) and his true servant.

The Prologue claims repeatedly that the scenes to follow present matter that is both sad and true (lines 9, 18, 21). In addition, the play's original title apparently was *All is True*.[15] This insistence on truth, I want to argue, refers not simply to the representation of historical characters and events, but to the collision of individual truths. Even more telling in this respect than the disturbing fates of Katherine and Wolsey is the figure of Sir Thomas More. When told that More has been appointed Lord Chancellor in his place, Wolsey replies:

> May he continue
> Long in his highness' favour, and do justice
> For truth's sake and his conscience. (3.2.396–8)

---

14 R[ichard] B[ernard], *Isle of Man* (London, 1627), p. 36.
15 In a letter dated 2 July 1613, Sir Henry Wotton refers to 'a new Play called *All Is True*, representing some principal pieces of the Reign of Henry 8.' The letter is printed in the Arden edition, p. 180. Additional evidence is summarized in the Oxford *Textual Companion*.

The ironically prophetic references to Henry's favour and More's conscience remind the audience that the new Lord Chancellor will shortly lose his head for 'truth's sake and his conscience'. Wolsey's advice to Thomas Cromwell, his companion in this scene, is similarly prophetic:

> Let all the ends thou aim'st at be thy
> country's,
> Thy God's, and truth's. Then if thou fall'st,
> O Cromwell,
> Thou fall'st a blessèd martyr.   (lines 448–50)

As More will fall a Catholic martyr, Cromwell will fall a Protestant martyr (at least according to Fox's *Acts and Monuments*). Having displeased Henry in arranging his marriage to Anne of Cleves, Cromwell was to be executed on charges of heresy. Cranmer's prophecy of peace and plenty at Elizabeth's baptism is also radically undercut by an historical perspective. Not only is the mother of the royal infant soon to be executed, but Cranmer himself will lose his life for conscience's sake in a reign he does not foresee, that of Katherine's daughter Mary.

The political implications are also unsettling. Robert Weimann has traced connections between the self-legitimating authority of early Protestant writings and the strategies of the English public theatre. 'On a certain level of generalization', he suggests, 'in Shakespeare just as in Luther's early Reformation texts, it may be said that the issue of authority in the textual representation of power gets deeply entangled with the inscription of self-authorizing standards and activities'. But while Luther 'distinguished between secular and spiritual forms of authority in order to keep asunder matters of political rule and questions of individual conscience', Shakespeare, 'far from avoiding the precariousness of the borderline between them, explored areas of contradiction as well as potential intertwining'.[16] As we have seen, *All Is True* represents Henry's divorce as an assertion of spiritual and political authority. Initially the King depends on Wolsey. According to the play's unusually detailed stage directions, Henry makes his first entrance 'leaning on Cardinal Wolsey's shoulder' (1.2). In contrast, when Cranmer is ignominiously kept waiting among 'boys, grooms, and lackeys' (5.2.17), Henry appears 'at a window, above' to comment ambiguously, ''Tis well there's one above'em yet' (line 26), and he enters the council-chamber as the protector not the dependent of the Church. Early in the play, Henry challenges his Council on the basis of precedent and law:

>   Have you a precedent
> Of this commission? I believe, not any.
> We must not rend our subjects from our laws
> And stick them in our will.   (1.2.92–5)

Later, he warns Cranmer that legal verdicts do not always issue in truth and justice, due to the malice of judges and perjury of witnesses (5.1.130–9). And he imposes his personal will on his Council, making it abundantly clear to them that their power derives from him.

Since the royal prerogative was a hotly contested issue in 1613, this display of Henry's intervention seems calculated to please King James. On the other hand, the dramatic representation grounds Henry's authority in his relationship to his subjects and in his personal conscience, a faculty common to all. Katherine and Henry demonstrate care and concern for his subjects, while Wolsey is villainized by his oppression of gentry and commoners alike. Before he ever appears on stage, Buckingham and Suffolk articulate the nobles' hatred of Wolsey, and from a more disinterested source, the Second Gentleman, we learn that:

>   All the commons
> Hate him perniciously and, o'my conscience,
> Wish him ten fathom deep. This Duke as much
> They love and dote on, call him 'bounteous
> Buckingham ...'   (2.1.50–3)

---

16 Robert Weimann, 'History and the Issue of Authority in Representation: The Elizabethan Theater and the Reformation', *New Literary History*, 17 (1986), 470, 472.

Anne Boleyn's rise to favour is endorsed by the joy of the citizens, and Thomas Cranmer's virtue is attested to by the 'common voice' (5.2.209). Sympathy for and from the common people, then, directs audience response to the changing fortunes on stage.

The support of the people figures also as a potential source of power. When reporting the people's suffering, Katherine's major concern is political danger. Their protest 'breaks / The sides of loyalty, and almost appears / In loud rebellion' (1.2.28–30). Crucial evidence in Buckingham's trial is testimony that he received this secret message:

> Bid him strive
> To win the love o'th'commonalty. The Duke
> Shall govern England. (1.2.170–2)

Wolsey also appreciates the causal connection implicit in this syntactical juxtaposition. When the King pardons the citizens who have refused to pay exorbitant taxes, Wolsey instructs his secretary:

> The grievèd commons
> Hardly conceive of me. Let it be noised
> That through our intercession this revokement
> And pardon comes ... (lines 105–8)

Political power, of course, does not proceed directly from the people. But the politicians' concern to court popular approval suggests they are a real force, and dramatically their sentiments justify Henry's authority and Wolsey's fall. The overarching pattern is the removal of Wolsey, 'a keech [that] can, with his very bulk, / Take up the rays o'th'beneficial sun' (1.1.55–6), so that the beams of royal authority nourish England and the 'royal minds' (4.1.8) of the people again are directed to the King with loyalty and obedience. But the dramatic action also suggests that the legitimacy of Henry's authority is insecure to the degree that it rests on the love of the people. 'This tractable obedience' could again become 'a slave / To each incensèd will' (1.2.65–6).

The impermanence of social ideologies is evident in the play's treatment of the concept of individual merit. The nobles' hatred of Wolsey is expressed largely as contempt for an upstart. To them, the Cardinal is an insolent 'Ipswich fellow' (1.1.138), this 'butcher's cur' (line 120), who 'not propped by ancestry' claims a 'place next to the King' on the 'force of his own merit' (lines 59–66). In the course of the play, Wolsey is humbled and left 'naked to [his] enemies' (3.2.458) while his adversaries are exalted. THE ORDER OF THE CORONATION describes in detail the emblems of this victory:

the Earl of Surrey bearing the rod of silver with the dove, crowned with an earl's coronet, and also wearing a collar of Esses ... the Duke of Suffolk as High Steward, in his robe of estate, his coronet on his head, and bearing a long white wand. With him enter the Duke of Norfolk with the rod of marshalship and a coronet on his head. Each wears a collar of esses. (SD, 4.1.).

This display of aristocratic regalia announces the end of a time when a 'beggar's book / Outworths a noble's blood' (1.1.122–3). But as one of the spectators observes, such stars are 'sometimes falling ones' (4.1.56), and the triumph of blood and birth over individual merit is temporary, according to Cranmer. He predicts a future when English men and women will learn 'the perfect ways of honour, / And by those claim their greatness, not by blood' (5.4.37–8).

At the beginning of the play, the English people are represented as victims. The nobles are humiliated, their fortunes and their lives at risk through Wolsey's machinations. The common people are on the verge of rebellion, 'compelled by hunger / And lack of other means' (1.2.35–6). Desperate from poverty and unemployment, they are potentially dangerous, but primarily they are regarded as weak and oppressed. But by the coronation, they evoke images of strength and fertility. The crowd's roar of approval for Anne is like the noise 'the shrouds make at sea in a stiff tempest, / As loud and to as many tunes' (4.1.74–5). As a group, they embody a force that obliterates individual distinctions:

Great-bellied women,
That had not half a week to go, like rams
In the old time of war, would shake the press,
And make'em reel before'em. No man living
Could say 'This is my wife' there, all were
    woven
So strangely in one piece.   (lines 78–83)

The celebration of Elizabeth's baptism is even more enthusiastic and more uncontrollable. The penultimate scene is devoted entirely to efforts to restrain the crowd surging toward the entrance to the court. The Porter and his assistant complain of the impossibility of dispersing them 'Unless we sweep'em from the door with cannons' (5.3.13). They are as immovable as St Paul's, as irresistible as the tide (lines 16, 18). Again they create an impression of energy and fertility: 'what a fry of fornication is at door! On my Christian conscience, this one christening will beget a thousand' (lines 35–7).

All Is True represents the people as overwhelmingly loyal to the King, but it does so amid reminders that political ideologies and configurations of power change and that the Christian conscience is a powerful and potentially subversive phenomenon. These ironies also destabilize the allusions to the contemporary context. The play's theatrical display of royalty may serve to celebrate and support contemporary authority, but it may also, as Thomas Wotton observed, 'make greatness very familiar, if not ridiculous'.[17] Cranmer's vision of James I, rising 'star-like' to 'stand fixed' and 'flourish, / And like a mountain cedar reach his branches / To all the plains about him' (5.4.46, 47, 52–4) may be either a fulsome compliment to James or a portrait of an ideal Christian monarch, depending on one's critical perspective. But its truth must have been of a distinctly non-literal sort to the audience seeing the play in 1613 and aware that the peace of the commonwealth was threatened by the dissatisfied consciences of both Catholic recusants and Protestants advocating a more thorough reformation of the English church. In the year of the Armada, the King, as James VI

of Scotland, had identified the Pope as antichrist and urged armed warfare 'to fight against antichrist and his upholders'. '[S]ince with a good conscience we may ... stand in our defence', he argued, it is a duty 'to use lawful resistance ... for the maintenance of the good cause God had clad us with.'[18] Within thirty years of the first production of *All Is True* the Stuart monarchy will be challenged by men acting on their Christian consciences. The same arguments that James used against the Armada are soon to be used against his son by the men who cut off his head.[19]

The reading I am arguing for, then, is analogous to a collaboration between a Whig historian and a revisionist – a joint production by A. G. Dickens and Christopher Haigh perhaps. The play portrays the reign of Henry VIII as the gradual triumph of progressive, nationalist Protestantism, in which Englishmen under the leadership of a godly prince and clergy escape from lordly prelates and oppressive ecclesiastical authority. Simultaneously, it displays those events as the results of factional competition for power and influence and contingent on individual sexual and political ambitions. It shows the changes initiated by

---

[17] Foakes, p. 180. Several critics have argued that *Henry VIII* celebrates Jacobean ideals of monarchy and compliments James I. See, for example, Foakes, 'Critical Introduction', xxxix–lxiv, John D. Cox, 'Henry VIII and the Masque', *ELH*, 45 (1978), 390–409; Edward I. Berry, 'Henry VIII and the Dynamics of Spectacle', *Shakespeare Studies*, 12 (1979), 229–45. Critics who see implicit criticism of James include Lee Bliss, 'The Wheel of Fortune and The Maiden Phoenix of Shakespeare's King Henry the Eighth,' *ELH* (1975), 1–25; Stuart M. Kurland, 'Henry VIII and James I: Shakespeare and Jacobean Politics', *Shakespeare Studies*, 19 (1987), 203–18; F. Schreiber-McGee, '"The View of Earthly Glory": Visual Strategies and the Issue of Royal Prerogative in Henry VIII', *Shakespeare Studies*, 20 (1988), 191–200.

[18] James VI, *A Fruitful Meditation* (1588), pp. 78, 80, quoted in Paul Christianson, *Reformers and Babylon* (Toronto: Univ. of Toronto Press, 1978), pp. 95–6.

[19] Christianson, p. 96.

Henry's case of conscience strengthening the state at the expense of the church, and it also suggests that eventually their effects may destroy the political order Henry represents. *All Is True* embodies the sardonic but compassionate perception that to follow one's conscience – that is, to act according to one's personal under-standing of moral law while attending to particular circumstances and probable consequences – is the only way to live at peace with oneself, but may also incur and inflict suffering. The individual conscience, instead of redeeming the Stuart monarchy, could, and in fact would, destroy it.

SHAKESPEARE'S ROMANTIC INNOCENTS AND THE MISAPPROPRIATION OF THE ROMANCE PAST: THE CASE OF *THE TWO NOBLE KINSMEN*

RICHARD HILLMAN

In what is probably the most influential discussion to date of the relation between *The Knight's Tale* and *The Two Noble Kinsmen*, Philip Edwards leans heavily on 'a Chaucerian view of the frailty of our determinations'[1] in making his case for a fundamental continuity of vision. Shakespeare and Fletcher, apparently, are far from misappropriating the romance, even if they skew its rueful irony regarding human subjection to chance, coincidence, and above all Venus, to match the intensely personal bitterness of a Shakespeare 'looking dim-eyed at innocence and seeing salvation disappear with puberty' (p. 104). It is as if the world-weary bard, having just recently bid farewell to the imperfect magic of his art in *The Tempest*, returns for a curtain call in the role of Theseus, presiding sagely over the fading of another insubstantial pageant:

> O you heavenly charmers,
> What things you make of us! For what we lack
> We laugh, for what we have are sorry; still
> Are children in some kind. Let us be thankful
> For that which is, and with you leave dispute
> That are above our question. Let's go off
> And bear us like the time.   (5.4.131–7)

Indeed, Theseus' magisterial resignation might appear to take us beyond the threat of 'despair' that troubles Prospero's 'ending' (*The Tempest* Epi.15) to something like the pallid stoicism of *King Lear*'s concluding lines (either Edgar's or Albany's, depending on the text preferred): 'The weight of this sad time we must obey, / Speak what we feel, not what we ought to say' (*Lear* F 5.3.299–300). Still, in *King Lear* it is obvious – even to the sometimes obtuse Albany – that the 'present business / Is general woe' (5.3.295), whereas Theseus' exhortation to obey the mixed messages sent by the gods seems an impossibly tall order, and thus an evasion of underlying issues:

> A day or two
> Let us look sadly and give grace unto
> The funeral of Arcite, in whose end
> The visages of bridegrooms we'll put on
> And smile with Palamon; for whom an hour,
> But one hour since, I was as dearly sorry
> As glad of Arcite, and am now as glad
> As for him sorry.   (5.4.124–31)

We recall that Gloucester's heart could 'bear / Affliction' (4.5.75–6) unmitigated but '[b]urst smilingly' when torn ''[t]wixt two extremes of passion, joy and grief' (5.3.190–1). It may take, paradoxically, a less capacious heart to respond

> as 'twere with a defeated joy,
> With one auspicious and one dropping eye,
> With mirth in funeral and with dirge in marriage,
> In equal scale weighing delight and dole
> (*Hamlet* 1.2.10–13)

At least on first reading, a refreshingly dispassionate corrective to the construction of authorial disillusion is E. Talbot Donaldson's

---

1 Philip Edwards, 'On the Design of *The Two Noble Kinsmen*', *Review of English Literature*, 5, no. 4 (1964), 89–105; p. 99.

recent argument[2] that *The Two Noble Kinsmen* decisively shifts responsibility for the bitter-sweet outcome by portraying the gods, not as agents of fatality, but as emblems of destructive desires and values 'in the hearts of Theseus, of Hippolyta, of Palamon, and of Arcite' (p. 72). Only Emilia, in his view, remains 'helpless before chance' (p. 73) in the Chaucerian manner. Yet this exception points to a recuperation of Edwards' basic position. For by taking at face value Emilia's sustained exaltation of same-sex friendship over heterosexual love, Donaldson rejoins the critical mainstream (even more recently swollen by the contribution of Eugene M. Waith),[3] which locates the tragic component of the tragicomedy essentially in the loss of an ideal of innocence. Even if that ideal is characterized in terms of lesbian sexuality, as in one approach to the play '[a]s a dance of shifting sexual kind',[4] it remains *de rigueur* for criticism in the latter half of the twentieth century to deal in terms of 'the healing superiority of Emilia's values'.[5]

It ought to put us on our guard that, in order to sustain such an essentially nostalgic approach at once to this play and to Shakespeare's final dramatic word, commentators are eager to accept the standard division of authorship and prone to make large allowances for what Clifford Leech calls 'Fletcher's deflating hand'.[6] Thus Waith cites the younger dramatist's 'taste for sudden turns' ('Shakespeare and Fletcher', p. 244), downplaying elements in the composite text that threaten to bear harshly on either the friendship of Palamon and Arcite or the ingenuousness of Emilia. Ann Thompson considers that, instead of 'mocking and deflating his subject matter', as she takes Chaucer to do, adopting the satirical reading of a minority of modern critics, 'Shakespeare treats it seriously' but is 'occasionally at odds with his collaborator'.[7] For Donaldson, it would seem, the entire subplot of the Jailer's Daughter intrudes impertinently between the 'swan' and the 'well'; though Shakespeare is credited with introducing the character, the developing action is dis-missed as 'handled almost exclusively by Fletcher, and hence not included in my discussion' (*Swan at the Well*, p. 69).

But it is also possible, especially in a post-modern critical climate, to take the play's internal jars, whatever their origin – and I have no quarrel with the widely accepted distribution of authorship[8] – as integral to the text we have, not as blocking the text that might have been.

2 E. Talbot Donaldson, *The Swan at the Well: Shakespeare Reading Chaucer* (New Haven, Connecticut, 1985), pp. 50–73.
3 Eugene M. Waith, 'Shakespeare and Fletcher on Love and Friendship', *Shakespeare Studies*, 18 (1986), 235–50.
4 Richard Abrams, 'Gender Confusion and Sexual Politics in *The Two Noble Kinsmen*', *Drama, Sex and Politics*, ed. James Redmond, Themes in Drama, 7 (Cambridge, 1985), 69–76; p. 73. Abrams takes his cue from the allusions to homosexuality in the Jacobean court detected by M. C. Bradbook, 'Shakespeare and his Collaborators', *Shakespeare 1971: Proceedings of the World Shakespeare Conference, Vancouver, August 1971*, ed. Clifford Leech and J. M. R. Margeson (Toronto, 1971), pp. 21–36, and Glynne Wickham, '*The Two Noble Kinsmen* or *A Midsummer Night's Dream. Part II*?', *The Elizabethan Theatre VII: Papers Given at the Seventh International Conference on Elizabethan Theatre Held at the University of Waterloo, Ontario, in July 1977*, ed. G. R. Hibbard (Hamden, Connecticut, 1980), 167–96. While Abrams' observations on the patriarchal structure of the play-world are just and I appreciate his sensitivity to the sexual dimension of characters' attitudes, I believe that only by a highly selective and literal-minded use of the evidence can Emilia be painted as a frank and self-conscious lesbian.
5 Abrams, 'Gender Confusion', 75. As Wickham points out ('*Two Noble Kinsmen*', 168–9), earlier criticism tended high-handedly to denigrate Emilia together with the play as a whole. He, too, exalts her, as well as what he takes to be other emblems of 'the purity and innocence of youthful friendship' (p. 194). In general, Wickham's approach to the play as an allegory of events at court – the death of Prince Henry and the marriage of the Princess Elizabeth – unduly flattens and confines the text, although his view of the play's relation to *A Midsummer Night's Dream* is illuminating.
6 Clifford Leech, Introd. to *The Two Noble Kinsmen*, by William Shakespeare and John Fletcher, The Signet Classic Shakespeare (New York, 1966), p. xxxii.
7 Ann Thompson, *Shakespeare's Chaucer: A Study in Literary Origins* (Liverpool, 1978), p. 166.
8 See Leech, Introd., p. xxiv.

The notorious 'tensions and inconsistencies' (Thompson, *Shakespeare's Chaucer*, p. 166) then emerge as highly functional. Consistently, they expose as disingenuous and destructive, not merely the ideals of all the characters – notably including Emilia – but, more provocatively, idealism itself. Collaboratively, then, the dramatists went beyond shifting the *Tale*'s emphasis; they produced a radical discontinuity. That discontinuity, moreover – and this would seem to rule out the possibility that Shakespeare and Fletcher themselves took the romance to be satirical – is kept current by idealistic elements claiming a Chaucerian paternity. A running dialogue with the precursor text is initiated by the Prologue, which expresses anxiety about sustaining the 'nobleness' (15) of the original, in view of the literary ideal achieved by its author: 'it were an endless thing, / And too ambitious, to aspire to him' (Prol. 22–3). This disclaimer notwithstanding, the play displays a strong stylistic aspiration to forms of decorum reminiscent of the *Tale* – a tendency that continually runs up against unruly assertions of dramatic flux, notably including the comic subplot. This aspiration matches the cultivation of self-image practised by its characters, to the point where the prayer-scenes become virtual emblems of narcissism, with the terrestrial 'charmers' upstaging the 'heavenly' ones, as is certainly not the case in Chaucer. Precisely by endlessly trying and failing to measure up to the inherited images of romance perfection, these pale Jacobean imitations deconstruct the very business of image-making. They are trapped by their own attempted appropriation of a medieval past.

From this perspective, Theseus' responses to the challenges posed to his moral authority – not only, as we have seen, by the gods' final judgement but initially by the supplicant queens and later by the kinsmen themselves – differentiate themselves from their Chaucerian precedents in a way that has not been fully appreciated. It is not just that Chaucer's commanding figure becomes infected with a chronic (if low-grade) indecisiveness, which tends to issue in abrupt and contradictory resolutions as inadequately conceived as they are platitudinously delivered. More significantly, the struggles of the second Theseus – at times nearly comical – to keep on top of unfolding circumstances are infused with a new dimension of self-consciousness, largely by way of the dramatic technique, which abruptly juxtaposes action and stasis. The scenes of importuning that so smoothly fit the pacing of Chaucer's narrative are structured here as awkwardly overextended tableaux, and they focus sceptical attention on the Duke's image of himself as preternaturally wise, virtuous, and compassionate – in effect, as thoroughly Chaucerian.

In the opening supplication scene, the play's Theseus, wavering as his precursor certainly does not ('This gentil duc doun from his courser sterte / With herte pitous, whan he herde hem speke' (952–3)[9] is flattered into action by precisely such a portrait of himself:

> Remember that your fame
> Knolls in the ear o'th'world; what you do quickly
> Is not done rashly; your first thought is more
> Than others' laboured meditance; your premeditating
> More than their actions. (1.1.133–7)

The First Queen thus shrewdly overcomes the Hamlet in Theseus by painting him as a sort of anti-Hamlet, uniting the 'rashness' that Hamlet comes to praise (5.2.6 ff.) with the all-seeing 'divinity that shapes our ends' (5.2.10). It is left open whether the noble duke is also swayed by the conspicuously less heroic argument that follows – 'Now you may take him, / Drunk with his victory' (1.1.156–7) – an echo of Hamlet's decision, though 'Now [he] might do it pat' (3.3.73), to defer action until he can catch

---

[9] *The Knight's Tale* is cited from *The Riverside Chaucer*, ed. Larry D. Benson et. al., 3rd ed. (Boston, 1987).

Claudius '[w]hen he is drunk asleep' (3.3.89). At any rate, once Theseus has yielded, the Queens assure him, 'Thus dost thou still make good the tongue o'th'world. / ... And earn'st a deity equal with Mars – / ... If not above him ...' (1.1.225–7). Regard for self-image is commensurately prominent in his response, which graciously absorbs the 'deity' thus earned into his humanity:

> As we are men,
> Thus should we do; being sensually subdued,
> We lose our human title.   (1.1.230–2)

The narrative space where this posturing and this exposure take place is opened up, we should note, by a conflict between duty and sexual temptation not present in the original, where Theseus and Ypolita are already married. Shakespeare and Fletcher would appear to have found more useful the impatience for his marriage of the Duke in *A Midsummer Night's Dream*. That impatience is, of course, unflatteringly set off against his rejection of the validity of Hermia's desire, as he threatens to sentence her either to death or to the 'livery of a nun' (1.1.70).

Vanity becomes absurdity when Theseus, in a virtual parody of his Chaucerian original's second swift but dignified access of mercy ('For pitee renneth soone in gentil herte' (1761)), is pulled in several directions after his discovery of Palamon and Arcite hacking at each other in the forest. His abrupt command, 'None here speak for 'em' (3.6.183), is immediately flouted by Hippolyta, Emilia, and Pirithous ('Nay, then, I'll in too' (3.6.201)) in an orgy of supplication that 'make[s his] faith reel' (3.6.212). Emilia dismisses his instantaneous oath that 'both shall die' (3.6.136) as 'rashly made' (3.6.277), thus retracting the First Queen's praise and restoring him to indecisiveness. She then cites him against himself by invoking his prior vow to grant her any wish '[f]it for my modest suit' (3.6.235) – a qualification that does not wholly cancel this promise's resemblance to the sort notorious in romance as 'rash'. But if Theseus' words are

quick, his feelings are sluggish. He admits first to the possibility of feeling compassion, then, some sixty lines and much supplication later, to compassion itself. And his thoughts still lag behind: 'What may be done?' (3.6.270). At last, the stubborn chivalrous extremities of the two combatants puzzle his good intentions into a scheme that, unlike the relatively bloodless counterpart devised by Chaucer's Theseus, promises to save the life of one of them only at the cost of four certain deaths. Theseus ratifies this notably defective solution with a convenient redeployment of his honour:

> Thus I ordain it,
> And by mine honour once again it stands,
> Or both shall die.   (3.6.287–9)

This display of Theseus as frustrated, indeed all but helpless, in the face of absurdly conflicting noble gestures and motives is directly preceded by another equally chaotic, if less challenging, May Day encounter. He can receive the bumbling homage of the Schoolmaster's rustic dance with all the aplomb that his avatar in *A Midsummer Night's Dream* claims for himself ('Where I have come, great clerks have purposèd / To greet me with premeditated welcomes ...' (5.1.93–4)) because he is oblivious of the *Pyramus and Thisbe*-like subversion involved in celebrating his godlike perfections. Pyramus' epithet, 'dainty duck' (5.1.276), is recycled for this 'dainty Duke,' whose 'doughty dismal fame / From Dis to Daedalus' (3.5.116–17) hints at the darker side of the classical figure. The dance itself, redolent of sexuality and folly, makes an apt parodic anticipation of the serio-comic ballet shortly to be staged by Palamon and Arcite – a performance which is similarly made possible and completed by the fortuitous arrival of the missing female. It is suggestive that the Jailer's mad Daughter accepts her part in the dance with a mixture of unconsciousness and, in her own private (literally, idiotic) terms, enthusiasm ('I'll lead' (3.5.91)).

To this extent, the much-discussed parallel

between the Jailer's Daughter and Emilia points beyond the hazards of subjection to Venus, vividly depicted though they are, to the active part played by the dogged devotee of Diana in the pageant of mortal folly which Theseus, with rather less success than the posturing pedant, attempts to put in order. Obviously, the forest scene confronts Emilia with a fearful responsibility she had not sought and initiates the process by which her commitment to virginity becomes untenable. In effect, the knights, having lapsed from the pre-sexual 'innocence' emblematized by their friendship by constructing her as love-object, now put pressure on her, supported by patriarchal authority, to follow their example – to join their dance. On the other hand, Emilia's victimization is also problematized, both indirectly and directly.

Apart from the subversion of the Duke's status as fount of wisdom and model of virtue, the idealism of Palamon and Arcite appears in a highly sceptical light from start to finish. Their quarrel in the prison scene – a scene sometimes discounted on the grounds of Fletcher's authorship[10] – is immediately preceded, as it is not in Chaucer, by extreme professions of perfect friendship. The absurdity of the quarrel itself is developed from the gentler irony of Chaucer so as to bring out, pointedly, the childishness of the very response that marks their supposed fall from youthful purity: 'I saw her first. / ... That's nothing. ... But it shall be. ... I saw her too' (2.2.163–4).[11] The knights' concern with purity, which goes beyond self-consciousness to near-obsession, is an entirely non-Chaucerian element, present in both their professions of friendship here and in their conversation when we first see them in Thebes (a scene generally assigned to Shakespeare, incidentally). In both instances, a strain of 'outdoing' lends their fraternal bond a competitive edge. As for the moral claim itself, it runs afoul of the locker-room reminiscences that accompany the temporary renewal of their companionship during the rustic drinking episode

(3.3.28 ff.). Rather than write off this anomaly, too, as a Fletcherian aberration, we might allow it to signal that the 'innocence' of the two kinsmen conveniently accommodates sexual self-indulgence without responsibility. In any case, there remains the notoriously problematic prayer to Venus apparently provided by Shakespeare for Palamon (5.2.9 ff.), whose exaltation of love is darkly ambivalent and who, in a single breath, boasts of his chivalrous regard for female honour and makes a gratuitous salacious jest about a woman's virtue.

What seems most significant about the knights' ideal of noble friendship, however, is its escapist thrust, which is twice coupled, in exhortations by Arcite, with a sense of their vulnerability to corruption:

> let us leave the city,
> Thebes, and the temptings in't, before we further
> Sully our gloss of youth. (1.2.3–5)

> Let's think this prison holy sanctuary,
> To keep us from corruption of worse men.
> We are young, and yet desire the ways of honour
> That liberty and common conversation,
> The poison of pure spirits, might, like women,
> Woo us to wander from. (2.2.71–6)

On both occasions, tellingly, the impulse to preserve the ideal intact through withdrawal from temptation is immediately frustrated by intrusive circumstances – the news of war, the sight of Emilia. Their very resistance to the moral complexities that come with maturity appears to provoke the onslaught of experience, yet experience merely intensifies their evasive childishness – witness Arcite's dying double-talk, 'I was false, / Yet never treacherous' (5.6.92–3). It is the play's final irony that

---

[10] See, e.g., Waith, 'Shakespeare and Fletcher', 239–42.

[11] Abrams, 'Gender Confusion', 70–1, brings out the narcissism of the knights and relates it to the suggestion of a homosexual bond. It is not clear why he should take similar elements in the portrayal of Emilia as unequivocally positive.

Theseus uses an acknowledgement of human childishness ('still / Are children in some kind') to endorse an attitude of passive irresponsibility ('Let us be thankful / For that which is').

This, then, is the rather shaky scaffolding provided for the value that stands at the pinnacle of the play's absolutism – Emilia's ideal of innocence and same-sex friendship. It is an ideal that Shakespeare, at least, is generally taken to celebrate, if not to share personally, even by critics who note the similarity between her reminiscence of the perfect harmony she enjoyed with Flavina as a young girl (1.3.49 ff.) and Polixenes' idyllic portrayal in *The Winter's Tale* of himself and Leontes as

> Two lads that thought there was no more behind
> But such a day tomorrow as today,
> And to be boy eternal. (1.2.64–6)

To speak sympathetically of these characters' 'sense that an Eden was lost when they grew up and took wives'[12] is to ignore the intimate relation between that sense and the savage jealousy of Leontes, who imaginatively imposes upon his pregnant wife the burden of his fall into sexual maturity and adult responsibility. Yet the parallel with Emilia's nostalgia is undeniably close. Her account, too – so emotionally charged that it makes her, according to Hippolyta, 'out of breath' (1.3.82) – evinces a specific longing for her pre-sexual days; the plucked flower that later betokens her loss of virginity is prefigured by

> The flower that I would pluck
> And put between my breasts – O then but beginning
> To swell about the blossom – (1.3.66–8)

Nor is jealousy, albeit in muted form, beside the point. By calling attention to the response of Pirithous to Theseus' absence, Emilia has just encouraged Hippolyta to think of her bond with Theseus in terms of a competition with his male friend. In effect, she casts her sister in the potential rôle of Hermione, the victim of rejection, while herself remaining aloof – an aloof-

ness she will maintain when she is made the intrusive member of a similar triangle. In her enigmatic and oblique response to her sister's new sense of her vulnerable position, we may even catch an echo of Iago's tickling of Othello's jealous vein:

> Doubtless
> There is a best, and reason has no manners
> To say it is not you. (1.3.47–9)[13]

Of course, the most obvious intertextual affiliation of Emilia's picture of girlhood friendship is with the claim of Helena in *A Midsummer Night's Dream* that she and Hermia 'grew together, / Like to a double cherry' (3.2.209–10). (So Palamon anticipates that the souls of Arcite and himself will 'grow together' (2.2.66) in prison; both images deny the proliferation and separation associated with natural growth by Camillo in *The Winter's Tale*, when he attributes to the two kings 'an affection which cannot choose but branch now' (1.1.24).) To speak of 'a merely gentle picture of two girls together'[14] misses both the immediate comic point and the larger serious one. Helena's idyllic vision is a self-serving fiction that she herself is about to retract unceremoniously ('She was a vixen when she went to school' (3.2.325)) as part of the process by which the lovers' multifarious naïveté is broken down by the darker feelings and tensions of mature experience. Under the fairies' influence, idealization of sexual innocence joins other self-indulgent postures as discredited, in keeping with the initial equation of a 'maiden pilgrimage', however 'blessèd' (1.1.74–5), with death.

Yet *A Midsummer Night's Dream* also suggests that to die in the course of nature is something

---

12 Leech, Introd., p. xxviii.
13 Even Abrams, who speaks of 'Emilia's mannerly attempt to reassure her sister', notes that her 'graphic description of the men's intimate bond ... aggravates with sexual innuendo, rather than removing, anxiety' ('Gender Confusion', 72). Wickham ('*Two Noble Kinsmen*', 182) is upset by the whole exchange.
14 Leech, Introd., p. xxx.

else altogether – a matter of accepting, rather than resisting, the flux of time. Another neglected analogue is the Fairy Queen's recollection of her intimacy with her votaress (2.1.123 ff.), whose death in childbirth Titania participially invests with a sense of inevitability: 'she, being mortal, of that boy did die' (2.1.135). The ultimate source of discord in both Fairyland and the 'mazèd world' (2.1.113) of mortality is Titania's attempt to retain her hold on that idyllic past through her friend's child. Again, pregnancy is used to present entry into the conditions of adulthood, for better and worse, as a natural process. A similar significance is attached to the pregnant Helena in *All's Well That Ends Well*, who drags Bertram, if not kicking and screaming, at least leering and stammering, into the sexual responsibility that marks maturity.

More provocatively to the point is the contrast between *Measure for Measure*'s Juliet, on the one hand, whose pregnancy is stigmatized by a hypocritical society but fulfils a mature relation with Claudio, and, on the other hand, the ferociously chaste Isabella. As the only Shakespearian female figure besides Emilia to embrace Hermia's threatened punishment by making a cult of her virginity, only to forfeit it ambivalently in the end (assuming that this Duke, too, is not to be refused), Isabella makes for some instructive intertextuality. It has become a critical commonplace to view her attempt to preserve her innocence at all costs to others, to isolate herself from the world of sexuality and moral responsibility, as self-deluding and destructive. Lucio is backhandedly right, as often, to recognize her 'renouncement' as rendering her 'enskied and sainted', an 'immortal spirit' (1.4.33–4), rather than a human being, and thus implicitly to endow her coldness with a dimension of power – a natural enough psychological compensation, one might add, for real powerlessness. That power, of course, has a sexual dimension. In the two scenes where Angelo finds himself chilled into helpless attraction, her 'speechless dialect'

(1.2.171) and her speech itself, initially with Lucio's encouragement, come close to making supplication an obscene act. And in proportion as her predicament bespeaks victimization, her anti-sexuality serves her as a weapon, albeit a defensive one. This is made apparent through her notorious display of a range of most unsaintlike feelings – from simple self-righteousness to aggressive lack of charity ('Take my defiance, / Die, perish'! (3.1.144–45)) to vindictiveness ('O, I will to him and pluck out his eyes!' (4.3.116)) – but at the core lies her much-discussed erotics of martyrdom:

> Th'impression of keen whips I'd wear as rubies,
> And strip myself to death as to a bed
> That longing have been sick for (2.4.101–3)[15]

Once the pressure of moral choice is conveniently removed, thanks to the Duke and Mariana, and Isabella is restored, as she supposes, to the secure position of detached emblem of spiritual perfection, such outbursts naturally subside. Yet her very resumption of the ideal image as she asks mercy for Angelo, kneeling on behalf of Mariana in a way that anticipates the tableaux of *The Two Noble Kinsmen*, balances with exquisite ambiguity her claim to chaste humility and her sense of sexual potency:

> I partly think
> A due sincerity governed his deeds,
> Till he did look on me. (5.1.442–4)

Now even if Emilia's initial passionate defence of her anti-sexual 'faith' (1.3.98) entails some discomfiting of her sister, never does her purity reveal such Duessa-like nether parts. But then neo-Chaucerian Athens is a very different world from Vincentio's Vienna, and Isabella's desperate case is not Emilia's. Indeed, in keeping

---

[15] See, for example, the recent treatment of these lines in (rather reductive) psycho-sexual terms by Carolyn E. Brown, 'Erotic Religious Flagellation and Shakespeare's *Measure for Measure*', ELR, 16 (1986), 139–65; pp. 164–5.

with the fundamental paradox of courtly love, Emilia's very construction as the object, however unwilling, of honourable desire superficially enhances her status. Chaucer's narrative stresses Emelye's confinement within that paradox, giving her conspicuously little attention – and no direct speech at all – before her prayer to Diana, which is sandwiched between the orisons of her suitors. At that point, the emotional depth of her dedication to maidenhood is suddenly communicated, in explicit terms of the preservation of freedom:

> I am, thow woost, yet of thy compaignye,
> A mayde, and love huntynge and venerye,
> And for to walken in the wodes wilde,
> And noght to ben a wyf and be with childe.
>
> (2307–10)

However, with Diana's negative decree the narrator imposes silence ('This is th'effect; there is namoore to seye' (2366)), and Emelye again has nothing to say from this point on. A parenthetical comment casually assimilates her response to the victory of Arcite into an antifeminist stereotype: 'And she agayn hym caste a freendlich ye / (For wommen, as to speken in comune, / Thei folwen alle the favour of Fortune)' (2680–2). Subsequently, she is gathered smoothly into the successive rôles of Arcite's mourner and, in the happily-ever-after conclusion, Palamon's loving wife.

Shakespeare and Fletcher highlight Emilia's victimization by compressing the tragi-comic ending. They also give that victimization a psychological dimension by linking her loss of sexual independence with self-abasement. Emilia is made to insist that no woman would be worthy of a compound of the two knights (5.5.85 ff.) and later, even more extremely, that all women collectively fall short of one of them (5.5.143). Once we shift into the psychological mode, however, the rôles of victim and victimizer become less distinct, for we gain access to the compensatory mechanisms by which Emilia attempts – with the pitiful futility of the Jailer's Daughter's mad fantasies – to shift the balance of power. The consequences – a subtle form of self-destruction – are no less poignant for the family resemblance to other Shakespearian figures who react manipulatively against a lack of control over the basic conditions of their lives.

Emilia's humility can also be read as a case of protesting too much, for it displays something very like the double edge of Isabella's pleading for Angelo: such cataclysms, and all on account of poor little *her*. Moreover, while Emilia's innocence may not crack under pressure, as does Isabella's, she is shown, not merely as clinging defensively to the virginity that is her only claim to power, but as keenly sensible of that power. This sensibility reaches a height late in the play, but it is present from the start. Understandably enough, when the knights are discovered fighting on her account, she will not choose between them in order to save only one. Remarkably, however, she supplicates Theseus, not on the grounds of her maiden 'faith', but in terms that invest virginity with an implicitly sexual potency: 'By that you would have trembled to deny / A blushing maid' (3.6.204–5). This is, in fact, an oblique echo of her initial plea on behalf of the Queens, which implies an early appreciation of self-withholding as a manipulative technique:

> from henceforth I'll not dare
> To ask you anything, nor be so hardy
> Ever to take a husband. (1.1.202–4)

More obviously problematic is Emilia's inability to make a choice before the tournament, when her marriage to either Palamon or Arcite is assured and when she actually could prevent all the bloodshed she ostentatiously deplores:

> Yet I may bind those wounds up that must open
> And bleed to death for my sake else – I'll choose,
> And end their strife. Two such young handsome men
> Shall never fall for me (4.2.1–4)

To make her choice, she continues, is her duty to their mothers – that is, to her own sex. Yet as she compares the knghts' images and sways absurdly between them in terms that remind us of the Jailer's Daughter, she again becomes powerless – the self-constructed victim now, not of male desire, but of female fickleness, lack of *will*-power. She does not betray her sex; rather, in her view, her sex confounds itself:

> O, who can find the bent of woman's fancy?
> I am a fool, my reason is lost in me,
> I have no choice   (4.2.33–5)

This episode is recognizably Fletcher's excessive handiwork, but the aberrant style points to a continuity in her exploitation, indeed cultivation, of weakness itself as a source of manipulative strength.

If one takes it seriously, Emilia's admission here that her 'virgin's faith has fled' her (4.2.46) makes rather a mockery of the prayer to Diana in the following scene – a scene apparently written by Shakespeare. Perhaps, in contrast with Chaucer's version, the reason for Diana's refusal lies, not in the stars, but in the heroine herself. There is also an irony reminiscent of Palamon's shaky assertion of pure thoughts in addressing Venus a few lines before. Diana, Emilia emphasizes, is not amused by bawdy sights ('thing maculate' (5.1.9)) or sounds ('scurril term', 'wanton sound' (5.1.11–12)), yet we may recall that the kinsmen were first dazzled by the distant sight of an Emilia who was not rambling silent and solitary, as in Chaucer, but encouraging her maid in risqué conversation (2.2.120 ff.).[16] This, too, as some commentators hasten to insist, is Fletcher's contribution. Yet the Shakespearian prayer also undoes itself more fundamentally by altering the emphases of its Chaucerian model. Emilia reduces her precursor's intense feeling for virginity to a few formulaic phrases, while introducing and focusing on her powerlessness and its powerful consequences. Indeed, that powerlessness is presented as an index of innocence, an article of faith:

> Out of two, I should
> Choose one and pray for his success, but I
> Am guiltless of election.   (5.3.16–18)

Making this the last of the three prayers and the dramatic climax of the scene confirms the ambivalent centrality of her position: in proportion as she is totally dependent, everything depends on her.

Emilia's sense of her simultaneous impotence and importance is strikingly focused again in her decision not to witness the combat on the grounds that 'The title of a kingdom may be tried / Out of itself' (5.5.33–4). She also thereby gains the freedom to renew successive Fletcherian fantasies about the two knights, while they are fighting off-stage. This time her near-ridiculous resemblance to the Jailer's Daughter, erotically obsessed with Palamon, clearly invests her power of life and death with an eroticism that tends, by erasing the self as both focus and locus of desire, to convert Isabella's masochism to its closely allied opposite:

> Arcite may win me,
> And yet may Palamon wound Arcite to
> The spoiling of his figure. O, what pity
> Enough for such a chance! If I were by
> I might do hurt, for they would glance their
>   eyes
> Toward my seat, and in that motion might
> Omit a ward or forfeit an offence
> Which craved that very time. It is much better
> I am not there.   (5.5.57–65)

All in all, Emilia, overdetermined as passive love-object – doubly chosen, twice given away – extracts from her very deferral of choice the same sort of gratification that we associate with the male power to choose, and with two

---

[16] Abrams, 'Gender Confusion', 70, is surely right to bring out the homoerotic overtones of this conversation, but the lines make it clear that sex is assumed actually to occur between men and women. To see Emilia as 'prompting flirtation which ends in the women going to bed together' is to convert the play abruptly and irrevocably into burlesque. At the opposite extreme is Wickham, '*Two Noble Kinsmen*', 185, who needs to preserve Emilia as an emblem of chastity in order to identify her with the Princess Elizabeth, and who therefore ignores her sexual remarks.

highly sinister Shakespearian exponents of that power in terms of self-withholding: 'I'll have her, but I will not keep her long' (*Richard III* 1.2.217); 'Which of them shall I take? – / Both? – one? – or neither? Neither can be enjoyed / If both remain alive...' (*Lear* F 5.1.48–50). It is typically Shakespearian that nostalgia should have its most potent negative consequences for, and through, the character who, in effect, desperately takes refuge in the rôle of Chaucer's pure and simple victim. The stately dance to unheard heavenly music that is *The Knight's Tale* gives way, thanks in part to the stylistic tension between stasis and motion, to a bumbling pageant, like that of *Pyramus and Thisbe*, presided over by a pompous patriarch in love with his own false learning. To *aspire* to join that dance, far from being 'too ambitious', is the ultimate madness.

Despite the affiliation of the play's evasive nostalgia with the darker side of *The Winter's Tale*, such a frankly interrogative adaptation of the very premises of romance might appear a fundamental departure from Shakespeare's final dramatic practice. After all, in the latter half of *The Winter's Tale*, the tragedy produced, in effect, by resistance to time is redeemed for romance through human suffering within time. The dramatist's gift of this time, and of the capacity to profit from it, makes the difference between wish-fulfilment and wish-frustration. Yet the gift is a pointedly arbitrary one, as is signalled by the abrupt intervention of Time as Chorus, and in this sense of textual charity lie the seeds of the subversion of romance.

It is useful to parallel the two adaptations Shakespeare made of material from *The Knight's Tale* with his two appropriations, also at opposite ends of his dramatic career, of Gower's version of the tale of Apollonius of Tyre, related in the *Confessio Amantis*. In both *A Midsummer Night's Dream* and *The Comedy of Errors*, a mystical, extra-human element – fairy magic in the first case, error-as-comic-process in the second – subverts and overrules destructive human tendencies as a matter of course, a

function of genre. Higher powers naturally fill the gap left by frankly powerless mortals. In *Pericles*, on the other hand, it may be argued that the interventions of divinities are ultimately contingent on human actions, as in *The Two Noble Kinsmen*. I have made the case elsewhere[17] that the first of the last plays integrates a text illustrating the arbitrary operations of fortune with a pattern of personal development analogous to that followed by Amans over the whole course of the *Confessio Amantis*. Amans' difficult extrication from the power of Venus – something achieved by the characters in neither *The Knight's Tale* nor *The Two Noble Kinsmen* – provides the model for Pericles' progressive abandonment of image-making and image-worship. That model brings responsibility down to earth. Yet as in *The Winter's Tale*, a dramatic world of lavish proportions and impossible conditions is ostentatiously provided in order to make redemption possible. In *The Two Noble Kinsmen*, such compensation for human responsibility is just as conspicuously withheld. Chaucer's generous expanses of time have been drastically and systematically circumscribed.

Such a restricting of the wide-open narrative spaces characteristic of romance may be compared, however, to the imposition of the dramatic unities in *The Tempest* by way of Prospero's 'rough magic' (5.1.50) – a sign, as I have also argued elsewhere, of that character's misappropriation of his own romance past.[18]

---

17 'Shakespeare's Gower and Gower's Shakespeare: The Larger Debt of *Pericles*', *Shakespeare Quarterly*, 36 (1985), 427–37.

18 '*The Tempest* as Romance and Anti-Romance', *University of Toronto Quarterly*, 55 (1986), 141–60. See also my proposal, in 'Chaucer's Franklin's Magician and *The Tempest*: An Influence Beyond Appearances?', *Shakespeare Quarterly*, 34 (1983), 426–32, that *The Tempest* as a whole appropriates Chaucerian romance – specifically, *The Franklin's Tale* – but that Shakespeare takes the numinous and nebulous figure of the magician, the instrument of a librating grace that resonates retroactively through the world of the tale, and effectively cuts him down to human size.

What in *Pericles* and *The Winter's Tale* had emerged – in both cases, through idealized female figures – as an ideal involving reconciliation through suffering becomes susceptible to self-serving and self-deluding manipulation: Marina and Perdita give way to Miranda, firmly under her father's thumb. Putting the playwright's magic into human hands is a step towards eliminating it altogether, and a step towards tragedy. The next step logically entails the deconstruction of the female icon of romance values. And so the overtones of 'despair' in Prospero's 'ending' give way, not only to the Boethian bird's-eye view claimed by the philosophical Theseus, but to the banal paradigm of mutual self-destruction that makes such a philosophy at once imperative and absurdly irrelevant. In so far as the chivalric content of *The Two Noble Kinsmen* specifically alludes to the court-ethic associated with Prince Henry, as various commentators have proposed, what is lamented goes well beyond that Prince's untimely death. Like *Romeo and Juliet*, this text refuses to accept as compensatory the impulse of its survivors to produce images of blasted promise 'in pure gold' (*Romeo* 5.3.298). Rather, it takes the part of a wiser Prince than is contained within it: 'All are punishèd' (5.3.294).

THE HAND OF JOHN FLETCHER IN
DOUBLE FALSEHOOD

STEPHAN KUKOWSKI

In 1728 Lewis Theobald published *The Double Falsehood; or, The Distressed Lovers*, a play he claimed to be 'Written Originally by W. SHAKESPEARE; And now Revised and Adapted to the Stage by MR THEOBALD...' Even a cursory reading of the play would seem to discount the possibility that Theobald's claim has any merit. Yet one or two facts seem to demand we give the claim further attention. The play is based on the story of Cardenio in *Don Quixote*. *Cardenno* is the title of a play twice acted by Shakespeare's company at the court of James I during 1612–13.[1] Among unpublished manuscripts of that company acquired by Humphrey Mosely was one entered to him in the Stationers' Register in 1653 as 'The History of Cardenio, by Mr Fletcher & Shakespeare.'[2] This information did not come to light until long after Theobald's death; it is unlikely that Theobald knew it; he certainly never made use of it to justify his claims, even in the face of a campaign of ridicule.

In his preface to the play, Theobald gives an account of the source of one of the three manuscripts he claims to have had in his possession; John Freehafer[3] has examined this account and found it credible. Freehafer provides a detailed and convincing provenance for Theobald's oldest manuscript, which Theobald said was 'of above Sixty Years Standing, in the Handwriting of Mr Downes, the famous old Prompter; and, as I am credibly inform'd, was early in the possession of the celebrated Mr

Betterton, and by Him design'd to have been usher'd into the World.'

If Theobald's claim was not a lie (and, as Freehafer points out, 'He could not safely have made a misstatement in 1727 about Betterton, who had remained active virtually until his death in 1710 and had appeared with many members of the original cast of *Double Falsehood*'[4]), then his oldest copy was made at a time when Downes, Betterton, and Sir William Davenant were producing a much revised version of Fletcher's and Shakespeare's *The Two Noble Kinsmen* (which they entitled *The Rivals*).[5] It is interesting that Davenant's revision of this play left not a line of the passages most confidently ascribed to Shakespeare intact, although several of Fletcher's passages survive with only minor alteration.[6]

Note: Quotations from *Double Falsehood* are from the first edition (1728). Plays of Beaumont and Fletcher are quoted from Fredson Bowers's edition (Cambridge, 1966) except that *A Very Woman* is quoted from *The Plays and Poems of Philip Massinger* eds. Philip Edwards and Colin Gibson (4 vols., Oxford, 1976; vol. 4), *The Faithful Friends* from the Malone Society reprint (Oxford, 1970), and *The Loyal Subject*, *The Pilgrim*, and *The False One* from A. H. Bullen's edition.

[1] Malone Society *Collections*, VI (Oxford, 1965), 55–6.
[2] W. W. Greg, *Bibliography of the English Printed Drama to the Restoration* (London, 1939–59), I, p. 61.
[3] John Freehafer, 'CARDENIO, by Shakespeare and Fletcher,' *PMLA*, 84 (1969), 501–13.
[4] Freehafer, '*Cardenio*', p. 502.
[5] Acted in 1664.
[6] See A. C. Sprague, *Beaumont and Fletcher on the Restoration Stage* (Cambridge, MA, 1926), Part I.

Thus, even if Theobald is being scrupulously honest, he may well have had in his possession no more than an already much adulterated version of *Cardenio*.

In contrast to pre-twentieth century commentators,[7] most of those who have examined the play more recently have been prepared to give some credit to the possibility of Shakespeare's partial authorship of *Double Falsehood*.[8] The play has rarely, however, been subjected to detailed analysis, and comment has been guarded and general in nature. Kenneth Muir deals with it in a brief final chapter of his *Shakespeare as Collaborator*.[9] He suggests that there is a chance that a few traces of Shakespeare's hand might be found in the play, and quotes some of its better lines. He finds, in 1.2.58 ff. and 1.2.101 ff., 'at least two passages which strike the reader as genuinely Elizabethan, though definitely not Fletcherian'. He remarks that the imagery and rhythm here are 'either Shakespearian or a remarkably clever imitation'. Harriet Frazier[10] has no doubts at all that the whole play is indeed an imitation by Theobald. It is this possibility, first suggested by Pope and his allies, that has perhaps led critics to shy away from considering the play too closely. Muir's conclusion may well express the consensus view: 'It is clearly impossible to come to any definite conclusions about *Double Falsehood*... But one can understand the desire to relieve Shakespeare of all responsibility for a play which, at least in its present form, can add nothing to his reputation.'[11]

One can indeed. But this is hardly the point. And I believe that some definite conclusions about *Double Falsehood* are in fact possible. One needs to start, however, by asking the right questions. It is not most useful to start with: 'Is there evidence of Shakespeare's presence in this play?' even though, in the end, this represents our prime interest in it. Our starting point ought instead to be: 'Is there any evidence of Fletcher's presence in the play?' That should be easier to answer, since Fletcher's lines would be more likely to survive an extensive revision (as we can see from Davenant's *The Rivals*). Our answer to this new question will then bear on the issue of Theobald's honesty. If we find definite evidence of Fletcher's presence, then we may question Theobald's judgement, but not his honesty. And if Theobald was not in fact lying, then it is hard to see how *Double Falsehood* can be anything other than a genuine, if corrupted, version of *Cardenio*.

The most detailed examination of *Double Falsehood* has been conducted by Harriet Frazier,[12] who has been quite single-minded in her determination to prove Theobald an abject forger. In these attempts, she never once considers the play from the point of view of Fletcher's authorship, and in this she is only the most extreme example of a tendency in nearly all previous commentators. Her argument is that Theobald, determined to make a great contribution to Shakespearian knowledge (beyond even his *Shakespeare Restored*, whose contribution to Shakespeare scholarship can hardly be overrated), and in particular obsessed

---

[7] The entry for *Double Falsehood* in W. Jaggard's *Shakespeare Bibliography* (Stratford-upon-Avon, 1911), p. 304, reads: 'Malone attributed this play to Massinger, Farmer to Shirley, and Reed thought that Theobald himself was the writer. Reed's surmise was probably the shrewdest.'

[8] See Gamaliel Bradford Jr, 'The History of Cardenio by Mr Fletcher and Shakespeare', *MLN* xxv (Feb. 1910), 51–6; Edward Castle, 'Theobald's *Double Falsehood* and the *History of Cardenio* by Fletcher and Shakespeare', *Archiv für das Studium der Neueren Sprachen und Literaturen*, 169 (1936), 182–99; John Freehafer, 'Cardenio'; the introduction to *Double Falsehood*, ed. Walter Graham (Cleveland, 1920); Alfred Harbage, 'Elizabethan-Restoration Palimpsest', *MLR*, 35 (1940), 287–319; E. H. C. Oliphant, *The Plays of Beaumont and Fletcher* (New Haven, CT, 1927), 282–302.

[9] Kenneth Muir, *Shakespeare as Collaborator* (London, 1960), p. 148–60.

[10] Harriet C. Frazier, 'The Rifling of Beauty's Stores – Theobald and Shakespeare', *Neuphilologische Mitteilungen*, 69 (1968), 232–56.

[11] Muir, *Shakespeare as Collaborator*, p. 160.

[12] 'The Rifling of Beauty's Stores'; also 'Speculation on the Motives of a Forger', *Neuphilologische Mitteilungen*, 72 (1971 287–96); *A Babble of Ancestral Voices: Shakespeare, Cervantes, and Theobald* (The Hague, 1974).

with trying to prove that Shakespeare had read Cervantes, forged the whole thing from beginning to end. She believes that he must have known about the entries in the Stationers' Register (Theobald could hardly have chosen the Cardenio plot by chance); she offers no explanation as to why Theobald then did not use those entries to provide a most effective defence against the ridicule of Pope. (It is worth noting that Pope later claimed he had 'never supposed' the play to be Theobald's, but took it to be 'of the age of Shakespeare'.)[13]

Frazier examines Theobald's poem *The Cave of Poverty* (1715), declared by the author to be 'Written in Imitation of Shakespeare'. She gives fifteen examples of Theobald's borrowing, all from *Venus and Adonis* and *The Rape of Lucrece*. The first (and typical of the rest) is:

O unseen shame! invisible disgrace!
O unfelt sore! crest-wounding, private scar!
(*Lucrece* 827–8)

Oh faulty Riot, and Crest-wounding Shame!
(*Poverty* 205)

Thirteen of these fifteen quite obvious borrowings are in the same hyphenated form; significant, then, that not one of the alleged borrowings in *Double Falsehood* is in this form, and neither are any of them this obvious. Rather than using the poem to show Theobald's forthrightness when imitating Shakespeare, she uses it instead to attempt to establish a 'pattern' of Theobald's dishonest practices. In the same spirit, she ignores the fact that Theobald not only admits but is evidently proud of the fact that *Double Falsehood* was 'Revised and Adapted for the Stage' by him; some of the lines he specifically claimed as his own.

Frazier finds almost forty 'echoes' of Shakespeare in *Double Falsehood*. Four or five of them may be significant (these are all listed in Kenneth Muir's treatment of the play; most of them derive from Leonard Schwartzstein[14]); the bulk of them are not echoes at all. Typical of the examples she cites are:

Oh,
That a Man could reason down this Feaver of the Blood
Or sooth with words the Tumult of his Heart.
(*Double Falsehood* 2.1.38–40)

O, that this too too solid flesh would melt,
Thaw, and resolve itself into a dew!
Or that the Everlasting had not fix'd
His canon 'gainst self-slaughter!
(*Hamlet* 1.2.129–32)

Treacherous, damn'd Henriquez
(*Double Falsehood* 3.1.5)

Remorseless, treacherous, lecherous, kindless villain
(*Hamlet* 2.2.608)

This World is full of Coz'ners, very full;
Young Virgins must be wary in their Ways
(*Double Falsehood* 4.1.92–3)

We are arrant knaves all; believe none of us.
Go thy way to a nunnery
(*Hamlet* 3.1.130–1)

Frazier also cites:

Thou can'st not tell me the Way
To the next Nunnery?
(*Double Falsehood* 4.1.201–2)

noting that 'There is no near or distant nunnery in the Cardenio narrative in *Don Quixote*.' This is true; but the suggestion that Theobald would have made such a plot alteration in order to be able to employ so 'Shakespearian' a line seems rather far-fetched!

The fact that there are echoes of Shakespeare in *Double Falsehood* is hardly proof of a Theobald forgery. After all, if the play is not a forgery, then Shakespeare might have been its part-author. On the basis of Frazier's exceptionally vague evidence, it would be hard indeed to distinguish between Theobald echoing Shakespeare and Shakespeare echoing Shakespeare. Furthermore, since Theobald

---

[13] Alexander Pope, *Correspondence*, ed. George Sherburn (Oxford, 1956), IV, 102.
[14] Leonard Schwartzstein, 'The Text of *The Double Falsehood*', *Notes and Queries*, 199 (1954), 471–2.

claims to have revised and adapted the play, occasional imitative echoes, if such they be, can hardly be taken as indicating wholesale forgery. Finally, it needs to be noted that the plays of Beaumont and Fletcher are full of Shakespearian echoes far more distinctive than Frazier's examples from *Double Falsehood*; several examples must stand for several hundred:

> Go on, fair beauty, and in your orisons
> Remember me
> (*Four Plays in One*, Death. 4)

> Oh that same whoreson conscience, how it
>   jades us?   (*Philaster* 1.1.168)

> The Revel's ended now
>   (*Women's Prize* 1.2.198)

> our gorgeous Buildings
>   (*Faithful Friends* l. 2176)

>   What shall appear
> Is but a weak apparition and thin air
>   (*Chances* 5.3.21–2)

>   Not all the showers of rain
> The heavy clouds send down can wash away
> That foul unmanly guilt
>   (*The Faithful Shepherdess* 4.1.12–14)

>   My guiltles bloud
> Shall dye the greene grasse crimson
>   (*Faithful Friends* ll. 2376–7)

[Explaining that she, too, is a mere mortal:]

>   Prick my hand
> And it will bleed
>   (*The Faithful Shepherdess* 4.1.12–13)

Thus we see that echoes of Shakespeare, if they are not evidence of Shakespeare's authorship, might as easily be the work of Fletcher as of Theobald. Luckily there is a wealth of more conclusive evidence to suggest at least the presence of Fletcher, which we may now examine.

The most distinctive feature of Fletcher's versification is his fondness for the feminine ending,[15] which has been used to separate his contributions from Shakespeare's in *Henry VIII* (*All Is True*) and *The Two Noble Kinsmen*. The portion of feminine endings in the plays generally acknowledged to be by Fletcher alone is consistently above 50 per cent and as high as 75 per cent. *Double Falsehood* contains a large percentage of feminine endings: about 35 per cent. Graham[16] calculated that the second half of the play (from 3.3) contains a higher percentage than the first half, and concludes that the second half of the play is by Fletcher, and the first half by Shakespeare.

While most of the evidence for Fletcher's part-authorship of the play is to be found in this second half, I do not consider such a straightforward division satisfactory. The proportion of feminine endings is inconsistent throughout the whole play (suggesting revision), and in several places in the first half of the play we find passages that not only contain a large number of feminine endings, but seem to have the distinctive Fletcherian rhythm, very end-stopped and displaying an easy rhetorical tone; for example:

HENRIQUEZ
> Julio, alas, feels nothing of my passion:
> His love is but th'Amusement of an Hour,
> A short relief from Business, or Ambition,
> The Sport of Youth, and Fashion of the Age.
> O! had he known the Hopes, the Doubts, the
>   Ardours,
> Or half the fond Varieties of Passion,
> That play the Tyrant with my tortur'd Soul;
> He had not left thee to pursue his Fortune:
> To practice Cringes in a slavish Circle,
> And barter real Bliss for unsure Honour.

LEONORA
> Oh, the opposing Wind,
> Should'ring the Tide, makes here a fearful
>   Billows:
> I needs must perish in it.
>   (*Double Falsehood* 2.3.73–85)

---

[15] This was, I believe, first used to differentiate the verse of Fletcher from that of Shakespeare by Henry Weber in his postscript to *The Two Noble Kinsmen* (*Works of Beaumont and Fletcher*, Edinburgh, 1812, vol. XIII, p. 166). See also F. G. Fleay, 'Metrical Tests as Applied to Dramatic Poetry, Part II, Beaumont, Fletcher, and Massinger', in *Transactions of the New Shakspere Society*, I (London, 1874), 61–72.

[16] Walter Graham, *Double Falsehood*, Introduction.

Fletcher re-uses the same images and ideas continuously (as Gayley unkindly puts it,[17] 'Usually his ribbons (from a scantly furnished, much-rummaged wardrobe) are carelessly pinned on'); the listing, especially in threes (as in line 77), the short-cuts (as in line 78), the favourite idea of line 81, are all consistent with Fletcher's habits. The image of lines 83–5 seems to belong to a great store of billows images.[18] Of course none of this is conclusive, but the occurring together of several Fletcherisms amidst a high proportion of feminine endings, here as in other passages in the first half, should make us beware of dividing the play up too squarely at 3.3.

Perhaps the one word that should trigger us to expect Fletcher's presence is 'fling'. It is not, of course, an uncommon word, but Fletcher's use of it is most distinctive. It occurs at least once in nearly every play in which he had a hand; it occurs eight times in one of his first plays, *The Faithful Shepherdess*, and nine times in one of his last, *The Wild-Goose Chase*, and at an average of about four times per full play. More important than the mere number of occurrences is the use Fletcher puts the word to. While Shakespeare, in his rare uses of the word, generally uses it literally ('Here I'll fling a pillow' – *Taming of the Shrew*, 4.1.201) Fletcher generally uses it figuratively, in a rather stretched manner:

> The day that flings his light upon my kingdom
> (*Maid's Tragedy* 1.2.268)

> to fling off this case of flesh
> (*Bonduca* 4.4.128)

> Cromwell, I charge thee, fling away ambition
> (*All Is True* 3.2.440)

> a thousand envious souls fling the foams on me
> (*The False One* 2.1.46)

> that my bondness
> Should fling itself upon his desperate follies
> (*Monsieur Thomas* 1.3.43–44)

> fling on me what aspersions you please, sir
> (*Wild-Goose Chase* 2.2.143)

> I'll take you, with those faults the world flings
> on you   (*Wild-Goose Chase* 3.1.41)

The following is thus wholly consistent with Fletcher's style:

JULIO   If the curst Henriquez
Had Pow'r to change you to a Boy, why, Lady,
Should not that Mischief make me any Thing,
That have an equal Share in all the Miseries
His Crimes have flung upon us?
VIOLANTE   Well I know it:
And pardon me, I could not know your Virtues,
Before your Griefs.

> (*Double Falsehood* 4.2.93–9)

Fletcher's favourite oath is 'on my conscience' or 'o' my conscience', which occurs only once in all of Shakespeare's work (*Cymbeline* 5.4.200). The oath occurs in the majority of Fletcher's plays, and usually several times. It occurs twice in Act 3 Scene 3 of *Double Falsehood*, amidst a swelling of feminine endings.

The word 'extremely' is used a great deal by Fletcher, but hardly at all by Shakespeare. Of the eight occurrences in the Shakespeare canon, five are in Fletcher's portion of *The Two Noble Kinsmen* and *All Is True*. The other three include one in the non-Shakespearian portion of *Timon of Athens*. In the two Shakespearian occurrences (*Love's Labour's Lost* 5.2.740; *A Midsummer Night's Dream* 5.1.80) the adverb comes before the verb, the reverse of Fletcher's distinctive habit.

> I love your wife extremely
> (*Coxcomb* 2.1.103)

---

[17] Charles Gayley, *Beaumont the Dramatist* (New York, 1914), p. 276.

[18] Fletcher's imagery makes much use of the sea (sometimes perhaps even suggesting actual maritime experience), and 'billows' occurs at least once in most of his plays; see Gayley, *Beaumont the Dramatist*, 274. Shakespeare's use of sea imagery, particularly sea-in-storm imagery, has been noted by Wilson Knight, and 'billows' does occur several times in his work. However, without being able to supply exact figures here, I would suggest that Fletcher's use of 'billows' is much more frequent; it is his most common image for conflict or difficulty.

at your letter he laughed extremely

(*Scornful Lady* 5.2.31)

Do we not love extremely?

(*Valentinian* 3.3.103)

He weeps extremely

(*Humorous Lieutenant* 5.3.43)

'She weeps extremely' occurs also in *Double Falsehood*, in a passage rich with feminine endings, a passage which, as Muir has remarked, 'recalls, without actual echoing, the laments of Aspatia in *The Maid's Tragedy*':[19]

VIOLANTE   You maidens that shall live
To hear my mournful Tale, when I am Ashes
Be wise; and to an oath no more give Credit,
To Tears, to Vows, (false Both!) or any Thing
A man shall promise, than to Clouds, that now
Bear such a pleasing Shape, and now are
   nothing.
For they will cozen, (if They may be cozen'd,)
The very Gods they worship. – Valour, Justice,
Discretion, Honesty, and all they covet,
To make them seeming Saints, are but the Wiles
By which these Sirens lure us to Destruction.
JULIO   Do not you weep now? I could drop
   myself
Into a Fountain for her.
GENT.   She weeps extremely.

(*Double Falsehood* 4.2.62–74)

Julio's reaction has the typical Fletcherian ring to it also. This passage recalls not only Aspatia's lament, but all the laments of Fletcher's numerous 'ruin'd maids', who typically see themselves as exempla for future dramas. The above may be compared with:

And what a lover's vows, persuasions, tears,
May, in a minute, work upon such frailty,
There are too many and too sad examples.

(*A Very Woman*[20] 1.1.214–17)

Again in *Double Falsehood* we find:

I have read Stories
(I fear too true ones;) how young Lords, like
   you,
Have thus besung mean Windows, rhymed
   their
                        Sufferings
Ev'n to th'Abuse of Things Divine, set up

Plain Girls, like me, the Idols of their
   Worship,
Then left them to bewail their easy Faith,
And stand the World's Contempt.

(*Double Falsehood* 1.3.41–7)

'He ly'd extremely' (*Double Falsehood* 5.1.65) also occurs in a passage with many feminine endings.

Typically Fletcherian is:

You deal unkindly; misbecomingly,
I'm loth to say

(*Double Falsehood* 1.2.110–11)

'To deal' and 'to be loath', though admittedly common enough anywhere, are constructions heavily employed throughout Fletcher's work. Compare the above with:

'twas done indiscreetly,
I would be loath to say, maliciously

(*A Very Woman* 1.1.191)

E. H. C. Oliphant remarked of Fletcher:[21] 'Senseless repetitions are as intentional and even

---

[19] Muir, *Shakespeare as Collaborator*, p. 153.

[20] *A Very Woman* is considered (by Hoy amongst others) to be a Massinger revision of a play originally by Fletcher. This scene is given by Hoy to Massinger. Although there has been some speculation that Massinger was in this portion of the play revising his own work, there is evidence against this – such as the Fletcherian use of 'fling' in the next scene, which is also speculated to be Massinger revising Massinger (Massinger, in all his solo plays, uses 'fling' only twice, each time in the phrase 'to have a fling'). Certain parallels between Massinger's writings and the first half of *Double Falsehood* suggest that he may have been a principal reviser. Notable among these is a precedent for the line in *Double Falsehood* which Pope singled out for ridicule: 'Is there a Treachery, like This in Baseness, / Recorded anywhere? It is the deepest: / None but Itself can be its Parallel' (*Double Falsehood* 3.1.157). Massinger is inordinately fond of the word 'parallel', and his uses of it are sometimes unusual, as in: 'Her goodnesse does disdaine comparison, / And but herself admits no paralell' (*Duke of Milan* 4.3.39–41). (It may also be interesting to note that the pair of lovers in *A Very Woman* are called 'Don Martino Cardenes' and 'Leonora', which led to speculation, by Gifford amongst others, that this play was a revision of *Cardenio*.)

[21] Oliphant, 'Beaumont and Fletcher', 37.

more irritating than his verse methods', and cites as an example:

> O ye have played the fool,
> The fool extremely, the mad fool
> > *(Bonduca* 3.5.125–6)

What Gayley calls 'elocutionary after-thought'[22] may also be illustrated by:

> Yes, and good women too, very good
> > women,
> Excellent honest women
> > *(Loyal Subject* 3.2.125–6)

> How does your woman,
> And a fine woman she is, and a good woman
> > *(Love's Pilgrimage* 2.4.33–4)

> Makes me forget an honest man, a brave man,
> A valiant, and a virtuous man, my country-man
> > *(Island Princess* 3.1.226–7)

Clear examples of this are to be found in *Double Falsehood*:

> This is a fine Hand,
> A delicate fine Hand, – Never change Colour;
> You understand me, – and a Woman's Hand
> > *(Double Falsehood* 4.1.168–70)

> And dare you lose these to become Advocate
> For such a Brother, such a sinful Brother,
> Such an unfaithful, treacherous, brutal Brother?
> > *(Double Falsehood* 5.1.16–18)

Hoy, in his work on separating the shares of the authors of the Beaumont and Fletcher canon,[23] only once departs from his confinement to purely linguistic evidence when using the distinctive Fletcherian mannerism which he illustrates with:

> she is a right good Princes, and a just one
> > *(Women Pleased* 1.1.1)

> I have a close ward, and a sure one
> > *(Loyal Subject* 3.2.71)

> This is a new way of begging, and a neat one
> > *(Pilgrim* 1.2.47)

We have an example in *Double Falsehood*:

> I have a witness, and a noble one
> > *(Double Falsehood* 5.2.168)

Several passages in *Double Falsehood* can almost be reconstructed from pieces to be found elsewhere in Fletcher's work. A brief example might be 'some fair-snouted skittish Woman' (*Double Falsehood* 4.1.17–18), which recalls 'some snout-fair piece' (*Coxcomb* 4.3.44) and 'A skittish filly will be your fortune' (*Scornful Lady* 3.1.349). (Shakespeare, it might be noted, never uses 'snout' of a person's appearance (it is the name of a male character in *A Midsummer Night's Dream*, and refers to a boar in *Venus and Adonis*).)

There appears to be an echo of Shakespeare's Sonnet XVIII in one of Leonora's better speeches:

> First, welcome heartily;
> Welcome to th'Ending of my last good Hour:
> Now Summer Bliss and gawdy Days are gone,
> My Lease in 'em's expired.
> > *(Double Falsehood* 3.2.31–3)

Shakespeare is here echoed by Fletcher, I think. The use of the first 'welcome' as a springboard for the next line is a technique used very often by Fletcher; compare, for example, 'Farewell? A long farewell to all my greatness' (*All Is True,* 3.2.35). Leonora's speech has the same sense of looking at oneself almost as a character, and seeing there something pathetic, that is so typical of Fletcher's lamenting strain. It can again be found in Buckingham's farewell, where again we have the consciousness of 'the last good hour' (*All Is True* 2.1.133). In that speech we also find 'All good people' (*All Is True* 2.1.132) which is found several times elsewhere in Fletcher and again in one of Violante's plaints: 'All good People / Are fal'n asleep for ever' (*Double Falsehood* 4.2.41–2). The phrase 'all good people' is not found in Shakespeare's work.

The linguistic evidence of the play, such as it is, neither definitely confirms nor denies

---

[22] Ibid., p. 267.

[23] Cyrus Hoy, 'The Shares of Fletcher and His Collaborators in the Beaumont and Fletcher Canon v', *Studies in Bibliography*, XIII (1961), 83–91.

Fletcher's part-authorship. Fletcher's fondness for 'ye' and ''em', his preference for 'has' over 'hath', and 'does' over 'doth', has been extensively documented by Hoy.[24] *Double Falsehood* contains three 'ye's and ten ''em's'.[25] This is certainly not a frequency typical of Fletcher's solo productions but, given the play's length, neither is it inconsistent with the frequencies of many of the Beaumont and Fletcher collaborations; Hoy suggests that in these cases a reviser (presumably Beaumont) reduced this most noticeable of Fletcherian preferences.

Perhaps more interesting is the dominance in the play of 'has' (forty times) over 'hath' (ten times), while 'doth' occurs three times against three occurrences of 'does'[26] (this includes two occurrences of h'as' and one of 'sh'as', the former, but not the latter, being taken by Hoy as Fletcher's common usage). In itself, this may not be particularly significant. But in the light of the crucial question of forgery by Theobald, it gains added importance. If Theobald were attempting to forge Shakespeare, why would he not imitate his most obvious preference? 'Any schoolboy' attempting a quick imitation of Shakespearian English automatically peppers his speech with 'hath' – see, for example, William-Henry Ireland's *Henry II* and *Vortigern*. Why then would a forging Theobald imitate not Shakespeare's obvious practice, but Fletcher's?

There are long passages without the appearance of a single 'hath' or 'doth'. The last two acts contain only two occurrences of 'hath' and none of 'doth'. When they do appear, they usually do so in clusters; could these clusters suggest fragments of a Shakespearian original? One concentration of 'hath' and 'doth' occurs in the brief opening scene which is also, perhaps, the most Shakespearian in the play. Another example might be:

LEONORA   Your Absence hath giv'n Breeding
   To what my letter hath declar'd, and is
   This instant on th'effecting, Hark! the Musick
         [Flourish within]
   Is now on tuning, which must celebrate
   This Bus'ness so discordant.

This is certainly like Shakespeare; Spurgeon[27] would no doubt underline both 'breeding' and the music image, while one might also point out that the lines are, unlike so much of the play, notably not end-stopped. This could, of course, be a rather good imitation by Theobald – which makes the argument against forgery just as well: if Theobald were creating a deliberate forgery, he would be attempting to produce more lines that sound like Shakespeare, and fewer that sound like Fletcher.

The audience of 1728 might be expected to know the 'sound' of Fletcher; 1711 had seen the publication of an octavo edition of the Beaumont and Fletcher plays, following hard upon Rowe's 1709 edition of Shakespeare; and in the 1720s there were plenty of productions of his plays. Though Beaumont and Fletcher were no longer as popular as in the days of Dryden when, he claimed,[28] they were performed with twice the frequency of Shakespeare, nevertheless in the month of the first performance of *Double Falsehood* (December 1727), London playgoers could have seen *The Scornful Lady* and *Rule a Wife and Have a Wife*, along with versions of Shakespeare's *Hamlet*, *Richard III*, *Troilus and Cressida* and *King Lear*.[29] It was this audience whose reaction, recorded by Theobald

---

[24] Ibid., part I (SB vol. VIII, 1956), 85–91.

[25] 'ye' occurs at : 2.3.125, 2.3.128, 3.3.149; 'em' occurs at: 1.2.105, 1.3.3, 2.4.11, 2.4.34, 3.1.12, 3.2.35, 4.1.160, 5.2.221, 5.2.238, 5.2.239.

[26] 'has' occurs at: 1.2.105, 1.2.195, 2.3.38, 2.3.101, 2.4.12, 3.2.2, 3.3.65, 3.3.80, 3.3.92, 3.3.103, 3.3.122, 3.3.154, 4.1.8, 4.1.57, 4.1.59, 4.1.82, 4.1.85, 4.1.123, 4..140, 4.1.142, 4.1.245, 4.2.25, 4.2.37, 4.2.88, 5.1.4, 5.1.7, 5.1.10, 5.1.37, 5.2.27, 5.2.49, 5.2.68, 5.2.58, 5.2.157, 5.2.158, 5.2.200, 5.2.201, 5.2.222, 5.2.232, 5.2.235, 5.2.257; 'hath' occurs at: 1.1.26, 1.1.32, 1.2.20, 1.2.50, 3.2.11, 3.2.35, 34.2.40, 3.2.159, 4.1.52, 4.1.200; 'does' occurs at: 1.3.57, 3.3.71, 4.1.145; 'doth' occurs at: 1.1.37, 1.2.76, 1.3.71.

[27] Caroline Spurgeon, *Shakespeare's Imagery and What It Tells Us* (Cambridge, 1935), p. 75.

[28] John Dryden, *The Art of Dramatick Poesie, An Essay*, 1668,

[29] Emmet L. Avery *The London Stage 1660–1800* (Illinois, 1960), part 2, vol. 2, pp. 947–52.

in his preface, has provided perhaps the best one-sentence critique of the play to date: 'Others again, to depreciate the affair, as they thought, have been pleased to urge, that tho' the Play may have some Resemblance of Shakespeare, yet the Colouring, Diction, and Characters, come nearer to the Style and Manner of FLETCHER.'

Harriet Frazier notes:[30] 'Theobald's edition of Shakespeare ... suggests that Theobald had superabundant talent to create a very clever imitation of Shakespeare.' Precisely. Then why would he produce a very clever imitation of Fletcher? Although it is somewhat obscured by revision, the evidence we have is that the metre, the collocation of certain words, and the stylistic mannerisms of large parts of the play are distinctively Fletcherian. This does more than suggest Fletcher's presence in the play: it makes it clear that the play cannot be a forgery (unless, that is, Theobald had inadvertently forged the wrong writer); if the play is not a forgery, then the case for it being a relic of *Cardenio* is very strong. Furthermore, if indeed we have no reason to doubt Theobald's honesty, then his description of the source for what might have been the oldest of his manuscripts goes some way to explaining the nature of the play which he 'revised and adapted'.

Had *The Two Noble Kinsmen* never been published in the form we have now; had instead Theobald revised and adapted Davenant's *The Rivals* and claimed – in good faith – that it was by Shakespeare, we would no doubt have had the same debate about that play as we have had about *Double Falsehood*. We would have a play in scenes some reminiscent of Fletcher, but with no evidence of Shakespeare's hand.

It is, however, just possible that we might be a little more fortunate. Theobald claimed to have had three manuscripts; one of them, he said, was 'much more perfect, and has fewer Flaws and Interruptions in the Sense'. Perhaps, from the various stages of revision by the team of Davenant, Betterton and Downes, Theobald managed after all to salvage a few scraps of a Shakespearian original.

---

[30] Harriet Frazier, 'Speculation on the Motives of a Forger', *Neuphilologische Mitteilungen*, 72 (1971), 288.

'THE DUKE MY FATHER'S WRACK': THE INNOCENCE OF THE RESTORATION *TEMPEST*

MATTHEW H. WIKANDER

'What care these roarers for the name of Duke?' exclaims Trincalo, the Boatswain in *The Enchanted Island*, Dryden and Davenant's adaptation of the *Tempest*; 'to Cabin; silence; trouble us not' (1.1.22).[1] The temptation to see this as one of the absurdities of restoration royalism is strong. Driven by the desire to expunge any critique of monarchy from the plays of an earlier generation, the adaptors replaced the name of king with the name of duke. The ocean's 'roarers' no longer suggest a crowd resentful of divine right claims, and the Boatswain is guilty of a certain rudeness to a duke but not of the more frightening crime of lèse-majesté. The duke's notion that his 'name' might still the storm becomes itself absurd; only the name of king can match the force of nature. And it is a name that is not spoken in Dryden and Davenant's play.

The traumas of civil wars, regicide, and restoration seem to have locked the theatre into a state of denial, at least until the 1680s, when opposition voices would again be heard in Parliament and (briefly) upon the stage. Heroic dramas indeed concentrated upon conflicts of allegiance and impossible divisions of loyalties, but did so in exotic settings, where an Amurath might succeed an Amurath, never a Harry a Harry, or a Charles a Charles. In *The Tempest*, Alonzo, King of Naples in Shakespeare's play, becomes Duke of Savoy in Dryden and Davenant; Prospero has lost his dukedom through the intrigues of a rival duke. The Boatswain's brusqueness to Alonzo, instead of being anti-

royalist, merely marks his recognition that a duke is not a king. The possibility that the 'roarers' might in fact care for a regal name is left open. As is, equally, the possibility that they might not.

But Dryden and Davenant have not merely increased the number of dukes in the play by one. Alonzo himself is a double duke, having usurped the dukedom of Mantua – apparently with the help of Antonio. Hippolito, right heir to the dukedom of Mantua, is thus an 'excellent contrivance' in two ways, being both a man who has never seen a woman and a duke who has never seen his dukedom. Miranda in Shakespeare's play moves up the social scale when, as daughter of a duke, she marries the son of a king. In Dryden and Davenant, she contents herself with the heir to a dukedom, and her sister Dorinda marries a restored duke. Trincalo's line at his final entrance in the play points to the adaptors' awareness of the new situation: 'What, more Dukes yet?' (5.2.205). The super-

---

[1] Dryden and Davenant's *Tempest* is quoted throughout from *The Works of John Dryden*, vol. 10, *Plays: The Tempest, Tyrannick Love, An Evening's Love*, editor, Maximillian E. Novak, textual editor, George Robert Guffey (Berkeley, Los Angeles, London: University of California Press, 1970). Shakespeare's *Tempest* is quoted from *The Complete Works* ('Original-Spelling Edition'), general editors, Stanley Wells and Gary Taylor (Oxford: Clarendon Press, 1986). The operatic *Tempest* is quoted from Christopher Spencer, *Five Restoration Adaptations of Shakespeare* (Urbana: University of Illinois Press, 1965).

abundance of dukes in this *Tempest*, like its absence of kings, sets the adaptation apart from its model, and suggests that some political ideas in Shakespeare's *Tempest* might have been too embarrassing (or subversive) for the adaptors to touch.

The most notable side-effect of the demotion of Alonzo is, curiously, a demotion of Prospero as well. Recent historical criticism of Shakespeare's *Tempest* is more than willing to see James I's absolutist politics figured in Prospero, as father, ruler, and sage. As Stephen Orgel has put it, 'family structures and sexual relations become political structures in the play, and these are relevant to the political structures of Jacobean England'. Orgel quotes James's description of himself in *Basilikon Doron* as 'a loving nourish father' to his kingdom: James 'conceives himself as the head of a single-parent family', and so has closer ties than are immediately apparent to Prospero.[2] Noticing the remarkable lack of mastery over the situation exhibited by the restoration Prospero, Katharine Maus has argued that 'the play redefines the limits and uses of sovereignty'. For Maus, the new Prospero reflects a restoration spirit of compromise: 'Prospero with all his faults is a just and orderly ruler, and the postwar royalists consider justice and order the primary virtues of a good sovereign.'[3] Both the guilt-ridden Duke Alonzo and the Prospero who sinks into despair as Hippolito appears to die truly do seem limited in their powers. The renunciation of magic in the adaptation is far harsher than that in Shakespeare's play: 'I am curs'd because I us'd it', Prospero mutters in parentheses as his scheme to marry Miranda to Ferdinand collapses in the wake of the young rivals' duel (4.3.160).

Ariel saves the day: and to Maus, this points the play in a Whiggish direction. 'The potential for a creative political order resides not with the benevolent monarch but with the loyal, resourceful subject', she argues.[4] But this argument avoids the insistence, on the part of both Prospero and Ariel, upon the rôle played by the

divine will in furnishing Hippolito's recovery. Prospero's success in the play is not dependent, as Maus would suggest, upon a spirit of compromise with and among his subjects, but upon the deity.

The adaptors are eager to resolve what in Shakespeare's play remains murky: the extent to which Prospero's powers are black or white magic. Therefore they excise his abjuration of his art, with its famous (or infamous) echoes of Medea. Prospero blames his use of magic for the collapse of his plans, and Ariel, summing up the situation at the end of the fourth act, blames all the play's inversions of social order upon magic:

> Harsh discord reigns throughout this fatal Isle,
> At which good Angels mourn, ill spirits smile;
> Old *Prospero*, by his daughters rob'd of rest,
> Has in displeasure left 'em both unblest.
> Unkindly they abjure each others bed,
> To save the living, and revenge the dead.
> *Alonzo* and his Son are Pris'ners made,
> And good *Gonzalo* does their crimes upbraid.
> *Antonio* and *Gonzalo* disagree,
> And wou'd, though in one Cave, at distance be.
> The Seamen all that cursed *Wine* have spent,
> Which still renew'd their thirst of Government;
> And, wanting subjects for the food of Pow'r,
> Each wou'd to rule alone the rest devour.
> The Monsters *Sycorax* and *Caliban*
> More monstrous grow by passions learn'd from
>   man.
> Even I not fram'd of warring Elements,
> Partake and suffer in these discontents.
> Why shou'd a mortal by Enchantment hold
> In chains a spirit of aetherial mould?
> Accursed Magick we our selves have taught
> And our own pow'r has our subjection
>   wrought!   (4.3.256–77)

This key speech continues the play's assault on magic. Ariel blames himself for his enslavement

[2] Stephen Orgel, 'Prospero's Wife', *Representations*, 8 (Autumn, 1984), 7, 9.

[3] Katharine Eisaman Maus, 'Arcadia Lost: Politics and Revision in the Restoration *Tempest*', *Renaissance Drama*, 13 (1982), 190, 197.

[4] Maus, 'Arcadia Lost', 206.

to the warring elements of the play's human world. Natural order is inverted, and a spirit is bonded to a mortal.

But Ariel remains a higher being. Where Prospero is confounded and determined to pursue his punishment of Ferdinand through to the death, Ariel, noticing that Hippolito was not quite dead, sets out to find a cure. 'I prun'd my wings', he tells Prospero,

and, fitted for a journey, from the next Isles of our *Hesperides*, I gather'd Moly first, thence shot myself to *Palestine*, and watch'd the trickling Balm, which caught, I glided to the *British* Isles, and there the purple Panacea found. (5.1.51–5)

The journey is an ambitious one: from the world of Ancient Greece to the land of the Old Testament to Britain. According to the editors of the California Dryden, the 'trickling Balm' closes wounds made by swords, and the 'purple Panacea' might well be *Panax coloni* or 'all-heal' (p. 374). Both would be appropriate medications for Hippolito, but moly is the herb that renders Odysseus invulnerable to the spells of Circe. Identification of those spells with desire – and desire out of control has been Hippolito's problem – magnifies the kind of cure attempted here. Not only the wounds but the imbalance that led to the duel will be cured.

Ariel's journey from the old world to Britain is not unlike the journey undertaken by the daughters of Niger in Jonson's *Masque of Blackness*. They follow a prophecy that leads to a land whose name ends in Tania: after Mauritania, Lusitania, and Aquitania they are finally taken to Britannia. In *Blackness*, the beams of James's own 'light scientiall' bleach them white; likewise, here, the 'purple Panacea' has a linkage to the imperial theme. 'To substantiate the semi-divine nature of kingship', Ronald Hutton reminds us of the first days of the restoration, 'Charles spent two June days touching nearly a thousand sufferers from scrofula, who were presented gold pendants and assurances of miraculous recovery.'[5] Britain becomes once again home to the royal,

purple, heal-all. This densely allegorical speech, needless to say, was cut in the operatic, 1674 *Tempest*. There Ariel gathers the simples and balms by himself; in the 1667 *Tempest*, he needs the help of Hippolito's good angel to mount to the level of the planets and mix the proper medicines. Cutting out the supernatural dimension might be secularization on the part of Shadwell, trimming the play to meet the demands of opera, or it may be Whiggish revision; in the Dryden/Davenant version, the spirit cannot save the mortals without divine aid.

The limitations upon human power in the 1667 *Tempest*, then, do not point in the direction of constitutional compromise or reform. Rather, the inability of Prospero to control events on his island and the impotent guilt of Antonio and Alonzo suggest that human means alone are too flawed to untangle the play's complexities. Since all three are dukes, along with the moribund Hippolito, the play links their human failings and incapacities with that rank. Again, the possibility is left open that a king might not be so inept. In the heroic plays of Roger Boyle, first Earl of Orrery, popular in the 1660s, a strict line of demarcation distinguishes the powers of kings (intellectual and amorous) from those of mere subjects, among whom dukes find themselves numbered. Where Shakespeare's Prospero is aligned with *Midsummer Night's Dream*'s Theseus and *Measure for Measure*'s Vincentio in the order of absolute dukes, Dryden/Davenant's dukes are haunted, Prospero by his cursed use of magic and the others by their crimes. They see their failures as just retributions. Hippolito, lacking the taint of a past, none the less falls prey as natural man to indiscriminate sexual appetites. Good government in Shakespeare, in heroic plays, and in this *Tempest* is equated with control over desire, and Hippolito cannot be

---

[5] Ronald Hutton, *The Restoration* (Oxford: Clarendon Press, 1985), p. 128.

satisfied with one woman until the 'purple Panacea' has been applied.

Less in control yet, of course, are the sailors who make up the underclass of the play. The editors of the California Dryden point out that the comic business of the sailors has been greatly expanded in the new version of the play. Their 'thirst of government' is also exaggerated, as they compete for position in the new situation. 'This Isle's our own, that's our comfort', says Ventoso, 'for the Duke, the Prince, and all their train are perished.' 'Our Ship is sunk, and we can never get home agen', rejoins Mustacho; 'we must e'en turn Salvages, and the next that catches his fellow may eat him' (2.3.46–50). The interchange greatly expands the single sentence in Shakespeare: 'Trinculo, the King, and all our company else being dround, wee will inherit here' (2.2.1081–2). The important Shakespearian issue of inheritance is elided as Dryden and Davenant instead focus on the disorderly governments the sailors propose. With Stephano self-elected as duke and Mustacho and Ventoso as viceroys, the symmetry becomes complete when Trincalo proclaims himself duke as well. The four dukes of the main plot – Prospero, Alonzo, Antonio, and Hippolito – are mirrored in the two dukes and two viceroys of the comic plot. The adaptors have taken the course of multiplying complications rather than simplifying; the Shakespearian Tempest has a much cleaner neoclassical structure. The drunken shifts of allegiance of the island's two native subjects, Caliban and his sister Sycorax, like the dukes' and viceroys' vain boasts, compound the instability of Prospero's island. Their scene of quarrel and fighting instantly precedes Ferdinand's and Hippolito's duel.

Much recent criticism of Shakespeare's Tempest has emphasized the connection between the play and the colonial ventures of the late sixteenth and early seventeenth centuries. Of special importance have been early accounts of shipwrecks, in which the order of command collapsed on desert islands, as seamen refused to obey those who would have been their governors had they successfully arrived at their destination or those who had the right to command them at sea. The new situation led to mutinous outbreaks and challenges to accepted order; cannibalism and piracy, both proposed by the sailors in the Restoration Tempest, were recorded. By multiplying the number of seamen and by exaggerating their ambitions, Dryden and Davenant make even more explicit reference to the problems of colonialism. 'I am a free Subject in a new Plantation, and will have no Duke without my voice', explains Ventoso, demanding a bribe of liquor (2.3.60). The word 'plantation', which in Shakespeare's use refers to Gonzalo's Utopian plans for plantation of the isle, here takes on its specific colonial meaning.

'I will speak for the people', says Mustacho, 'because there are few, or rather none, in the Isle to speak for themselves' (67–8). Davenant himself had been appointed by the king, during the Interregnum, to a position on the Council of Virginia. His journey to take up that post, however, ended in a species of island exile, as his ship was taken by Parliamentary forces and he himself was imprisoned on the Isle of Wight.[6] Satirizing the politics of the colonist as well as the mutineer, Dryden and Davenant are able to allude to the conflicting claims of authority over the colonies in the Interregnum.

The discovery of new peoples in the new world, as Stephen Orgel has argued, forced the old world to reconsider its image of itself.[7] Dryden and Davenant, again, conquer the problem of Caliban by dividing, first by making male and female versions of the servant-monster. The two aspects of Shake-

---

6 Mary Edmond, Rare Sir William Davenant, The Revels Plays Companion Library (New York: St Martin's, 1987), pp. 103–4.
7 Stephen Orgel, 'Shakespeare and the Cannibals', in Cannibals, Witches, and Divorce: Estranging the Renaissance, Selected Papers from the English Institute, New Series, no. 11, ed. Marjorie Garber (Baltimore: Johns Hopkins University Press, 1987), 40–66.

speare's Caliban – his uncanny mingling of characteristics of the noble savage and the irredeemable brute – are also separated in the adaptation. Caliban continues to be the wild brute, while Hippolito is given the characteristics of the noble savage, the natural man. Ariel's cure points him on the way to civilization. Dryden and Davenant's Caliban promises to 'be wise hereafter' (5.2.231) but does not get to finish the sentence in Shakespeare 'and seeke for grace'. Nor does the Restoration Prospero acknowledge the 'thing of darkness' his. Both Calibans reject their worship of Stephano and Trinculo, but Dryden/Davenant's does so because now he sees the real dukes: 'What a dull fool was I to take those Drunkards / For Gods, when such as these were in the world" (5.2.231–2). This Caliban remains bounded by the limits of his own experience.

The treatment of Caliban is more strictly comic in the Restoration version, and the satire of the seamen is more pointedly political and more sustained. Like the proliferation of the dukes, this works to an overall effect of heightening the instability of Prospero's island. The marriages at the end of the play, too, seem perfunctory by comparison to the magnificent masque that celebrates marriage in Shakespeare's play. The adaptors left out this specimen of Prospero's art and instead tormented the guilty dukes with a dance of Pride, Fraud, Rapine, and Murder. Unlike the victims of the 'three men of sin' anti-masque in Shakespeare's *Tempest*, these men are already overwhelmed with guilt, even to the point of recognizing that their recent crusade into Portugal against the Moors has no effect on the condition of their souls.[8] What in Shakespeare's play features as an anti-masque to usher in the marriage masque becomes the central moral spectacle in Dryden and Davenant.

The result is a secularization of the marriage of Ferdinand and Miranda; its undercutting by the comic unwitting bawdry of Hippolito and Dorinda works to the same end. The marriage

masque permits Shakespeare's play to look towards a reconciliation in which, through Ferdinand and Miranda, Milan and Naples will again be one. They and their children will inherit a world in which the rift between Prospero and Alonzo is dissolved. In the Restoration *Tempest*, Alonzo only finds his son to lose him to Prospero's sense of justice. Ferdinand is restored to his father as Hippolito is restored to life by the intervention of Ariel. Hippolito and Prospero are restored to their dukedoms. For an emphasis on stability by succession and inheritance, the Dryden/ Davenant play substitutes an emphasis on political stability through restoration. Only the usurping Antonio loses his dukedom, which he willingly gives back to Prospero.

The downplaying of the Shakespearian *Tempest*'s interest in family and inheritance speaks as much to its context as Shakespeare's play did. James I saw *The Tempest* at court twice, in November 1611 and in the winter of 1612–13. On the second occasion, he had just lost a son and heir in Prince Henry and was in the process of marrying off a daughter.[9] The play's selection for this occasion would have the effect of equating the king's situation with that of the grieving Alonzo. Dryden and Davenant may be seen to avoid dealing with the matter of succession by demoting Alonzo and changing the purpose of his journey into a crusade. But none the less the abundance of dukes may remind us that the heir to Charles II was the Duke of York and that in 1663 Charles's bastard son had been created Duke of Monmouth. Thus we have a situation in which a pair of royal brothers (one the king, one a duke) and a pair of dukes (one the heir to the throne, one the king's son) entertained the public's eye and provoked their speculation. In 1667, too, there was concern about the queen's failure to

---

[8] As Maus neatly puts it: 'This Prospero torments people who are conscious of their crimes,' 'Arcadia Lost', 197.

[9] See Stephen Orgel's introduction to *The Tempest* (Oxford: Clarendon Press, 1987) for full discussion.

provide Charles with a son and heir; divorce and remarriage or legitimation of Monmouth were rumoured as possibilities.

Hippolito's problem in the play – his uncontrolled sexuality – and his sudden elevation to a dukedom embody different aspects of the Restoration scene, depending, as is so often the case with applications of this sort, upon the angle of approach. The play's emphasis on divine will suggests that everything will work out in the end, but this *Tempest* shares the fascination with the succession that persisted on stage in the form of royal rivals in heroic drama. Buckingham's two kings of Brentford in *The Rehearsal* are a comic comment on this trend. In *The Tempest* the confusions of the age led Dryden and Davenant to alter the pattern of family bonds in Shakespeare into a pattern of symmetrical dukes. In so doing, they no doubt bore in mind, as Charles always did, the king his father's wrack. For if Hippolito seems to contain aspects of York and Monmouth, he is also something of a Charles, waiting to be restored to his proper lands.

All of these suggestions pale, however, beside the fact that the part was played in November 1667 by a woman. Jocelyn Powell argues that Dryden's assertion that 'dearth of Youths' (Prologue, 29) led to this casting is 'clearly disingenuous': 'The whole part is set up for it, as the woman on stage asks the mixed audience what women are like.'[10] The 'innocent' bawdry of the character winks at the audience through the experienced actress. If Montague Summers' guess that this was Moll Davis is correct, the complications multiply. By January 1668, Pepys reported, she was the king's mistress; on May 29, the queen walked out of a performance at court rather than stay to watch Moll Davis dance. The portrayal of a natural man who must learn to rule his lusts before he can rule his dukedom by this actress must have been richly ironic, as the object of royal lusts portrays a duke whose frenzy to possess all women has led to his near death at the hand of a more experienced rival. The sexual misconduct of the royal

brothers and its danger to the realm is represented, but only playfully. Moll Davis as Hippolito is not a serious threat.

Summers's guess, however, is only that. *The London Stage* proposes for Moll Davis the rôle of Ariel, and gives that of Hippolito to Jane Long.[11] Here we can see the royal mistress portraying the part of the ingenious spirit who seeks out the 'purple panacea' and saves the injured duke, and who repines at the dangers of human passions. Again, the casting subverts comically a clear moral reading of the play's message, leaving its solution not in the hands of a loyal subject but of a royal whore. The insatiable sexual appetites of Hippolito become, as the part is played by any woman, Moll Davis or Jane Long, joking matters rather than serious issues. Ariel's transcendence of the human realm and his union in faithful love with the mate provided for him by Dryden and Davenant are likewise open to mockery. The Restoration audience, always sensitive to the disparity between the moral status of characters and the reputations of actresses, is free to make serious applications or to indulge in salacious debunking.[12] Whatever the casting, the choice would have remained open.

The 'radical shrinking of Prospero', James Winn argues, also undercuts another threat: the

---

10 Jocelyn Powell, *Restoration Theatre Production* (London: Routledge and Kegan Paul, 1984), p. 72.

11 *The London Stage: 1660–1800; Part One: 1660–1700*, ed. William van Lennep with a critical introduction by Emmet L. Avery and Arthur H. Scouten (Carbondale: Southern Illinois University Press, 1965), p. 123. This casting is based upon John Harold Wilson's suggestions in *All the King's Ladies: Actresses of the Restoration* (Chicago: University of Chicago Press, 1958), pp. 140, 166. Wilson notes that Moll Davis was particularly noted for singing and dancing; Jane Long had just begun to specialize in breeches parts in 1667.

12 Peter Holland sees this phenomenon as closely related to the intimate design of the Restoration playhouse: 'The closer the actor is to the audience the stronger is the audience's recognition of the actor as an individual behind the role', *The Ornament of Action: Text and Performance in Restoration Comedy* (Cambridge: Cambridge University Press, 1979), p. 63.

strategy 'might possibly have reflected [the adaptors'] desire to avoid any potential analogy between the banished Duke of Milan and the recently deposed Chancellor', Sir Edward Hyde, the Earl of Clarendon.[13] Winn admits that his point is 'speculative', and it is also possible to speculate that the inability of Prospero to control the island, especially to control the robust appetites of his daughters and the dukes they desire, does conjure up Hyde's image. The Duke of York's marriage to Hyde's daughter was the unfortunate result of youthful indiscretion; and if Hyde was unable to control his own daughter, he was equally unable to urge Charles into any conspicuous propriety of behaviour. Prospero's vain counsels of self-control to the young quartet under his charge lead only to internecine rivalries. Miranda's marriage to a duke in exile could well be seen as a reflection of Anne Hyde's marriage. The confusions of the isle may match the confusions of the court.

The sympathy of Dryden and Davenant for Clarendon in 1667 may show through in Ariel's cure of Hippolito: the forces Prospero has sought to control simply defy human capability. The divine will sent Prospero into exile, and it has called him back. Nor does the exile need to exact any revenge, for those who have wronged him are paralyzed by their guilt. Hyde returned from exile as mentor to the royal brothers at the Restoration, but he was no magician, and his daughter's marriage to the Duke of York not only earned him close ties to the royal family, but provoked much hostile criticism. The play as a whole counsels that justice, in the long run, will prevail, despite human failures.

Dryden and Davenant removed the most openly subversive moments in Shakespeare's *Tempest*, excising Gonzalo's mildly republican plans for the island and Sebastian's intrigue against Alonzo. But to say, as Winn does, that the play thereby becomes politically 'innocent' (twisting Pepys's original meaning) seems to belie the play's elaborate strategies of dis-placement. The Restoration *Tempest* is not political allegory, but in its persistent doubling it shares a common language of duplicity with the literature of the period in general. Suggestion and evasion of specific reference, not to mention downright lying, is endemic to Restoration political and literary practice. Stephen Zwicker links the style of Dryden's *Annus Mirabilis* specifically to the age's willingness to disconnect words from meanings: 'The posture is crucially reminiscent of the king's own Act of Oblivion – a denial of the language and facts of opposition – and it anticipates the portrait of the king in the poem, not a man embattled by sharp criticism but the crown as beloved servant and redemptive saint.'[14] Similarly, by belittling the whole redemptive agenda of the Shakespearian *Tempest*, the adaptors paradoxically make the play theodicean. A clear pattern of poetic justice supplants the Shakespearian ambiguities of the unregenerated Antonio and the Caliban who seeks for grace.

But as in *Annus Mirabilis*, this drive towards abstractness is a denial of the facts and language of the play itself. Prospero's exile is not Clarendon's, and Ferdinand and Hippolito are not Charles and James, nor are they York and Monmouth. The seamen are not mutinous colonists nor are Caliban and Sycorax Indians. The more vehemently we make these denials, the clearer it becomes that the play is suffused with the duplicity of the language of its own age. The restoration play withholds from Prospero his Stuart absolutist dimension. The idea of the self-mastering sage, father, and monarch is absorbed in the general atmosphere of guilt and repentance. The operatic version of the play went further in dissociating the play from its earlier connection with Stuart

---

13 James Anderson Winn, *John Dryden and his World* (New Haven: Yale University Press, 1987), p. 189.

14 Stephen N. Zwicker, 'Politics and Literary Practice in the Restoration', in *Renaissance Genres* (Harvard English Studies, 14) ed. Barbara Kiefer Lewalski (Cambridge, Mass.: Harvard University Press, 1986), 280.

ideology. The published version of the 1684 opera places the arms of the British royal house where they belong: on the proscenium arch, outside the play, but framing and containing it. The opera, like the play, both is and is not about the limitations of Stuart absolutist ideology. Dryden and Davenant, trying hard not to see in their *Tempest* a too familiar tale of island and exile, of confused succession, of a king's father's wrack, of a disgraced and powerless sage, of old world and new, of promiscuity and indiscretion, succeeded. But the play protests its

innocence in the same way that Moll Davis or Jane Long, playing Hippolito, wonders 'What are women like?' (2.4.44). The ignorance is affected, and the audience is invited to share it or not as they please. Pepys, himself dependent upon the Duke of York, may have protested too much in finding it 'the most innocent play that ever I saw'.[15]

---

[15] *The Diary of Samuel Pepys*, ed. Robert Latham and William Matthews, 11 vols. (Berkeley: University of California Press, 1970–83), VIII, p. 522.

'REMEMBER/FIRST TO POSSESS HIS BOOKS': THE APPROPRIATION OF THE TEMPEST, 1700–1800

MICHAEL DOBSON

The eighteenth century inherited two versions of *The Tempest*. One was an established classic, immensely popular in the theatre and the subject of countless allusions outside it: *The Tempest, or the Enchanted Island*, adapted by Dryden and Davenant in 1667 and provided with further operatic embellishments by Shadwell in 1674. The other was the play which appears first in the Shakespeare Folio, *The Tempest*, which had not been performed since its author's lifetime and would not be revived in anything like its original form until 1746. The history of these competing texts in eighteenth-century culture, which this paper will endeavour to illuminate, is not a simple matter of the Restoration's spurious, usurping *Enchanted Island* gradually succumbing to the inevitable rise of Bardolatry in favour of the true, Shakespearian *Tempest*, although this is how it has always tended to be represented. It is rather the history of how new concepts of Shakespeare – new ideas of the meanings and uses of Great English Literature – conspire both with and against new readings of *The Tempest* to produce a series of new Prosperos, new Mirandas, and new Calibans over the course of the century – whether in fresh stage versions like Garrick's operetta of 1756, the puppet version of 1780 or Kemble's play of 1789, or in other media: novels, statues, poems, literary criticism. In this short essay I hope to suggest what issues were at stake for the eighteenth century's various appropriators of *The Tempest*, and quite why this text, frequently hailed from

the nineteenth century onwards as perhaps the most artistically (and indeed typographically) reliable of all Shakespeare plays, should have been one of the most unstable in the repertory during precisely the period which both identified Shakespeare with Prospero and installed him as 'the god of its idolatry'. In effect I shall be using eighteenth-century responses to *The Tempest* to sketch a history of the cultural pressures under which this text was enabled to function alternately as a fiction of gender relations and a fiction of racial mastery, developments which have been discussed with particular pertinence and urgency in the context of the twentieth century by Ania Loomba in *Gender, Race, Renaissance Drama*.[1]

On the stage, *The Tempest* entered the eighteenth century as a play which addressed the issue of power primarily in terms of patriarchal authority within the family. Davenant

This article began life as a paper presented to the Special Session 'Alternative Shakespeares: Adaptation and Interpretation, 1660–1900' at the MLA conference in New Orleans, 1988, and I am especially grateful to the panel's organizer, Professor Jean Marsden (University of Connecticut), and to my fellow panellists, notably Professor Nicola Watson (Northwestern University), for many valuable suggestions. Since then different versions have elicited further helpful advice from Professor Stanley Wells (Birmingham University) and Professors Marjorie Garber and Stanley Cavell (Harvard University).

[1] Ania Loomba, *Gender, Race, Renaissance Drama* (Manchester: Manchester University Press, 1989): see especially chapter 6, 'Seizing the book', on colonial and post-colonial appropriations of *The Tempest* in India.

and Dryden's adaptation *The Enchanted Island* (first performed in 1667), perhaps as a result of its post-Restoration uncertainties about Prospero's political status within the state,[2] displaces the whole question of government on to the proper socialization of sexuality, compensating for its qualms about Prospero's authority as a father-king with a remarkable degree of enthusiasm for his authority as a father *tout court*. In its extended scenes between Ferdinand, Miranda, and the added characters Dorinda (Miranda's younger sister, equally ignorant of men) and Hippolito (Prospero's ward, 'one that never saw Woman, right Heir of the Dukedom of *Mantua*')[3] *The Enchanted Island* sets out to prove, in a manner half way between that of a court masque and a Royal Society experiment, that patriarchal authority can be rationally deduced from nature; to demonstrate, in effect, that *Basilikon Doron* may not be entirely incompatible with *Leviathan*. Even the most cursory summary of Davenant and Dryden's additions to *The Tempest* may suggest the degree of insistence with which this enduringly popular play sets out to demonstrate the 'naturalness' of contemporary gender rôles to an audience increasingly aware of the contingency of all social institutions. On their first appearance Miranda and Dorinda are represented as unpromptedly eager to be subjected to mates who will assume Prospero's paternal authority, even before they learn of Ferdinand and Hippolito's existence – 'Methinks indeed it would be finer, if we two / Had two young Fathers,' speculates Dorinda[4] – and Dryden goes so far as to have Miranda unconsciously consent to undergo labour pains as part of the cost – 'I had rather be in pain nine Months, as my Father threatn'd, than lose my longing'.[5] Having displayed these exemplary young women's innate aptness for precisely the functions to which contemporary society consigned them,[6] the play moves on to justify the ways of marriage to men. Hippolito, after his first forbidden meeting with Dorinda, seems unproblematically to embrace monogamy as the condition of

possession – 'I'd quit the rest o'the'world that I might live alone with / Her ..,'[7] he tells Prospero – but it transpires that this unprompted willingness to forsake all others is premised on his ignorance that any others exist. When Ferdinand lets this vital piece of information slip, Hippolito is overjoyed, declaring that 'I'le have as many as I can, / That are so good, and Angel-like as she I love. / And will have yours ...,'[8] and the two young princes are soon engaged in a proto-Freudian primal struggle for dominion over the women. Ferdinand, defending his property rights in Miranda, kills Hippolito in a duel, and only a magic resurrection effected by Ariel prevents Prospero from executing him in revenge: after this solemn display of the disadvantages of the sexual 'state of nature', the four young lovers, all together on stage at the start of the last act for the first time in the play, are able to deduce (even on purely mathematical grounds) that the adoption of conjugal fidelity on all sides is the best expedient to prevent further violence. At this convenient point in their experiments legitimate paternal authority arrives on the stage to ratify these agreements in the persons of Prospero and Alonzo, and thus despite its other principal subplot's dutiful attack on Hobbes

2 Persuasively analysed in Katharine Eisaman Maus, 'Arcadia Lost: Politics and Revision in the Restoration *Tempest*', *Renaissance Drama* (new series) XIII, 1982, 189–209, and further illuminated by Matthew Wikander elsewhere in this volume.

3 Sir William Davenant and John Dryden, *The Tempest, or the Enchanted Island* (London, 1670), 'Dramatis Personae'.

4 Ibid, p. 13.

5 Ibid., p. 28. There is an interesting submerged pun at work here, as Miranda's willingness to undergo 'labour' as the price of having Ferdinand takes the place of Ferdinand's Adamic labour (carrying logs) as the price of having Miranda in the original.

6 On empiricism and gender in *The Enchanted Island*, see Catherine Belsey, *The Subject of Tragedy: Identity and Difference in Renaissance Drama* (London and New York: Methuen, 1985), pp. 81–6.

7 *The Enchanted Island*, p. 47.

8 Ibid., p. 50.

(the mutinous and quarrelsome sailors repeatedly misquote *Leviathan*), the play can achieve comic resolution in a fashion surprisingly congruent with the emerging political doctrines of contractualism, patriarchal monogamy proving to be a rational contract made between men in a state of nature for their mutual self-preservation and the protection of their property.

So thoroughgoing is *The Enchanted Island* in its emphasis on gender that it virtually occludes Caliban altogether: in Davenant and Dryden's adaptation he gets drunk so thoroughly during his first encounter with the sailors that so far from leading an attempted coup against Prospero he neglects even to alert his new comrades to the Duke of Milan's existence. He is in effect rewritten as a potentially unruly woman by the provision of a sister, Sycorax, over the possession of whom Trincalo and Stephano struggle in a deliberate reiteration of the Hippolito / Ferdinand duel of the romantic subplot. Thomas Duffett's illuminating travesty of *The Enchanted Island*, *The Mock-Tempest* (1674), which transfers the action of the play to contemporary London low-life, is similarly uninterested in colonialism, translating Caliban perfunctorily into class terms (he features, briefly, as a lower-class hired bully, Hectoro), and preferring to gloss, in a strikingly Foucauldian fashion, Davenant and Dryden's overriding concern with gender politics by casting Prospero as the keeper of the Bridewell prison, the state's official punisher of prostitutes. Discussing Caliban in the preface to his subsequent adaptation *Troilus and Cressida; or, Truth Found Too Late* Dryden simply mystifies him as an example of the supernatural grotesque rather than a dispossessed native ('[Shakespeare] *there seems to have created a person who was not in Nature*'),[9] and this neglect of the racial issues raised by Shakespeare's 'salvage and deformed Slave' seems to have persisted in the early eighteenth-century theatre, one production of *The Enchanted Island* at Drury Lane in 1729 having apparently omitted Caliban altogether.[10]

With or without Caliban, the first decades of the eighteenth century found *The Enchanted Island* achieving virtually annual revivals, reaching a level of popularity which, paradoxically, would ultimately be its undoing. Preserving what is virtually the sole potentially subversive aspect of Dryden and Davenant's adaptation – their original transvestite casting of Hippolito and Sycorax – and frequently compounding these disruptive aspects of its presentation by casting an actress as Ariel (so that at the play's conclusion Prospero appears to sanction two pairings of women, the cross-dressed Hippolito with Dorinda and the cross-dressed Ariel with her/his added spiritual partner Milcha), the play, acquiring new musical and visual accretions each season, became a carnivalesque holiday entertainment, a familiar set-piece revived (often for actors' benefits, a sure sign of broad popularity) for the socially heterodox audiences attracted to the theatre between New Year's Eve and Twelfth Night.[11] The English theatre now has a specific name for plays of this kind, spectacular Christmas performances of stories so familiar that they have come to constitute part of the ideology of their audiences, inexplicably featuring middle-aged men dressed as comic women: pantomime. Already equipped with a Principal Boy in Hippolito and a Dame in Sycorax, and possessing a Wizard in Prospero and a Good Fairy in Ariel, *The Enchanted Island*'s assimilation as the standard festive treat of the early eighteenth-century theatre identifies *The Tempest* as the ultimate source of Panto as the London stage still knows it. In the new cultural climate of the early 1700s, however, both the

---

9 John Dryden, *Troilus and Cressida; or, Truth Found Too Late* (London, 1679), 'The Grounds of Criticism in Tragedy'.

10 See Emmett L. Avery et al, eds., *The London Stage, 1660–1800* (5 pts. in 11 vols., Carbondale: Southern Illinois University Press, 1960–8), pt. 2 p. 1006.

11 See C. B. Hogan, *Shakespeare in the Theatre, 1701–1800* (2 vols, Oxford: Clarendon Press, 1952), I, pp. 423–4.

explicitly sexual content of *The Enchanted Island* and its 'low', hybrid dramatic form could only result in its slow but inevitable demotion from the status of literature, and by the 1740s (during the early years of Garrick's reign at Drury Lane, as the Theatres Royal sought increasingly to present themselves as impeccably decorous social spaces) it was already on its way to being banished from the legitimate theatres altogether. After a few last Christmas revivals, the very last in the 1749–50 season, *The Enchanted Island* was driven out to less gentrified arenas, first to the illegal New Wells Theatre in Goodman's Fields for one production in 1745, and ultimately to that definitive site of lowness and transgression, Bartholomew Fair itself, where it was staged at Phillips's Great Theatrical Booth opposite Cow Lane from 1749 onwards.[12] After this the play was exiled to even darker fringes of the theatrical world, achieving regular revivals at the John Street Theatre in New York between 1774 and 1788, where its dramatization of the issues of absolutism and contractualism, and its admittedly attenuated interest in the structures of colonialism, must have seemed particularly to the point.[13]

Meanwhile, the return of the repressed colonial plot had to take place, for the time being, in other media. Alexander Pope, for example, follows Davenant and Dryden in appropriating *The Tempest* as a text about the policing of female sexuality, borrowing Ariel as the chief sylphic guardian of Belinda's chastity in *The Rape of the Lock* (1714), but his heroine is additionally a Miranda deeply implicated in the fate of offstage Calibans in that her beauty is conspicuously adorned, if not constructed, by a glittering catalogue of luxury items represented as the spoils of England's growing mercantile imperialism.[14] Five years later a text still more closely associated with the rise of capitalist imperialism would expel Miranda entirely to place the Prospero/Caliban relationship centre stage. In an article published nearly twenty years ago, J. W. Loofbourow noticed some incidental similarities between *The Enchanted Island* and Defoe's *Robinson Crusoe* (1719),[15] and I would argue that Defoe's desert island episode constitutes in itself a radical, bourgeois response to Davenant and Dryden's familiar play. Defoe simply deletes women as vigorously as the adaptors had imported them, enabling Crusoe and Friday, left alone on their conspicuously unenchanted island, to get on with the serious business of the colonial plot (complete with its crucial language lessons), and although he grudgingly retains *The Enchanted Island*'s mutineers he carefully banishes them to the ship which finally comes to Crusoe's rescue.[16]

---

[12] See Mary Margaret Nilan, *The Stage History of The Tempest: A Question of Theatricality* (PhD thesis, Northwestern University, Evanston, Illinois, 1967: Ann Arbor: University Microfilms International, 1980), Chapters 2–4: *The Daily Advertiser*, 23 August 1749.

[13] See George C. D. Odell, *Annals of the New York Stage* (15 vols., New York: Columbia University Press, 1927–49), I, p. 163.

[14] As Laura Brown remarks: 'Of all the major works of its period, *The Rape of the Lock* does the most to match imperialism and commodity fetishism, and the most to place the commodification of English culture in the context of imperial violence.' Laura Brown, *Alexander Pope* (Oxford: Blackwell, 1985), p. 22.

[15] 'Robinson Crusoe's Island and the Restoration Tempest', *Enlightenment Essays* 2 (1971), 201–7. Loofbourow notes that the polarizing of Crusoe's island into 'garden' and 'barren' areas, and the prominence of his cave, derive from the stage set of Dryden and Davenant's play, and adduces its Masque of Devils as a source for the earthquake and the accusing vision which follows it. The connections between Defoe's novel and the Davenant and Dryden adaptation are perhaps further suggested by *Robinson Crusoe*'s ultimate assimilation to the same pantomime tradition, from Sheridan's *Harlequin Friday* (1780: published anonymously, 1795) onwards.

[16] For at least one other contemporary novelist, however, *The Enchanted Island* remained a text concerned almost exclusively with untutored sexuality: the desert island adventures which proliferated in the wake of *Crusoe*'s success included *The Force of Nature; or the Loves of Hippollito and Dorinda. A Romance* (Northampton, 1720), which in keeping with its mildly salacious transcription of Davenant and Dryden's plot purports brazenly to be 'Translated from the FRENCH Original, and never before printed in ENGLISH'. Reprinted, with a short introduction, in Charles C. Mish, 'An Early

Neither of these printed derivatives of *The Enchanted Island* acknowledges Shakespeare by name: to be redeemed as a reputable, publishable Author in Augustan culture Shakespeare had to be cleared of his association with Davenant and Dryden's interpolated hanky-panky. Nicholas Rowe's pioneering six-volume edition of the Complete Works (1709) accordingly restores *The Tempest* to propriety (printing Shakespeare's unadulterated text, following the Folio, as the first play in the canon) and identifies it as Shakespeare's exclusive literary property: the essay appended by Charles Gildon in a spurious seventh volume, 'Remarks on the Plays of Shakespeare', opens fittingly with a scathing attack on *The Enchanted Island*, concluding with the remark that its additional scenes are 'scarce guilty of a Thought, which we could justly attribute to *Shakespeare*'.[17] Gildon's construction of a stable authorial presence behind and beyond the play, in his critical quest for such thoughts as we could justly attribute to Shakespeare, is entirely in tune with one of the most notable features of this edition, Rowe's provision of a biographical memoir by way of general preface. By 1746 it had become possible once more to stage *The Tempest* in something like its original form, only a few of Shadwell's added touches of pageantry remaining.[18]

Nevertheless, even the 'original', Jacobean *Tempest* came to address similar contemporary issues to those canvassed in Defoe's demystified prose version of *The Enchanted Island*, Prospero the island colonist soon being adopted as an acutely timely figure for Shakespeare's 'timeless' originality. The explicit adoption of Prospero as an unmediated Shakespearian self-presentation is initiated by Gildon just a year before *Crusoe*'s publication, when his 'Shakespeariana: or Select Moral Reflections, Topicks, Similies and Descriptions from SHAKESPEAR',[19] the first example of this particular way of commodifying Shakespearian drama for bourgeois home consumption, quotes the 'Our revels now are ended. . .' speech under the ten-

dentious heading beneath which it has been brandished so often since: it is offered as Shakespeare's own definitive statement on 'Humane Nature'. This now traditional stroke of biographical criticism was nationally institutionalized in 1741 by the chiselling of a garbled fragment of the same speech onto the scroll displayed by the statue of Shakespeare erected that February in Westminster Abbey:

> *The Cloud cupt Tow'rs,*
> *The Gorgeous Palaces,*
> *The Great Globe itself*
> *Yea all which it Inherit,*
> *Shall Dissolve;*
> *And like the baseless Fabrick of a Vision*
> *Leave not a wreck behind.*

Although the committee which supervised the design and installation of this monument was predominantly aristocratic, if not positively Jacobite (it was led by Lord Burlington, and included Pope),[20] the impetus behind the project was chiefly mercantile: during the late 1730s Shakespeare had been proclaimed repeatedly, by bourgeois pressure-groups such as the Shakespeare Ladies' Club, as an exemplar of unfallen Elizabethan Protestantism, a cultural figurehead pressed into the service of the growing campaign for full-scale trade war against Spain.[21] The monument thus simul-

---

Eighteenth-Century Prose Version of *The Tempest*', in Shirley Strum Kenny, ed., *The British Theatre and the Other Arts* (London: Associated University Presses, 1984). On this novel's relation to *Robinson Crusoe* see p. 241. n. 11.

17 Nicholas Rowe, ed., *The Works of Mr William Shakespear, in Six Volumes* (6 vols., London, 1709; 7 vols., London: Edmund Curll, '1709' [1710], vol. 7, p. 264.

18 See Nilan, *The Stage History of the Tempest*.

19 Published as part of his *Complete Art of Poetry* (2 vols., London, 1718).

20 On this statue, see Morris R. Brownell, *Alexander Pope and the Arts of Georgian England* (Oxford: Clarendon Press, 1978), pp. 354–6: David Piper, *The Image of the Poet: British Poets and their Portraits* (Oxford: Clarendon Press, 1982), pp. 78–82.

21 See especially the epilogue, addressed to the Shakespeare Ladies' Club, of George Lillo's Richardsonian adapta-

taneously identifies Shakespeare with Prospero the prince, a symbol of the lost splendour of the English monarchy (Burlington's committee insisted that the statue's pedestal should incorporate likenesses of Elizabeth I and Henry V), and with Prospero the private, magically creative proto-playwright, patron of a new and specifically culturally-based strain of nationalism. The latter perspective heavily predominates in the considerable number of mid eighteenth-century poems dedicated to celebrating Shakespeare as the type of home-grown British genius, poems which frequently both repeat the identification of Shakespeare with Prospero canonized by the Abbey monument and take a new pride in the Bard's humble market-town origins. *AVON, a Poem in Three Parts* (1758),[22] written by John Huckell (who characteristically accounts for Shakespeare's imaginative power by describing how as a youth he saw Nature bathing naked in the Avon), states that the Bard is 'Possess'd of more than his own PROSP'RO's skill';[23] the Scottish poet John Ogilvie's *Solitude: or, the Elysium of the Poets, A Vision* (1765)[24] presents Shakespeare, attended by Ariel, sharing poetic dominion over Britain with that other untaught native genius, Ossian. If Shakespeare is Prospero, the pastoral, provincial Britain he inhabits must be his island, a surmise confirmed in the 'VERSES on reading SHAKESPEAR' printed in *The Gentleman's Magazine* for June 1753: here the Bard summons us

> to rove
> With humble nature, in the rural grove,
> Where swains contented own the quiet scene,
> And twilight fairies tread the circled green,
> Drest by *her* hand, the woods and valleys smile,
> And spring diffusive, decks th'inchanted isle.

More famously, Garrick's *An ode upon dedicating a building, and erecting a statue, to Shakespeare, at Stratford upon Avon*, recited in front of a copy of the Westminster Abbey monument at the climax of the Stratford Jubilee of 1769, links the grammar-school prodigy with Prospero

repeatedly, perhaps most remarkably in its opening patriotic rhetorical questions:

> To what blest genius of the isle,
> Shall Gratitude her tribute pay,
>   Decree the festive day,
> Erect the statue, and devote the pile?
>
> Do not your sympathetic hearts accord,
>   To own the 'bosom's lord?'
> 'Tis he! 'tis he! that demi-god!
> Who Avon's flow'ry margin trod,
>   While sportive *Fancy* round him flew,
> Where *Nature* led him by the hand,
>   Instructed him in all she knew,
> And gave him absolute command!
>   'Tis he! 'tis he!
> 'The god of our idolatry!'[25]

In the service of Prospero/Shakespeare, the genius of the isle, attended by sportive Fancy as Ariel, Garrick has here not only taken over the rhetoric of royal panegyric but outdone it: as the father of English Literature, Shakespeare is claimed as a national deity, whose special middle-class revision of absolutism is sanctioned by that quintessentially bourgeois virtue, sympathy.

If the identification of Shakespeare with Prospero serves here to claim *The Tempest* for what may look like a form of Little Englandism, it also presses it more strenuously than ever into the service of imperialism. Garrick's own version of *The Tempest*, an operatic abbreviation which ran for only six performances in 1756, was staged at the height of the Seven Years War, as Britain vied with France for control over vast colonized territories in

tion of *Pericles, Marina* (London, 1738). On the Ladies' Club, see Emmett L. Avery, 'The Shakespeare Ladies' Club', *Shakespeare Quarterly*, Spring 1956, 153–8.

[22] Published anonymously (Birmingham, 1758).

[23] Cf. Joseph Wharton's journal *The Adventurer*, no. 93, 25 Sept. 1753: 'The poet is a more powerful magician than his own PROSPERO ...'

[24] (London, 1765).

[25] David Garrick, *An Ode upon Dedicating a Building, and Erecting a Statue, to Shakespeare, at Stratford upon Avon. By D.G.* (London, 1769), p. 1.

India, the Far East, and the Americas: eschewing the interpolated pleasures of the Dorinda/Hippolito scenes, and cutting Sycorax, this adaptation restores the rebellion and punishment of Caliban to prominence in the subplot, and is additionally prefaced by a prologue which cites English opera as an ideal patriotic stimulus to its audience to commit deeds of valour against the French.[26] The Shakespeare Jubilee itself, staged in the interim between the colonial gains of the Seven Years War and the losses of the American War of Independence, featured reiterated boasts of Shakespeare's domination of World Literature, and it is hard not to regard the 'gratitude' Garrick's climactic Ode showers so fulsomely upon the Bard as largely inspired by Britain's recent imperial acquisitions. A song in Garrick's subsequent pageant-play *The Jubilee* (1769) succinctly underlines this point: 'Our Shakespeare compared to is no man / No Frenchman, nor Grecian, nor Roman.'[27] Culturally superior to all major modern and classical competitors, Shakespeare's artistic triumph is here neatly congruent with the imperial triumph of his modern fellow Britons. Prospero, as both playwright and colonist, rules the waves.

Both *The Enchanted Island* and Garrick's operatic *Tempest* had by 1769 long been laid aside in the theatres in favour of Shakespeare's original text, and that this shift away from the adaptations, contemporary with the definitive appropriation of Shakespeare/Prospero as a figurehead for imperial expansion, is also a shift away from a gender-oriented and towards a race-orientated reading of *The Tempest* is perhaps suggested by the sole illustration of the play in performance which survives from this period. The frontispiece to the play in Bell's acting edition of 1774 ignores Miranda, Ariel, Ferdinand, and indeed Prospero to illustrate the moment in Act 2 when Trinculo and Stephano force the newly-drunk Caliban to swear allegiance – a primal scene of colonialism if ever there was one, and significantly the actor playing the kneeling Caliban is made up not as

Dryden's supernatural freak but, perfectly representationally, as a Negro.[28] Garrick, too, chooses this scene as the central moment of the play in the procession of Shakespearian characters which marks the climax of *The Jubilee*, having Prospero, preceded by Ariel 'with a wand, raising a tempest' and a model 'ship in distress sailing down the stage', march triumphantly downstage ahead of Miranda, and Caliban 'with a wooden bottle and 2 Sailors all drunk':[29] contemporary engravings depicting this procession similarly record Caliban's representation as a black slave.[30] Prospero here serves as a living emblem of the proper jurisdiction of Englishmen over not only women and the incipiently mutinous lower classes (as he certainly does in *The Enchanted Island*) but also over the subject races newly compelled to pledge allegiance to the Empire.

This is not to say that Dryden and Davenant's adaptation, or the uses of *The Tempest* it initiates, had been forgotten. The editor of Bell's edition, Francis Gentleman, considered that Shakespeare's text was '*an odd, improbable, agreeable mixture ... more nervous and chaste, but not so well supplied with humour or business, as Dryden's*', and opined that '*by properly blending ... a better piece than either, might be produced*'.[31] In 1780 just such a hybrid, the anonymous

---

26 See *The Plays of David Garrick*, ed. Harry William Pedicord and Frederick Lois Bergmann (6 vols., Carbondale and Edwardsville: Southern Illinois University Press, 1981), vol. 3, pp. 272–3.

27 David Garrick, *Songs, Choruses, &c. which are introduced in the New Entertainment of the Jubilee* (London, 1769), p. 4.

28 *Bell's Edition of Shakespeare's Plays* (9 vols., London, 1774), vol. 3, 'The Tempest', frontispiece.

29 *The Plays of David Garrick*, vol. 2, p. 116.

30 See, for example, J. Johnson and J. Payne, publ., *The Principal Characters in the Procession of the Pageant Exhibited in the Jubilee at Drury Lane Theatre* (London, 1770). This and Bell's illustration tend to disprove Ania Loomba's assertion that 'Not until 1934 was [Caliban] represented as black on the British stage.' (Loomba, *Gender, Race, Renaissance Drama*, p. 143).

31 'Introduction' to *The Tempest* in *Bell's Edition of Shakespeare's Plays* (9 vols., London, 1774), vol. 3.

puppet play *The Shipwreck*, enjoyed considerable success at the 'Patagonian Theatre' on the Strand: more concerned with the disciplining of female sexuality than ever, this version pits Prospero against a whole team of insurgent witches in the main plot and, allowing Sycorax to upstage Caliban once more, expands the sailors' scenes to include a diatribe against masquerades.[32] More remarkably, another reworking of the old Davenant/Dryden adaptation would nine years later replace Shakespeare's original as the standard acting text employed in the Theatres Royal, namely *The Tempest; or the Enchanted Island. Written by Shakespeare; with additions from Dryden: as compiled by J. P. Kemble.*[33]

This 'relapse' to what is in effect a slightly respectablized version of *The Enchanted Island*, more than four decades after the restoration of Shakespeare's original *Tempest*, has long puzzled stage historians, and I should like to close by suggesting some reasons why Kemble should have chosen to follow Gentleman's advice at this particular time. By the 1780s *The Tempest* was no longer the most prominent example in contemporary libraries of a text interested in describing the natural innocence of a woman brought up by an ideal guardian outside conventional society: it was competing as such against a text with potentially far more radical implications, namely Rousseau's *Emile*. Miranda is specifically held up as a counter-example to Rousseau's 'child of nature', Sophie, in the most noteworthy piece of Shakespeare criticism published in the year of Kemble's adaptation, William Richardson's *On Shakespeare's Imitation of Female Characters*,[34] and in one of the acting editions of Kemble's adaptation she is contrasted with another Rousseauistic heroine of sensibility, Amanthis, the protagonist of the radical Elizabeth Inchbald's play *The Child of Nature*.[35] In the aftermath of the storming of the Bastille – and Kemble's *Tempest* was one of the first new productions mounted in London in the season which followed it – *The Tempest* was, in effect,

mobilized to discipline susceptible English womanhood and to warn the youth of Albion against the temptations of French libertinism. The reaction against the Revolution characteristically figures its enemy as female sexual transgression, and thus Dryden and Davenant's adaptation, with its redoubled pro-patriarchal love plot, was self-evidently better suited to Kemble's right-wing purposes than Shakespeare's original text. In effect the task of civilizing Caliban abroad was temporarily laid aside, the immediate threat of Revolution causing *The Tempest* once more to be deployed as a text enforcing law and order within the family.[36] A last example of this counter-

---

32 *The Shipwreck* (London, 1780). See George Speaight, *The History of the English Puppet Theatre* (London: Harrap, 1955), pp. 149ff. On the masquerade as a locus for anxieties about female sexual transgression, see Terry Castle, *Masquerade and Civilization* (Stanford: Stanford University Press, 1986).

33 (London, 1789).

34 Richardson's essay, largely devoted to the praise of Miranda, anxiously notes that 'the history of modern Europe will attest, that even politics, a science of which men are particularly jealous, is not beyond the reach of adventurous females', and goes on to offer a terrible warning against the delusive attractions of free love:
In all situations whatever, where the tendency to extreme profligacy becomes very flagrant, the respect due to female virtues, and confidence in female affection, decline and decay. So great are the obligations of the fair sex to those institutions, which, more than any other, by limiting the freedom of divorce, and by other proper restrictions, have asserted the dignity of the female character.
(Reprinted in *Essays on Shakespeare's Dramatic Characters*, 6th edn., London, 1812, pp. 342–3).

35 William Oxberry, ed., *The New English Drama*, vol. 17 (London, 1823), 'The Tempest', p. vii. Oxberry hails Miranda as 'the abstract of purity personified' (p. vii).

36 Racist readings of *The Tempest* would return emphatically in the early decades of the following century, first of all in the wake of the West Indian slave mutinies: J. H. Fawcett's ballet adaptation (1803), for example, endlessly replays Caliban's attempted rape of Miranda. The most striking such version remains the Brough brothers' travesty *Raising the Wind* (1848), which, conflating racism and counter-revolution, portrays Caliban as a caricatured Negro abolitionist who brandishes a red flag and sings the *Marseillaise*.

revolutionary appropriation of the play is found in Mary Ann Hanway's conservative novel *Ellinor, or The World As It Is* (1798): here once more Shakespeare's play is invoked to police female sexual licence, when our heroine Ellinor is induced, like Sycorax in *The Shipwreck*, to attend a masquerade. Sir James Lavington, the upright member of the gentry who will prove to be Ellinor's rightful father, has been pressurized into attending the same masquerade by his wicked other daughter, Augusta: as a sign of his virtuous parental authority, and his true English moral superiority to such Continental excess, he comes dressed not mendaciously but as his true self: as Prospero.[37]

Obscure as Hanway's novel may be, Sir James Lavington provides in many ways a completely appropriate final incarnation of the late eighteenth-century Prospero. Over the course of the eighteenth century's transmission of *The Tempest*, Prospero's ambivalently royal prerogative has been used to sustain the changing versions of authority developed during the century's steady takeover by the merchant classes of the symbols of national power. Just as power relations themselves were being rewritten, so *The Tempest*, already deeply involved with them by 1700, had to be rewritten too. From sustaining Stuart patriarchy it had come to certify the enchantedness of Stratford and the cultural superiority of the English bourgeoisie, eventually being invoked to defend family life and property against the threat of Revolution. Deployed alternately as a figure for paternal jurisdiction, racial mastery and successful counter-revolution, Prospero, and by extension his creator, had been variously but securely appropriated as the defender of prosperity. Two centuries later, Miranda, Caliban and the mutineers have yet to depose him.

---

[37] Mary Ann Hanway, *Ellinor, or The World As It Is* (4 vols., London, 1798), vol. II, p. 217.

THE TEMPEST AND AFTER

INGA-STINA EWBANK

As a child, did you never hold a shell to your ear and listen ... hear the surge of your heart's blood, the murmur of the thoughts in your brain, the snapping of a thousand little worn-out fibres in the tissues of your body?[1]

This essay addresses itself to some works by three Scandinavians who in various ways wrote 'after *The Tempest*'. It also examines that play's tendency to turn, in the hands of writers and critics, into a seashell. What you hear when you hold a shell to your ear are processes of life within yourself – as, in the lines quoted above, Indra's daughter explains to the Poet in the Fingal's Cave scene of Strindberg's *A Dreamplay*. The neurobiological details of her image may be somewhat dubious, but the bearing of the image itself is clear. In its context it becomes particularly self-reflexive, for in the cave, which is shaped both like a shell and an ear, the god listens to humans and humans listen to winds and waves, trying to find a language to define 'reality', 'poetry', 'dreams'.

It so happens that *A Dreamplay* is one of many works, from many cultures and languages, in which *The Tempest* is present, not necessarily as a verbally identifiable 'source' or 'influence' but as a shell which the writer has held to his or her ear. That peculiar quality of *The Tempest* which Anne Barton identifies, in her Introduction to the New Penguin edition of the play, as 'secretive', depending 'upon the suppressed and the unspoken', this quality also, as she puts it, 'compels a peculiarly creative response'.[2] Of course all literary and dramatic criticism is to a greater or lesser extent both subjective and creative, but *The Tempest* presents a gap between text and meaning which gives the play a particularly shell-like nature: so much of what you hear in it – be it Shakespeare's autobiography or a colonial discourse – is yourself.

This essay, then, is not so much a retrospect of *Tempest* criticism as a discussion of 'after': a word which, in its deceptive simplicity, rates eight columns in the OED. As the terms of the definitions of 'after' slide from place to purpose (*adv.* & *prep.* 4: 'following with intent to overtake, pursuing, in pursuit of'), to time, to causality (9: 'of temporal and logical sequence') and to generativeness (14: 'after the manner of; in imitation of; like'), so the movement of the word becomes a kind of paradigm of literary history and criticism. To engage in either, after (*sic*) all, is to attempt a process of defining 'after', even if that process does not lead to as self-conscious or systematic a definition as T. S. Eliot's 'tradition' or Harold Bloom's 'anxiety of influence'. To attempt a survey of everything written 'after' *The Tempest* would be like trying to construct a Key to all (Shakespearian) Mythologies. I cannot pretend that my few

---

[1] August Strindberg, *Samlade Skrifter*, ed. John Landqvist, 55 vols. (Stockholm, 1912–20) (hereafter referred to as *SS*): vol. 36 (1916), p. 297. In this paper, translations are my own, unless otherwise indicated.

[2] *The Tempest*, ed. Anne Righter (Barton), New Penguin Shakespeare (Harmondsworth, 1968), p. 19.

examples have been chosen only for their intrinsic interest; my subtext is a plea for openness in the reading of the play – in an after-age when the concern for seeing plays as subject to historical contingencies (in itself laudable) has tended to veer towards over-interpretation and closed readings ('following with an intention to overtake'). Implicitly, too, there is a plea for remembering that 'after' can extend into space as well as time: that Shakespeare has been a creative force outside insular culture and involved in making not only English men of letters[3] but also lettered men and women of other tongues and cultures. It would seem that, if your own native literature is that much less rich, you are that much more likely to turn to Shakespeare, albeit read in translation, and to hear in his works the voice of the essential poet. And if your own country has not, in recent centuries, wielded imperial power, you are that much less likely to hear him through the reverberations of a post-colonial conscience.

At the same time, my chosen examples are not without connection with English critical tradition, if only through coincidences in time. In November 1957, as volume 11 of *Shakespeare Survey* was going to press, containing Philip Edwards's retrospective article, 'Shakespeare's Romances: 1900–1957', in which he identifies approaches through myth, symbol and allegory as typical of then current readings of *The Tempest*, the Danish author Isak Dinesen was seeing John Gielgud in Peter Brook's production of *The Tempest* at the Shakespeare Memorial Theatre. She went away and wrote a story, 'Tempests', in which Shakespeare's play itself serves as myth, symbol and allegory.[4] The year 1906 saw the first publication in book form of Lytton Strachey's notorious essay on 'Shakespeare's Final Period', in which the image of a bored and disgusted bard replaces the prevailing one, of the author of *The Tempest* as serenely 'On the Heights', while the autobiographical interpretation as such, perhaps best epitomized by Morton Luce's introduction to his Arden edition (1901), remains unquestioned.[5] In the same year Henrik Ibsen died, and August Strindberg began to use Shakespeare as a stick to beat him with. In the first volume of *A Blue Book* (begun in 1906, published in 1907) Strindberg composed for Ibsen the cruel epitaph of 'The man who rests here hated flowers, children and music'; and he was soon to amplify this by contrasting, in his 1909 essay on *The Tempest*, Shakespeare's play with Ibsen's 'Dramatic Epilogue' *When We Dead Awaken*:

[*The Tempest*] ends with a general amnesty, all are given grace and forgiveness ... Prospero (Shakespeare) forgives even Caliban ... It cannot be denied that Shakespeare's farewell to humanity is more beautiful than that of the Nora Man who, in his last play, sticks his tongue out at his audience ...[6]

---

[3] See Terence Hawkes's witty essay, 'Swisser-Swatter: Making a Man of English Letters', in John Drakakis, ed., *Alternative Shakespeares* (London, 1985), pp. 26–46.

[4] Philip Edwards's essay appeared in *Shakespeare Survey* 11 (Cambridge, 1958), 1–18. John Gielgud, in *An Actor and his Time* (London 1979; Penguin edition 1981), p. 105, apparently misremembers the order of events; he writes that Isak Dinesen (pseudonym for Baroness Karen Blixen) 'adored the play but had never seen it performed, and one of the stories in her new collection *Anecdotes of Destiny* had been inspired by reading it'. *Anecdotes of Destiny* was published, in Danish and English, only in 1958; and the *Notater om Karen Blixen* by her companion/secretary Clara Svendsen (Copenhagen, 1974) makes no reference to the story existing before the Stratford visit. It seems to have been written in the winter of 1957–8. See also Judith Thurman, *Isak Dinesen: The Life of a Storyteller* (New York, 1982), pp. 410–16.

[5] Lytton Strachey's essay, 'Shakespeare's Final Period', *Independent Review*, III (1904), was reprinted in his *Books and Characters* (London, 1906).

[6] August Strindberg, *Shakespeares Macbeth, Othello, Romeo och Julia, Stormen, Kung Lear, Henrik VIII, En Midsommarnattsdröm* (Stockholm, 1909), pp. 41–2. These essays formed the fourth of Strindberg's *Open Letters to the Intimate Theatre*, although, according to Landqvist (*SS*, vol. 50, notes), they did not actually go to the company. The only complete English translation of the *Open Letters*, by Walter Johnson (Seattle and London, n.d.), tones this passage (and others) down: 'the Nora Man', e.g., becomes just 'Ibsen' (p. 202).

1906 was also the year in which *A Dreamplay*, written in 1900, was first staged. Out of this strange medley of coincidences – and I emphasize that they are timely but not necessarily causal – I wish to disentangle some of the effects of listening to *The Tempest* as to a seashell.

August Strindberg is of course an extreme example of someone hearing himself in *The Tempest*. His essay on the play builds on the assumption that Prospero is identical with Shakespeare and that the play is 'the poet's last confession, vision of life, farewell, thanks and prayer'.[7] But the poetic career he describes sounds strikingly like his own, and his comments on 'Our revels now are ended' become unashamedly personal:

This is indeed how it is when you are beginning to grow old; if then you turn around and look at the things you have experienced, it all looks so terrible that you 'hardly think it is real', and even the best things, which did have a certain reality, gradually dissolve, like smoke. Is it strange then if you begin to doubt the reality of reality?[8]

Strindberg's appropriation of material was always blatant and self-confessed,[9] and so was his blurring of dividing lines: between different kinds of source material, different genres, different modes of discourse. One such line which he persistently blurs is that between 'creative' and 'critical' writing: his own critical essays move as a matter of course between, on the one hand, highly specific practical criticism and, on the other, interpretative statements which are so evocative as to become fiction. So, for example, in the essay in volume I of *A Blue Book* entitled 'The Self-Sacrifice of the Writer', Shakespeare becomes the type of the artist to whom art and life are one:

What would Shakespeare have been like as a poet if he had lived like a good boy, carried on in his father's respectable trade and written in his spare time, about his narrow conditions? Though we don't know much about the great Briton, we can tell from his writings what a stormy life he must have led; there is scarcely anything nasty and sordid which he hasn't lived through, not a passion which he hasn't known; hatred and love, revenge and lust, murder and fire – all these he seems to have experienced, as a poet. And a real poet should, ought to, must sacrifice his person to his poetry. I would therefore like to imagine a Shakespeare monument depicting Hercules lighting his own funeral pyre on Mount Oeta, offering his rich life as a self-sacrifice to humanity![10]

This notion of authorship as 'self-sacrifice' is central to Strindberg's poetics. There is a lexical difficulty in translating Strindberg's noun, as the Swedish *självoffring* holds in suspension the notions both of an offering forth of the self in a triumphant, even exhibitionist, sense and of the immolation of the self as a sacrificial victim. But clearly, when Strindberg, in 1909, writes that 'the calling of the writer is a self-sacrifice',[11] he is describing the total use of his own personality as raw material for his art. By itself the sentence sounds deceptively like T. S. Eliot's *dictum* that 'the progress of an artist is a continual self-sacrifice'; but Eliot, in 1919, preaching the impersonality of art, continues his sentence by defining self-sacrifice as 'a continual extinction of personality'.[12] This is not the place to explore the connection between this creed and later, more formalist, approaches to Shakespeare. The point is that, in the first decade of this century, Strindberg's preconceptions would find confirmation in such Shakespeare criticism as he read.[13]

---

[7] *Shakespeares Macbeth*, p. 42.

[8] *Shakespeares Macbeth*, p. 42–3.

[9] He makes the point repeatedly in his autobiographical writings; and in *To Damascus III* (1901) his *alter ego*, the Unknown, proudly claims 'What I have read has become mine, because I smashed it, like glass, smelted it down and blew new glass with it, into new shapes' (*SS*, vol. 29, p. 322).

[10] *SS*, vol. 46, p. 72.

[11] Postscript to the 1909 edition of his autobiography, *Son of a Servant* (*SS*, vol. 18, p. 460).

[12] T. S. Eliot, 'Tradition and the Individual Talent' (1919), in *Selected Essays* (London, 1932; new ed. New York, 1950), p. 7.

[13] Twice in his life-time Strindberg had to sell all his books; his third library (books acquired between 1892

When the Danish critic Georg Brandes wrote his monumental study of Shakespeare, which Strindberg read and which was influential well beyond the borders of Scandinavia, he had no doubt that he was writing about the man himself:

The William Shakespeare who was born at Stratford-on-Avon in the reign of Queen Elizabeth, who lived and wrote in London in her reign and that of James, who ascended into heaven in his comedies and descended into hell in his tragedies, and died at the age of fifty-two in his native town, rises a wonderful personality in grand and distinct outlines, with all the vivid colouring of life from the pages of his books, before the eyes of all who read them with an open, receptive mind, with sanity of judgment and simple susceptibility to the power of genius.[14]

The creed enunciated in this peroration informs the study as a whole and most explicitly the chapters on *The Tempest*. Brandes quotes with approval Richard Garnett's reading of the play in the critical introduction to the Irving Edition: 'Prospero is not Shakespeare, but the play is in a certain measure autobiographical'; and the qualifying 'certain measure' is soon forgotten in a wholesale identification of Shakespeare as man and creator with Prospero:

He sees into the soul of mankind with as sure an eye as Shakespeare himself, and plays the part of Providence to his surroundings as incontestably as did the poet to the beings of his own creation ...
Like Prospero, [Shakespeare] had sacrificed his position to his art, and, like him, he had dwelt upon an enchanted island in the ocean of life.[15]

Even in 1906–7 there were sceptics embarrassed by this kind of detailed analogy. Perhaps the most interesting among them is Henry James who confesses to a 'bewildered credulity' before Dr Brandes's reading and who backs away from it in a series of labyrinthine paragraphs typical of his late style, to emerge at the end with an amazingly straightforward statement that 'we shall never touch the Man *directly* in the Artist'.[16]

That James's Shakespeare was not Strindberg's is, of course, not merely a matter of different artistic temperaments. Many cultural layers separate Strindberg's reception and understanding of Shakespeare from James's. They involve the transmission of Shakespeare as a Romantic and post-Romantic, North-European cultural phenomenon: through Goethe and Schiller, through the Schlegel–Tieck translation, through the Scandinavian poet-dramatists of the early nineteenth century (notably Oehlenschläger), and through mid-nineteenth-century Swedish translations which themselves owed much to the German. The significance of this cannot be dismissed with a condescending reference to 'unser Shakespeare'; Brandes is deadly serious when he states that Schlegel's Shakespeare relates to the original 'with the similarity which the perfect has to the perfect'. What this means, he goes on to say,

is in reality no less than that it is as if in the middle of the eighteenth century – at the side of Goethe and Schiller – Shakespeare too had been born in Germany. He was born in 1564 in England; he was re-born in 1767 in his German translator. In 1597 *Romeo and Juliet* was published in London; in 1797

---

and his death in 1912), now at the Strindberg Museum in Stockholm, contains a number of works on Shakespeare in Swedish, German and English, many of them annotated by him. Apart from an 1854 edition of Hazlitt's *Characters of Shakespeare's Plays*, there were, e.g., Charles Knight's *Biography* (London, 1851); B. Wendell's *William Shakespeare, A Study in Elizabethan Literature* (London, 1894); G. G. Gervinus, *Shakespeare*, 4 vols. (Leipzig, 1849–50); H. Ulrici, *Über Shakespeare's dramatische Kunst* (Halle, 1839); and K. Bleibtreu, *Der wahre Shakespeare* (Munich and Leipzig, 1907). For a catalogue, see Hans Lindström's invaluable *Strindberg och böckerna* (Stockholm, 1977).

[14] Georg Brandes, *William Shakespeare* (London, 1898), p. 690. Published originally in Danish (Copenhagen, 1895–6), the work was translated partly by William Archer and partly by Diana White, both assisted by Mary Morison; but Brandes himself revised the proofs of the whole work.

[15] Brandes, p. 662 (citing Garnett) and pp. 666–8.

[16] Introduction to vol. 16 of the Renaissance Edition of *The Complete Works of William Shakespeare*, ed. Sidney Lee (London 1907); reprinted in Morris Shapira, ed., *Henry James: Selected Literary Criticism* (Harmondsworth, 1968), pp. 343–57.

this tragedy was published in Berlin as a newly-born work.[17]

Within these assumptions – however remote they may seem to us – it is the author, rather than the words, of the text that is being transmitted: the poet, not the poetry, of *The Tempest*. Strindberg could – and sometimes did – read Shakespeare in the original. When he died in 1912, his library contained two complete editions of Shakespeare in English as well as eight volumes of *The Temple Shakespeare*, including *The Tempest*.[18] His own handling of language – his bold innovations in vocabulary and experiments with syntax, and his richly associative imagery – was a-typically Swedish and strangely Shakespearian. But most of his encounters with Shakespeare texts were through the translations by Karl August Hagberg which he admired (justifiably so, as translations go) and sometimes had the audacity to find superior to the original.[19] Though a dramatist, and keenly interested in contemporary developments in staging – he frequently refers to the work of Jocza Savits at the Munich Shakespearebühne, and the designs of Gordon Craig[20] – he rarely went to the theatre, in Sweden or abroad, and so had *seen* little Shakespeare.

And yet, from beyond what may seem to us insuperable barriers, 'Shakespeare' was to Strindberg not a monolithic 'influence' but, throughout forty or so years, an ever-varying combination of stimuli, some of which seem contradictory, and some surprisingly modern. His autobiographical writings and letters tell us of continuing and evolving responses, of specific points of impact and of periods of sustained study.[21] One of the latter was in the late 1890s, out of which – he was later to explain – he wrote his own history plays 'after my teacher Shakespeare'.[22] The years of the composition of his *Blue Book* (1906–8), with its essay on Shakespeare as the self-sacrificing and self-exhibiting artist, were also the years that, thanks to the efforts of the young actor-manager August Falck, saw the establishment of the Intimate Theatre in Stockholm as a realization of Strindberg's dream of a theatre for his own plays. By the time he came to write his *Open Letters to the Intimate Theatre*, Shakespeare was utterly woven into his thinking about drama and theatre, so that it seemed to him natural to celebrate the first anniversary of the opening of the theatre, in 1908, with a pamphlet on *Hamlet*; and altogether in the five *Letters* essays on single Shakespeare plays (of which the *Tempest* is one), and on aspects of Shakespeare's art, rub shoulders with advice to the young actors in Falck's company. His approach is pluralist: he can write a splendidly objective study of the 'polyphonous' structure of *A Midsummer Night's Dream*, and he can describe the way in which Act 4 of *Hamlet* introduces 'new motifs', reversing old ones 'in a contrapuntal fashion';[23] but he can also totally appropriate Shakespeare the man *and* the artist.

Thus, for example, an essay on 'Old Age: Beautiful and Ugly', published both in *A Blue Book* and as part of the second *Open Letter*, turns on Prospero's warning to Ferdinand not to

[17] Georg Brandes, *Hovedstrømninger i det nittende Aarhundredes Litteratur*, 6 vols. (Copenhagen, 1872–1890): vol. 2 (new ed., Copenhagen, 1966), pp. 56–7.

[18] See Lindström, p. 144.

[19] For example, he thinks the song in *Henry VIII*, 3.1.3–14, 'Orpheus with his lute', sounds like 'dry narrative prose' in the original and is improved by the vocabulary of Hagberg's translation. Similarly, in Iago's lines about 'good wine' (*Othello*, 2.3.302 ff.) he finds 'exclaim' to be 'abstract and colourless' and much surpassed by Hagberg's '*trät*' (literally 'quarrel') – incidentally, a common reaction, from inside a Germanic language, to the Latin elements of English. Both examples are from *Shakespeares Macbeth*, p. 78.

[20] Particularly in his discussions and correspondence with August Falck over the Intimate Theatre. See Falck, *Fem år med Strindberg* (Stockholm, 1935).

[21] In 1908 he was actually planning to write a book on Shakespeare (see letter to Karl Börjesson of 10 November 1908).

[22] *Ur några förord till de historiska dramerna* (Stockholm, 1909), pp. 7–8. (This 'Preface' to his own history plays is part of Strindberg's fifth *Open Letter*.)

[23] *Shakespeares Macbeth*, p. 67; *Hamlet: Ett Minnesblad* (Stockholm, 1908), *passim*.

'break [Miranda's] virgin-knot before / All sanctimonious ceremonies may / With full and holy rite be minist'red'.[24] Strindberg reads this as an expression of the poet's wish to hand on his own sexual experience, 'won dearly but too late', and so to 'teach his children to win the happiness he himself has wasted' – a sign, that is, of the 'beautiful' and generous wisdom of Shakespeare's old age. Here, as when singling out 'King Lear's Wife' as the subject of an essay, he is asking much the same questions as far more recent psychoanalytical critics have done, though coming up with more obviously self-echoing answers. Like Coppélia Kahn he sees the absent mother as a sign of 'male anxiety'.[25] But in the end, of course, it is his own anxiety that he sees:

For good and ill, with her root in dung and her flower in the light, the most beautiful grafted onto the most ugly, the masterpiece of creation but utterly spoiled, loving when she hates and hating when she loves, thus Shakespeare depicts woman, the sphinx, whose riddle cannot be solved, since it is unsolvable or does not exist![26]

If then Strindberg listens to *The Tempest* as to a seashell, what he hears is still not a simple self-echo. Although he hears in the text his own anxieties and his own wish-fulfilments, and although he says that he does not want to see the play performed, only 'to read it and make my own scenery out of mere air and light', he also has an awareness of the play in the theatre which anticipates modern theories of reception. His essay on *The Tempest* begins:

It seems to me sometimes as if a work of poetry or fiction does not have a fully independent life of its own but needs, for its existence, to be part of an energy circuit, or has to draw its power from a dynamo of minds or an accumulator of sympathies.[27]

The Tempest, he goes on to say, is particularly dependent on such a power circuit. But he then blurs his general insight into the way an audience is actively involved in the production of meaning, by turning it into a specific onslaught on what he sees as the Ibsen tradition in the theatre. The reason why a recent Swedish production of *The Tempest* was so successful was that

it cleared the air, dispersed the mists from the Dovre mountains and melted the ice. It resurrected what is good in mankind, buried as it was under Norwegian avalanches and French glaciers; it dared to use the words 'the golden age', and it snapped back at the Nora Man: 'No marrying 'mong his subjects? – None, man; all idle; whores and knaves.'[28]

Miranda is the antitype to 'the shrews of the 1880s'; her tears at her own 'unworthiness' and her words to Ferdinand, 'I am your wife, if you will marry me; / If not, I'll die your maid', are to an audience 'a discovery at the end of a century in which the followers of the Dovre poet had recently proclaimed the fury and the whore as being the only "true women" '.[29] It is now not a power circuit but a power game that *The Tempest* is part of, and Strindberg goes on to win the game by appropriating Shakespeare into his image of himself as a 'real poet', one to whom life and art merge in a glorious Herculean 'self-sacrifice'.

In all its cruelty, and for all its special pleading, this use of *The Tempest* to place the art of Ibsen may have been closer to the mark than Strindberg knew. At the end of his creative life Ibsen was, I believe, quite ready to see himself as an antitype of Shakespeare. I also believe that what may directly have prompted him to do so was not the plays of Shakespeare but Brandes's book on Shakespeare which, like Strindberg, he

[24] *The Tempest*, 4.1.15–17.

[25] Coppélia Kahn, 'The Absent Mother in *King Lear*', in Margaret W. Ferguson et al., eds., *Re-Writing the Renaissance* (Chicago, 1986), pp. 33–49. Cf. also Stephen Orgel's less exclusively psychoanalytic essay on 'Prospero's Wife' in the same volume, pp. 50–64.

[26] *SS*, vol. 50, p. 95. This essay appeared both in *A Blue Book* (*SS*, vol. 47, pp. 758–9) and as part of the second *Open Letter* (1908).

[27] *Shakespeares Macbeth*, p. 39.

[28] *Shakespeares Macbeth*, p. 40.

[29] *The Tempest* 3.1.83–4; *Shakespeares Macbeth*, pp. 43–4.

read – but read differently, hearing in it not his own voice but the voice of the man and author he never was.

Ibsen's career, unlike Strindberg's, was not marked by a series of evolving responses to Shakespeare. Unlike Strindberg he was never able to read the texts in English, but we can be fairly sure that he read some translations in his youth, and we know that he borrowed Shakespeare plays from the library of the Scandinavian Club in Rome in 1867. Most of his direct contacts with Shakespeare were early: he saw a number of the plays (not *The Tempest*) on his study tour to Copenhagen and Dresden in 1852, during which he also completed his own Midsummer's Night play (*Sancthansnatten*) which he later disowned. In 1855 he directed an unsuccessful production of a version of *As You Like It* at the Bergen Theatre, and the same autumn he gave a lecture to a literary society in Bergen of which, tantalizingly, only a record of the title survives: 'W. Shakespeare and his influence on Scandinavian art'.[30] Scholars have traced Shakespeare influences in his own early and historical plays (*Catiline, Lady Inger, Pretenders*),[31] but this is 'Shakespeare' very much transmuted via German and Scandinavian translations and imitations. It is also the 'Shakespeare' which epitomizes what he deliberately rejected – historical subjects, artificial conventions, verse as a medium – when in the 1870s he turned to 'the far more difficult art' of writing contemporary prose plays.[32] He may have continued to read works by and about Shakespeare, but – again unlike Strindberg – he was always reticent about his reading, unwilling to make critical pronouncements on others' works, and ready to describe himself – as in a letter to Georg Brandes in 1871 – as 'a very bad critic'. His reaction, in 1896, to Brandes's book on Shakespeare is therefore all the more striking:

I have not only read the whole of your great monumental work on Shakespeare, but I have been absorbed by it as I have hardly ever been by any other book. I feel that not only Shakespeare and his

age but also you yourself are alive and breathing in this work of yours – a work of genius.[33]

'Work' is an inadequate translation of Ibsen's virtually untranslatable word '*digtning*' which signals that he is thinking of Brandes's book as a creative work, like a poem or a novel. Indeed, two years later he was to tell Brandes how well he could understand why Brandes no longer wrote poems,

for it is after all the same poetic power that you have employed in your magnificent epos on Shakespeare, in your poem about Disraeli ... and in everything else you have written.[34]

The 'poem' (*digtet*) about Disraeli is of course a critical-biographical study, based on the same assumption – that the work is the man – as the book on Shakespeare, the purpose of which was 'to declare and prove that Shakespeare is not thirty-six plays and a few poems jumbled together and read *pêle-mêle*, but a man who felt and thought, rejoiced and suffered, brooded, dreamed and created'.[35] Ibsen would have been particularly receptive to Brandes's 'poem' about a playwright and his *corpus*, as he was in these same years labouring

---

30 These are well-known biographical facts, recorded in standard Ibsen biographies (e.g. Halvdan Koht's and Michael Meyer's) and in the excellent introductions and appendixes to *The Oxford Ibsen*, ed. J. W. McFarlane.

31 Sverre Arestad, 'Ibsen and Shakespeare: A Study in Influence', *Scandinavian Studies*, 19 (1946), 89–104, is typical of the view of Shakespeare as a crutch which the mature Ibsen threw away.

32 See Ibsen's letter to Lucie Wolf, 25 May 1883, in *Henrik Ibsens Samlede Verker*, ed. Francis Bull, Halvdan Koht, Didrik Arup Seip, 21 vols. (Oslo, 1928–57) (hereafter referred to as *SV*): vol. 17, p. 511. There have been interesting comparative studies of the last plays of Shakespeare and Ibsen: Kenneth Muir, *Last periods of Shakespeare, Racine and Ibsen* (Liverpool, 1962) and David Grene, *Reality and the Heroic Pattern: Last Plays of Ibsen, Shakespeare and Sophocles* (Chicago, 1967); but these do not examine the nexus of indirect involvements with Shakespeare which is my concern here.

33 Letter of 3 October 1896 (*SV*, vol. 18, p. 385).

34 Letter of 30 December 1898 (*SV*, vol. 18, p. 421).

35 Brandes, *William Shakespeare*, p. 689.

to make sure that his own works would not be read 'pêle-mêle', preparing a collected edition which appeared in both Norwegian and German in 1898. In the preface to the Norwegian edition he insisted that the reader should see 'my entire output as a consistent and continuing whole' and thus read his plays, in effect, as Brandes has read Shakespeare: 'not to skip anything, but to absorb the works – to read through them and to live through them, in the same order in which I wrote them'.[36] In the light of this it is not surprising that he also revived a long-abandoned idea of writing an autobiography – 'a book that will link my life and my authorship together into an illuminating whole'.[37] But by the summer of 1898 this project had been superseded by the composition of the play which was to become his last, *When We Dead Awaken*. He could read himself, and expect to be read, through the 'continuous whole' of his works; and this, it turned out, was also the only way he could write himself: not the Brandes type of 'poem' linking life and authorship together 'into an illuminating whole', but a play about an ageing artist's ambivalent relationship to both art and life. The question whether artistic creativity has to mean a sacrifice of all that we think of as a fulfilled human life – friendship, love, sex, marriage, children – was one that had haunted Ibsen from such early poems as 'On the Heights' (1859) and had come to the fore in his late plays, from *The Master Builder* (1892) onwards. His 'Dramatic Epilogue', *When We Dead Awaken*, does not solve the question but sharpens it into a tragic *impasse*. The sculptor Rubek's refusal to see Irene as anything other than a model for his art has turned her existence into a living death, and at the same time losing her has meant to Rubek the loss of his artistic vision, the death of his creative power. 'When we dead awaken', Irene says at the end of the penultimate Act, 'we see that we have never lived.' And their attempt at a mountain-top resurrection ends in the deadly avalanche. As a paradigm of the life and death of the artist, this

tortured self-questioning is the antithesis of the serene acceptance of 'awakening' which Brandes attributes to Shakespeare: 'a deep sleep, from which we awaken to life, and again, a deep sleep hereafter'.[38]

I do not know whether Ibsen knew Shakespeare's last plays at first hand, but in Brandes's 'poem' he would read of a winter's tale without snow and avalanches but with 'flowers, children and music', a tale in which a beloved woman's statue is resurrected into 'warm' life, and in which the disappearance and return of that woman are as strangely accounted (or unaccounted) for as Irene's, and yet as necessary:

It would be absurd to seek for a psychological reason for Hermione's prolonged concealment. She reappears at the end because her presence is required, as the final chord is needed in music or the completing arabesque in a drawing.[39]

Brandes sees *The Winter's Tale* as a much less engaged work than *The Tempest*, the product of an author detachedly making a pattern out of fairy-tale materials. But it is not difficult to imagine Ibsen, who himself said that *When We Dead Awaken* began as a 'basic mood',[40] being struck by Brandes's analysis of the play as a pattern of moods, in a paragraph which ends with the lines just quoted and which begins:

---

36 English translation by J. W. McFarlane in *Henrik Ibsen*, Penguin Critical Anthologies (Harmondsworth, 1970), p. 171.

37 Speech at a banquet in honour of Ibsen's seventieth birthday (Christiania, 23 March 1898); translation by McFarlane, in *Oxford Ibsen*, vol. 8, p. 352.

38 This is Brandes's paraphrase of 'We are such stuff / As dreams are made on' (which he also reads as Shakespeare's 'underlying thought'): *William Shakespeare*, p. 668. Without pressing the point of a possible verbal echo, the original Danish text which Ibsen read – '*dyb Søvn, før vi vaagner til Liv, og dyb Søvn derefter*' – has a haunting resemblance to the title of Ibsen's play, *Naar vi døde vaagner*. His original idea had been to call it *Opstandelsens dag* (The Day of Resurrection).

39 Brandes, *William Shakespeare*, p. 639.

40 Letter to his wife, 13 June 1897 (*SV*, vol. 19, p. 392).

Looked upon from a purely abstract point of view, as though it were a musical composition, the play might be considered in the light of a soul's history.

In Brandes's chapters on *The Tempest* Ibsen would read of a play that was its author's own 'soul's history'; in which Ariel is 'the emblem of Shakespeare's own genius' and his 'longing for freedom after prolonged servitude has peculiar and touching significance as a symbol of the yearning of the poet's own genius for rest'.[41] The last thing we hear at the end of *When We Dead Awaken* is Maia, Rubek's wife, triumphantly singing 'I am free! I am free!' Earth-bound and following her bear-hunter down the mountain, she is not an Ariel; and her song, here and at the end of Act 2, is a symbol, not of Rubek's 'genius' but of his confining and stultifying effect on her life. His own longing is not for 'rest'; he is much more the bored and disgusted artist of Lytton Strachey's Shakespeare essay, lamenting a wasted life in which his art has degenerated from the Resurrection statue to portrait busts of 'striking likeness' to their subjects but with animal faces underneath. This is no doubt what Strindberg referred to when he wrote of Ibsen sticking his tongue out at his audience. While this is more malicious than fair, there is clearly a world of difference between the prayers which conclude, respectively, *When We Dead Awaken* and *The Tempest*: the Nun's '*Pax vobiscum*' which seals Rubek and Irene into their own world of death, and Prospero's call for the audience's prayer which throws his fate into their lap, bridging the gap between art and life – much as Shakespeare, according to Brandes, had bridged it throughout his career.

The point then is not that *When We Dead Awaken* is in any commonly accepted sense 'influenced' by Shakespeare's last two Romances, but that the play shows peculiar signs of being written 'after' Shakespeare: that is after Ibsen had seen himself in Brandes's 'poem' as the negative of the image of the serene and fulfilled bard. His 'Epilogue' is a richer and sadder work if, as an undertone in it, we hear

'I am not Shakespeare, nor was meant to be'.

Fifty-eight years after the appearance of *When We Dead Awaken* Isak Dinesen wrote her story 'Tempests' after seeing John Gielgud as Prospero. She, too, was near the end of her creative career: 'Tempests' helped to complete her last collection of stories, *Anecdotes of Destiny* (1958). She, too, owed much to Georg Brandes, through whom she had 'discovered' Shakespeare at fifteen and developed a '*personal enthusiasm*' which was to last her all her life.[42] In her seventeen years in Africa, lived mainly in the English language, she read and discussed Shakespeare with Denys Finch Hatton and others; and as a writer of stories – almost all of which she first composed in English – she would claim an affinity with Shakespeare as the creator of the late Romances.[43] She borrowed from him the title for her second collection of stories, *Winter's Tales* (1942). But the affinity was with the art of the *text* – the self-conscious artifice; the meeting of the comic and the marvellous – not with the person.

Sadly, there seems to be no first-hand record of how Isak Dinesen responded to Peter Brook's production of *The Tempest*, or to the acting by Gielgud and the rest of the cast.[44] In the story, as we shall see shortly, her response is mainly to the verbal poetry of the play; and this may well have something to do with Gielgud's delivery. The story itself, set in the mid nineteenth century, is of an old actor and theatre director who gives up a career at the Royal Theatre in Copenhagen in order to tour the small Norwegian coastal towns with his own company, because 'he was a man of a mighty,

---

41 Brandes, *William Shakespeare*, pp. 563–4.
42 See her letter to her Aunt Bess, 19 April 1924, in Anne Born's fine translation, *Isak Dinesen, Letters from Africa 1914–1931* ((London, 1983; new ed. 1986), p. 209.
43 Robert Langbaum, in *The Gayety of Vision: A Study of Isak Dinesen's Art* (London, 1964), which seems to me still the best critical study of Isak Dinesen, makes a good deal of this affinity.
44 Clara Svendsen's *Notater* (see note 4, above) describes only the social side of the visit to Stratford.

independent character, which demanded the creation and control of his own world around him'. Naturally, then, a production of *The Tempest*, with himself as Prospero, is the realization of 'a life-old dream'. He casts as Ariel a girl, Malli, who becomes the focus of the story. She so identifies herself with her part that, when the ship in which the company is sailing is caught in a terrible snowstorm off Christiansand, she believes that this is the opening scene of the play and so, by her apparent courage, in fact saves the ship. Fêted as a heroine and engaged to be married to the son of the ship's owner, she is nearly drawn into happy domesticity and lost to the theatre, but is brought back to it by the death of the real-life Ferdinand – a sailor who had helped to keep the ship afloat – and by the consequent realization that, as an artist, she is doomed to affect other human beings as does the city of Ariel in Isaiah, 29: 1-8:

Woe to Ariel, to Ariel! ... It shall even be as when an hungry man dreameth, and, behold, he eateth; but he awaketh, and his soul is empty; or as when a thirsty man dreameth, and, behold, he drinketh; but he awaketh, and, behold, he is faint, and his soul hath appetite.[45]

She returns to Soerensen in a scene where, *via* several of Ariel's speeches, she also returns into her part, and enables him to become Prospero and speak the lines which set Ariel free:

My Ariel, chick, then to the elements
be free, and fare thou well![46]

Only, of course, for this Ariel freedom means a life-time's commitment to her artistic vocation and sacrifice of ordinary human happiness – just as this Prospero deliberately left his wife, who loved him, so that she could be re-married to 'a good man' and have a home and children.

This account leaves out all the rich, and often comical, local details of a story in which *The Tempest* has been used very selectively. We hear more of Prospero's wife than we do of Miranda, and nothing of Caliban. Isak Dinesen had written her own Utopian colonial discourse in *Out of Africa* (1937) and was soon to

publish an epilogue to it in *Shadows on the Grass* (1960; English version 1961); and clearly Shakespeare's play did not speak to her of colonialism. It gave her, as a myth, a structure in which to write about her own art: 'Tempests' is as self-reflexive as *When We Dead Awaken* and as much about the self-sacrifice of the artist. But her thematic thrust is different from Ibsen's: what she seizes from *The Tempest* is not a dramatic poet's farewell to his art but the immense power of the artist in creating and controlling a world of his own, and the power of language in this creation. Soerensen embodies the first when, with the returning and grieving Malli, he begins by casting the two of them as Lear and Cordelia, and then becomes 'fully conscious of his authority ... He once more became the man powerful above others: Prospero'.[47] Malli embodies the second. Her native gift is developed in ruthless rehearsals by Soerensen, who – unlike most directors – believes that it is wrong 'to let Ariel come swooping onto the stage on a wire':

It is the words of the poet which are to make Ariel fly. Ought we, who are our William's servants, to rely more on a bit of steel than on his heavenly stanzas![48]

And, though the story never puts Malli to the test before an audience, in Soerensen's eyes, and ears, she achieves the miraculous transformation of herself into Ariel. In the Danish text – for this was an almost unique case of Isak Dinesen writing the story first in Danish and then translating it into English: the opposite of her normal procedure – the fifth section of the story ends with two paragraphs omitted in the English version. In these Soerensen's excitement rises to a kind of apotheosis. Shakespeare, he cries out to Malli, sees the two of them and

---

45 *Anecdotes of Destiny* (Vintage Books edition, New York, 1974), pp. 147–8.
46 *Anecdotes of Destiny*, p. 145. It will be obvious that Dinesen takes some liberties with Shakespeare's text.
47 *Anecdotes of Destiny*, p. 141.
48 *Anecdotes of Destiny*, p. 77.

smiles upon them. They are no longer 'an old, bald, provincial theatre director' and a small-town girl: 'Oh no, we are his children and partake of his immortality!'[49] It would seem that Isak Dinesen, when re-thinking these paragraphs in English, found them toppling into sentimentality, in a story which otherwise holds the ridiculous and the exalted in remarkable balance; and so she left them out – thus depriving English readers of this example of Shakespeare quite literally making a Danish man and woman of letters. But she kept, later in the story, Malli's reading of 'Full fathom five' in which her change of pronouns shows her identification with far more than Ariel's part in the play:

> Those are pearls that were my eyes,
> Nothing of me that doth fade,
> But doth suffer a sea-change
> Into something rich and strange.[50]

Isak Dinesen was soon going to expound her own reading of those lines, in a talk she gave to the American Academy of Arts and Letters in 1959:

We may make use of the words – even when we are speaking about ourselves – without vainglory. Each one amongst us will feel in his heart the inherent richness and strangeness of this one thing: his life.[51]

Ariel's song works on the listener much as does the seashell in another late story of Isak Dinesen's. 'The Immortal Story' – a shell which also comes to symbolize the refusal of life with its contingencies to fit into the pre-determined patterns of fiction.[52] Like Strindberg and Ibsen she hears herself in *The Tempest*; unlike them she tells us all to go and do the same. I would not wish to set the clock of *Tempest* criticism back to 1960, even less to 1906, and thus forgo the advantages which neo-historicism and other modern readings have bestowed on us. But it is a poor reading which does not acknowledge at all the power of *The Tempest*, through barriers of time, space and even language, to evoke 'the inherent richness and strangeness' of life.

---

[49] *Skaebne-Anekdoter* (Copenhagen, 1958), p. 92 (my translation). Exactly which language Isak Dinesen imagines Soerensen and Malli as speaking is sometimes – perhaps deliberately – unclear. In the Danish text, the Shakespeare quotations are all in Danish translation; in both texts, when Soerensen makes his climactic speech (his retort to Malli's question of what the artist receives in return for his/her sacrifice of 'life'), 'he was not aware that he continued in his chosen, sacred tongue'. Judith Thurman reads 'Tempests' psychoanalytically, as the story of Dinesen's search for her lost father (*Isak Dinesen*, pp. 410–16); and no doubt there is a strong autobiographical element – part of which, however, is also a story of Dinesen's love-affair not only with Shakespeare but also with the English language.

[50] *Anecdotes of Destiny*, p. 144.

[51] Isak Dinesen, *Daguerrotypes and Other Essays* (Chicago, 1979), p. 15.

[52] *Anecdotes of Destiny*, pp. 155–231.

POETRY'S SEA-CHANGES: T. S. ELIOT AND *THE TEMPEST*

MARTIN SCOFIELD

Full fathom five thy father lies.
  Of his bones are coral made;
Those are pearls that were his eyes;
  Nothing of him that doth fade
But doth suffer a sea-change
Into something rich and strange.
Sea-nymphs hourly ring his knell:
[SPIRITS] (*within*) Ding dong.
  Hark, now I hear them.
[SPIRITS] (*within*)   Ding-dong bell.
              (*The Tempest* 1.2.400–9)

I

What part does poetry play, characteristically, in the mental life of its readers? I suggest that a primary function of poetry is simply to provide the reader with the memory of words, phrases, lines, images, impressions and occasionally complete poems. On the other hand it is sometimes seen as providing myths or structures for comprehending life as a whole: the Romantic poets, Blake, Wordsworth and Shelley have been seen in this way. That is to say their work as a whole has been seen as amounting to a comprehensive structure, a vast myth which comprises a view of life, or a 'philosophy' more or less (usually less) precisely formulable. It has also been seen, more recently, as a part of discourse in general, upon which ideological interpretation can get to work to disclose the workings of a particular society. This last rôle can, I think, be relegated to a subordinate position: something you can do with poetry after reading it and thinking about it as poetry (which is not to say that politics and ideology may not be also part of our immediate response to it as poetry). The second idea of its function (the creation of myths) is more important, but still subordinate: we may still read the individual poems long after discarding the myths (Milton and Wordsworth might be cases in point). What we get out of poetry first of all is words, phrases and images, which may preserve a life in our minds. They may also, particularly in the case of practising poets, develop a life beyond their original context, and change significance and sometimes shape in the process.

What do we remember?

    I remember
Those are pearls that were his eyes.
       (*The Waste Land*, lines 124–5)[1]

Eliot's speaker in 'A Game of Chess' voices (probably silently) the memory of a line from Ariel's song in Act 1 Scene 2 of *The Tempest*, though because there are no quotation marks he is also saying 'I remember *that* those are pearls that were his eyes.' The possibility that the line is a noun-clause means that the memory has an ambiguous status as either a quotation or the memory of a fact: it inhabits (for the speaker) equally literature and life. He voices the line inwardly, as a silent reply to utterances of despair. It is a reply that keeps him going, and keeps the poem moving, growing. It is partly

---

[1] Quotations of Eliot's poems are from *The Complete Poems and Plays*, London, 1969, repr. 1982.

an inspiration, and partly, remembering the drowned bones, it grows out of what has gone before:

> I think we are in rats' alley
> Where the dead men lost their bones. (115–16)

This first 'reply' to the lady in this scene of marital non-communication is a memory from some urban scene, or perhaps from the trenches of the Great War. But why '*lost* their bones'? In the deepest despair there is nothing there, not even the presence of a skeleton or a heap of bones which might turn into coral or, one day, as in the valley of Ezekiel come together bone to his bone and have breath come into them and stand upon their feet; or sing, as in *Ash-Wednesday*. But the thought of the bones leads on to the memory of the song from *The Tempest*, a memory that has already occurred earlier in the poem, at the session with Madame Sosostris:

> Here, said she,
> Is your card, the drowned Phoenician Sailor,
> (Those are pearls that were his eyes. Look!)
> (46–8)

The parenthesis suggests, I think, that it is the protagonist who is speaking, or thinking, here, rather than Madame Sosostris herself; though it could be the latter, whose charlatanry sometimes hits on some uncannily suggestive things: for Phlebas the Phoenician will, of course, reappear in 'Death by Water'.

But why *The Tempest*, and why this line in particular? For the metamorphoses of memory are not simply mechanical. It is not a question of a mere Hartleyan association of ideas, or a Hobbesian matter of imagination as decayed memory. Mere memory can produce only imitation or parody (as we shall see later): here something new is at work, a process in which the line, simply 'stolen' is put to work in a completely new context. Eliot's mother, Charlotte Stearns Eliot, wrote in a letter of 1905, when Eliot was sixteen: 'He has always been a student, and read extensively in English literature, especially Shakespeare. He has read prac-

tically all of Shakespeare, whom he admires, and retains much in memory.' So perhaps Ariel's song had been in Eliot's head for many years. But it needed pressure of experience for it to be used creatively. As Eliot wrote of the last quatrain of Canto IV of the *Inferno*:

[it] . . . gives an image, a feeling attached to an image, which 'came', which did not simply develop out of what precedes, but which was probably in suspension in the poet's mind until the proper combination arrived for it to add itself to. The poet's mind is in fact a receptacle for seizing and storing up numberless feelings, phrases, images, which remain there until all the particles which can unite to form a new compound are present together.[2]

Eliot's accumulated experience, around 1921–22, was of course too complex for summary. But it included among other things: an upbringing in a (to him) arid and stultifying rationalistic faith, with more than a touch of puritanism towards sexuality; the thin air of New England public duty and respectability; the reading of Laforgue and Frazer and Weston, as well as Shakespeare; an increasingly unhappy marriage; a bent towards philosophy and anthropology as well as poetry; intimations of religious mysticism and anguish; the death of his father in 1919; and 'the smell of steaks in passageways'. Only poetry could put all these together into a complex whole, which might include also 'the mermaids singing each to each' ('Prufrock') or 'An old crab with barnacles on his back' ('Rhapsody on a Windy Night'). Elements like the latter may be associated with Ariel's song (and there are doubtless others); but in the end we have to recognize an inexplicable charm and mystery in the poem which cannot be traced to their constituents in our own responses, let alone in those of a poet writing sixty or so years ago. Eliot might, for example, have responded particularly to Laforgue's assertion: 'Et j'ai des mines riches, des

---

2 *Selected Essays*, Glasgow, 1934, repr. 1966, pp. 18–19.

gisements, des mondes sous-marins qui fermentent inconnus.'[3]

II

Ariel's song is both an element in, and an emblem of, the transformations of Eliot's imagination. Firstly the emblem:

What every poet starts from is his own emotions. And when we get down to these, there is not much to choose between Shakespeare and Dante. Dante's railings, his personal spleen – sometimes thinly disguised under Old Testament prophetic denunciations – his nostalgia, his bitter regrets for past happiness – or for what seems happiness when it is past – and his brave attempts to fabricate something permanent and holy out of his animal feelings – as in the *Vita Nuova* – can all be matched out of Shakespeare. Shakespeare, too, was occupied with the struggle – which alone constitutes life for a poet – to transmute his personal and private agonies into something rich and strange, something universal and impersonal. The rage of Dante against Florence, or Pistoia, or what not, the deep surge of Shakespeare's general cynicism and disillusionment, are mere gigantic attempts to metamorphose private failures and disappointments. The great poet, in writing himself, writes his time.

('Shakespeare and the Stoicism of Seneca')[4]

Perhaps Shakespeare started 'from his emotions': but we may question whether we can be sure of this, and how we might know. Dante's 'rage' may be readily pointed to but Shakespeare's 'disillusionment', if it existed, is impossible to distinguish (except in the Sonnets, and perhaps even there) from that of his characters. But what is undoubtedly true is that this account of poetic creation can be applied to Eliot himself. The idea behind 'Tradition and the Individual Talent', despite its seemingly greater emphasis on the impersonal, is just such an idea of literary metamorphosis: 'the more perfect the artist . . . the more perfectly will the mind digest and transmute the passions which are its material'.[5]

And it is significant that Eliot turns to *The Tempest* for images in this passage; not only for

'something rich and strange' but also, perhaps by association, for the 'deep surge' of Shakespeare's cynicism and disillusionment, the tempest, like Lear's 'tempest in the mind', of tragedy, violence and revenge (the storm on Lear's heath, the ominous storm between Othello's Venice and Cyprus, or on the night of Duncan's murder) which in *The Tempest* expresses Prospero's anger but also blows the sky clear for eventual forgiveness and repentance (or partial repentance) and 'clear life ensuing'. For Prospero has to try to transcend tragedy (this at any rate seems to be Shakespeare's intention) and to learn that

> The rarer action is
> In virtue than in vengeance.   (5.1.27–8)

and Eliot to transcend the despair and disillusion of *The Waste Land* and

> to construct something
> Upon which to rejoice   (*Ash-Wednesday*, 1)

just as Eliot's Dante had to 'fabricate something permanent and holy out of his personal animal feelings'. ('Fabricate', on the other hand, is a tricky word, and the critical question here would be how far Eliot's later poetry is a genuine 'construction' and how far a mere fabrication.) Eliot uses *Tempest* images here in his prose because he had used them five years before in the personal struggle of writing *The Waste Land*, the struggle which gave him the authority to make those pronouncements about the transmutation of the personal and the private into something rich and strange.

III

To return to *The Tempest* as an element in the poem: Madame Sosostris touches off in the protagonist's mind something which will grow

---

[3] Editions de la Connaissance, II, 41, Paris, 1920–1. Quoted in the Introduction to *Derniers Vers*, eds. M. Collie and J. M. L'Heureux, Toronto, 1965, p. 7.

[4] Eliot, *Selected Essays*, p. 137.

[5] Eliot, *Selected Essays*, p. 18.

and transmute. After the man's silent reply to the woman with bad nerves ('I remember/ Those are pearls that were his eyes'):

> 'Are you alive, or not? Is there nothing in your
> head?'

(Is Alonso alive or not? Are there eyes, or pearls, or nothing, in his head?)

>   But
> O O O O that Shakespeherian Rag –
> It's so elegant
> So intelligent . . .   (126–30)

If the protagonist is still thinking about Ariel's song the words 'Rag' and 'elegant' and 'intelligent' are just the words he would use to be 'clever' and 'sophisticated' about it in a 'Twenties' or Noel Coward manner. The lines are also, as Terence Hawkes has pointed out,[6] a near-quotation from a jazz hit of 1912, 'That Shakespearian Rag' by Buck, Ruby and Stamper:

> That Shakespearian Rag,
> Most intelligent, very elegant,
> That old classical drag,
> Has the proper stuff, the line 'Lay on Macduff'

– they bring Ariel's song into counterpoint with the jazz song in a way that is exhilarating but disconcerting: the protagonist's mind is alive, mobile, responsive to the new as well as the old (or at least responsive to what he might have danced to in Boston nine years ago in 1912); but however much you like jazz you can't deny that the modern song, applied to Ariel's, dispels the latter's sadness and beauty. Such mobility of mind and quickness of response can be jarring, nearly manic. Like Hamlet's it can modulate in an instant, from the depths of anguish to a light humour, to save itself from itself, but also because it cannot bear very much reality.

But the poem's memories of *The Tempest*, and lines that chime with the music of *The Tempest*, are not dispelled. Ferdinand in Act 1 Scene 2 of the play hears Ariel's first song, 'Come unto these yellow sands,' and says:

> Where should this music be? I' th'air or
>   th'earth?
> It sounds no more; and sure it waits upon
> Some god o'th' island. Sitting on a bank,
> Weeping again the King my father's wreck,
> This music crept by me upon the waters,
> Allaying both their fury and my passion
> With its sweet air. Thence I have followed it –
> Or it had drawn me rather. But 'tis gone.
> No, it begins again.   (1.2.390–8)

In 'The Fire Sermon'

> By the waters of Leman I sat down and wept . . .
>   (182)

and soon the echoes become explicit:

> A rat crept softly through the vegetation
> Dragging its slimy belly on the bank
> While I was fishing in the dull canal
> On a winter evening round behind the gashouse
> Musing upon the king my brother's wreck
> And on the king my father's death before him.
> White bodies naked on the low damp ground
> And bones cast in a little low dry garret,
> Rattled by the rat's foot only, year to year.
>   (187–95)

The speaker, becoming Ferdinand, also changes him, and becomes, too, Prospero and even perhaps Sebastian thinking of 'the King [or Duke] my brother's wreck'. Why the change from father to brother? And why Ferdinand and *The Tempest* at all?

It would be foolish to think one could answer these questions, but certain indeterminate answers or suggestions increase the poem's resonances. The protagonist of *The Waste Land* is a disinherited prince, '*La Prince d'Aquitaine à la tour abolie*' as well as a questing knight from the Grail legends seeking a means to cure the King and restore the land; he is also a seeker after love and the player of a game of chess, both of which Ferdinand will soon become. At the same time he is Prospero intensely aware of

---

[6] Terence Hawkes, *That Shakespeherian Rag*, London, 1986, pp. 80–1. (Citing B. R. McElderry Jnr, *American Quarterly*, 9 (1957), pp. 85–6.)

the sins of the world; and a Sebastian (brother to the King of Naples) who is himself a sinner 'musing upon the king my brother's wreck' in a particularly sinister way. (The bodies could as well be murder victims, like Sebastian's intended victims, in 'White bodies naked on the low damp ground / And bones cast in a little low dry garret.') He is even, as we shall see later, an Alonso who listens to What the Thunder Said, or to what

> the thunder,
> That deep and dreadful organ-pipe,
> pronounced.   (3.3.97–8)

Into this mixture of multiple references, it is also not irrelevant to add the fact that Eliot's own father died in 1919, and that he was worried about his brother's career:[7] it is impossible to know how much weight to give such facts but 'what a poet starts from is his own emotion' and the latter idea may not seem so far-fetched if we recall the curious fact (recorded by Valerie Eliot in the first volume of Eliot's letters) that Eliot said he had his brother in mind when writing the lines in 'Preludes':[8]

> The notion of some infinitely gentle
> Infinitely suffering thing.

'Just as the one-eyed merchant, seller of currants, melts into the Phoenician Sailor, and the latter is not wholly distinct from Ferdinand Prince of Naples' (Eliot's note), so all the men are one man and melt into figures of Eliot's life. The poem is capacious, and opens up possibilities rather than closing them into a fixed set of meanings.

But the poem is not just an echo chamber: certain primary meanings are distilled, and certain directions taken. The echoes are gone, then they begin again. And the direction the poem has followed them, or they have drawn it rather, is revealed in the extraordinary turning point of line 257, this time a quotation in inverted commas as if to signal it more clearly as a memory in the protagonist's mind:

> 'This music crept by me upon the waters.'
>   (257)

It is an outstanding example of how the memory of past literature can have a decisive effect at a crucial moment of the poem, can be a turning point, or better, a hinge, between two moods, turning the poem from boredom and disgust (or boredom and horror) to a moment of glory. It is 'the intensity of the artistic process, the pressure, so to speak, under which the fusion takes place, that counts'. The moment is the end of the arid scene between the typist and the house-agent's clerk, and the turning point is reached *via* Goldsmith, who already slightly dislodges the reference from its fixity in the present:

> When lovely woman stoops to folly and
> Paces about her room again, alone,
> She smoothes her hair with automatic hand,
> And puts a record on the gramophone.
>
>   'This music crept by me upon the waters'
> And along the Strand, up Queen Victoria
>   Street.
> O city city, I can sometimes hear
> Beside a public bar in Lower Thames Street,
> The pleasant whining of a mandoline
> And a clatter and a chatter from within
> Where fishmen lounge at noon: where the
>   walls
> Of Magnus Martyr hold
> Inexplicable splendour of Ionian white and
>   gold.   (253–62)

The music is first the music of the gramophone (perhaps 'that Shakespeherian rag' as in the earlier scene between lovers?) as it drifts out of the flat window over the Thames and along the Strand; but it metamorphoses into the beautiful music of the song Ferdinand heard ('Come unto these yellow sands'), and this lifts the mood and allows the love poem to the City,

---

[7] See for example Eliot's letters to his mother of 28 May 1917 and 13 February 1921, and to his brother Henry, 2 July 1919. In the second letter to his mother he wrote 'I am always worried about his health and happiness and future.' (*The Letters of T. S. Eliot, 1892–1922*, ed. Valerie Eliot, London, 1988, pp. 182, 437 and 310.)

[8] *The Letters of T. S. Eliot*, p. 54 n.2.

[9] Eliot, *Selected Essays*, p. 19.

the music of the mandoline from those other seafarers, and the momentary vision of Magnus Martyr. Each image 'was probably in suspension in the poet's mind until the proper combination arrived for it to add itself to ... until all the particles which unite to form a new compound are present together'.[10] And the new compound constitutes a metamorphosis of experience.

IV

But the metamorphosis of past literature and past experience into a new form can sometimes fail of realization. This is what happens in the lyric discarded from *The Waste Land*, 'Dirge', 'probably written in 1921' (according to Valerie Eliot) and marked with a double query and the word 'doubtful' by Pound. Here *The Tempest* is evoked in a parodic, satirical way reminiscent of the allusions in *Poems 1920*, but without the wit and sardonic polish of that volume, and without the extent of fusion achieved there. Eliot's well-known remarks about imitation in his essay on Massinger are relevant here:

Immature poets imitate; mature poets steal; bad poets deface what they take, and good poets make it into something better, or at least something different. The good poet welds his theft into a whole of feeling which is unique, utterly different from that from which it was torn; the bad poet throws it into something that has no cohesion.[11]

By these criteria 'Dirge' is certainly 'immature', bad parodic imitation rather than clean theft (one might note that no line is actually quoted from Ariel's song, unlike in the finished *Waste Land*); and it would have had no cohesion with the rest of the poem. It remains simply a distasteful aberration which was judiciously discarded:

> Full fathom five your Bleistein lies
> Under the flatfish and the squids.
> Graves' Disease in dead jew's eyes!
> When the crabs have eat the lids.

> Lower than the wharf rats dive
> Though he suffer a sea-change
> Still expensive rich and strange
> That is lace that was his nose
> See upon his back he lies
> (Bones peep through the ragged toes)
> With a stare of dull surprise
> Flood tide and ebb tide
> Roll him gently side to side
> See the lips unfold unfold
> From the teeth, gold in gold
> Lobsters hourly deep close watch
> Hark! Now I hear them
> scratch scratch scratch.[12]

What seems to have happened here is that the memory of Ariel's song, which is generally a positive and redemptive note in the poem, is here taken over by those critical and essentially dissolvent elements in Eliot's imagination, the elements that produced 'Burbank with a Baedeker, Bleistein with a Cigar'. The unpleasant anti-Semitism of that poem ('The rats are underneath the piles. / The Jew is underneath the lot') is intensified and made more morbid. And as often happens in *The Waste Land*, an allusion to traditional beauty is soured by parody. One feels that the poet's imagination is poised so precariously and yet finely between disgust and the awareness of beauty that any image could be swayed in either direction. It is a remarkable example of how swift and dynamic Eliot's development was between 1919 and 1922, when fragments of verse of such sharply differing tone and quality were being produced side by side, and when the metamorphosis of past literature could take such violently different shapes from moment to moment.

For what finally emerged as a kind of dirge in the finished *Waste Land*, recalled from 'Dans le Restaurant' of 1917, was 'Death by Water', where the drowning of Phlebas the Phoenician,

---

10 Eliot, *Selected Essays*, p. 206.
11 *The Waste Land: A Facsimile and Transcript for the Original Drafts including the Annotations of Ezra Pound*, ed. Valerie Eliot, London, 1980, p. 121.

though it has no direct verbal echoes of *The Tempest*, has something closer to the quiet lyric mood of Ariel's song. The ghastly crabs and the grotesque bones of 'Dirge' have been replaced by the only slightly sinister (and even potentially cleansing) image 'A current under sea / Picked his bones in whispers', and the rising and falling of the bones have an altogether more tranquil feeling than the mocking 'Roll him gently side to side'. And the 'dead jew' of 'Dirge' (with the insulting lower case 'j') has been given full equality and humanity in the address 'Gentile or Jew / O you who turn the wheel and look to windward'. The sea-changes of the poet's imagination have worked through to a broader and saner vision.[12] What the passage does not have, however, is any suggestion of metamorphosis or transfiguration of Phlebas himself. Ferdinand has become Phlebas, but in becoming him he has lost the hope of transfiguration or resurrection. If there is sea-change in the process of poetic composition in *The Waste Land* there is no final sea-change in the spiritual state of the protagonist.

But there is a further fusion of 'sources' and inspirations. Phlebas the Phoenician is not totally remote from *The Tempest* in another way, when we remember that Alonso and Ferdinand were returning from Carthage to Naples after the marriage of Claribel to the King of Tunis ('This Tunis, sir, was Carthage', as Gonzalo assures Antonio and Sebastian). Colin Still, in his book *'The Tempest': Shakespeare's Mystery Play*,[13] which Eliot found interesting and which was published in 1921, suggested that this voyage echoed Aeneas's voyage from Carthage to Naples (or literally Cumae) and added to the accumulation of suggestions which related the play to the pattern of eleusinian initiation ceremonies (for at Cumae Aeneas descends into the underworld). The protagonist of *The Waste Land* also comes to Carthage (line 307 – though of course mainly *via* St Augustine), and descends into a kind of underworld of 'bats with baby faces in the

violet light' (lines 377–84). He is a kind of quester, and a candidate for initiation who listens to what the thunder says. But his initiation is a failed one: his replies to the thunder suggest only his past failure; and unlike Aeneas he receives no guidance or revelation from a goddess. In a cancelled passage of 'The Fire Sermon' the image of divine revelation is undercut by being compared to its modern alternative, the worship of the film star:

> To Aeneas, in an unfamiliar place,
> Appeared his mother, with an altered face,
> He knew the goddess by her smooth celestial
>   pace.
> So the close rabble in the cinema
> Identify a goddess or a star.[14]

V

At the end of *The Waste Land* the protagonist listens to the voice of the thunder, as Alonso does:

>   O, it is monstrous, monstrous!
> Methought the billows spoke and told me of it,
> The winds did sing it to me, and the thunder,
> That deep and dreadful organ-pipe, pronounced
> The name of Prosper. It did bass my trespass.
>
>   (3.3.95–9)

The Waste Land quester also hears his trespasses implied in the commands of the thunder; the failure to give, sympathize and control. But there is no note of final forgiveness and reconciliation at the end of *The Waste Land*: these things must be striven for in later poems. There are 'aethereal rumours' which though they revive 'a broken Coriolanus' may also recall *The Tempest* and Ferdinand ('Where should this

---

[12] For a discussion of these passages in relation to Eliot's anti-Semitism see Christopher Ricks, *T. S. Eliot and Prejudice*, London, 1988, pp. 38–40 and 72–3.

[13] Colin Still, *'The Tempest': Shakespeare's Mystery Play*, London, 1921, pp. 20ff. Eliot refers to the book in his Introduction to Wilson Knight's *The Wheel of Fire* (Oxford, 1930), p. xx.

[14] *The Waste Land: A Facsimile*, p. 29.

music be? I'th'air or th'earth?'). But 'The awful daring of a moment's surrender / Which an age of prudence can never retract' is followed by no sign of the possibility of redemption or atonement, unlike Prospero's initial surrender of his power in Milan, which now has the opportunity to be redeemed. Ferdinand in *The Tempest* marries, and plays a game of chess which images a harmonious conflict, and friendly opposition, unlike the desperate 'game of chess' in *The Waste Land* with its echoes of Middleton and seduction. In the last paragraph of the poem the quester still sits upon the shore fishing; he is still *'Le Prince d'Aquitaine à la tour abolie'*. 'Shall I at least set my lands in order' might recall Prospero returning to Milan; but the poem's protagonist is finally Hieronymo rather than Prospero or Ferdinand. *Pace* Grover Smith, he can expect little 'triumph' and as yet neither 'the joy of Ferdinand' nor 'the liberation of Prospero'.[15]

VI

In Eliot's later poems *The Tempest* largely disappears as a source of images, to be replaced by other of Shakespeare's late plays: *Pericles*, of course, in 'Marina' and, probably, *The Winter's Tale* in *The Hollow Men*. 'Marina' springs from the recognition scene in *Pericles* but also retains something of *The Tempest* in the mention of 'islands', alongside the predominant mood of hope, 'the new ships'.

> What seas what shores what granite islands
> towards my timbers.

The feeling of Eliot's

> ... let me
> Resign my life for this life, my speech for that
> unspoken,

owes as much to Prospero as to Pericles, who, although he gives the throne of Tyre to his daughter and son-in-law, has a life reunited with Thaisa ahead of him. And

> The awakened, lips parted, the hope, the new
> ships

recalls Miranda's wonder at this 'brave new world', Ferdinand's wonder at 'admired Miranda' and the ship 'in all her trim' which will take Prospero, Miranda and Ferdinand back to Milan. But the fact that the speaker of the poem is a Pericles, a father speaking to his daughter, rather than a Ferdinand as in *The Waste Land* is a measure of how far Eliot's poetic sensibility had moved between 1922 and 1930: instead of the (seemingly) bereaved son, and the aspirant to married love, we have the father who has suffered from 'those who sharpen the tooth of the dog' and 'those who suffer the ecstasy of the animals' but has now been freed of them. It is the difference between a beleaguered and despairing youth (one of the elements, among many others, of *The Waste Land*) and an awakening to a calm and experienced maturity.

In *The Hollow Men* the repeated collocation of eyes and stars, and the metamorphosis of eyes into a star, must surely recall Leontes. The hollow men are

> Sightless, unless
> The eyes reappear
> As the perpetual star
> Multifoliate rose
> Of death's twilight kingdom

Leontes in Act 5 laments he did not follow Paulina's counsel:

> Then even now
> I might have looked upon my queen's full eyes
> *(The Winter's Tale* 5.1.52–3)

Paulina replies that should Leontes marry another wife she would, were she the ghost of Hermione,

---

15 Grover Smith, *T. S. Eliot's Poetry and Plays*, Chicago, 1961, p. 98. ('But the very act of recognition, the deliberate acknowledgement of humility points towards ultimate triumph, if not for society, nevertheless for himself. He can expect, if not the joy of Ferdinand, then at any rate the liberation of Prospero.')

                    bid you mark
Her eye, and tell me for what dull part in't
You chose her ...   (5.1.63–5)

And Leontes:

                    Stars, stars,
And all eyes else, dead coals! Fear thou no
     wife.
I'll have no wife, Paulina.   (5.1.67–8)

It is perhaps not quite a transfiguration of eyes into stars as in *The Hollow Men*, but Hermione's eyes are like stars in contrast to those of others, and may have suggested the connection to Eliot. In 'Marina', too, the glimpse of a new face and intimation of a new feeling is 'more distant than stars and nearer than the eye' – something infinitely distant and as if divine, and at the same time indivisibly close, intimate and human.

Beyond any mere verbal echoes, there is in Eliot's later poems (from 1925) a general preoccupation with the transfiguration or metamorphosis of experience in the light of divinity.

                    See, now they vanish,
The faces and the places, with the self which, as
     it could, loved them,
To become renewed, transfigured, in another
     pattern.   ('Little Gidding' III)

His last two plays, though hardly successful, are concerned with similar matters to Shakespeare's: recognition (the rediscovery of parents and children), reconciliation, forgiveness and the discovery of self-identity. In the later poetry there is a diminution of emphasis on the vivid surface of place and character, and a movement inward toward more impersonal and 'abstract' realities. In an unpublished lecture on 'The Development of Shakespeare's Verse' given at the University of Edinburgh in 1937,[16] Eliot spoke of the characterization in Shakespeare's last plays. He argued that we arrive at a sense of the characters through a sense of the play as a whole and not vice versa; and that it is pointless to call Miranda or Perdita insipid in comparison to Juliet, because the judgement employs a wholly irrelevant standard. Some emotions have been purified away, so that others, ordinarily invisible, may be made apparent. And in his essay on John Ford he writes: 'we can hardly read the later plays attentively without admitting that the father-and-daughter theme was one of very deep symbolic value to him in his last productive years: Perdita, Marina and Miranda share some beauty of which his earlier heroines do not possess the secret'.[17] Now our reaction to the above pronouncements may be something like: 'But what emotions, and what kind of beauty?' Eliot does not elaborate, and many of us are left with our difficulties with Shakespeare's last plays, and perhaps too with Eliot's later works. Eliot may be justified in his claim that it was right and inevitable that Shakespeare in his last plays should proceed into regions into which the audience cannot follow him and Eliot may have been tempted to claim similar rights for himself. But such a claim makes the ordinary processes of criticism difficult. For most of us, I would guess, the 'sea-change / Into something rich and strange' stands as a rich metaphor for the transmutation of life into art. Whether it can stand for something like the transcendence at which Eliot hints, is another question.

---

[16] The typescript of the lecture is part of The John Hayward Collection in the library of King's College, Cambridge.

[17] Eliot, *Selected Essays*, pp. 194–5.

THE NEW FUNCTION OF LANGUAGE IN SHAKESPEARE'S *PERICLES*: OATH VERSUS 'HOLY WORD'

ELENA GLAZOV-CORRIGAN

Pericles occupies a conspicuous position in the Shakespearian *corpus*. The play marks its author's departure from the tragic genre in its plot, its characterization, and the sheer time span encompassed. More importantly, however, *Pericles* departs from the mode of tragedy in its re-examination of the power of language, for when facing the starkness of his misfortune, Pericles refuses to speak and, thus, suppresses a mode of language which has nourished a great number of the preceding plays. When the king finally speaks, his language is no longer that of the tragic character; it is a language of amazement, surprise and celebration. Thus, the play turns upon Pericles' resumption of speech – an action which bears a significance beyond the immediacy of the plot. The king's speech is an affirmation of language in a much wider context, a celebration of its ability to break through the tragic vision. The question which we ask ourselves here, therefore, is most pertinent: is there a new trust in language, or rather a new vision of language's potential to be found in this first of the romances? We shall argue that *Pericles* not only employs a new pattern of interchange between its characters, but that it isolates a generative principle which lies at the heart of this newly found linguistic mode.

The purpose of this article, therefore, is, first, to appraise the importance Shakespeare attaches to the power of the word; second, to assess both the force and the significance of Marina's confrontation with the power of the oath; and

third, to indicate a new resurgent pattern of language developed in the play, namely, her power of persuasion. Consequently, we shall isolate an approach to the power of words which contrasts in a striking manner with that developed in the Shakespearian tragedies.

The troublesome question of authorship does not vitiate our argument. Most thematic analyses of *Pericles*, such as those of Knight,[1] Peterson,[2] Felperin,[3] or even Hoeniger,[4] are com-

---

[1] G. Wilson Knight, in a discussion of textual problems, observes: 'And, yet, as against these suspicions, we are forced to recognize that everything is organic in story-value.' See *The Crown of Life: Essays in Interpretation of Shakespeare's Final Plays* (London: Methuen, 1961), p. 32.

[2] Similarly, Douglas Peterson treats the play as a whole. See *Time, Tide and Tempest: A Study of Shakespeare's Romances* (San Marino, California: Huntington Library, 1973), pp. 71–107.

[3] Howard Felperin chooses to accept the inconsistency in order to examine the message of the play as a whole: 'Given that the play is consistent in detail, what are we to make of a self-consistency so strange and archaic?' See *Shakespearean Romance* (Princeton: Princeton University Press, 1972), p. 144.

[4] Hoeniger, who initially proposed the authorship of John Day for the first two acts, found it possible even then to examine the play as a unified work. See Hoeniger, in the Introduction to the Arden edition of *Pericles* (London: Methuen, 1963), pp. lxxviii–lxxxviii. In a more recent article, 'Gower and Shakespeare in *Pericles*' (*Shakespeare Quarterly*, 33 (1982), 461–79), he argues that the first two acts are an authentic work of Shakespeare. Yet it is unlikely that this is so; see Sidney Thomas, 'The Problem of *Pericles*', *Shakespeare Quarterly*, 34 (1983), 448–50.

pelled to recognize that there is little in the first two acts (by general agreement not written by Shakespeare) to threaten the play's unity. Moreover, a curious relationship exists between Pericles' initial reliance upon Marina's speech and Shakespeare's engagement in a new genre which takes place through his rewriting of a play which belongs to someone else. Here both the author and his protagonist-king approach language with a similar caution to find a new mode of speech, a mode which is precisely the subject of our investigation.

Our first step towards identifying this mode is an examination of Marina's initial display of eloquence – her pleading with Leonine (4.1.190ff.). The scene in question contains several unusual characteristics which will afford our first clue to understanding the place which Shakespeare assigns to verbal power in *Pericles*. It is necessary to observe that Shakespeare differs in two curious details from his main source, the eleventh chapter of *The Pattern of Painful Adventures* by Lawrence Twine.[5] First, he makes Marina *plead* for her life in a lengthy speech, whereas the Tharsia of Twine only *enquires* as to the cause of her impending death. Since the future fate of both girls is to protect their virginity through pleading, it seems at least strange that Shakespeare should alter the more logical version of his source, in which the young girl *never* shows herself incapable of the art of persuasion. However, he *does* alter his source by showing how Marina fails in a situation which is for her of the utmost importance. The cause of her failure is most significant: it is an *oath* which binds her assailant: 'I am sworn, / And will dispatch', says Leonine (4.1.90–1).[6]

Leonine's recollection of his oath is Shakespeare's second important deviation from the episode in Twine. The 'villaine' of *The Pattern of Painful Adventures* is intent on murder in order to save his own life, since Dionisiades (the prototype of Dionyza) gives him little alternative: '...doe as I command thee, or els I sweare by God, thou shalt dearely repent it'.[7]

Leonine in *Pericles* shows himself a more 'independent' murderer who refuses for his own reasons to release Marina. The fact that Marina's pleading does not outweigh the strength of Leonine's vow is even less complimentary to Marina's art of persuasion than the simple fact of her failure. Almost immediately after Leonine's refusal, Shakespeare emphasizes that Leonine is a liar and fears little to be forsworn. When Marina is abducted by the pirates, we hear Leonine thinking to himself: 'There's no hope she'll return. I'll swear she's dead / And thrown into the sea' (4.1.98–9).

What are Shakespeare's reasons for introducing such changes from his source, changes which do indeed call into question Marina's art as a speaker? Anne Barton cites this scene between Leonine and Marina, and suggests that it provides clear evidence of Shakespeare's deep pessimism concerning the power of words.[8] I propose instead that when Shakespeare shows the failure of Marina's power with words in the scene with Leonine, he does so not to downplay the power of language, but to emphasize the importance of some vital change in her later discourses. Far from being simply pessimistic, Shakespeare in this scene sets up a background against which subsequent events will be displayed: in this early scene Marina tries to persuade by talking about herself, whereas in all her subsequent speeches until her meeting with Pericles she never speaks about her sentiments, her thoughts or her misfortunes. However, before discussing this in detail, we must examine the character of the power against which Marina directs her eloquence.

Leonine's oath is in no way an isolated occurrence in the play. When Shakespeare changes

---

[5] See Appendix A, Extract from Lawrence Twine, in the Arden edition of *Pericles*, p. 164.

[6] All quotations from *Pericles* in this essay are from the Arden edition of *Pericles*, edited by F. David Hoeniger.

[7] Appendix A, Arden edition, p. 164.

[8] Anne Barton, 'Shakespeare and the Limits of Language', *Shakespeare Survey 24* (1971), 118.

his source, he introduces what is to be a recurrent pattern in all of Marina's speeches: Marina's power will *always be displayed in a context closely associated with the idea of either curse or oath*. Dionyza, for example, in getting rid of Marina, breaks Cleon's oath and, thus, risks the danger of being affected by his self-curse (1.4.101–6).[9] Boult, in the brothel scene, summarizes Marina's behaviour in curious terms: 'Faith, I must ravish her, or she'll disfurnish us of all our cavalleria, and make our swearers priests' (4.6.11–12). Marina's overcoming of Pericles' silence could well be viewed as a victory over a well nigh deadly vow. And if Kenneth Muir is correct, as I believe he is, and the original Thaisa did make a vow of chastity to Diana[10] (there is an ambiguous allusion to this effect in 2.5.10–12), then the whole development of the last three acts lies in the emancipation of Thaisa from Diana's mastery. This is, of course, conjectural; but it does not affect the presence of the pattern in which two modes of language, oath and persuasion, confront each other and compete for victory.

Frances Shirley, who has observed a central rôle of oaths in many of Shakespeare's plays, comments upon the close connection between the plots of tragedies and the power of oaths or curses exercised by the play's heroes. Shirley shows conclusively how the structure of many early plays is dictated by a given oath, and, what is even more remarkable, how the tension of tragedies is often deepened by an accompanying vow. After presenting the importance of the oath in *Othello*, for instance, she wonders 'if Othello would have completed the murder had he not taken a vow'.[11] She further argues that in the romances Shakespeare's interest in oaths is practically non-existent. This she explains as the playwright's response to the censorship of 1606, which becomes in the romances 'a full blown compliance with regulations'.[12] This conclusion, however, is only partially correct. Shirley is undoubtedly right in her observation that the power of tragic vision has its linguistic counterpart in the word-

mode of an oath: a word which possesses in Shakespeare an unconditional power to bind the characters to events and to divest them of freedom, just as Hamlet's vow to the Ghost binds him to revenge and, thus, to death. She is, however, mistaken in her supposition that this significant pattern can be so easily obliterated in the romances. In *Pericles* Marina confronts the power of oaths, and our first step is to examine what we take to be the real nature of this confrontation.

The confrontation between the power of the oath and Marina's gift of persuasion has its most striking counterpart in a central event of the play, when the sailors throw Thaisa overboard because of their custom and Cerimon brings her back to life. The link between oath and custom is underscored by means of the idea of superstition, which defines both phenomena. 'That's your superstition', says Pericles (3.1.50), when the sailors refuse to keep the supposedly dead Thaisa on board. The same word is used when Dionyza tries to define the language of Cleon, a character who, as we shall see, is a primary bearer of the idea of the oath. 'Y're like one who superstitiously / Do swear to th' gods that winter kills the flies', says Dionyza (4.3.49–50). It has been pointed out by several critics that Marina and Cerimon exercise the same function in the play: through both the idea of hope and healing finds its way into the action.[13] Yet it is equally important to observe that both characters display their power against the same enemy – blind, pagan custom which admits of no exception and which professes a close link to supernatural power. 'Pardon us, sir; with us at sea it hath been still observ'd and we are strong in [custom]', the sailors reply to

---

9 See 3.3.25–7.
10 Kenneth Muir, *Shakespeare as Collaborator* (New York: Barnes Noble, 1960), pp. 80–1.
11 See Frances Shirley, *Swearing and Perjury in Shakespeare's Plays* (London: George Allen & Unwin, 1979), p. 118.
12 Ibid., pp. 140–7.
13 See, for example, Peterson, *Time, Tide and Tempest*, p. 96.

Pericles (3.1.51–2), making it clear that no reconsideration of the decree is possible. Cerimon, however, rejects this claim and before healing Thaisa, introduces a fresh viewpoint: 'They were too rough / That threw her in the sea' (3.2.81–2). Marina, of course, will show a similar ability to bring regeneration to what seems to be the most static of situations. Cerimon and Marina, therefore, literally unbind the binding superstitious custom. Moreover, this implicit connection between the forces these characters confront is sufficiently important for Shakespeare to summarize its main principle yet again in *The Tempest* in Gonzalo's remark to Boatswain, 'Now blasphemy / That swear'st grace overboard, not an oath on shore?' (5.1.219–19),[14] which restates in the most laconic manner Cerimon's disapproval of the sailors and Marina's confrontation with oaths. These words furnish not only the most concise overview of *Pericles*' plot; they restate the play's vision with full clarity: oaths are potent and victorious only at a time of tribulation, but on the shore 'after the tempest' they can give no direction and are, indeed, a threatening and sinister force.

Quite apart from the fact that oaths are a counterpart to the sailors' throwing of Marina overboard – an act which is the cause of all Pericles' misfortunes – the play presents a whole range of characteristics associated with the phenomenon of oaths. Firstly, there is the clear indication that oaths are being discouraged (obviously a pattern from which Shirley draws her conclusions). Thus, the first mention of an oath in the play is in Pericles' words to Helicanus: 'I'll take thy word for faith, not ask thine oath' (1.2.120). The same sentiment on Pericles' part reappears (in what is certainly Shakespeare's section of the play) when Pericles says to Cleon and Dionyza:

> I believe you;
> Your honour and your goodness teach me to't
> Without your vows. (3.3.25–7)

Moreover, there are other instances in the play when oaths, once made, are not followed up at all. Indeed, it is surprising how casually Shakespeare (who has structured a good number of his plays around the effects of wrongly made or forgotten oaths) treats Cleon's self-curse (1.4.101–6 and 3.3.23–5) and equally remarkable that no apparent consequences follow upon Simonides' reckless lie about Thaisa:

> One twelve moons more she'sll wear Diana's livery;
> This by the eye of Cynthia hath she vow'd,
> And on her virgin honour will not break it.
> (2.5.10–12)

All this seems to support Shirley's view that Shakespeare's interest in oaths is here minimal. A closer look, however, shows that the treatment of oaths has a remarkable inner consistency: it is not that they are depicted with half-hearted attention, but rather that their rôle and significance are closely investigated and the forces which stand behind this word-mode are shown to be in a process of declining power.

It can hardly be coincidental that the person who employs curses and oaths most frequently is Cleon, the most ineffectual figure in the play. What also characterizes his speech is a remarkable 'overloading' of language. In Act 1 (generally assumed not to have been written by Shakespeare), Cleon describes the hunger in his city with images whose intention is to shock:

> Those mothers who, to nuzzle up their babes,
> Thought nought too curious, are ready now
> To eat those little darlings whom they lov'd.
> So sharp are hunger's teeth, that man and wife
> Draw lots who first shall die to lengthen life.
> (1.4.42–6)

In subsequent acts Shakespeare takes up and develops this fondness for overstatement; it is, for instance, thrown into strong relief when met by Dionyza's common sense:

---

14 Apart from *Pericles*, textual citations throughout are from *The Riverside Shakespeare*, ed. G. Blakemore Evans (Boston: Houghton Mifflin Company, 1974).

DIONYZA Why [are] you foolish? Can it be
    undone?
CLEON O Dionyza, such a piece of slaughter
    The sun and moon ne'er looked upon!
DIONYZA I think you'll turn child again.
CLEON Were I chief lord of all this spacious
    world,
    I'd give it to undo the deed. A lady,
    Much less in blood than virtue ...   (4.3.1–6)

A similar connection between hyperbole and
oath is evident in another major event: the
epitaph written by Dionyza on what is supposedly Marina's monument. Here, however,
we find a new element, this time of great
significance, entering the equation. The epitaph
in question connects oaths not only to overstatement and elaborate description of the
disaster-in-view, it relates oaths directly to the
image of the tempest. Moreover, the importance of the epitaph's message is emphasized
when Gower breaks the established pattern of
his narrative to recite Dionyza's lie. The
epitaph, replete with over-emphatic imagery,
becomes almost unintelligible at its close:

> The fairest, sweet'st, and best lies here,
> Who wither'd in her spring of year.
> She was of Tyrus the king's daughter,
> On whom foul death hath made this slaughter.
> Marina was she call'd; and at her birth,
> Thetis, being proud, swallowed some part o' th'
>   earth.
> Therefore the earth, fearing to be o'erflow'd,
> Hath Thetis' birth-child on the heavens
>   bestow'd;
> Wherefore she does, *and swears she'll never stint*,
> Make raging battery upon shores of flint.
>   (4.4.34–43; emphasis added)

Dionyza's intention here is clearly to cover the
lie with a 'battery' of phrases, to create verisimilitude by a sheer mass of eloquence carved on
stone in 'glittering golden characters' (4.3.44).
What remains surprising, however, is the image
of the quarrel between earth and sea, and the
vow of the latter never to cease warfare. On the
one hand, this image is obviously an overstatement used to conceal the truth. Yet, on the
other hand, the content of the vow is the central
image of the play, the source of many of
Pericles' misfortunes and the dominant force in
Marina's fate (4.1.17–20). The epitaph, therefore, interweaves the idea of swearing and
warfare with the image of the tempest, and,
perhaps, calls into question the authenticity of
the latter. One should also observe Pericles'
alienation from the very spirit of the storm
(2.1.1–11 and 3.1.1–14). This is excellently discussed by Hoeniger, who compares Pericles'
call for quietude with Lear's encouragement of
the storm and subsequent 'heroical challenge' to
it.[15] Thus, if in *King Lear* the artistic vision (and
the very temperament of the play) lies side by
side with the image of the storm,[16] in *Pericles* it
is closely related to the desire to soothe and bind
the quarrelsome 'elements'. The pagan notions
of protest, loud-mouthed fighting and displays
of strength are rejected by Pericles in his invocation of silence: 'O, still / Thy deaf'ning,
dreadful thunders; gently quench / Thy nimble
sulphurous flashes! ...' (3.1.4–6). Later, when
Pericles is shocked by Thaisa's death, it is
Lychorida's turn to remind him that explicit
protest is suicidal: 'Patience, good sir; do not
assist the storm' (3.1.19). Pericles obediently
concedes.[17]

---

15 See Hoeniger in the Introduction to the Arden edition
    of *Pericles*, pp. lxxxii–lxxxiii. For a further treatment of
    Pericles' withdrawal from any active and dramatic
    involvement see, for example, John Arthos, 'Pericles,
    Prince of Tyre: A Study in the Dramatic Use of
    Romantic Narrative', *Shakespeare Quarterly*, 4 (1953),
    269; Knight, pp. 73–4; Norman Rabkin, *Shakespeare
    and the Common Understanding* (New York: Macmillan,
    1967), p. 194; and Thelma N. Greenfield, 'A re-
    examination of the "Patient" Pericles', *Shakespeare
    Studies*, 3 (1968), 55.
16 Madeleine Doran, for example, writes about *King Lear*:
    'we feel that we are seeing a drama of human suffering
    through enlarging and filtering lenses; or that we are
    listening to the music of it, composed in unexpected
    keys with harsh dissonances and rare harmonies'. See
    Shakespeare's Dramatic Language (Madison: University
    of Wisconsin Press, 1976), p. 93.
17 In this confrontation between Pericles' silence and the
    violence of the storm there is also something reminis-

Thus, Pericles' mode of behaviour rejects the hyperbolic power of tragedy, the wrathful madness of Lear who has sealed the exile of Cordelia and Kent with 'Away, by Jupiter, / This shall not be revoked' (1.1.178–9). However, Pericles also makes a vow, even if that vow contrasts with the raging oath of Lear and even if in *Pericles* it is directly opposed to Cleon's hyperbolic vows and Dionyza's equally hyperbolic lie. Pericles' vow of silence clearly challenges the acts of fulsome protestation and open warfare. It also questions the very idea of hyperbolic expression. We can conclude that both types of oath, therefore, whether the over-explicit type of Cleon (and the oath of the storm evoked by the deceitful epitaph) or the silent vow of Pericles, signify the rejection of tragedy. Cleon reduces to absurdity the language which nurtures tragic art, Pericles' silence rejects and buries it. In this sense, Pericles' behaviour is a non-tragic way of presenting tragedy: he goes beyond the fighting language of Lear, he simply refuses to speak. Pericles' protest is, however, more complex than the simple rejection of a tragic mode of expression in that he rejects the art of words as such. He mistrusts words altogether, and therefore, questions the very art of his creator – the art of expression, and the underlying faith in language. Pericles' silence is, indeed, a stoical protest against the art of words.

Yet even before Marina confronts the problem of his silence and returns to language its vitality, there are indications that Pericles is mistaken in the very act of using vows. In both instances his vows follow upon incorrectly made decisions. When he swears not to cut his hair as he leaves Marina in Tharsus (3.3.25–32), he makes the mistake of trusting Cleon and Dionyza. He swears not to speak or wash his face when he wrongly accepts their version of Marina's death (4.4.23–9). Both of these events indicate that Shakespeare, on the occasion of each vow, emphasizes the interconnection between Pericles' blindness in judgement and his vow-making, since in both instances his mistaken act is accompanied by a vow/oath virtually within the same sentence. Thus, even when the usual, over-emphatic nature of the oath is controlled by Pericles' stoicism, oaths are still indicative of inner blindness. In *Pericles*, therefore, Shakespeare carefully weaves a pattern in which explicit and, hence, exaggerated vows, together with Pericles' own vow of silence, which signifies the loss of communication, are to be simultaneously rejected.

Blindness (Pericles), futility, overstatement (Cleon), indifference and falsity (Leonine, the epitaph) seem to exhaust the associations of oaths in the play. Yet, Shakespeare appears to suggest further that 'swearing' is also a sentimental and impotent anger against the gods.[18] It is remarkable how pregnant is the phrase with which Dionyza assesses Cleon:

> Ye're like one that superstitiously
> Do swear to th' gods that winter kills the flies,
> But yet I know you'll do as I advise. (4.3.49–51)

This idea of swearing against, or to, the gods in futile anger is a curious, implicit reflection upon the sanctity of vows, yet it would seem accurately to sum up the rôle of all the oaths in the play: wicked or noble, oaths are ultimately powerless. What seemed in the earlier plays to possess an almost supernatural magic is here only blind custom, and the idea of the magic power of words is transferred from curses and oaths to a completely new realization – the persuasive art of Marina.

---

cent of Hamlet rejecting the authenticity of Laertes' feelings because of the latter's loud protestations. 'For in the very torrent, tempest, and, as I say, whirlwind of your passion, you must acquire and beget a temperance that may give it smoothness,' – so the Prince of Denmark instructs the actors in a well known scene (3.2.5–8).

[18] It is relevant to our topic to point out that Marina's only vow in the play turns into a prayer:

> If fires be hot, knives sharp, or waters deep,
> Untied I still my virgin knot will keep.
> Diana, aid my purpose! (4.2.147–9)

This would seem to signify further the rejection of oaths as a pattern of speech.

As we have indicated, Marina's rôle in the play is related to that of Cerimon. Hence, it is necessary to examine the peculiarities of Cerimon's healing power before discussing Marina's art. It is important to observe how close Cerimon is in his generosity to that most magnanimous of all tragic characters, Timon of Athens, the protagonist of the preceding play and a character who in fact is bankrupt not only of money but also of language: 'what he speaks is all in debt; he owes / for every word' (1.2.198–9). Cerimon, in contrast, remains opulent:

> Your honour has through Ephesus pour'd forth
> Your charity, and hundreds call themselves
> Your creatures, who by you have been restor'd;
> And not your knowledge, your personal pain,
>   but even
> Your purse, still open, hath built Lord Cerimon
> Such strong renown as time shall never –
>
> (3.2.43–8)

Yet, there is little similarity between the two characters, because the key feature of Timon – his blindness – is totally absent from Cerimon. The rôle of Cerimon's power of observation cannot be overestimated in the exercise of his art (3.2.31–7). His cure of Thaisa is not the miraculous performance of a magician who knows no limit to his power. Even his first appearance in the play, when he predicts the death of his patient (3.2.7–9), intimates that he is cooperating with nature, not overcoming it. Thaisa is restored to life because there are signs she may be living. The main difference, therefore, between Cerimon and the sailors (and even Pericles) is that he notices these signs and they do not. There is little surprise, then, that Cerimon talks of 'virtue and cunning' as great endowments of his art.

Marina develops similar gifts when threatened by dishonour in the brothel. Whilst the Marina who talks to Leonine is both blind and self-centred (her pleading is merely an account of her life), and her call to virtue too schematic, the Marina of the brothel scene is, above all, shrewd; she changes her line of persuasion to suit the character of her interlocutor. Thus, the spell of blind virtue, as blind as that of Timon or of Pericles (in his dealings with Cleon and Dionyza), is broken. Marina's only hope of survival is in the full understanding of the people with whom she is brought into contact.[19] This is the major characteristic of her art with words. When Marina talks to Lysimachus, she speaks as if she were superior in education, a sarcastic woman of his circle, clever and abusive. In talking to Boult, she at once reminds him of his subservient position, scolds him severely, and only then explains in businesslike fashion that she can be of better profit 'amongst honest women'. The note that she strikes is acceptable even to Boult's 'master and mistress'. She speaks a 'holy word' – this is how Marina's art is characterized (4.6.133). If what she says is indeed 'holy', then its flexibility is remarkable. There is little that the brothel can offer to shock Marina's ear:

> BOULT   But can you teach all this you speak of?
> MARINA   Prove that I cannot, take me home
>   again,
>   And prostitute me to the basest groom
>   That doth frequent your house.
> BOULT   Well, I will see what I can do for thee; if
>   I can place thee, I will,   (4.6.187–93)

If Twine's Thaisa could protect her virtue by retelling the story of her own life, Marina, who has attempted this on one occasion and failed, develops a completely different ability in a similar predicament. She learns how to direct

---

[19] Inga-Stina Ewbank contrasts the Marina of *Pericles* and her prototype in Gower and Twine. She observes that the Marina of Gower is defensive and pathetic in giving 'full accounts of her sad fate', whereas Marina is 'aggressive and shines forth as verbal wit', '"My name is Marina": The Language of Recognition', *Shakespeare's Styles: Essays in Honour of Kenneth Muir*, ed. Philip Edwards, Inga-Stina Ewbank, and G. K. Hunter (Cambridge: Cambridge University Press, 1980), p. 116. Although such an analysis of Marina's speech is unmistakably correct, her linguistic power lies not so much in the fact of her aggressiveness as in her ability to reproduce precisely the inner world of her interlocutor.

her speech to the secret desires or fears of those whom she addresses without ever explicitly stating her own inner predicament; and she speaks in such a manner that her interlocutors need her to continue more than she herself needs to do so.[20] This 'holy' quality of Marina's art resides in her ability to make inner reality of her interlocutors explicit or, as I.-S. Ewbank puts it, Marina gives reality to what appears to a by-stander to be a merely metaphoric situation.[21] Pericles immediately recognizes this quality in her:

> in pace another Juno;
> Who starves the ears she feeds, and makes
>   them hungry
> The more she gives them speech.   (5.1.111–13)

And it is, of course, in her meeting with Pericles that this ability is displayed most fully.

Phylis Gorfain comments upon a conspicuous quality in this father-daughter confrontation: 'Marina represents the answer to all her father's queries.'[22] It is, indeed, noteworthy how in their conversation she becomes the most suitable partner, the mirror-image of his woeful self. After their equality is established, Pericles starts to talk:

> My fortunes – parentage – good parentage –
> To equal mine – was it not thus? What say you?
>   (5.1.97–8)

Marina mentions her parentage only because Pericles will not be well unless he knows who this girl is. Later, Lysimachus will say that Marina always refused to talk about herself and her past, which indicates that her speech has invariably been the reflection of her interlocutors' needs, which are seated so deeply that only she can articulate them. In her meeting with Pericles she seems even more distrustful of words than he: he questions, and she answers almost grudgingly, until the rôles are reversed and Pericles says, 'Prithee speak' (5.1.119). The full revelation of her own identity Marina does not grant until Pericles is brought step by step to the verge of discovering it himself. Marina is ever careful:

> Some such thing I said,
> And said no more but what my thoughts
> Did warrant me was likely.   (5.1.132–4)

Pericles is impatient until he is brought to full knowledge: it is his Marina, all signs are his. The power of the scene resides in Marina's ability to give back to Pericles a desire for language. Because he wants to hear her speak, she makes him talk. Thus, in a sense, by recognizing and stating each of Marina's qualities, Pericles creates her anew. The heavenly music that Pericles hears testifies to the fact that Marina has returned to him his creative power and vision. The feeling of stalemate and the bankruptcy in the language of the last tragedy and preceding play, *Timon of Athens*, is overcome: the mysterious harmony is again within reach.

Gorfain discusses at length the enigmatic quality of Marina's discourse, and suggests that she destroys the wicked spell of Antiochus' riddle. Gorfain sees Pericles and Marina in their confrontation as two pieces of a puzzle which together strike a heavenly note: 'The mutuality of father and daughter eventually restores the mother and wife, Thaisa ... Recognizing Marina's admittedly incredible tale as the corollary to his own history brings Pericles back to life; realizing Pericles' story complements her own, restores Thaisa as mother and wife.'[23] This is an illuminating suggestion. One may note, however, that Gorfain does not really take account of the important fact that the

---

[20] Anne Barton observes Marina's changing use of words in each situation, but she explains this as a dislocation between the character and her speeches: 'Shakespeare appears to be using Marina less as a character than a kind of medium, through which the voice of the situation can be made to speak'; 'Leontes and the spider: Language and Speaker in Shakespeare's Last Plays', in *Shakespeare's Styles*, p. 138.

[21] I.-S. Ewbank, 'My name is Marina'.

[22] Phylis Gorfain, 'Puzzle and Artifice: The Riddle as Metapoetry in *Pericles*', *Shakespeare Survey 29* (1976), 14.

[23] Gorfain, 'Puzzle and Artifice', 15.

discoveries of Marina and Thaisa are different in character.[24] Marina is ultimately found when each sign of her identity is re-examined with painful slowness and anxiety, whereas Thaisa is restored to Pericles when the signs are confidently enumerated. Thus, the return of Thaisa comes as a proof that the qualities Marina has healed are not illusory and that the speech which comes back to Pericles can generate life. What Pericles has made inert and frozen by shunning explicit words or statements, by hiding his face (his first vow: not to cut his hair) and refusing to speak, finally demands its full revelation: Diana appears to Pericles and orders him to relate his fate in public.[25] His creative power is at its highest peak and the theatrical allusions in Marina's speech are hardly inappropriate. For with Pericles, Shakespeare too has found a new mode in which the trust and service of language can again be given power.

> Before the people all,
> Reveal how thou at sea didst lose thy wife.
> To mourn thy crosses, with thy daughter's, call,
> And give them repetition to the [life].
> *Or perform* my bidding, or thou liv'st in woe;
> Do't, and happy; by my silver bow!
> Awake, and tell thy dream.
>
> (5.1.243–9; emphasis added)

The recovery of Thaisa at the end of the play is a sign that Pericles' 'performance' was for him a necessarily cathartic action. Like a charmed queen, Thaisa was unable to reunite with him without the awakening of his creative power, his power to perform. We may even suggest (without in any way insisting upon it) that a curious parallel may well exist between Marina's rôle in Pericles' life and the structure of the play as a whole. Marina returns to Pericles his power. She enumerates her parentage, he recognizes it as his own. In a similar fashion, half of *Pericles* is not written by Shakespeare. Something in this ready material attracted, revitalized and indeed gave him a different orientation to his art. Thus, words which have lost their power in *Timon of Athens* have in *Pericles* regained their strength, healed by the

'cunning' art of Cerimon and Marina, an art in which vitality comes through observation and nurture of the signs of life and of need in those whom they encounter. The bondage of blindness in this art has been overcome and the closed circle of self-centredness in tragic characters has been broken.

In *Pericles*, then, trust in the power of words is not destroyed. We may suggest that the metaphoric definition of the fullest expression of that power is not given until Prospero casts his spells over the enchanted island. However, a profound similarity exists between Marina's art of persuasion and Prospero's magic commands. The secret of the invincibility of their words does not reside in the power of oath, that is, in language's capacity to manipulate unconditionally by imposing an alien pattern upon those addressed. Both Marina and Prospero search for signs of regeneration in those with whom they come into contact. Their language is victorious because it imposes only what it uncovers.[26] It does not arrest natural potential, it senses nature's patterns and accelerates its appearance. Thus, in *Pericles*, we argue that there is a reawakening of trust in the capacity of language (despite its perversions of oath, curse, lie, sinister command, etc.) to re-create, recog-

---

[24] I.-S. Ewbank comments upon the difference in Pericles' recovering of Thaisa and Marina, 'My name is Marina', 145.

[25] Maurice Hunt perceptively suggests that the character of Pericles is based upon the denial of speech and the redemptive character of its final acceptance; 'Opening the Book of Monarch's Faults: *Pericles* and Redemptive Speech' in *Essays in Literature*, 12, 2 (1985), 155–70.

[26] One may suggest here that Prospero's treatment of Antonio and Sebastian does not contradict our main thesis. The punishment inflicted upon them by Prospero – loss of senses and distraction – is the natural development of their fate, a development which is here accelerated. It is relevant to observe that their predecessors in Shakespeare's earlier plays all ended their lives in either loneliness or madness: Richard III, Buckingham, Edmund, Iago, Macbeth, Lady Macbeth and the wicked queen of *Cymbeline*. Even Iachimo seems to imply that he is overtaken by melancholy: 'The heaviness and guilt within my bosom / Takes off my manhood' (5.1.1–2).

nize, and, above all, to restore life. Together with this new rôle of language which celebrates art as 'virtue and cunning', Shakespeare develops a new dramatic genre, thus leaving behind the long-standing association of oath and tragedy.

THE DISCOVERY OF THE ROSE THEATRE: SOME IMPLICATIONS

R. A. FOAKES

The remains of the Rose provide the first direct evidence concerning an Elizabethan public theatre. It will no doubt be some time before a full report on the excavations is available, and the significance of the finding can be fully established. The excavation nearby of a part of the foundations of the Globe may open up new perspectives on both this theatre and the Rose. It is possible, nevertheless, to begin to work out some implications provisionally of what is the most exciting theatre discovery in this century. The Rose was financed by Philip Henslowe in partnership with John Cholmley, and built by John Griggs, described in the deed of partnership as a carpenter, in 1587.[1] Henslowe lists in his account-book or diary expenses for refurbishing the playhouse in the spring of 1592. The remains include part of the brick, chalk, and clunch or soft stone foundations of the original theatre, and also the foundations of a substantial extension northwards, including a new stage, which were presumably added in 1592. Hitherto the only visual evidence available has been that provided by John Norden in his three panoramas of London engraved one in 1593 and the others in 1600, which show the Rose schematically as hexagonal or round.[2] The excavations carried out by the Department of Greater London Archaeology of the Museum of London have now brought to light what John Orrell and Andrew Gurr describe as 'the first really trustworthy evidence about any of the playhouses that flourished in Shakespeare's day' in their preliminary report on the findings in the *Times Literary Supplement*, 9–15 June 1989;[3] I have relied on their account for basic information.

1. The Rose was different from the other arena theatres about which we have any information. The surviving contracts for the Fortune and Hope playhouses, the De Witt drawing of the Swan, and the representations of theatres in views of London have been used to fortify a sense that all the theatres were more or less alike in most respects. With the exception of the square Fortune, modelled nevertheless in many details on the Globe, the arena playhouses have been assumed in many accounts of the theatres in Shakespeare's age to be roughly similar, large, perhaps up to 100 feet in diameter, accommodating 3,000 spectators, and designed with a large rectangular stage projecting into the middle of the arena. The remains of the Rose show that it was more modest in scale, about 74 feet in diameter, and had a small, tapered stage. It may well be that other theatres were far more different from one another than we have assumed. The discovery of the Rose

---

[1] *Henslowe's Diary*, ed. R. A. Foakes and R. T. Rickert (Cambridge, 1961), p. 305.

[2] R. A. Foakes, *Illustrations of the English Stage 1580–1642* (London and Stanford, 1984), pp. 6–7, 10–13.

[3] p. 636; a revised and expanded version of this article, with the same title, has been published in *Antiquity* 63 (1989), 421–9. Measurements of the Rose given in this article may need to be revised in the light of further excavation.

Plan of the Rose Theatre   Phase 1

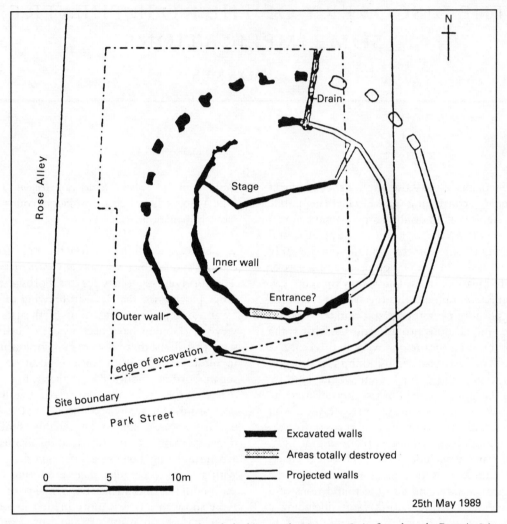

Plan of the Rose Theatre remains in Southwark, looking north, May 1989. In its first phase the Rose (1587) appears to have been a regular fourteen-sided polygon. The shape of the extended Rose (1592) remains conjectural, but it was probably an irregular polygon.

should ensure that if and when the standard survey by E. K. Chambers is revised, it will be entitled *Elizabethan Stages*, not *The Elizabethan Stage*.[4]

2. In particular, the Rose was unlike the Swan theatre. In spite of the difficulties it offers interpreters, De Witt's drawing of the Swan has been widely used as the central piece of evi-

dence about the interior of the arena theatres. Before the Rose was discovered, historians of the stage were pretty unanimous in concluding that 'Of all the pieces of evidence that can help us to fill in the details of the picture of public

---

[4] Andrew Gurr has signalled a necessary move in this direction in his article, 'The Shakespearian Stages, Forty Years On', *Shakespeare Survey 41* (1989), 1–12.

Plan of the Rose Theatre   Phase 2

Excavated walls
Areas totally destroyed
Projected walls

0   5   10m

25th May 1989

playhouses, incontestably the most important is Arend van Buchell's copy of Johannes de Witt's sketch of the interior of the Swan.'[5] The finding of the remains of the Rose means that this statement is no longer valid, but it is important to note how a sketch of the Swan has been taken as evidence about the 'public playhouses' in general. Because it is the only known illustration of the interior of a playhouse, scholars have wanted it to tell us more than it does, and to find in it evidence about

all the playhouses, as if all were alike. In particular, it has been used as a source of information about the Globe, for want of anything else, and perhaps understandably, it has acquired a strange authority, so that we have been urged to accept it 'at its face value without modification, interpolation or any other unwarranted

---

[5] Andrew Gurr, *The Shakespearean Stage* (2nd edn, Cambridge, 1980), p. 122.

change' as relevant not only to the Swan, but to other stages, especially the Globe.[6]

'Most commentators today are inclined to accept its accuracy' according to Andrew Gurr,[7] although the drawing has evident shortcomings and many features that are obscure or impossible to interpret with any certainty. Some have gone further to argue that van Buchell was 'unusually capable in drawing'.[8] However, further doubts have recently been cast on the quality of the drawing by the researches of Johan Gerritsen, who has shown that De Witt probably sent his friend van Buchell a half-size copy of his original, which the latter then scaled up in another copy. Moreover, the two men had different styles of draughtsmanship, and De Witt seems to have been a much better draughtsman than van Buchell, who had a hard time drawing buildings in such a way as to allow a 'coherent interpretation'.[9] The discovery of the remains of the Rose should encourage us to look again, more sceptically, at the Swan drawing, and to recognize that the features shown, so far as they make sense, relate possibly only to the Swan, and cannot be assumed to provide evidence about other playhouses.

3. The size and shape of the Rose in its first phase seem to have been dependent not on the number of sides, but on the unit length of each bay of the outer frame, which varied slightly, but was based on the measurement of one rod, perch, or pole (16 feet 6 inches). All speculation about the size of the public playhouses seems to have assumed that the number of sides of a wooden multisided theatre would inevitably be a multiple of four (12, 16, 20, or 24), and that a figure for the diameter of such a theatre could be assessed separately, as unconnected with the number of sides. Drawings of the theatres, and reconstructions, influenced perhaps by the well-known but inaccurate Visscher view of 1616, have posited a multiple of four sides, even though John Norden schematized the Bankside playhouses as hexagons in 1600. I suppose it

seems a natural assumption because of the tidy symmetry it suggests, and because of the symbolic resonances of the number four, the four elements, the four points of the compass, the four gospels, the four cardinal virtues, etc. C. Walter Hodges believed the second Globe had sixteen sides.[10] Richard Hosley thought the Globe had 24 sides, and assumed the diameter of the Globe was based on a 3-rod square, and was therefore 99 feet.[11] John Orrell, interpreting the Swan drawing as indicating a theatre with 24 sides, argued by analogy for 24 at the Globe as 'a satisfactory multiple of four and six'; he relied upon the accuracy of Wenceslaus Hollar's drawing for his 'Long View' (1647) to argue that the Globe had a diameter of 103.35 feet.[12] The figures seem arbitrary, but no more so than the diameter of the Rose, which we now know was about 74 feet. In view of our liking for multiples of four, the number of sides at the Rose, fourteen, is especially surprising on the face of it, and seems to demand explanation. John Orrell and Andrew Gurr suggest that the plan of the Rose was obtained by 'simply dividing the outer circle off into one-rod sec-

---

[6] Glynne Wickham, *Early English Stages*, vol. II, 1576–1660, part I (London, 1963), p. 204.

[7] *The Shakespearean Stage*, p. 124; Gurr himself in fact describes in some detail the problematic features of the drawing.

[8] John B. Gleason, 'The Dutch Humanist Origins of the De Witt Drawing of the Swan Theatre', *Shakespeare Quarterly*, 32 (1981), 324–38; the quotation is from p. 329.

[9] Johan Gerritsen, 'De Witt, Van Buchell, The Swan and the Globe, Some Notes', in *Essays in Honour of Kristian Smidt*, edited Peter Bilton et al. (Oslo, 1986).

[10] C. Walter Hodges, *Shakespeare's Second Globe* (Oxford, 1973), p. 45.

[11] Richard Hosley, 'The Shape and Size of the Second Globe', in *The Third Globe* (1981), pp. 84–5.

[12] John Orrell, 'Wenceslaus Hollar and the Size of the Globe Theatre', in *The Third Globe*, ed. C. Walter Hodges, S. Schoenbaum and Leonard Leone (Detroit, 1981), pp. 114, 116; in *The Quest for Shakespeare's Globe* (Cambridge, 1983), p. 201, Orrell estimated the diameter of the playhouse as between 101.37 and 103.32 feet.

tions, providing exactly fourteen gallery bays in all',[13] a scheme varied here and there to allow for entrances and passageways, so accounting for slight irregularities. It could have started with someone setting a pin in the ground and describing a circle with a radius of 37 feet. In other words, the design of the theatre probably originated not with the question that has most troubled modern scholars, how many sides did it have?, but with the question that for the builders determined the number of bays, what radius (or diameter) of a playhouse would best suit their purposes? For the number of sides was determined by the measurement of the circumference of the circle within which the sides were marked off.

The basic measure for the outer walls of the bays of the Rose was one rod, or 16 feet 6 inches, a considerable length for the quantity of oak beams required for horizontal timbers, but since each bay tapered towards the inner frame, down to 11 feet or so, it was probably desirable to make the sides of the outer frame as long as was convenient. The rod may have been a basis for determining the length of bays in other multi-sided theatres, for the surviving contract for the Hope specifies measurements for the dimensions of beams, the height of the galleries, and breadth between the inner and outer frame, but is silent on the length of each bay. The reason for choosing a diameter of 74 feet was that the resulting circumference (232 feet) divided by 14 gives almost exactly 16 feet 6 inches. It may be that this explanation for the size of the Rose has further implications in relation to other theatres. If the Theatre, and the first Globe, built using the main timbers of the Theatre, were conceived also in terms of bays a rod in length in the outer frame, then it would follow that the diameter of the Globe was also related to and in effect determined the number of its bays. The only measurements that seem to make sense in terms of rods would be a diameter of 95 feet, which gives a circumference of 298 feet, and corresponds almost exactly to eighteen bays of 16 feet 6 inches (297

feet); or alternatively a diameter of 105 feet, which gives a circumference of 329.8 feet, and corresponds almost exactly to twenty bays of 16 feet 6 inches (330 feet). Both Hosley's figure of 99 feet and Orrell's of 103.35 feet may therefore be inaccurate. Given that the Rose was smaller than anticipated, it is possible that the Globe was 95 feet rather than 105 feet in diameter; the first measurement would have provided a floor area within the outer frame of 7,087 square feet, the second an area of 8,658 square feet, more than twice the size of the Rose (4,300 square feet). If the Globe was built to the smaller of these two figures, it would mean that Hollar exaggerated the scale of the second Globe in his drawing, and that his representation is not as accurate as Orrell supposed.

4. The rear wall, or *frons scenae*, at the Rose seems to have been the inner frame of the polygonal theatre. The evidence of the remains of the Rose thus conflicts with that of the De Witt drawing of the Swan, which shows a flat rear wall with two large doors in it. Richard Hosley developed an elaborate theory that the stage façades of indoor theatres were based on the screens of great halls in houses, palaces and inns of court, which usually had two doors in them; Andrew Gurr sums up Hosley's conclusions:

Most screens had one or two doorways, and several had a gallery for musicians on top of the screen. Such an arrangement roughly conforms with the tiring-house layout of the indoor playhouse, which had a musicians' gallery 'above' and either two or three doors ... So, the argument goes, the players copied the screens of great halls for their tiring-house façades, because their idea of grandeur was to perform in front of such a façade.

By extension it can also be said that since plays were so readily interchangeable between one venue

---

[13] Orrell and Gurr, 'What the Rose can Tell Us', *Times Literary Supplement*, p. 636; *Antiquity*, p. 423.

and another, the public amphitheatres must have used a similar model.[14]

This theory looks very tidy, but it is based essentially, as far as the arena theatres are concerned, on the Swan drawing. The plans discovered by John Orrell for the conversion of the great hall of Christ Church, Oxford, into a theatre for a visit by James I and the court in 1605 show that in this instance the stage was erected at the opposite end of the hall from the screen. Indeed, there is no evidence for believing that the screen-ends of halls were commonly used for staging plays. The stage at the Rose tapered from 37 feet 6 inches at the junction with the inner frame to 24 feet 9 inches in the arena, and was about 15 feet 6 inches deep;[15] it was much smaller than that at the Fortune, which may have been rectangular (though this is not certain, since the 'plot thereof drawen', or plan, referred to in the contract no longer survives), and measured 43 feet wide and 27 feet 6 inches deep, according to the building contract.

It is possible therefore that the stage at the Fortune, and that at the Globe on which it was modelled, had a flat *frons scenae* erected at the rear; but there is no mention of such a wall in the contract for the Fortune. The tiring-house at the Rose must have been the space between the outer and inner frame behind the stage, as is confirmed by Henslowe's payment in 1592 for the building of a penthouse against the tiring-house wall, i.e. the outer wall of the theatre, presumably to provide more space. The contract for the Fortune calls for a 'Stadge and Tyreinge howse to be made, erected & settupp within the saide fframe',[16] and this could mean, as some have argued, that the tiring-house was free-standing and built within the inner frame. This would account for a flat stage façade, but would also cut the depth of the stage perhaps by half. However, the contract also calls for glazed windows to be provided for the tiring-house, and these were presumably in the outer wall of the theatre. So it is probable that at the Fortune, as at the Rose, the space between the inner and

outer frames at the rear of the stage was used for the tiring-house. Certainly at the Rose there is no reason to think Henslowe, or Griggs, his carpenter-builder, had any thought of hall-screens in designing their stage-area, since they used the inner frame of the theatre for the stage-façade. There is no archaeological evidence about the number of doors or their location at the Rose, but it would be unwise to assume that there were two placed as in the Swan drawing.

5. The stage at the Rose was tapered into the arena. The Swan drawing shows a rectangular stage, and it has been generally assumed that other public theatres likewise had rectangular stages. The contract for the Fortune specifies that the stage should be 43 feet 'in length' (i.e., measured at its widest point where it met the inner frame of the theatre?), and extend to the middle of the yard, but it is not clear that it would have been rectangular; it was to have been 'placed & sett' as indicated in a plan now lost. The contract for the Hope calls simply for a 'stage to be carryed or taken awaie',[17] and gives no indication of its shape. The vignettes on the title-pages of *Roxana* and *Messallina* (1632, 1640) depict a tapered stage,[18] which I once suggested might have originated in the conversion of octagonal cockpits into indoor theatres, but which may just as well have been copied from one or other of the public theatres. The tiny sketch in a copy of the Quarto of *2 Henry IV* in the Huntington Library, that

[14] Gurr, *The Shakespearean Stage*, p. 134.
[15] Orrell and Gurr, 'What the Rose can Tell Us,' *Times Literary Supplement*, p. 636; *Antiquity*, p. 425.
[16] Gurr, *The Shakespearean Stage*, p. 128.
[17] Ibid., p. 141.
[18] Foakes, *Illustrations of the English Stage 1580–1642*, p. 72; these vignettes also derive from earlier illustrations, such as those in the 1493 edition of the comedies of Terence; see *The Comedy of Errors*, ed. R. A. Foakes (London, 1962), pp. xxxvii–xxxix, and the article by John H. Astington on the *Roxana* and *Messallina* title-pages in this volume.

may be a blocking diagram, also depicts what appears to be a tapered stage.[19] It is conceivable therefore that a number of theatres had stages tapering into the auditorium, so providing more standing-room for spectators and offering a very workable kind of stage for actors, to judge from experience with a similar tapering stage in the Gulbenkian Theatre at the University of Kent in Canterbury.

6. In their report on the Rose findings, John Orrell and Andrew Gurr argued from the size of the auditorium, and allowing '18 inches laterally for each person' in accordance with 'the Elizabethan standard',[20] that the original Rose had a capacity of about 2,000, which was increased to about 2,425 after Henslowe extended the north end. Henslowe recorded payments for work on the Rose in March and April 1592, and since the theatre was in daily use for performances throughout this period, the payments, for bricks and chalk, putting in rafters, thatching, plastering, painting, etc., were presumably made after the work was completed.[21] The listings Henslowe began to make of sums in relation to performances commence in early March 1591 old style, i.e., 1592, so that we have no figures for receipts at the old Rose. At the newly extended Rose the figures Henslowe lists against plays performed range from £3 16s 8d down to 7s. If these represent his takings as owner of half the moneys paid in for entrance to the galleries, and if, as Thomas Platter said, spectators paid a penny to stand, and another penny to sit in the galleries,[22] then Henslowe's figures should represent in pennies half the number of spectators in the galleries at each performance. If Henslowe's figures for this period, on the other hand, represent, as Neil Carson suggests, 'money collected by him but due to the players',[23] that is to say the half of the gallery receipts he owed the players, then the highest figures recorded would still presumably indicate the maximum capacity of the theatre. Some plays are marked 'ne' (= newly entered?), and prices may have been raised for

them. Ignoring these, the highest figure for a popular play was £3 11s, or 852 pence recorded against *Jeronymo* (*The Spanish Tragedy*) on 14 March 1592, which would represent a gallery attendance that day of 1,704 people, as against the estimate of 1,579 by Orrell and Gurr. If the playhouse was unusually packed on this day, the working capacity in the galleries may have been somewhat less, say 1650, corresponding to Henslowe's normal maximum of 68 or 70s. If the arena held 500, then the total capacity would have been about 2,150, which is pretty close to the figure of 2,200 suggested by Orrell and Gurr.

7. Here might seem to lie an answer to the question why Henslowe went to such trouble and expense to demolish part of his theatre and extend it, reconstructing the stage end, in 1592. There would appear to be two possible reasons, one that the design of the theatre proved unsatisfactory, the other that Henslowe wished to increase his takings. There is nothing to show whether the earlier theatre had inadequacies as a building, but the fact that the extensions did not alter significantly the general design, and that a new stage was erected exactly on the plan of the earlier one, suggests that Henslowe was satisfied with the plan. It could be that part of the theatre collapsed, or some structural deficiency made partial rebuilding necessary. The second explanation is not convincing either, namely, that for popular plays spectators were being turned away, and the primary purpose of the enlargement of the playhouse was to increase audience capacity. Henslowe paid out 11s for painting his stage, and only 10s for old timber

---

[19] Ibid., pp. 156–7.

[20] Orrell and Gurr, 'What the Rose can Tell Us,' *Times Literary Supplement*, p. 649; *Antiquity*, p. 428.

[21] Neil Carson, *A Companion to Henslowe's Diary* (Cambridge, 1988), pp. 14–15; see also Carol Chillington Rutter, *Documents of the Rose Playhouse* (Manchester, 1984), pp. 49–51, 57–8.

[22] Gurr, *The Shakespearean Stage*, p. 197.

[23] Carson, *Companion*, p. 20.

to make a penthouse at the tiring-house door,[24] so he was not spending a lot on facilities for the players. As to audiences, enlarging the theatre would only make a difference when there were large attendances. At 89 performances listed by Henslowe between 19 February and 31 May 1592, he records £3 or more on eleven occasions, four of them marked 'ne'; he records between 50s and £3 on a further nine occasions. If Orrell and Gurr are right in assuming that the extensions raised capacity from about 2,000 to about 2,425, adding 250 spaces in the galleries, then Henslowe's additions would only have brought him in an extra 10s or so for a full house. And if the theatre was full only for about one in eight performances, as was the case for this period, then revenues would have been increased by at most about £20 a year, a poor return on an outlay of £108 in listed expenses, plus many items not priced. It would seem that there must be a better explanation therefore for the reconstruction of part of the Rose in 1592.

---

[24] *Henslowe's Diary*, pp. 11, 13.

THE ORIGINS OF THE *ROXANA* AND *MESSALLINA* ILLUSTRATIONS

JOHN H. ASTINGTON

The small engraved vignettes of stages published in the second edition of *Roxana* (1632) and in *Messallina* (1640) have fascinated stage historians since the beginning of this century (see Plates 1 and 2). Their depiction of small, polygonal, railed stages, with hangings forming the upstage façade, contrasts markedly with the large, bare rectangle of the Swan stage and its sturdy tiring-house doors, as rendered by De Witt and Van Buchell. They have therefore quite reasonably been taken to be pictures of indoor playhouses, although they have also been used as a theoretical stick to beat the evidence of the Swan drawing by those not disposed to accept it, and since the uncovering of the foundations of the Rose we have been presented with plain proof that the shape of stage they depict is neither fanciful nor solely confined to indoor theatres. The reconstructions of the Globe by Albright (1909) and John Cranford Adams (1942) owe a great deal to the features shown in the engravings. More recently, Glynne Wickham has attempted to revive interest in the relationship between these pictures and identifiable places by suggesting that they are temporary theatres built within cockpits, and hence related to the two well known conversions of such buildings to permanent playhouses, in Drury Lane and Whitehall Palace.[1] Wickham redrew the pictures to demonstrate his argument (compare Plates 3a/b and 4a/b), and his redrawings have since been given wider currency by Andrew Gurr.[2]

Such speculative interest in the pictures has tended to ignore a number of ascertainable facts about how and by whom they were made. The engravers of both can be identified: students of engraving have for over fifty years assigned the *Messallina* plate to Thomas Rawlins.[3] Mysteriously, this ascription has failed to find its way into the area of theatre history, although it has particular significance for those who wish to establish a physical identity for the playhouse shown in the picture.[4] Rawlins was not only an engraver, medallist, and artist employed by

---

[1] See *Early English Stages 1300 to 1660*, Vol. 2, Part II (London, 1972), pp. 82–9.

[2] Successively in the second edition of *The Shakespearean Stage, 1574–1642* (Cambridge, 1980), for the paperback edition of which Wickham's version of the *Roxana* vignette is also used as a jacket design, in *Playgoing in Shakespeare's London* (Cambridge, 1987), and most recently in *Rebuilding Shakespeare's Globe* (with John Orrell, London, 1989).

[3] See A. F. Johnson, *A Catalogue of Engraved and Etched English Title-pages* (Oxford, 1934), p. 51.

[4] G. E. Bentley describes Rawlins's career as engraver and employee of the Mint (*The Jacobean and Caroline Stage*, vol. V (Oxford, 1956), pp. 993–4), and identified him as 'probably' the engraver of Nathanael Richards's portrait which prefaces *Messallina* and is signed 'T.R. sculp': (ibid., pp. 1001–2). He has nothing to say about the *Messallina* title plate itself, but when one compares the decorated initial R of 'Richards' on both plates one is left in little doubt that the same craftsman produced both. For a reproduction of the portrait plate, see M. Corbett and M. Norton, *Engraving in England in the Sixteenth and Seventeenth Centuries. Part III. The Reign of Charles I* (Cambridge, 1964), plate 147.

1   John Payne, unsigned title plate to *Roxana*, 1632

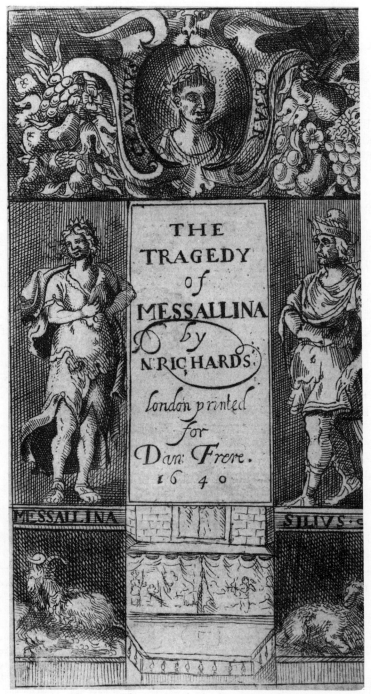

2   Thomas Rawlins, unsigned title plate to *Messallina*, 1640

the Mint, but also wrote at least one play, *The Rebellion*, which was printed in the same year and by the same publisher, Daniel Frere, as was *Messallina*. He was also closely associated, evidently, with Nathanael Richards, since each man provided prefatory verses for the other's play. Both *The Rebellion* and *Messallina* had been produced by the King's Revels company, the former 'acted nine days together, and divers times since with good applause', and although problems of dating make it difficult to be entirely certain, both appear to have been staged at the Salisbury Court theatre.[5] The circle of Rawlins and Richards included actors from the company, who contributed verses to their published plays, and it would therefore seem that the *Messallina* illustration is likely to be a particularly valuable document: a depiction by a trained artist of a theatre which he knew intimately as a dramatist and as an associate of players and other playwrights.

Unfortunately, there are compelling reasons to qualify our enthusiasm over the testimony of the engraving. Comparison with the *Roxana* vignette reveals that the earlier picture is likely to be the pattern for the later, as was pointed out long ago by J. Q. Adams.[6] In the following pages I will demonstrate exactly what elements Rawlins drew from earlier models: the *Roxana* page was certainly one of them. As we shall see, Rawlins's practice was an altogether traditional manner of composition: title-pages tend to be allusive and derivative in their design, and entirely original treatment is rare. Moreover, comparison of the two pages shows that the *Messallina* plate is fairly crude hack-work when put next to the relatively energetic and graceful style of the *Roxana* engraver. This impression extends to the depiction of the two stages: the one is lively and theatrical, the other empty, lumpy, and dull. Yet however inept Rawlins may have been, he did change the depiction of the stage and tiring house in several ways, and such changes *may* have arisen from his first-hand knowledge of a playhouse. This matter can be more sensibly discussed after a fuller

examination of the *Roxana* picture, and I therefore defer it. The chances of the *Roxana* picture itself being a depiction of the Salisbury Court playhouse – certainly in existence by 1632 when the engraving was published – will be defined by what follows.

In fact, the likelihood that the *Roxana* engraving represents *any* specific place is extremely slim. It might be taken to be making reference either to the academic stages at Cambridge, where Alabaster's play was presented in about 1592, or more loosely to some commercial playhouse of the early 1630s. I shall argue here that it is a confection of iconographic conventions deriving from earlier engravings, etchings, and woodcuts, and defined by material conditions quite different from those that governed De Witt's original sketch of the Swan. The *Roxana* illustrator was not a learned tourist in a fascinating foreign city, but a commercial craftsman in the pay of either publisher or author.

The publisher of *Roxana* is announced on the printed title-page which faces the engraved plate: William Jones, a London printer with a fairly long career (assuming we are dealing with one man). When one reads a biography into his published titles, the profile is of an individual who would be at home in the ambiance described in Christopher Hill's *The Intellectual Origins of the English Revolution*. Jones published works on mathematics and astronomy by Edmund Gunter, Henry Briggs, William Bourne, Richard Norwood, Pierre de

---

[5] Bentley, *The Jacobean and Caroline Stage*, attempts to associate *The Rebellion* with the Red Bull, on the strength of internal allusions which also mention the Globe and the Fortune, and seem far from convincing. The literary assumption of the following phrase also strikes me as ill-founded: 'the *naïveté* of *The Rebellion* does not suggest that private theatre [Salisbury Court]' (p. 996). The company that acted both plays is not known to have performed in any theatre other than Salisbury Court, as Bentley concedes.

[6] 'Four Pictorial Representations of the Elizabethan Stage', *JEGP*, 10 (1911), 329–33.

3a   Enlargement of stage vignette, *Roxana* page

3b   Redrawn version of *Roxana* stage, 1972

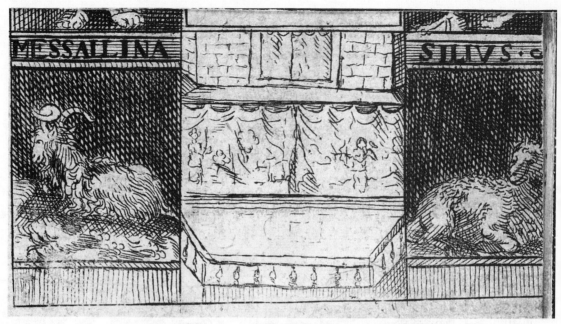

4a   Enlargement of stage vignette, *Messallina* page

4b   Redrawn version of *Messallina* stage, 1972

la Ramée, and Henry Gellibrand; he also published many sermons, devotional works, and religious treatises of a Puritan or anti-Papist slant. He was no regular publisher of plays, or indeed of any other form of imaginative literature. Apart from *Roxana*, the only other play with which he seems to have been concerned was the fourth quarto of *Philaster* in 1634. Between the two, far more typically, he was one of the printers involved in the infamous *Histriomastix*, and he had previously published other works by Prynne. He generally seems unlikely to have been familiar with the interior of playhouses, and is not a leading candidate for adviser to the engraver.

That rôle habitually fell to the author.[7] By 1632, I think, William Alabaster must have agreed with Jones on the publication of at least the initial works in a series of treatises, in Latin, on mystical theology, since over the next five years all his later published work, aside from the first edition of *Roxana*, appeared from Jones's press.[8] Two of these, *Ecce Sponsus Venit* (1633) and *Spiraculum Tubarum* (n.d.–1633), have elaborate title pages, recognizably engraved by the same craftsman who produced the *Roxana* page (compare Plates 1, 5 and 6), so that there would also seem to have been some agreement on lavish editions. *Spiraculum Tubarum* is signed on the plate with the initials IP, and *Ecce Sponsus Venit* is prefaced with an engraved portrait of Alabaster at the age of sixty-six, taken from a portrait by Cornelius Johnson, and signed 'Iohn Payne sculpsit'.[9] John Payne, who worked from about 1600 to 1639 or 1640, and who had trained with the brothers Van de Passe, is the engraver, if not the designer, of the *Roxana* stage. His style in lettering and the treatment of figures is easily recognizable when the page is compared with examples of his signed work.[10] We must therefore pay attention to his other work in the early sixteen thirties, and to that of his colleagues and contemporaries, if we are to understand what lay behind his art.

To turn back for a moment to Alabaster, it seems unlikely that the 'publication agreement' between the author and Jones, to entertain that hypothesis, would originally have included *Roxana*, which, for all that it is in Latin, is quite a different product of the author's learning from the ponderous millenarianism of *Ecce Sponsus Venit*. If Alabaster was emptying his drawers at the end of his career, then, Jones's publication of *Roxana* arose by accident, or perhaps by staged accident. That is to say that the play was entered on the Stationers' Register in May 1632 as the property of Andrew Crooke, and subsequently printed by 'R. Badger' for him. Alabaster then expressed genuine or feigned indignation, and prevailed on Jones to issue a correct text, including prefatory dedications and the well-known title page.

An engraved title page was usually the sign of an important and dignified edition, as in the Folios of Jonson and Shakespeare, and Alabaster's gesture, which he may have paid for himself, was intended to establish the worth and superiority of his corrected work. The instructions he gave to Payne cannot have been very detailed or prescriptive, however, since the title page as a whole has an oddly miscellaneous assembly of motifs, many of them having little to do with the play itself, which, as Boas tells us, is a sub-Senecan drama of revenge and murder, copied from an Italian original. The oddest feature of all, given the hypothesis

---

[7] See M. Corbett and R. Lightbown, *The Comely Frontispiece. The Emblematic Title-Page in England 1550–1660* (London, 1979), pp. 45–7.

[8] The *DNB* entry on Alabaster notices his early unpublished Latin verse, praised by Spenser, and two earlier mystical works, one printed in Antwerp and the second not extant.

[9] See Corbett and Norton, *Engraving in England*, p. 7, and plate 1a.

[10] 'On an engraved title plate the lettering also is the work of the artist and is not printed from movable type. It may be presumed that such lettering was the engraver's design, and it might be possible by a study of the hands of the chief engravers of a particular period to attribute some of the unsigned plates to their designers.' A. F. Johnson, *English Title-Pages*, p. ix.

6   John Payne, signed title plate to *Spiraculum Tubarum*, 1633

157

of authorial consultation with the engraver, is the scene on the stage, which 'cannot be identified ... with any of the episodes in *Roxana*'.[11] If Alabaster's instructions about the play itself were vague or confused, are we to assume that he was any more informative about the theatre? Perhaps, oddly, we are. Engravers worked from visual models, frequently transferring sketches of them directly to the plate, and a picture would have been far more use to Payne than any amount of verbal description: he is at his most convincing when copying portraits. One element behind the *Roxana* stage picture, I suggest, may have been illustrated editions of Terence, which provided the most widely known imaginative vision of stage action in the *theatrum*.[12] Alabaster's idea, in other words, was not to invoke the contemporary London stage, or the Cambridge college stages of the late sixteenth century, but the imagined theatre of classical humanism. From the beginning, the illustrations in printed editions of Terence had blended contemporary costume and stage technique with imagined Roman practice.[13] The seminal early Lyons edition (by Treschel, 1493) shows a variety of stages: those for *Heautontimoroumenos* and *Phormio* are polygonal, and polygonally projecting booths are shown in both these plays and in *Adelphi*. The *Phormio* stage booth seems to have a polygonal tower projecting above it, which could be taken as a prototype of the *Messallina* arrangement. All these pictures, and the subsequent imitations of them in Venetian editions, show curtains forming the upstage façade, which is frequently divided by pillars not dissimilar to that shown dividing the balcony in Payne's engraving. Subsequent Italian editions illustrate the plays being performed on scenic stages,[14] and they add an observing audience: a portrayal of heads and shoulders seen from the rear, as in Payne's foreground. There is no one picture from any given illustrated Terence which is an obvious and direct source for Payne's composition, but there are enough similarities to the tradition of Terentian illustration to assume that Payne had

looked at such pictures; William Alabaster himself, a learned clergyman, may have lent him, shown him, or otherwise arranged for him to have access to the books from which they came.[15] In recognition of the visual allusions which are being made in the *Roxana* design, Payne's scheme was immediately copied by the engraver William Marshall, on the title page of an edition of Terence published in the following year, 1633.[16]

The relationship between Payne and Marshall was evidently close: at the very least they each kept a careful eye on the other's work, and the connections between their designs will concern us in what follows. I return first to the composition of the *Roxana* page, viewed within the context of other engraved pages produced between 1631 and 1633. If the Jones edition of *Roxana* was produced late in 1632, or even early in 1633, given that the Crooke edition appeared at some time after May, it seems likely that Payne's work on it was preceded by an important title page, which he signed, for a translated edition of Virgil published in 1632 (Plate 7). This book, incidentally, was printed in Cambridge by Thomas Buck, who subsequently published Marshall's Terence plate, and who was therefore a likely

---

[11] F. S. Boas, *University Drama in the Tudor Age* ((1914) New York, 1966), p. 286.

[12] The similarity of the *Roxana* stage to Terentian illustrations has been noted by both Wickham, *Early English Stages*, and by Richard Leacroft, *The Development of the English Playhouse* (rev. ed., London, 1988), p. 28.

[13] For a sceptical analysis of the relationship of Renaissance editions to contemporary staging of the plays, see T. E. Lawrenson and E. Purkis, 'Les Editions Illustrées de Térence dans l'Histoire du Théâtre', J. Jacquot, ed., *Le Lieu Théâtral à la Renaissance* (Paris, 1964), pp. 1–24. This article includes a thorough selection of reproductions of the illustrations referred to here.

[14] They simultaneously introduce depictions of stage costume which in some cases is classical in style.

[15] Payne evidently had Cambridge connections: see Corbett and Norton, *Engraving in England*, p. 6. Alabaster may have arranged for his access to college libraries, for example.

[16] Corbett and Norton, *Engraving in England*, Plate 81(b).

The
XII Aeneids
of Virgil, *the*
most renowned
Laureat-Prince
of Latine-Poets;
Translated
into English
deca-syllables,
By
Iohn Vicars.
1 6 3 2 .

Æneas.

Turnus.

Are to be sold by Ni. Alsop at the Angell in Popes head ally. IP

7 John Payne, signed title plate to *The XII Aeneids*, 1632

source of contact between the two engravers. Marshall fairly quickly copied the Virgil engraving on the title page of Philemon Holland's *Cyrupaedia*, a translation of Xenophon, turning Payne's Aeneas into Cyrus (and creating a pictorial scheme he would repeat in the Terence plate).[17] I assume here that Marshall follows Payne, and do so largely on the basis of the confidence and assurance of Payne's style. I recognize that this is not altogether a convincing argument, and certainly Payne copied Marshall, as we shall see, but the relationship between these particular engravings is not a crucial issue, and is introduced only to show how thoroughly allusive and repetitive the visual language of title pages habitually was.

In any event, the Virgil plate was strongly influential upon two engraved pages which followed, those for *Roxana* and for *Ecce Sponsus Venit*. (Compare the treatment of the waves and flames in the two vignettes on each page, Plates 7 and 5). The general scheme of the division of the rectangle of the page into nine smaller units – a common enough plan generally speaking – is established in the Virgil plate, and followed in a more rigid fashion in the *Roxana* page. A central panel of text is flanked by supporting figures in Roman military dress, which turns up at least in the costume of Mars in the top right vignette of the *Roxana* page. Payne's source for his Aeneas and Turnus may have been Achilles and Hector as first engraved by William Hole in 1610 for Chapman's translation of *The Iliad*, and reworked for *The Whole Works of Homer*, which appeared in 1616. Behind the reworked design, it has been suggested, lay drawings by Inigo Jones.[18] Once again, it is probably impossible to designate a precise original for Payne's figures, but it should be clear that his work is thoroughly imbued with the Stuart taste for figures costumed *à la Romaine*.

The goddesses flanking the upper vignette, Venus on the left and Juno on the right, are partly the model for the group of gods in the upper right vignette of the *Roxana* plate.[19]

Venus and Cupid reappear there, not depicted in quite such sensual detail, and Juno is absent, although her crown and sceptre in the Virgil plate appear to be the models for the rain of royal emblems in the bottom left frame of *Roxana*. Generally the treatment both of nude female figures and of draperies can be compared with that of all the female figures in *Roxana*, with the exception of the female character on stage, which has a different source. Fame (centre top) is also intended for a female figure, I think, despite her mighty thigh.

The figures in the lower central vignette of the Virgil page, Aeneas with Anchises and Ascanius fleeing burning Troy, wear costumes more directly related to the male figures on the *Roxana* stage, and to the man in the lower right panel. Aeneas wears Roman sandals, fastened around the calf, and the military skirt; Ascanius and Anchises wear cloaks or draperies which billow out behind them. (See Plates 7 and 1.) Anchises also appears to be wearing a Phrygian cap, which will concern us in another connection below. Generally the Virgil page is a far more accomplished piece of design than the *Roxana* page, but even here Payne is not afraid of incongruity and anachronism: Aeneas's vessel is unashamedly a seventeenth-century ship, and may perhaps be modelled on Simon Van de Passe's famous title page for Bacon's *Instauratio Magna* (1620).[20]

Payne's scheme for the *Roxana* page is far less unified. He must have had a fair amount of freedom in composing generally suitable motifs to match vague directions. He knew, evidently, that he was dealing with a play, but didn't

---

17 Corbett and Norton, *Engraving in England*, Plate 80.

18 See Corbett and Lightbown, *The Comely Frontispiece*, pp. 112–18, and Roy Strong, *Henry Prince of Wales and England's Lost Renaissance* (London, 1986), pp. 129–33.

19 They are in turn partly modelled, apparently, on Thomas Cecill's design for an edition of Ovid's *Metamorphoses* in 1626: see Corbett and Norton, *Engraving in England*, Plate 23(a).

20 The pillars on the title page of *Ecce Sponsus Venit* seem to be another allusion to the same design.

know too clearly what it was about, and hence the visual language is ambiguous and rather odd. One idea apparently was to oppose tragedy and comedy as flanking motifs (despite the engraved generic label, which even a non-Latinist might be expected to understand). Ignoring the top row of pictures for the moment we have the severe personified *Tragedia* to the left, wearing cothurnoi, and the more dishevelled, genial, unbuttoned *Comedia* to the right. Below them are motifs appropriate to their auspices: a little sport with Amaryllis on the right, and, rather lamely, a *de casibus* shower of crowns and sceptres on the left. Between the two, appropriately, the stage shows a scene ambiguously caught between gallantry on the right and violence on the left. The supporting figures are evidently not derived from Hole's engraving for the Jonson Folio, although the general idea may be. Their classical robes are a commonplace of Renaissance design in engraving and other visual arts – they are also the dress of the daughters of Jerusalem in the right-hand panel of *Ecce Sponsus Venit* – but if Payne was copying any specific source he may have taken Simon Van de Passe's portrait of Paul Van Somer (1622) as a model.[21] The supporters in that engraving are Painting and Poetry, but their dress is exactly that of Payne's figures, and there are even some echoes of pose.

It is when we attempt to read the balanced halves of the composition in the top row of frames that the design falters badly. Fame as a central figure is something of a ready-made motif, suitable to all occasions. Payne gives her the black and burnished trumpets of ill and good fame, and a value judgement on comedy and tragedy is introduced – inadvertently, I suspect. His design is unlike that of Renold Elstrack for Raleigh's *The History of the World* (1614), and seems to have older iconographic roots, in the engravings, for example, of Joost Amman for the Frankfurt publisher Sigmund Feyerabend (1560s and 1570s).[22] Above *Comedia*, and invaded by the blast of ill fame, sit the Olympian gods. Venus is the central figure,

but it is otherwise difficult to see their relevance to the column below. They seem a rather vague reference to the power of destiny, and something of an assemblage of figures and themes from the Virgil page. One might read the whole of the top row to the effect that Christian order is being praised over pagan superstition, but the scene of temporal submission to the throne of Peter (Canossa?) is in vertical line with the tragic scheme, which certainly would be William Jones's interpretation of the frame. The top left picture has least to do with Payne's design, and is even further from Alabaster's play than the other motifs. It is richly ambiguous, and clearly directly related to the figures on the left of the page of *Ecce Sponsus Venit*. (Compare, on each page, the seated pope with crozier and the tonsured monks). To the contemporary English eye, the top left *Roxana* vignette taken alone could only be a dreadful warning. Rome is unambiguously hell, Babel, and outer darkness in the 1633 engraving. I would explain the scene in *Roxana* by guessing that Payne had already begun work on the later – and, once again, more artistically unified – plate when he was asked to produce the title page for the play. Evidently scratching around for material (see bottom left), his wise virgins are drafted for dramatic service, and his Roman monks and prelates for another vignette rather generally illustrating the vicissitudes of fortune, and the fall of princes.

All this has perhaps taken us no nearer the frame in which we are all interested, although I take it to have demonstrated Payne's eclectic approach. I want now to push that argument rather further. First the composition itself. If the stage is not a composite of motifs from Terentian illustrations, but represents an actual place – an engraving from a drawing either of

---

[21] See A. M. Hind, *Engraving in England in the Sixteenth and Seventeenth Centuries. Part II. The Reign of James I* (Cambridge, 1955), Plate 160.

[22] See, e.g., A. F. Butsch, *A Handbook of Renaissance Ornament* ((1878, 1880) New York, 1979), plates 162 ff.

Beeston's Cockpit in Drury Lane or of the Salisbury Court playhouse, let us say – it is very clumsy in its representation of structure. We are looking centrally at a stage which appears to have a regular shape, with sides retreating diagonally at the same angle to the front. Yet the stage left side is shorter, and its rail lower, than that on stage right, and yet there is the same distance between their upstage ends and the rear of the stage. This is evidently a geometrical impossibility. There are more. Produce either edge of the stage to the point below the corner posts – both points are obscured by the heads of the audience – and you will find the sides of the stage don't meet. In itself this may be a footling point, but it does show the order of composition: the figures were sketched in first, and the stage drawn around them. It also shows Payne's precedence of interest in the composition: it is the human life of the theatrical scene which convinces us, from the pointing hand of the foreground left-hand figure, through the athletic and lively gesture on stage, even to the tilt of the otherwise perfunctory bald heads in the balcony. That very balcony has obviously been drawn to fit within the frame of the rectangle, without regard to the structural irrationality it introduces: the accommodation for seated bodies in the balcony would result in stage entries about three feet high.

Before I had looked carefully at the context of the engraving, I always distrusted the probability of its direct connection with the theatre because the style seemed to me continental. It was the work of a Flemish engraver, perhaps, who either did not frequent the London theatre or even worked outside England. We now know that Payne had picked up his fluidity of style, partly at least, from the Van de Passes. The only thing remotely like the spring and energy of the stage movement, I used to think, was to be seen in Callot, and he evidently was not working for London publishers in 1632. Yet his etchings were known to Inigo Jones, who used a number of his designs from the *Balli*

di Sfessania (*c.* 1621–22) and other etchings in the 1630s.[23] The *Balli* designs, interestingly, begin with a title sheet showing a small (rectangular) stage with three extravagantly cavorting characters performing. They are watched by audience at the sides, and by two other actors peering through rear curtains. Could it be that Payne had seen Callot's etchings of theatrical (and other) scenes?

It appears that William Marshall certainly had access to Callot's prints as early as 1631, which is exactly the year of Jones's first use of them, in *Love's Triumph through Callipolis*. As might be expected, Marshall copied them, although they had no permanently improving effect on his technique. His title page to Richard Brathwaite's *The English Gentlewoman* (Plate 8) is a rather clumsy compilation of vignette frames, following the format of the engraving by Robert Vaughan for Brathwaite's companion volume *The English Gentleman* (1630).[24] The third down in the left-hand column, labelled 'Complement', is a rendering of two of Callot's figures from the series *La Noblesse Lorraine* (*c.* 1620–23), the graceful and charming bowing gentleman (Plate 9) and the masked gentlewoman (Plate 10). Marshall simply reverses the former, retaining the walled garden as a background, and adapts the latter slightly. Payne in turn took this composition as the basis for the two right-hand figures on the *Roxana* stage: they are performing a scene of 'compliment', having nothing whatsoever to do with Alabaster's play, or with the contemporary theatre. Callot's gentleman has been recostumed, roughly, in the clothes of Aeneas and Anchises, but retaining the hat, the cloak over the shoulder, and the telltale pointed beard. He wears rather ambiguous footwear, halfway between cothurnoi and contemporary boots,

23 See J. Harris, S. Orgel, and R. Strong, *The King's Arcadia: Inigo Jones and the Stuart Court* (London, 1973), pp.74–7.

24 Corbett and Norton, *Engraving in England*, Plate 35(b).

8   William Marshall, signed title plate to *The English Gentlewoman*, 1631

and his hand has been dropped to his breast. His central position matches his visual ambiguity, halfway between the formalized classical dress of the iconographic tradition and the elegant French fashion of the mid 1620s. The puzzle of the female stage figure is explained by the source. Within the composition her clothes don't match the other stage costumes, nor those of the other female figures around her on the page. As female stage costume in 1632 her dress has always struck me as archaic. Why the ruff, when fashionable women (and men) had adopted the falling collar? Callot's female figures, however, are frequently depicted with a raised rear collar, if not a full ruff, and often it seems quite exaggerated, almost as if it were a personal stylistic affectation by the artist. The masked gentlewoman has quite a modestly elevated collar, but Marshall's English Gentlewoman, who generally seems something of a stick-in-the-mud, wears a full ruff in most of her vignette appearances, and it may be that the posture and costume of the figure in the frame above 'Complement', 'Behaviovr', was Payne's model for the stage left figure, although her puffed sleeves certainly come from the Callot etching via Marshall. It also seems entirely likely that Payne had looked directly at Callot etchings, and quite possibly the *Balli*, since he absorbs their grace and vitality far more directly than does the hamfisted Marshall.

If the two figures on the right were conceived of as an independent group invented by William Marshall, what of the character on the left, or stage right? The figure is male, since the costume roughly matches that of the central bowing actor, although the stage-right figure does not wear a cloak (toga?) over the shoulder, but is apparently dressed in a flowing surcoat over the basic skirted tunic, which flies out behind him as he moves. His forearms are bare, where those of the central figure, after Callot, are not. He possibly wears a cap, he is unbearded, giving him a rather androgynous appearance, and he wields a rather unconvinc-

ing curved sword (it has a handle almost as long as its blade). What gives him interest is his elastic, complex posture. He possibly has a rather oriental air, designed to match the play's setting in Bactria, but a glance at the *Ecce Sponsus Venit* plate reveals that he is also very like the daughters of Jerusalem brandishing their palm leaves in ecstasy, and may be another adapted importation from that engraving.

There is one further title page which may have a bearing on this figure, and which certainly was a source for the *Messallina* engraving. It is an unsigned page from 1632, and was almost certainly done by Payne. It was engraved for Matthieu's *Vnhappy Prosperitie* (Plate 11). The supporting figure of Sejanus is instantly recognizable as the model for 'Silivs' on the *Messallina* page (Plate 2). The general pattern is once again related to the Virgil page, and it includes the (reversed) motif of the ship under sail, in the bottom right roundel, with Payne's characteristic curving, hooked waves, also to be seen in the ark vignette in *Sponsus*. The male faces shown in profile, those of Sejanus and the double-headed 'Janus' at lower centre, are similar to those of Turnus in the Virgil engraving, and to the Callot-influenced bowing actor in the *Roxana* engraving. The treatment of the distant figures in the bottom central scene of Sejanus' fall may be compared with Payne's handling of the figures immediately below Calvary in the *Sponsus* picture, or those in the balcony in *Roxana*: his background figures tend to become bald marionettes. The costume and sword of Sejanus are what immediately concern us. Apart from the cap, his dress appears to be very close to that worn by the stage-right figure in *Roxana* (and by the male figure in the bottom right vignette), while the sword is a model for that brandished by the actor: curved blade, curved hilts, and a hooked beak giving a curve to the end of the handle. The small scale of the stage vignette results in a rather clumsy, badly-proportioned rendering of these features, but Payne's intention is revealed by the Sejanus sword.

9 Jacques Callot, Bowing Gentleman,
La Noblesse Lorraine, c. 1620–1623

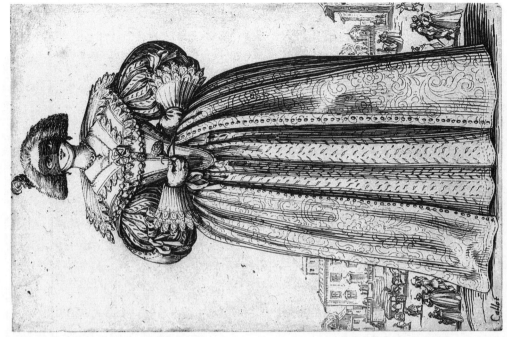

10 Jacques Callot, Masked Noblewoman,
La Noblesse Lorraine, c. 1620–1623

11   John Payne, unsigned title plate to *Vnhappy Prosperitie*, 1632

To sum up, most of the elements of the *Roxana* engraving can be accounted for as coming from elsewhere. The picture is not in any sense an original or particular depiction, but a job of work by one of the most accomplished contemporary engravers, who was probably not given a great deal of guidance by Alabaster himself. Asked to illustrate a stage, he invented a lover and a tyrant from visual types he knew. His general intent was to classicize, but not with any reference to classicism on the contemporary stage.

Aside from the level over the stage, which is at least hinted at in the Treschel Terence woodcuts,[25] one important feature of the *Roxana* picture remains: the stage railings, which are occasionally referred to in plays but for which we have no other pictorial evidence.[26] Was Payne here at least relying on his memory of visits to the playhouse? Judging by the weight of evidence assembled here we might be justly hesitant to say so. There is at least no known earlier picture of a railed stage which he might have copied.[27]

It should by now be evident that the *Messallina* engraving has no independent authority as a depiction of a theatre, real or imagined. Like so many other title pages, it copies existing visual models, and the central pattern is the *Roxana* page. Rawlins wisely disposes of Payne's puzzling top row of frames, and replaces it with a central oval frame with a bust of Claudius, badly done; the side panels become badly drawn heaps of greengrocery. The supporting 'Messallina', to the left of the central title panel, is essentially Payne's *Comedia* reversed, with hints of the costume of Philippa from the *Vnhappy Prosperitie* engraving. (See Plates 1, 2, 11). From the same page comes 'Silivs', the figure on the right, who is simply Sejanus reversed, cap and all, if a little more squat and stout in the leg.[28] The lower side panels are a pair of uninspired goats, obviously 'filler' material, which may have been suggested by the bottom left panel of the Jonson Folio page of 1616, reissued in 1640 with the

second volume of the *Works*. The *Roxana* stage is the basis for the bottom centre vignette, but has been rather badly redrawn, removing Payne's lively actors and gesturing audience, and showing only the stage and tiring house.

All in all, the *Messallina* page is hack work, but is no worse than many another contemporary engraving, and it was assembled in much the same way as was the *Roxana* page. J. Q. Adams acidly dismissed its depiction of the stage as the feeble effort of someone who couldn't draw figures, and if we have a certain aesthetic sympathy with his opinion our knowledge of Rawlins's career should make us more cautious. Was he adapting Payne's picture to represent more closely what he knew of the conditions at Salisbury Court? That he did not change it entirely is suspect, of course, given the largely fictional basis of Payne's composition, but perhaps he too wished to retain some kind

---

[25] Treschel's marvellously fanciful 'Theatrum' shows three galleries of audience, with the 'aediles' perched in a high box above and to the side of the 'Proscaenium'. In this connection, John Cranford Adams remarks that one cannot tell whether the *Roxana* audience is standing or sitting (*The Globe Playhouse*, 2nd. ed. (New York, 1961), p. 93); on the contrary it seems clear that Payne intends us to infer rows of ranked degrees – see the head at a lower level between the shoulders of the third and fourth figures from the left.

[26] They are shown in plan, but not in elevation, in both of Inigo Jones's theatre projects.

[27] Professor Alan Nelson has pointed out to me that a railed platform and an audience seated behind the stage were both features of Cambridge college stages. It is possible, therefore, that Payne was following Alabaster's directions in showing these details. Although Rawlins retains the railings in the *Messallina* picture, his entire elimination of human figures doesn't allow one to argue that he is depicting a London playhouse rather than a Cambridge college.

[28] The original headgear seems to be a version of a Phrygian cap, and is unlikely to be intended as 'a modern hat': see R. A. Foakes, *Illustrations of the English Stage 1580–1642* (Stanford, 1985), p. 80. Rawlins's choice of an illustration of Sejanus was perhaps prompted by Richards, whose play includes learned footnoted quotations on Roman decadence, much in the style of Matthieu's book, which he had perhaps read.

of reference to the classical stage, at least through its conventional Renaissance iconography. Yet Rawlins knew theatres, actors, and playwrights in a way that Payne, so far as we can tell, did not, and there seems to me every reason to think that his adaptations to Payne's design were made to match what he knew of the playhouse, or at least what he expected of it. By this I mean that the staging requirements of *The Rebellion* and of *Roxana* are similar in a number of respects: both, for instance, use the trap and an acting level over the stage, and it is precisely these features that Rawlins adds or adapts in his version of Payne's engraving.

The rather indefinite lines on the stage surface in the *Messallina* picture have been championed with more or less enthusiasm as our only pre-Restoration depiction of a stage trap. Wickham inks them in boldly, and Gurr boldly presents his redrawing as definitive, whereas Foakes is more cautious.[29] Despite the perfunctory and careless execution – it seems unlikely that any stage trap would be off-centre, as it is depicted – I believe that Rawlins is showing a theatrical feature which he knew was required in *Messallina*, as it was in his own play, and which existed at Salisbury Court, as it did at most other playhouses. Such an addition hardly turns the picture into a detailed portrayal of the playhouse, although the more radical change Rawlins makes to the tiring house perhaps comes closer to a specific representation.

Rawlins's treatment of the hangings on the lower and upper levels of his façade evidently derives from Payne. His depiction of decoration on the lower curtain may come from what he knew of playhouse fittings – equally it may be some slight decorative compensation for the missing figures of actors and audience. As a theatrical structure, however, what he shows behind the stage is a far more likely arrangement than that of Payne. Payne's balcony must be a cantilevered projection from some unseen support behind his curtain line, or is simply a further instance of the essentially

decorative nature of his scheme: he takes a Terentian curtained façade and makes it bear the weight of a stage gallery. Although less elegant in appearance, Rawlins's stage is more practicl. He shows the tiring house wall only at the upper level; on the stage a projecting curtained enclosure with a practical acting level forming its roof has been built out, possibly as a temporary arrangement for a particular play, in a fashion which has frequently been suggested by modern stage historians.[30] The upper level, entirely free of any visual restrictions in the way of balusters and railings, is accessible from the permanent central opening in the upper level of the tiring house. Any scene involving complex or protracted action above would benefit enormously from such an arrangement.

Yet one is prepared to trust Rawlins's grasp of practicality only so far. Not only does his use of Payne's fanciful theatre make his own suspect as primary evidence, but if, as I have suggested, the staging requirements of *The Rebellion* and *Messallina* govern what he shows, he plainly ignores certain demands in both plays which would involve a more radical recomposition of Payne's engraving. Both use the descent machine, for example, and there is no hint in the picture of any stage ceiling over the playing area; less extravagantly, both contain passages which make practical reference to stage doors, of which there is no sign in his engraving. Equally, from a practical point of view one distrusts the lateral suggestions of a polygonally projecting tiring house, and the even less likely continuation of the projecting booth along these walls. Lacking other evidence about Salisbury Court, one must be cautious, yet the polygonal stage comes from the eclectic invention of Payne, and it seems as if Rawlins is

---

[29] See Plate 4a/b; *The Shakespearean Stage*, p. 139; *Illustrations of the English Stage*, p. 81.

[30] Particularly in the seminal post-war studies of C. Walter Hodges and Richard Hosley. More recently, Scott McMillin has suggested the need for a similar structure at the Rose: see *The Elizabethan Theatre and The Book of Sir Thomas More* (Ithaca, 1987), chapter 6.

improvizing on the geometrical theme he has accepted by redrawing Payne's stage as his prominent foreground.

On balance, therefore, both illustrations must be relegated to the position of secondary evidence about the seventeenth-century stage. In histories of the theatre they should henceforth be identified by their engravers, and if they are used to speculate about particular theatres or types of theatre their nature and origin should be carefully considered. One is tantalized by the knowledge that the *Messallina* picture was made by a man who wrote a successfully produced play, frequented theatres, and knew actors. The disappointing awareness that as illustrator he made very little use of his theatrical knowledge should remind us of the conventional nature of so much pictorial evidence relating to the theatre of Shakespeare and his contemporaries.

RECYCLING THE EARLY HISTORIES: 'THE WARS OF THE ROSES' AND 'THE PLANTAGENETS'

LOIS POTTER

John Barton and Peter Hall reduced the three parts of *Henry VI* to two (Stratford, 1963), not only because of their length but also because they believed them to be, as Hall put it, 'a mess of angry and undifferentiated barons, thrashing about in a mass of diffuse narrative'.[1] When Terry Hands produced the most recent British stage version of the three plays in an unadapted form (Stratford, 1977) he converted some spectators but left others longing for the clarity and consistency of the Barton-Hall version. The key to the problem may lie in a remark made by Helen Mirren, the Queen Margaret of the production: 'One isn't playing in three plays, one is playing in a single long play – like a TV serial, or a serialized novel by Dickens.'[2] The success of Jane Howell's BBC production of 1982 resulted partly from the fact that Howell, like Mirren, recognized the affinity of the tetralogy to a TV series: at one point she compared it to *Dallas*.[3] Audiences of a serial which has several writers easily come to terms with the characteristics of the genre: cameo appearances of minor figures, inconsistencies of plot and characterization, even the writing in and out of characters to take account of casting changes. Moreover, the video recorder allows audiences to arrange viewing times to suit themselves, thus solving the purely practical difficulty of fitting in so many theatre visits in the right order. Television may well turn out to be the best home for the Henry VI plays.

Meanwhile, it seems likely that the live theatre will continue to condense and adapt them. Both the English Shakespeare Company *Wars of the Roses* (1987–9) and the Royal Shakespeare Company *Plantagenets* (1988–9) reduced the three Henry VI plays to two (now renamed) and wrote in bridging and clarifying passages, though not to the extent of Barton and Hall. Michael Bogdanov (ESC) came to the plays after directing *The Henries* (the Hal plays of the 'second tetralogy') in 1986; in the following year, when he added *Richard II* and the earlier histories to the group, all seven plays were carefully linked together, sometimes with the aid of interpolated lines. For instance, in the opening scene of *Henry V*, the Bishop of Ely reminded the Archbishop of Canterbury that Henry's claim to the French throne was dangerously similar to Mortimer's claim to the English throne. Adrian Noble (RSC), on the other hand, treated the adaptation as a self-contained work with little reference to past or future. The ESC sequence was designed for touring, which meant that both the cast and the set had to be as versatile as possible. *The Plantagenets* could be more elaborately staged and there was less doubling, which meant that more actors were available for crowd scenes and large-scale effects.

Given the difference of their contexts, the two adaptations (the ESC's by Bogdanov and

---

[1] *The Wars of the Roses*, BBC, 1970, p. vii.
[2] Homer D. Swander, 'The Rediscovery of *Henry VI*', *Shakespeare Quarterly*, 29 (1978), 146–63; p. 152.
[3] *Henry VI Part One*, The BBC Shakespeare, 1983, p. 22.

Michael Pennington, the RSC's based on a version by Charles Wood) were less different than might have been expected. Condensation in both largely affected the number of battle scenes, especially in the French episodes, and the plays lost colourful anecdotes like the Countess of Auvergne's attempted capture of Talbot and the combat between the Armourer and his apprentice. The RSC actually did more cutting and transposing,[4] but the ESC version probably *seemed* freer because of its more casual production style and because its interpolations were in easily recognizable modern English. The ESC directors also modernized the young princes' lines in *Richard III* to make them easier and to save rehearsal time, as the children who played these parts were recruited locally at the various touring venues.

The effect of both adaptations was, curiously, to darken the tone of the sequence. Individually, each of the *Henry* plays originally ended on an up-beat note: Part One with a truce in France and the Dauphin swearing fealty to the English king, Part Two with the Yorkist victory at St Albans, and Part Three with Edward IV in triumph hoping that war has given place to 'lasting joy'. Of course, all three of these happy endings are provisional and ironic, but, as is clear in the case of *Henry V*, hindsight need not diminish the theatrical satisfaction when a character orders, 'Sound drums and trumpets.' All two-part versions, however, place the 'victory' in France at the halfway point of the first part and end the play with the deaths of Cardinal Beaufort and the Duke of Suffolk and the King's growing awareness of the failure of his reign. In the second part, York's rebellion, like Cade's, rises and falls in the course of a single play, and Edward's triumph is followed by a reminder that Richard's play is to follow. Though the *Wars of the Roses* script of 1963 may be the main influence on these restructurings, they can be traced further back in time. The ending of the first play can be found even in the otherwise very different adaptation by John Crowne (1680),

while the end of the second play, where Richard Gloucester seems about to take the audience straight into the famous opening soliloquy of his own play, was used in Barry Jackson's Birmingham Repertory Theatre production in 1952.[5]

The pessimism implied in this progression was reflected visually in the 1963 *Wars of the Roses*; as the designer John Bury wrote, 'Colour drains and drains from the stage.'[6] In the theatre, this means that as the audience gets more tired the plays become more tiring, a fact which particularly affects *Richard III*. It is usually argued that this play, above all, benefits from cycle production, which can make sense of its numerous references to the past. It is also true, however, that reintegrating it into its context often makes it into a pretty bleak experience. Reviewers of both the Hall–Barton *Wars of the Roses* and of Jane Howell's television production felt that the actor who had been successful as the young Richard Gloucester was a disappointment when he came to what was supposed to be his own star vehicle.[7] This was not really the fault of either actor. The rôle has become mythical; audiences expect a great love-hate relationship with a star actor and a sensational fight at the end. Taken on its own, the play can be a psychological tragedy or fantasy or dream. Linked with its predecessors, however, it becomes part of historical time; its characters and their motives become explicable. Richard must be the

---

4 Elizabeth S. C. Brandow, 'History, Royal or English: A Study of the Royal Shakespeare Company's *The Plantagenets* and the English Shakespeare Company's *The Wars of the Roses*', unpublished MA thesis, University of Birmingham, 1989. I am grateful to Ms Brandow for letting me see this thesis, which is the result of the study of far more performances than I was able to attend.

5 See Barry Jackson, 'On Producing *Henry VI*', *Shakespeare Survey 6* (1953), 49–52; pp. 51–2.

6 *The Wars of the Roses*, p. 237.

7 See, e.g., *The Times* review of 21 August 1963, reprinted in John Elsom, ed., *Postwar British Criticism* (1981), pp. 130–1, and Bingham, p. 228, on its 'unfortunately anticlimactic' effect in the BBC series.

symbol and product of his society, not an exhilarating star turn. Nor does the end of the play relieve the gloom. When Bosworth Field is seen in the context of so many other bloody battles, it is hard to believe that the death of one ruler, or the advent of any other, can possibly make the slightest difference to the future of the country. Historically, this is certainly arguable, but audiences are getting tired of downbeat endings. The problem of balancing the demands of history and of the theatre was solved by both Bogdanov and Noble, but in very different ways.

In the 1986 *Henries*, Bogdanov had already combined a belief in 'history' with a distrust of 'costume drama' as such. The war in *Henry V* was essentially a conflation of most of the wars that have happened this century, most notoriously the one in the Falklands. When he added *Richard II* and the second tetralogy to the scheme, Bogdanov avoided imposing too clear a 'design concept' on the overall sequence. Instead, Chris Dyer (sets) and Stephanie Howard (costumes) suggested a double time scheme. One covered a period of roughly 200 years; the other was keyed to the atmosphere of particular scenes and characters. Richard II's reign was set in the age of the Prince Regent and the Gothic revival. Richard's relationship with Bolingbroke was partly a conflict between Regency and Victorian values, while in Henry IV's relationship with Hal Victorianism confronted the modern age. The later plays covered some of the same ground chronologically, but retold the history of the twentieth century from a more sinister angle. Henry VI and his council looked like figures from pre-1914 photographs. Edward IV hinted variously at both Edward VIII and George VI. Queen Margaret was probably intended at times – but not always – to remind audiences of a contemporary Margaret; hence, her Frenchness was not much emphasized. The war in France and the Wars of the Roses represented a merging of the first and the second World Wars: 'Plus ça change, plus c'est la même

guerre.' The low point of the sequence was the second half of the Henry VI cycle, where the horror and noise of the battle scenes certainly proved that war was hell but came close to making one feel the same about the theatre. The production's historical sense allowed some development of weaponry, but frequently the relationship of swords to guns was part of the production's sign language: those who used guns were associated with *Realpolitik* (a number of characters were shot in the back); swords were used for duels – vestiges of an old value system – but also for brutal killings like those of young Rutland and York himself.

After the military atmosphere of the other two plays, the beginning of *Richard III* showed all the characters back in civilian life, where the uneasy attempt to reconcile York and Lancaster took the form of a cocktail party, attended by the entire cast. Barry Stanton, the popular Falstaff and Chorus in *Henry V*, combined these rôles as, carrying a clipboard with notes on it, he wandered among the guests, telling the audience about their appalling past histories and the awful fates that awaited most of them. The scene was probably necessary, since audiences for *Richard III* generally included many people who had not attended the other plays, but its tone was deliberately comic. Margaret's first appearance in this civilian world, in an old khaki uniform absurdly covered with medals, showed her unwillingness to forget the past and her inability to learn from it. Her society, likewise unable to learn, would be condemned to repeat the same errors over and over. Against this gruesome background, however, the anarchic humour of Richard of Gloucester (Andrew Jarvis), and his deliberate, deceptive self-presentation as the blunt Yorkshireman ('eh, by gum!') emerged as a positive relief. Whereas Prince Hal's 'modern' world was a pub full of punks and dropouts, *Richard III* combined a number of worlds familiar to most film-goers; the sinister higher reaches of Big Business, with their metaphorical back-stabbings (Richard's throne room was an office

12   *The Plantagenets (Edward IV)*. Royal Shakespeare Company at The Royal Shakespeare Theatre, 1989.
Oliver Cotton as Jack Cade

with a personal computer on the desk); gangsterland, as when Richard's bodyguard ludicrously attempted to impersonate holy churchmen; and the spy thriller, suggested when Stanley made his treasonable telephone call to Richmond and then left the receiver off the hook. By this time, the tone had darkened to the point where the production risked losing its momentum, but Bogdanov managed to bring excitement to the final scenes without glamourizing fighting and violent death. Bosworth Field was Armageddon, or the final nuclear explosion; a few lines from the battle scenes were shouted in complete darkness, then, in what seemed a time-warp, the lights came up on two fully armed medieval figures miming the combat between Richard and Richmond – *then*, in another startling change of scene, we were in a television studio where the victorious Tudor and his relatives were being made up and groomed for their post-coup interviews. The dazzling theatricality of all this counteracted the sense of anticlimax usually felt when Richmond's victory speech is treated cynically. Here, he could speak it with conviction, but it was clearly a media event, reflected in tiny images on all the studio monitors.

The great strength of the ESC production was the clarity with which it told its story. The production avoided letting any one character dominate the plays. For instance, whereas the 1960s and 1970s generally treated the pacifist Henry VI with great sympathy, the ESC saw him as just one of many characters involved in a power struggle. Because the production was basically in favour of effective political action, the emphasis seemed, if anything, to favour characters who were successful, however ruthless: York and Richard Gloucester came out as well as anyone. Many of the best moments, however, involved ordinary people. A good example was the treatment of the Three Citizens in *Richard III*. I shall quote a description that gives more detail than I could do:

To the sounds of traffic off-stage, a youthful newspaper seller entered, in jeans and sneakers, holding up a paper on which the six inch banner headline was clearly visible; 'KING DEAD'. He shouted, 'King Dead! King Dead! Ed's dead! King shuffles off mortal coil!' in a raucous cockney and sold a paper to Second Citizen, middle-aged, cheerful and optimistic, clad in fake sheepskin jacket and cloth cap, carrying a supermarket shopping bag. Third Citizen was elderly, possibly a retired insurance clerk, wearing a full-length sober grey overcoat and homburg hat, clearly given to pompous pronouncements; he took possession of the newspaper and proceeded to pour authoritative gloom and doom on the other two. This production made clear that his fatuous aphorisms ('When clouds are seen') are exactly that, not gems of folk-lore, and his penultimate line: 'But leave it all to Gawd' [sic] (line 45) made his passivity and vulnerability to manipulation painfully obvious.[8]

This account illustrates two important aspects of the ESC interpretation: its willingness to take the non-noble characters seriously and its distrust of the moral and fatalistic generalizations which have sometimes been taken for the 'message' of the plays. However, most characters were allowed to die with dignity, and the pious sentiments which come so automatically to their lips were not ridiculed. The coexistence of these sentiments with their ruthless ambition and political cynicism was allowed to speak for itself. The naturalness and quietness of the actors' delivery was particularly striking in scenes that are normally played more emotionally, like York's harrowing death, and the materialist approach worked surprisingly well even where one would have least expected it, as with the ghosts in *Richard III*. They behaved in the familiar yet grotesque way of figures in dreams; Richard even welcomed some of his former friends, forgetting, until they turned on him, both that they were dead and that he had killed them. They had no reality outside his nightmare. It was only in the treatment of Joan of Arc that cutting and rewriting was needed in order to maintain the

---

[8] Brandow, '*History, Royal or English*', pp. 41–2.

rationalist emphasis of the production. Joan was innocent and rather fey, and her lines were altered so that she did not condemn her own country or (in soliloquy) reveal herself as a witch. Her responsibility was further lessened when Burgundy, in a ten-line speech which was 'the only substantial non-Shakespearean passage in the trilogy',[9] showed that he already had doubts about his alliance with England before Joan's approach to him. The production simply refused to believe in witchcraft.

The Plantagenets, on the contrary, constantly stressed the power of the irrational. Bob Crowley's brilliant designs were derived from the emblems so often mentioned in the plays (rose, sun, boar), but their visual excitement mattered much more than their meaning. The symbolic language was one of contrasts, even polarities. The throne not only appeared to extend all the way to heaven but also continued below the stage to become a prison cell. The sun of York turned black in *Richard III*, then began to roll, its rays suggesting a circular saw or the cogs in the Grand Mechanism which was Jan Kott's description of the historical process. The contrast between the winter of our discontent and the sun of York was unmistakable. When Margaret lamented to Louis of France the change from her queenly status 'in former golden days', she was standing, in black velvet, on a white floorcloth, confronting a golden court; Edward's court dress was also the glittering gold of stage finery. The white floorcloth became the snow-covered battlefield of Tewkesbury, where it was stained with blood; later it was hauled up to become the backcloth to the rest of the play. Winter came back with a vengeance in Richard's reign, as Elizabeth and the other women made their way to the Tower in falling snow. The white world was also the landscape in which the ghosts appeared. The effect of these strong contrasts was heightened by rapid cutting (in a cinematic sense), with bits of one scene remaining visible in the next one. Talbot's body was one of the corpses that rose to become the evil spirits invoked by Joan; it

remained onstage to the end of the first half, Joan's body later hanging above it in a parody of a crucifixion. The effect was to draw attention to parallels between characters and to remind one of the extent to which the past weighed on the present.

Leslie Fiedler suggested in 1972 that the recent theatrical success of the *Henry VI* plays might be linked to a current revival of interest in the occult.[10] He was thinking primarily of the female witches – Joan la Pucelle, Margery Jourdain, the Margaret of the cursing scenes. *The Plantagenets*, however, took the concept of witchcraft further. For example, in the scene where Joan seduces Burgundy away from England, he was initially so revolted by her that he was on the point of running her through with his sword. She fearlessly urged him on, and then – desperately, as if bewitched – he threw it on the ground in front of her. This obvious inversion of the scene between Richard and Anne was only one of several ways in which the other plays were made to point forward to *Richard III*. When Eleanor of Gloucester held her illicit conference with Margery Jourdain, both productions supplemented the Duchess's questions in the text with the one that is so curiously absent: what is going to happen to her husband? But, whereas the ESC version asked and answered about the Gloucester known as the 'good Duke Humphrey', the RSC, borrowing an idea from Barton's *Wars of the Roses*, made the spirit palter with Eleanor in a double sense, as Margery shrieked that 'Gloucester shall be king!' In case the point was lost on the audience, the second play of the trilogy had its interval just after the point where the victorious Edward gives his brothers their new ducal titles and Richard shows reluctance to take the name of Gloucester.

Richard III thus was the Anti-Messiah who

---

9 Brandow, 'History, Royal or English', p. 53.
10 *The Stranger in Shakespeare*, 1972; Croom Helm 1973, Paladin 1974, p. 55.

13   *The Plantagenets*. Royal Shakespeare Company at the Royal Shakespeare Theatre, 1989; *Richard III, His Death*.
Hastings's head is revealed: Anton Lesser (centre) as Richard, Oliver Cotton (far left) as Buckingham

fulfilled all the earlier prophecies of evil. In keeping with this ghoulish vision, the scene in which he appears between two supposed churchmen was played as a kind of black mass: his dining table had been hastily turned into an altar, with a large cross, a huge Bible, and a covered silver salver. Besides the slapstick frequently used in productions of this scene, there was also blasphemy: at the end, Richard stood on the Bible and the formerly recalcitrant citizens, who had just discovered that the salver bore Hastings's decapitated head, agreed with a hasty 'Amen' that he should assume the throne. Like a medieval Vice, Richard himself addressed the audience with the Scrivener's line, asking who could fail to see the deception being perpetrated. The appearance of a theatrical curtain was perhaps intended to remind the

audience of its own complicity in the deception of the stage. The most obviously illusory characters, the ghosts, were powerful figures here, bringing with them both airs from heaven and blasts from hell. In the opening play, the bright red and blue heraldic stage backdrop had collapsed to the floor, revealing blackness behind it, as Exeter prophesied disaster for England. In the nightmare scene, it was Richard's heraldic tent which collapsed, revealing the ghosts in their eerie white landscape behind it. Rather than entering his world, as in the ESC production, they seemed to beckon him into theirs. They were also present on the battlefield, and largely responsible for his defeat; they remained there until the end of the play.

As in Noble's *Duchess of Malfi* and *Macbeth*,

the production showed a strong contrast between the humanly domestic on the one hand and the horrific on the other. In the first part of the cycle the horror dominated. The dying Cardinal Beaufort was covered with leeches; the deaths of all the 'witches' took place onstage (Margery repeated the incantation already used by Joan); the rebels placed the severed heads of Cade's victims on poles and made them conduct a grotesque conversation in the air. The domestic tone entered the trilogy only in its second part. Elizabeth Woodville, at her first appearance, was accompanied by her children and her brother, and it was evident that she always saw herself as part of a family group. York's son Rutland had been played by an adult actor, but from this point on children became increasingly important: little Richmond, little George Stanley, the little princes. Increasingly, too, they became part of the horror. A chilling moment at the end of the second part came when, as Edward hoped that his wife had 'a son for me', he stumbled over the body of the young Prince Edward, whom he and his brothers had just hacked to death, and was fleetingly disturbed by the omen. In Elizabeth's last appearance in *Richard III*, she was carrying a doll, a pathetic substitute for her lost children; Richard grabbed at it when he urged her to win her daughter for him. In his smallness and unpredictability, Richard (Anton Lesser) was himself like a demonic child, and this quality was duplicated in his nephew, the small, malicious young York (also named Richard). The paper crown used to humiliate York reappeared as a toy for this child; prominent among the Christmas presents brought to the Tower by Elizabeth and the other women was a rocking horse, a miniature of the one for which Richard would call on the battlefield.

In contrast to the mainly naturalistic *Wars of the Roses, The Plantagenets* used a larger, more emotional acting style. Character contrasts were broader: a tall, icy-cold Somerset (Tom Fahy) confronted a calm, genial Warwick (David Lyon) and a stocky, passionate York

(David Calder), whose warmth and enthusiasm could be seen, in his sons, turning to sensual and emotional self-indulgence. The characters were on the whole emotional beings, individuals rather than representatives of particular views. Margaret (Penny Downie) was prepared to use her sexuality to get her way with her husband; Henry (Ralph Fiennes), despite his unworldliness, was in love with her and pathetically grateful for any signs of affection. The death of Suffolk changed her, though she never became as unrelievedly cold and fiendish as her ESC counterpart; Henry also acquired a disillusioned clarity of vision which, without playing for sympathy, nevertheless won it.

Comparisons between the two productions naturally looked first for their political implications, and the game of 'more subversive than thou' was widely played. Both Michael Pennington's programme note for the ESC and Alan Sinfield's for the RSC argue for a politically 'radical' interpretation of the plays. Presumably the RSC agreed with Sinfield's insistence that a production of the plays should show power systems as man-made, historically rooted rather than timeless, and capable of change. In this respect, it could be argued, the RSC's locating of the plays in a generalized 'medieval' setting was more genuinely 'radical' than the ESC's frequent implication that Shakespeare had really been writing about the twentieth century. The RSC's positive treatment of Richmond's victory also contrasted with the ESC's cynicism about it. Surely both interpretations can be justified politically. It is true that, as Sinfield points out, Richmond's victory is not a change of power-system but only 'another coup by violent magnates'. It is also, however, the plays' one example of successful action against an oppressive régime. Is it preferable to suggest that there is no point in taking such action, since the only effect must inevitably be the replacement of one corrupt ruler by another?

It was of course in their treatment of the common people that the politics of the two

14 *The Wars of the Roses.* English Shakespeare Company, on tour, Michael Pennington (left), as Jack Cade, with citizens

productions could most easily be compared. Both, it seemed to me, brought out the 'Brechtian' qualities of the episode of Saunder Simpcox: it balances Gloucester's 'judgement' on Simpcox against the judgement soon to be pronounced on him, shows that the couple perpetrated their fraud for 'pure need', and, by making Queen Margaret laugh when Simpcox is whipped, ensures that we will be uncomfortable if we have just done so ourselves. The scene between the disguised Henry VI and the two gamekeepers who arrest him is another example. It sets the king's belief in his spiritual crown of content against the two commoners'

obvious cynicism about it. Though the text appears to favour Henry's view of 'the lightness of you common men', both productions presented this attitude as the product of human bitterness rather than Christ-like resignation and implied that he did not really have the content that he claimed. The Jack Cade scenes, of course, are the main problem. The fact that Cade himself is really only a tool of the Duke of York is made clear in the text, but both he and his rebellion quickly take on a life of their own. Both directors seemed to be depicting him, along the lines suggested by Sinfield, as a parody of the unscrupulous ambition of his betters. The ESC played Cade's speeches as National Front propaganda. The lynching of the Clerk of Chatham was particularly horrifying because he was not merely an innocent passer-by but an interested lower middle-class sympathizer trying to be part of a working-class crowd. But even the most sympathetic of the crowd's victims, Lord Say, was not allowed to go unanswered: when he asked rhetorically, 'Is my apparel sumptuous to behold?' someone in the crowd replied, 'It's bettr'n ours, though, innit?' It is unlikely, however, that audiences took these scenes as anything but a comic-horrific depiction of mob behaviour. Isobel Armstrong put her finger on the problem in her analysis of the ESC production of *The Henries*: the 'low-life' scenes may constitute a subversive critique of the ruling class, but, since characters who lack an enlightened awareness of their situation cannot convey it to the audience, 'the brutalization which is the result of oppression can actually appear to justify the ruthless power exercised to control it'.[11] And, as Sinfield admits in the RSC programme, 'it wouldn't be easy to get a positive political vision out of *The Plantagenets*'.

The real reason why *The Plantagenets* gave the impression of being relatively conservative is that the political meaning of a production is inseparable from its theatrical effect. Theoretically, there is no reason why a lavish production should not make a radical point, just as a production built round a star (I am thinking of Derek Jacobi's *Richard II* and *Richard III*, which I have no space to discuss properly) can make a statement – both theatrically and politically relevant – about the infinite capriciousness which absolute power permits and the hypnotic attraction exerted by it. But the expensive decor of the stage at Stratford and the Barbican was itself a statement about the kind of audience that might feel at home there. Not only was it easier on the eye and ear, it allowed spectators to ignore the meaning and enjoy the spectacle. One obvious example was the end of the first half of the first play, which cut rapidly

between the making of peace with France and Henry's decision to marry Margaret of Anjou. As Suffolk told the audience his intention of governing the kingdom through Margaret – in lines which are as cynical about love as they are about politics – the English army, behind him, raised their banners and, to a great burst of triumphant music, gave a shout of victory. The juxtaposition was obviously ironic, but the effect, in practice, was to drown out Suffolk's lines in an operatic finale.

One of the reasons that the plays have been seen as Brechtian is that a cycle production, with its need for extensive doubling between plays, tends to displace interest from the characters to the actors themselves. As if to avoid this response, reviewers generally tried to see a thematic meaning in the doubling. In 1988, I noted the appropriateness of John Castle's playing both Bolingbroke and York, 'the successful and unsuccessful usurper'.[12] When the plays underwent partial recasting in the following year, the ESC changed its doubling patterns so that Barry Stanton now doubled Falstaff with York and with the Chorus in *Henry V*. Needless to say, one could justify this triple too: Falstaff and York represent different kinds of rebellion against authority; Falstaff and the Chorus both provide a perspective on the action. But I now feel that most of this search for patterning is really a refusal to accept the actor-centred nature of these plays. One piece of casting that was common to both productions was the combination of Suffolk, Cade and Buckingham, played by Pennington (in 1989) for the ESC and by Oliver Cotton in *The Plantagenets*. But neither production ever doubled York and Cade, which would have made a thematic point and which has, moreover, a theatrical precedent (James Ander-

---

[11] 'Thatcher's Shakespeare?', *Textual Practice*, 3 (1989), 1–14; p. 11.

[12] *Times Literary Supplement*, 1–7 April 1988, p. 360.

son in 1864).[13] There is a sense in which doubling is itself a theme of the *Henry VI* saga. Characters sometimes deliberately assume the rôles of others, as when Talbot vows, after Salisbury's death, to 'be a Salisbury' to the French, or York takes up the claim to the throne bequeathed him by the dying Mortimer, or York's youngest son says, 'Richard, I bear thy name; I'll venge thy death.' But none of these reincarnations could have been indicated by the doubling of parts. It would seem, rather, that the effect of doubling is usually to draw attention to the skill rather than to the 'message'. This was particularly true in the small-cast ESC productions, where easily recognizable ESC actors, like Michael Pennington and Andrew Jarvis, aroused audience interest in whatever parts they played.

The shock effect of Bogdanov's production did not really reside in its politics – which, in any case, were those of much of its audience. Everyone who sees the Henry VI–Richard III group knows that they are mostly by Shakespeare and that Shakespeare did not write about the police force, the BBC, or World War I. The production's theatrical style and its occasional interpolations, did, however, have the power to shock. This is because Shakespeare's words are normally the object of so much reverence that any obvious alteration of them – or any comic juxtaposition of Elizabethan English and modern situations – can seem like an attack on a god. Professor Armstrong ended up wondering 'how far it is ever possible to control the way you are interpreted'.[14] There are some things about audience reaction which seem unchangeable: the readiness to be distracted by the visual at the expense of the verbal, the tendency to confuse good acting with a good rôle. In short – and this must be why many political critics seem to dislike the theatre – people have a way of missing the point. Given the difficulties of being genuinely subversive, virtually the only genuinely shocking activity that remains is to label Shakespeare as part of the Establishment and then encourage the audience to ridicule Shakespeare himself.

---

13 A. C. Sprague, *Shakespeare's Histories: Plays for the Stage*, London: Society for Theatre Research, 1964, p. 112.

14 Armstrong, '*Thatcher's Shakespeare?*', p. 12.

SHAKESPEARE PRODUCTION IN ENGLAND IN 1989

STANLEY WELLS

Since the demise of the Old Vic Company in 1963, Shakespeare production in England has been dominated by the work of the Royal Shakespeare Company operating mainly in Stratford-upon-Avon and London but also taking full seasons to Newcastle-upon-Tyne and touring the provinces. Other companies have come and gone – the Actors' Company (1972–83), Prospect Theatre Company (1961–79) – and the National Theatre has put on a number of productions, starting with John Dexter's *Othello* with Laurence Olivier (1964); but for two decades Shakespeare virtually disappeared from the West End and from the commercial theatre in general.

West End productions depend for their drawing power largely on the appeal of popular actors in leading rôles. A result of the dwindling of such productions has been the increasing dominance of the director. Whereas Gielgud directed a Shakespeare production at Stratford during the 1950s when another actor, Anthony Quayle, was joint Artistic Director, since Peter Hall took over in 1960 no leading actor or actress has directed a major production there. Another result has been an increasingly intellectual approach. West End theatre is aimed at a paying public looking to be entertained. The subsidized companies acknowledge a responsibility to the educational world, many of their directors are university trained, they have felt free, even perhaps obliged, to re-explore the plays, departing from performance traditions evolved in the popular theatre, re-

thinking the texts, creating new – and often longer – acting versions, experimenting with the application of theatrical techniques related to the work of avant-garde dramatists, and responding to contemporary intellectual currents in a manner that was not encouraged by the commercial theatre.

During the last two or three years a marked change has occurred. Shakespeare productions at the National Theatre have increased in number. The Old Vic has re-emerged with a company under the overall direction of Jonathan Miller performing generally 'classical' plays and with Shakespeare in its repertoire. Among companies without a permanent home (such as Cheek by Jowl, which has done several Shakespeare plays in excitingly experimental fashion) actors have taken increasing responsibility for direction and administration. The English Shakespeare Company has had the actor Michael Pennington in joint command with the director Michael Bogdanov for its productions of a cycle of English history plays; the actor Kenneth Branagh founded the Renaissance Theatre Company presenting productions of Shakespeare directed once again by leading actors – Judi Dench, Geraldine McEwan, Derek Jacobi, and Branagh himself. And in the West End, commercial managements have been putting on plays with popular actors in the leading roles – Derek Jacobi as Richard II and Richard III, Alan Bates and Felicity Kendal as Benedick and Beatrice, and the American super-star Dustin Hoffman as Shylock.

Shakespeare productions have been running in competition: in 1988 the National Theatre, the RSC, and Cheek by Jowl vied with each other in productions of *The Tempest*; *Cymbeline* could be seen both at the National and at the Barbican; the English Shakespeare Company's *Wars of the Roses* was challenged by the RSC with *The Plantagenets*, and both had plays in common with the Jacobi venture; in 1989 there have been simultaneous productions of *Hamlet* at both the National Theatre and the Royal Shakespeare Theatre.

The result has been a broadening of the range of production styles and of acting techniques, a greater eclecticism on the Shakespearian theatrical scene. But at the same time there has been a lot of cross-fertilization, and it would be misleading to write as if a great divide existed between subsidized and commercial theatre. Dustin Hoffman's Shylock was directed by Sir Peter Hall in his first commercial production of Shakespeare after nearly three decades of work for the major subsidized companies. Conversely, Trevor Nunn's production of *Othello* for the RSC represented a return to Shakespeare after several years of directing sensationally successful West End musicals. Both Michael Pennington and Michael Bogdanov have worked for the RSC, as has Clifford Williams who directed Derek Jacobi's West End productions. Many of the directors responsible for recent major productions have been prominent for twenty or thirty years in both commercial and subsidized theatre, and not all have significantly changed their methods.

A company putting on a play by Shakespeare enters into an implicit contract to engage the minds and hearts of its audience with a work of the distant past. As I have suggested, the tastes and capacities of audiences differ. Many of those who flocked to see Dustin Hoffman in a sumptuous production of *The Merchant of Venice* would have taken no interest in Deborah Warner's austere *King John*, playing simultaneously in The Pit. Persons of a scholarly bent looking forward to Elizabethan revival pro-

ductions in the promised reconstruction of the Globe might be repelled by updated versions of *A Midsummer Night's Dream* and *Hamlet* such as have been on offer during the current year. And of course style is no guide to quality. A production does not need to be aggressively modern to break through the time-barrier, engaging its audience through language, character, and action; and even productions employing thoroughly up-to-date methods may fail either because they have not found an appropriate metaphor for the tenor of the text, or through inadequacies of execution. Some of the productions seen in 1989 have been able to communicate with the spirit of the times while employing a variety of theatrical modes, others have seemed to exist in a kind of time-warp, as if emptily recreating styles and methods of an earlier period. At one extreme, Clifford Williams's production of *Richard II* seemed to me to resemble some of the less successful Old Vic productions of the immediately post-war period, whereas Ron Daniels's *Hamlet* and John Caird's *A Midsummer Night's Dream* brought the plays fully up-to-date in productions that could have been given at no other time. In the remainder of this essay I want to write about some of the more important productions of 1989 with particular attention to the variety of methods that can be used to bring a Shakespeare text to contemporary theatrical life.

Playing spaces are becoming increasingly varied. In spite of the growing interest in Elizabethan theatrical conditions inspired both by Sam Wanamaker's plans to reconstruct the Globe and by the discovery of remains of the Globe and Rose, no one has attempted an authentically Elizabethan production, but Stratford's Swan Theatre provides a setting that has important features in common with buildings for which the plays were written, and Terry Hands's production of *Romeo and Juliet* did nothing to disguise them. The setting was the wooden frame of the theatre itself, with its thrust stage and a balcony at the first gallery level against the back wall and another contiguous with the second gallery (that is to say, forward of the lower balcony). A few fronds of foliage hung from above the upper balcony, and stage lighting was generally warm and mellow. Musicians played out of sight, and the only stage furniture was an occasional stool or bench and, for the closing scenes, a bed that converted into a bier. In this setting one scene flowed uninterruptedly into the next, the auditorium itself being used for some entries and exits. The opening Chorus wore white slacks and a sweat shirt, donning a scarlet cloak and golden chain for his transformation into Prince Escalus; otherwise costumes, indeterminate in style though with hints both of late Renaissance Italy and of Japan, favoured beige and cream colours.

One of the most important factors in bringing Shakespeare's text to life in any production is the style of speech, especially of verse speaking. There is currently much debate about this. Peter Hall favours a distinctly formal approach, with upward inflections and even slight pauses at the ends of lines, a style that can verge on the artificial or even the eccentric (see *Shakespeare Survey 42*, p. 143). Terry Hands's approach, as demonstrated in this production, is far more conversational, sometimes descending into the casual, the sense often over-riding the line-endings and breaking up the rhythm. One of the Swan's temptations is to offer the spectator enough light to consult a text (which indeed is provided in the programme, though changes made during rehearsal have usually rendered its indications of cuts out of date by the time the production opens). This revealed that Hands had made internal cuts probably amounting to not more than a couple of hundred lines – the performance lasted for three and a half hours – and that some of the actors, particularly Margaret Courtenay as the Nurse (who spoke her reminiscences of Juliet's childhood as prose, as they are printed in the first quarto), often abandoned the verse structure and resorted to unrhythmical paraphrase. The result was a gain in naturalness but a loss in stylistic expressiveness. Other actors, especially Patrick Godfrey as Friar Laurence, were more successful in making the verse sound new-minted without losing its rhythms and music. He made me conscious as never before of the foreboding irony of Romeo's entrance immediately after the lines

> Two such opposèd kings encamp them still
> In man as well as herbs – grace and rude will;
> And where the worser is predominant,
> Full soon the canker death eats up that plant.
>
> (2.2.27–30)

The illusion of spontaneity in speech is one aspect of the actor's creation of a sense of individual character, a feat which must be the result of an interplay between the actor's personal characteristics and his sense of the demands of the rôle. As is revealed by many of the essays in the series *Players of Shakespeare* (Cambridge University Press, vol. 1, 1985, edited by Philip Brockbank; vol. 2, 1989, edited by Russell Jackson and Robert Smallwood), most actors in approaching a rôle seek sub-textual pointers to an underlying psychological consistency which will motivate their words and actions and guide them – and their audiences – through the diversities of the text. This gives a clue to another important factor in making the play live for modern audiences – the need to suggest that the words of the play well up from the character's inner being, not just that they have been learnt by the actor. For me, the most successful character in this respect was Mercutio, played by David O'Hara in an unremittingly Scottish accent but with insolently confident ease of timing – he would keep us and his onstage hearers waiting for just long enough to create the sense that precisely these words and no others were what had come into his mind – and with a sub-text, motivating the bawdy, of intense but undirected sexuality, conveyed in gesture and body language as well as vocal emphases. I didn't quite see the point of miming masturbation as he spoke of the parson's dream of another benefice – have I missed some obscure word play? – but the sense of male bonding not quite amounting to homosexuality was powerfully conveyed in one of Mercutio's bawdiest passages (2.1) full of fantasies about Romeo's sexuality, in which he leapt on Benvolio's back and groped his crotch as if impelled to mock the absent Romeo by the pressure of repressed impulses within himself. Later (2.4) he kissed Romeo on the lips, heartily if not lingeringly.

No other performance suggested such psychological complexity, though Mark Rylance, a genuinely young, freshly attractive Romeo, imbued the rôle with a strong sense of melancholic fatalism expressed partly through a lugubrious if musical delivery that did not entirely avoid monotony. His Juliet, Georgia Slowe, slim, raven-haired, and with big dark eyes, looked so naturally young that there was no need for her exaggerated enactments of girlish impetuosity. The ballroom scene froze to a standstill for the lovers' shared sonnet – an effective and legitimate way of suggesting the timelessness of their love, though there is equally a case for maintaining movement around them to suggest the contrast between two modes of experience. Similarly, though the placing of Juliet in the upper balcony stressed the obstacles the lovers have to overcome, it reduced one of the rare opportunities to suggest genuine communication between them. (And surely Juliet should be already visible on 'But soft, what light...'?) Particularly in the later part of the play, this Juliet failed to project her lines as the expression of inner emotions, relying too much on a generalized, over-shrill vehemence that gave no sense of Juliet's maturing capacity to master experience.

The Swan's upper levels, and the sophistication of its lighting equipment, were put to good ironic use in the staging of the play's climactic episodes. Juliet's bed was put forth at the beginning of the scene (4.3) in which she chooses her wedding garments (the 1597 ['bad'] quarto directs 'She fals vpon her bed within the Curtaines' at the end of the scene). She lay on the bed after taking the potion, and the lighting shifted to the Capulets' wedding preparations on the forestage, but a shaft of light fell on the bed again for the Nurse's attempt to waken her; the scene of mourning was played polyphonically, and the bed was withdrawn but again still visible upstage as Peter spoke with the Musicians while attendants quietly set up a gated wooden screen behind them; the bier was then pushed forward and the forestage area became the inside of the tomb, with the comatose Juliet visible as Romeo appeared in bright light on the upper balcony for his speeches of false optimism punctured by Balthasar's news of Juliet's supposed death and Romeo's purchase of poison from the Apothecary. The Friar John scene (5.2), too, was played above, then Paris and the Page appeared behind the screen and attention was directed back to the main stage for the final scene, played mostly in darkness but with a bright light shining from above on the white-clad figure of Juliet from Romeo's words 'O no, a lantern...' The spotlight remained on Juliet till the end, when Capulet and Montague clasped hands over her body.

In spite of the production's close relationship to Elizabethan staging methods, which placed it in the tradition advocated by William Poel, its effect was in no sense antiquarian. Peter Hall's *Merchant of Venice* at the Phoenix Theatre had something in common with the Victorian pictorial tradition against which Poel rebelled. Chris Dyer's handsome and beautifully lit set lined three sides of the stage with golden colonnades for the Venetian scenes but permitted fluid transitions to the blue skies of Belmont. The casket scenes were played with elaborate ritual, the entry of each suitor heralded by portentous music, the caskets held by black-veiled female attendants; Portia clearly lived up to her income. Sumptuous Renaissance costumes offset Shylock's black gaberdine.

But Peter Hall's production was unVictorian in its respect for the text, played virtually uncut, and still more so in its refusal to turn the

15   *Romeo and Juliet*. Royal Shakespeare Company at the Swan Theatre, 1989. Romeo (Mark Rylance) and
Juliet (Georgia Slowe)

play into the tragedy of Shylock. The casting of Dustin Hoffman in this rôle was certainly a major factor in the production's enormous commercial success. But Hoffman, a ferrety little figure, bearded and with long hair curling in ringlets over his ears, gave a light-weight performance stronger on irony than on passion. He was at his best in the scene with Tubal, where his quick alternations of mood created a complex comedy. As in Bill Alexander's recent RSC production (reviewed in *Shakespeare Survey 41*, pp. 162–5) the Christians were much given to spitting, and Hoffman tolerated these insults with impassive forbearance: 'Taking out his handkerchief, he calmly wipes off the gob of spittle and continues to talk to his assailants, quite as though the unpleasantness had been caused by a passing bird' (Paul Taylor, *The Independent*, 3 June 1989). But whereas in Alexander's production the spitting was one of many ways in which Venetian society was characterized, here it seemed rather an extraneous and (as several reviewers commented) therefore incongruous device, as if to remind us from time to time that the play's Christian community was open to criticism. A similar hint was given by Portia's obvious xenophobia on 'Let all of his complexion choose me so', but the suitors were not caricatured.

I had no sense that Peter Hall was in any way lowering his standards for a West End audience drawn largely by the lure of a famous film star. The cast was strong throughout with Geraldine James as a gracious, elegant Portia somewhat lacking in sparkle, Nathaniel Parker a handsome and well-spoken Bassanio, and Leigh Lawson cutting a fine figure as Antonio, played as not greatly older than his friend. There was no overt homosexuality in the relationship of Antonio and Bassanio, little of the social realism of Bill Alexander's production, no apparent attempt to link the play to contemporary racial issues. In these respects the production was in line with the same director's work at the National Theatre and may have been very welcome to playgoers who wish the text to be allowed to 'speak for itself'. This represents a shift in method from Peter Hall's work at the RSC during the 1960s, which was often politically committed. But whereas in the best of his more recent productions – especially his *Antony and Cleopatra* (1987) and his season of late plays (1988) – unobtrusive direction has been allied with deep thought about the text and achieved full realization of its capacities, of dramatic rhythms and character relationships, of thought and emotion expressed through gesture, action, and above all language, here there seemed to be a lower level of engagement, resulting in a thoroughly conscientious and scrupulous but ultimately rather uninspired journey through the text rather than a sustained illumination of it.

Like Peter Hall, Jonathan Miller has long experience of directing Shakespeare, and his 1989 Old Vic production of *King Lear* was his fourth (two were for television). It suggested not merely that he had exhausted most of what he had to say about the play (at least through performance) but also that his technical competence as a director was at a low ebb. Far too often, entries and exits seemed unmotivated and actors were left standing around the stage in predetermined positions during dialogue in which they were not directly involved, mugging unconvincingly or simply not reacting at all. Richard Hudson's set imprisoned the early scenes in high walls of peeling black brick with a narrow central opening that made for unimpressive entries: one was conscious of the effort that actors had to make to get on to the stage before they could start to act. Peter Bayliss's Fool, old, raddled, and obese, like an aged Andrew Aguecheek, came on with Lear – an old device, undesirable at the best of times considering how deliberately Shakespeare builds up the character's entry in Scene 4, but particularly unwise since once he had arrived he was left stranded stage left constantly grimacing in wordless dismay at Lear's folly. Acting styles were eclectic, resulting in 'an exhibition of cliché-ridden 19th century theatricality' (John

Peter, *The Sunday Times*, 2 April 1989). Some performers imposed personality on their rôles, but in the absence of a unifying concept tended to resort to caricature, Frances de la Tour, for instance, endowing Regan with the false smiles and empty courtesies of a society hostess. In a socially realistic production it might have worked, but here the actress seemed merely to be putting on a turn unrelated to the performances around her. Jonathan Miller is normally so averse to self-consciousness of verse speaking that it was astonishing to hear an Edgar who sounded 'so hollowly pious and musically sanctimonious' (Paul Taylor, *The Independent*, 30 March 1989) as Peter Eyre.

There were some striking visual effects. For the storm scenes, gauzes billowed, smoke swirled, and a brilliant white light shone straight into the audience's eyes as Lear entered centre stage, as from a blazing inferno. Some hint of an attempt to relate the play to modern life emerged in a hovel scene that evoked without explicitly representing the night life of modern London's vagrants and derelicts. Dimly-lit figures wrapped in blankets were all too reminiscent of the squalid and sordid scenes in the subways around Waterloo Bridge that confront those who approach the Old Vic on foot. (At least, this is what the production evoked in me; the inevitable subjectiveness of audience response is pointed by the fact that none of the eight newspaper reviews that I have read registers this impression.) More questionable was the decision to play the blinding of Gloucester off stage, its horror conveyed indirectly through the vicious goading of Regan (who remained in sight) and the compassionate, horror-stricken reactions of a servant. It provoked conflicting responses. Irving Wardle wrote that he 'had never experienced the horror of Gloucester's blinding more strongly than in Miller's treatment of it as an off-stage event, with Regan as a voyeuse looking on and directing the atrocity' (*The Times*, 30 March 1989), whereas for Michael Billington it was 'a cardinal error ... The

greatness of the blinding-scene is that Shakespeare juxtaposes the extreme of human cruelty with an instinctual goodness when the servant draws his sword on Cornwall. By denying us the sight of palpable evil, Miller removes one half of the equation.' (*The Guardian*, 30 March 1989). One problem was the fact that spectators who knew the plot were jolted into consciousness of an unexpected adaptation of the text; following on from this we started to wonder how exactly the episode would be handled, instead of simply responding to it as part of the action, and then became over-aware of the stage box where the supposed blinding was taking place; although the servant mimed his reactions well, the shift into another mode of dramatic representation was too abrupt to be convincing. Of course the on-stage blinding of Gloucester is difficult to represent successfully and may be either unbearably painful (as perhaps it should be) or grotesquely ludicrous, but surely both directors and audience should come face to face with the challenge that Shakespeare sets before them.

Within this context Eric Porter, battered and gnarled, offered a dry, unsentimental, somewhat prosaic reading of the title-rôle that was intelligent and powerful enough to create a sense of regret that the director had done so little to allow the performance to reach its full potential. Porter had played the rôle for the RSC in 1968 in a production that, memory suggests, did far more to bridge the gap between the theatre and real life than Miller's production of 1989.

Bill Alexander's RSC production of *Cymbeline* brought into focus the question of the relationship between playing spaces and production styles. In 1987 he had directed the same play in a studio theatre, The Other Place (see *Shakespeare Survey 42*, pp. 139–42), in a production that transferred successfully to a similar theatre, The Pit, in London. The intimate conditions seemed peculiarly suited to the play's frequently narrative mode, and almost all the actors – the exception played Cloten – found an appropriate scale of delivery; the result was a production that seemed exceptionally responsive to the play's frequent shifts of tone and that delicately balanced its mingled emotions. News that Alexander was to direct the play in the RSC's main house at Stratford-upon-Avon aroused ominous recollections of the disastrous failure of Trevor Nunn's 1976 *Macbeth*, brilliantly successful in The Other Place, to transfer to the large auditorium. In the event Bill Alexander wisely offered a largely different and completely recast production which nevertheless was largely a failure.

Timothy O'Brien designed a steely, semicircular, prison-like well of a set with many doors from which ten actors spilled at the play's opening as if they were being ejected from the court, providing a cue for the opening words 'There's not a man but frowns.' The expository speeches that Shakespeare gives to two anonymous gentlemen were broken up phrase by phrase among the ten actors in a manner reminiscent of the handling of narrative in the RSC's version of *Nicholas Nickleby*, and throughout the action many of the actors addressed the audience directly. So they had in The Other Place, where the effect was one of engaging intimacy that collaborated with the mode of the play, but here it degenerated too often into stridency. Though this may have been attributable in part to the size of the auditorium, it was not helped by Ilona Sekacz's appallingly percussive musical score, performed by groups of musicians competing with each other from either side of the stage as if determined to batter both audience and actors into submission. Perhaps it was intended to suggest the barbarity of ancient Britain in the same way that, at one point, Caius Lucius was offered a drink from a vessel fashioned from the skull of, presumably, one of his compatriots.

One reason for the production's overall failure, then, was a misjudgement of scale. This was reflected in the acting, in which very different styles co-existed uneasily together, most pointedly in the performances of Giacomo and Posthumus. David O'Hara, who played Posthumus, is a very 'modern' actor of the style that became acceptable during the 1960s. He has, for example, done nothing to tone down his pronounced Glaswegian accent, which he uses for every rôle. If it is naturalistically inappropriate we are expected to ignore it just as, more recently, we have been expected to ignore the blackness of black actors playing with white ones in 'integrated' casts. Here, some effort to make it seem not merely isolationist was made by giving Pisanio, too, a Scottish accent (assumed for the rôle, and sometimes slipping a bit). We also had a black actor for the Gaoler, and a black actress for the soothsayer Philharmonus (trans-sexed for the nonce to Philharmona.) David O'Hara's accent is only one aspect of a highly idiosyncratic stage presence which seems reluctant to adapt itself to the rôle: he tends to stare fixedly at the person he is addressing; he slouches in a somewhat simian stance; he wears his own hair, and his long dark locks fall over his face, so that he constantly has to shake them back. When he played Mercutio the idiosyncrasies of the actor seemed to match that of the character, but they fitted ill with Posthumus, whose attraction for Innogen was hard to comprehend and whose misogynist tirade (2.5) was bellowed with an embarrassing absence of vocal control. It is quite right that there should be considerable likeness within difference between Posthumus and Cloten, but this Posthumus had less charm even than David Troughton's portrayal of his brutal alter ego.

The faults of this performance were the more conspicuous because they stood in stark contrast to John Carlisle's Giacomo. Although Carlisle also has his idiosyncrasies – he wears his hair long, often in a pigtail – he is a 'classical' actor in the sense that he works very much with and through language, deploying a highly developed verse-speaking technique characterized by sensitiveness to rhythm, ease of delivery, and sustained breath control that enables him to achieve full communication even of Shakespeare's more involuted late verse. He was able to undercut the stridencies of the production to create a suavely elegant, worldly Giacomo. Lingering over the sleeping Innogen he spoke the words 'No more' in a manner that suggested to me that he was resisting sensual temptation in furtherance of his plot against Posthumus, but which the actor himself stated in public discussion he intended as an indication of self-disgust, in preparation for the character's penitence. Sub-text is not always easy to bring to the surface.

I have lingered over these two performances because I wanted to make some general points about acting styles. I will say no more about a generally undistinguished production other than to remark on one textual change. This was a long acting version of the play, lasting about three and three quarter hours, and some cuts might have been welcome, but not that of Jupiter, who disappeared entirely, and of the vision, reduced to a silent couple wearing blue and white robes who made a brief appearance as if to bless the sleeping Posthumus. In the studio theatre production the decision to reduce Jupiter to a disembodied voice had been understandable, but to cut him altogether, and on a stage which provided ample scope for a spectacular effect, not only made nonsense of Posthumus's later reference to Jupiter's descent but deprived the final scene of all the visionary exaltation, the fusion of emotional extremes, that had been so much more successfully achieved in the smaller-scale production.

The Other Place, which had been put out of commission at the end of 1988, was pressed into service again when Trevor Nunn found himself free to direct a special production of *Othello* for a short run there and at the Young Vic in London. The Stratford auditorium has various drawbacks for spectators. Seats are uncomfortable, there is no air conditioning, it's best not to go on Tuesday because that's when the nearby church has its bell-ringing practice, seats are unreserved, and, though it holds only about 140 people, many find their view of the playing area obscured by poles and railings, especially in the balcony. Backstage facilities are severely limited, too, but for all this the auditorium has endeared itself to both actors and spectators because of the opportunities it provides for a rare intimacy of communication and directness of emotional impact. Trevor Nunn capitalized on these qualities in a production of almost Ibsenite social realism which linked it with John Barton's main-house version of 1971. Whereas Nunn's famous Other Place *Macbeth* of 1976 had adapted and reduced the text, *Othello* was played virtually complete, even including the second (though not the first) Clown episode, where the Clown was played, ironically, as a Soldier ('for me to say a soldier lies, 'tis stabbing'.) With a short interval the performance lasted over four hours. (Were these texts really played in full to audiences of Shakespeare's time? And if so, must they not have formed some of the most intelligent, thoughtful, attentive, imaginative, and intellectually receptive audiences ever to have peopled the theatre?)

The setting was extremely simple: the audience sat round three sides of the playing area, the other side had a central entrance and, above, a slatted wall behind which Othello could lurk as he overlooked Cassio and Desdemona. Costumes and detailed properties created the impression of a predominantly military society, late nineteenth century in period and indeterminate in locality though with strong hints of American Civil War (reinforced by plangent music played on cornet and harmonium) and of *Death in Venice*.

A wealth of social detail – especially in the earlier part of the play – illuminated the characterization and played over and beneath the surface of the text to release its full emotional potential. Iago, a non-commissioned officer with a slightly plebeian accent, swigged beer from a bottle which he offered to a dandyish Roderigo who wiped its top with a handkerchief before drinking; military ritual signalled Othello's entrance; the Duke's court met in the early hours of the morning over brandy glasses around a baize-topped table; Brabanzio was a top-hatted Victorian paterfamilias, touching as he rejected Desdemona's tenders of affection on his departure; Iago pocketed a cigar left on the council table and finished off the remains of the brandy. A large telescope on a stand established the quay-side setting for Cyprus; Cassio gave Desdemona his overcoat to keep her warm; Emilia wiped the rain off a piece of baggage before sitting on it. Iago here was very much the conscious entertainer, making a great set-piece of 'She that was ever fair and never proud...' (2.1.151ff.); merriment rose to an almost hysterical climax followed by a long, long pause during which the overwrought Desdemona's anxiety rose to the surface in sobs; Cassio's attempts to console her provoked Iago's cynicism on 'He takes her by the palm...' The drinking scene took place indoors, with a couple of portable camp beds and washbasins into which Iago sloshed two bottles of wine simultaneously, adding brandy from a flask in Cassio's absence, tasting the mixture with a finger, then adding more brandy; this scene, too, worked up to a brilliant climax with the debagging of one of the company, after which Iago and his mates converged on Cassio with the same intention, to be thwarted by his assertion of a drunken authority. Othello entered to still the brawl with his shirt off but his men leapt instantly to attention; after his departure Cassio vomited into one of the basins, provoking Iago's 'What, are you hurt, Lieutenant?'; he slept on one of the camp beds during Iago's 'And what's he then that says I play the villain...', addressed challengingly to the audience. The 'temptation' scene had a double setting, a workmanlike table and camp chairs to the back for Iago and Othello, with further forward a little outdoor table and chairs for Emilia and Desdemona where they mixed lemonade which Desdemona gave jokingly without sugar to Othello; she sat cajolingly on his knee as she spoke with him of Cassio. The sound of cicadas was heard as Othello and Iago worked on their papers. Entering to tell Othello that his dinner was ready, Desdemona plonked a watch before him to remind him of the time, then dropped her handkerchief. They went off together; a moment later she returned, anxiously seeking what she had left behind, and sighed with relief when she found – the watch. It was a brilliantly ironic end to the first part.

Social detail dwindled in the second part as passion mounted, but the production remained rooted in naturalism; indeed, a fully written account of this production would read like a Victorian novel. Searching Desdemona's dressing table for evidence of Desdemona's infidelity, Othello found only the box of sweets with which Cassio had tried to cheer her up on the quayside. As he reviled her with the name of whore he made her stand on a table, pacing around her like a beast tormenting its prey. At 'Swear thou art honest' (4.1.40) he dragged her to a prie-dieu, and there, at the end of the willow scene, she knelt to say 'God me such uses send / Not to pick bad from bad, but by bad mend!', momentarily recalling Verdi's insertion of an 'Ave Maria' at this point. For the murder Othello wore an elaborate Moorish gown and carried a scimitar. He smothered her orgasmically on a large bed, rolling off her unconscious body as if after sexual climax.

The production style, like the auditorium, encouraged naturalistic acting, and, rather as in Terry Hands's *Romeo and Juliet*, speech style tended to the colloquial. The cast was exceptionally strong. Imogen Stubbs's Desdemona was young, beautiful, vulnerable, deeply, physically in love with Othello, and no less loving to her father, so that the sense of her 'divided duty' was touchingly conveyed. The depth of her love was most apparent after her fate was sealed, as she listened entranced to Othello's tale of the handkerchief and for a moment one sensed a return to an earlier stage of their relationship, when she would listen with similar fascination to his traveller's tales.

Othello was played by the black opera singer Willard White, with whom Trevor Nunn had worked on *Porgy and Bess* at Glyndebourne. (It

16   *Othello*, 1989. Royal Shakespeare Company at The Other Place. 4.2: Othello (Willard White) berates Desdemona (Imogen Stubbs)

was a complicating irony of the production that the black Othello was played by a negro called White, while Bianca – whose name means 'white' – was played by a black actress.) White is an imposing figure of great natural nobility with a darkly resonant speaking voice of unforced power and authority. Though he never seemed anything less than highly accomplished as an actor, his own speech rhythms were sometimes at odds with the iambic patterns of Shakespeare's verse, resulting in a less than thorough exploration of verbal meaning. For example, in 'Thou dost conspire against thy friend, Iago' (3.3.147) only the second syllable of 'conspire' received a (heavy) accent, so there was no sense of paradox; 'I am bound to thee for ever' was merely a polite statement, and 'Set on thy wife to observe' had none of the sense of self-abasement that Donald Sinden found in it. But Othello's suffering came powerfully to the surface on 'Why did I marry?', his 'farewell', punctuated with the tearing of papers and the drumming of fists on the table, reached an impressive climax, and sheer emotional sincerity won through in the final scenes in which we suffered with him as he made Desdemona suffer. 'Where should Othello go' was a magnificent cry, his final speech both pathetic and noble. The emotional truth of this performance overcame its technical limitations.

And it was matched by Ian McKellen's Iago, a tall, trim figure of military bearing, so professionally disciplined that he was obviously a strong candidate for Cassio's lieutenancy. In Othello's presence he was always under iron control, though his eyes narrowed to slits in intense concentration as he observed anything that might serve his purpose. Only in relaxation, with Roderigo or Cassio, or above all Emilia, did his coarseness of spirit reveal itself. Zoë Wanamaker's subtle portrayal of bemused, long-suffering, but still not quite hopeless incomprehension reminded us that the play is about Emilia's marriage as well as Desdemona's. Iago's contempt for her was barely concealed, yet it was clear why he would have

attracted her. McKellen's insolent scorn extended even to the audience in his baleful, challenging gaze. There was a frightening sense of danger in the final scene as he rushed to escape over the bed in which Desdemona lay, and after he had been brought back, captive, he stared fixedly at her body, unresponsive to Lodovico's 'This is thy work', still staring at the dead Desdemona, advancing closer to the foot of the bed to gaze on his handiwork, still staring in impassive, unflinching fascination as the lights went down. It was a chilling conclusion to a fascinating production.

Two large-scale productions of *Hamlet*, one by Richard Eyre for the National Theatre in the Olivier auditorium, the other by Ron Daniels for the RSC in the main house at Stratford, provided illuminating contrasts in the variety of effect and the differing degrees of engagement that may derive from a single text. Eyre's production, his first on taking over the directorship from Peter Hall, marked no decisive break from the traditions established by his predecessor for the performance of classic plays in this difficult auditorium. He was faithful to an edited text, he worked to no obtrusive interpretative concept, and he used largely unfurnished settings (beautifully designed by John Gunter) which, like those in Peter Hall's *Merchant of Venice*, combined neo-Victorian pictorialism with Elizabethan flexibility, mingling the symbolic with the picturesque. A vast statue of old Hamlet with armour and truncheon dominated the action from beginning to end. Generally the actors ignored it, but it constantly reminded the audience of the nature of Hamlet's task, was spectrally illuminated through the walls of Gertrude's room as the Ghost made his last appearance, and served as young Hamlet's last resting place when, after death, he was spreadeagled upon its base, a visible sacrifice to filial piety. The broad, open Olivier stage poses problems, but scene transitions were smoothly managed and big concerted episodes were expertly manipulated to fill its ample spaces.

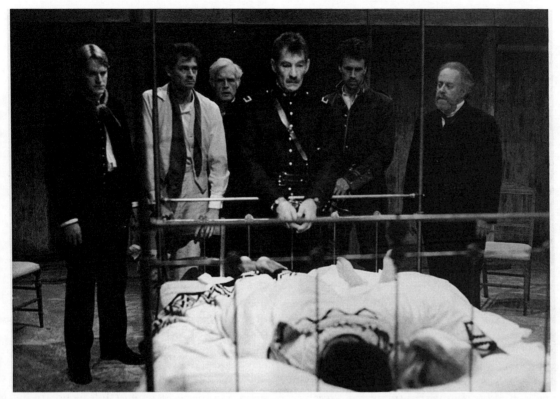

17   *Othello*, 1989. Royal Shakespeare Company at The Other Place. 5.2: Iago (Ian McKellen) (centre) looks 'on the tragic loading of this bed'

As if in deference to the demands of the even broader auditorium, the style of performance was presentational, formal rather than intimate. After the greys and blacks of the opening scene on the battlements, where mists swirled and drained down the trap through which the guards had entered, the court erupted onto the stage in a burst of blood-red light. Gertrude was Claudius's adoring new wife; onlookers showered the bridal pair with confetti as they performed a weird dance to the accompaniment of drums and trumpets. The stage was fully peopled, but Claudius addressed himself to us, not to his courtiers. Daniel Day-Lewis's tall, saturnine Hamlet, baritonally musical but lacking a sharp edge of wit, spoke most of his soliloquies firmly planted at stage centre with scarcely a gesture (though as he

recalled old Hamlet's funeral his hands touchingly mimicked the steps with which his mother's shoes followed his father's body to the grave). Polonius stood ten feet distant from Ophelia as he talked with her of Hamlet; Ophelia spoke her descriptions of Hamlet's mad behaviour with no movement, and though Hamlet was physically close to Horatio as he declared his affection, his delivery was formal, betraying no intimacy.

It was a distancing style, holding the audience at arm's length, encouraging observant neutrality rather than involvement in the characters' emotions and in the excitement of the action. In the play scene we watched the inset play rather than responding to the counterpointing tensions between spectators and actors; the graveyard scene remained a succession of distinct episodes rather than a sequence in which Hamlet moves inexorably from jesting abstractions about death to the emotional purgation of his anguished response to the sight of the corpse of the woman he had loved. In the final scene it was a measure of the audience's detachment that, at the performance I saw, John Castle's Claudius raised laughter with 'It is the poisoned cup; it is too late.'

The presentational mode and an excess of acting from the neck upwards resulted in colourless characterization and inadequate exploration of relationships. Only two of the leading actors broke through the barriers to engage our imaginations as well as our minds. Michael Bryant played Polonius as a father whose authoritarian exterior barely concealed deep love for his children. The most striking moment of his performance, commented on by several reviewers, came with his absent-mindedness at 'What was I about to say? By the mass, I was about to say something.' Bryant created a complex effect by suggesting that Polonius had not simply become entangled in the web of his own verbosity but had actually lost his memory in a moment of aphasia foreshadowing the onset of senility in a manner that would be particularly damaging to an elderly politician. The fact that the moment occurred in a play added an extra layer of complexity by momentarily embarrassing the audience with the thought that not the character but the actor had lost his memory.

The other outstanding performance was Judi Dench's Gertrude. The heart of this production lay in her relationship with Hamlet. Whereas too much of the earlier part of the play had seemed to be formally recited, full body language came into play in the closet scene. As Hamlet's passion mounted he bestraddled his mother; her evident tenderness for him sought physical expression, and their climactic kiss was a naked and mutual acknowledgement of desire that shocked her. She addressed 'What shall I do?' to herself, not to Hamlet, acknowledging the discovery within herself of unsuspected

depths she could not fathom. As Hamlet left she collapsed, and for the rest of the play was a broken woman. Her flinching from the King's touch was instinctual, not willed; she showed deep compassion as she told Laertes of his sister's death. This was acting that communicated emotional complexity with great economy of means, and that set the play's heart beating as it should.

Ron Daniels's Stratford *Hamlet*, heavily expressionistic and consistently interpretative, was at the opposite extreme from Terry Hands's *Romeo and Juliet* and pretty far distant, too, from the National's generally unengaging, Establishment version of the same play. The stage was surrounded by a disjointed frame, its sides sloping outwards. The ceiling of the stateroom in which much of the action took place sloped at a vertiginous angle, reminiscent of the sinking of the Titanic: clearly the ship of state had been torpedoed. From time to time a turbulent painting of sea enraged by storm could be partially seen through windows or even revealed as a complete backdrop. Lighting was atmospheric, constantly shifting not on any naturalistic principle but to suit the mood of the episode. Costumes, eclectic in period, were suggestive mainly of the 1930s, but Claudius wore a plum-coloured suit in dubious taste and Ophelia had a Victorian style funeral with black umbrellas and long black bombazine dresses for the ladies. There were few of the appurtenances of royalty.

The aim throughout seemed to be to play an emotional subtext, at whatever sacrifice to literary values. The speech style was naturalistic, remote from that advocated by Peter Hall, and much of the acting took place during pauses or between lines. Even the Ghost, assisted by atmospheric gusts of wind, eerie music, and a red glow under the stage that brought us close to the world of melodrama, was nevertheless intensely human, throwing himself to the ground as he recounted his sufferings to Hamlet and poignant especially in his love for Gertrude. As Hamlet berated her in

18   *Hamlet.* Royal Shakespeare Company at The Royal Shakespeare Theatre, 1989. 3.4: Hamlet (Mark Rylance) and
Gertrude (Clare Higgins) with the Ghost

the closet scene the curtains began to blow, at first only a little, then increasingly as mysterious music sounded and the light changed, then a shadow fell on them, and at last the Ghost emerged during Hamlet's ravings and protectively cradled the unknowing Gertrude from behind as if to protect her from Hamlet's violence, even his lust.

The text was cut internally by some nine hundred lines, so that for example Polonius lost the passage with which Michael Bryant had made such an effect, and there were occasional adaptations, the nunnery scene occupying its First Quarto position before the arrival of the players (so that 'To be or not to be' came before 'O what a rogue and peasant slave'), and 'Speak the speech' became a rehearsal, Hamlet interrupting the player as he instructed him. The

insistence on psychological verisimilitude, on an emotional expressiveness that left no distance between the actor and the language, reduced the play's variety of style and so narrowed its expressive range, but made for great intensity and a high degree of emotional involvement.

Mark Rylance was even more melancholy on his first appearance as Hamlet than he had been as Romeo, skulking in a dark raincoat and sitting on his suitcase as he waited for Claudius's attention, obviously hoping to catch the next train to Wittenberg; he spoke the opening lines of his first soliloquy with his back to us in a state of clinical depression. Short, fresh-faced, essentially tender-natured but emotionally volatile, ranging from the depths of despair to hysterical, mocking insolence, this was a warmly human, often very funny, never heroic Hamlet.

From his entry to speak 'To be or not to be' till his departure for England he wore pyjamas, as if he were under medication, and at times his emotional disturbance choked his utterance as he spoke of, for example, 'the dread of ... *long pause* ... something ... *a shorter but still lengthy pause* ... after death'. Though he was brutal with Ophelia, casting her down and spitting in her face, at the close of the nunnery scene he kissed her with real tenderness, leaving no doubt that he had indeed loved her once, and might do so again if he could regain his equilibrium.

Hamlet's satirical intelligence was evident in his mocking of Polonius, mimicking him to amuse Rosencrantz and Guildenstern, even twice baring his behind at him (Irving, thou shouldst be living at this hour) in contempt. In the play scene (during which he wore a white jacket with his pyjama trousers) he jestingly trained a pair of opera glasses on the actors, and Claudius and Gertrude treated him with condescending indulgence. After Claudius had rushed off, Hamlet put the player's crown on his head and stuffed a pillow up his jacket, bouncing in mockery of Claudius on the bed which the players had used for the enactment of the murder of Gonzago as he exulted over the success of his scheme. In the closet scene Polonius concealed himself close to the bed and was stabbed on it wrapped in the sheets with which he had become entangled. Hamlet's portraits of his father and uncle were snapshots which he pulled from his pockets, and after the Ghost had vanished Hamlet solicitously tucked his mother up in the blood-stained sheets in a manner that provoked disturbed laughter in the audience. Here too there was an Oedipal embrace between mother and son, arousing guilt in both. A tin bath was brought on stage for 'Safely stowed'; Hamlet was washing his sword with the sponge that gave the cue for his insult to Rosencrantz, 'Besides, to be demanded of a sponge'; rubbing Polonius's blood from his vest he stood in the bath as Claudius entered. As in, for example, Trevor Nunn's 1970 production,

Claudius's frustrated anger at Hamlet found vent in physical violence – he forced the squirming Hamlet's head under the water till he nearly drowned, and reacted with fury to Hamlet's suggestion that he seek Polonius 'i'th' other place' himself. On 'Farewell, dear mother' Hamlet kissed Claudius on the lips (male kisses are in fashion at Stratford), and in a brilliantly comic climax to the episode jumped into the bath and mimed paddling himself in a boat on 'Come, for England'. The stormy backcloth was visible for the Fortinbras scene (4.4), and Fortinbras and his soldiers remained on stage for 'How all occasions...'

Peter Wight's Claudius was an emotional King, far from efficient as a ruler, who threw himself against the wall in impotent fury at hearing of Hamlet's return to England. Efforts to play the plotting scene between him and Laertes for psychological verisimilitude seemed somewhat redundant; tension is apt to sag here in any case, and it seems best to get on with the action as rapidly as possible. On his return from England Hamlet wore a red shirt, white trousers, and a neckerchief (provoking the gibe that he seemed to have escaped from *The Pirates of Penzance* rather than from the pirates), and gave many indications of having recovered his wits; even the lighting was steadier than before. There was deep tenderness in his jesting over Yorick's skull, which he kept about him, even placing it on the mantelpiece, turning it so that its eyeless sockets faced the action, as a talisman during his duel with Laertes. There was sweetness and even a touch of nobility in his final speech, spoken directly to the audience; this Hamlet made a touching end.

The interpretative commitment of this production provoked wide-ranging reactions in its audiences. One critic, finding that 'No opportunity for crude shock effect is missed', declared that 'The only tragic aspect of the evening ... is that this fiasco is the work of the RSC' (Peter Kemp, *The Independent*, 28 April 1989); another declared that 'The Royal Society for the Prevention of Cruelty to Shakespeare has another

19 *Hamlet*. Royal Shakespeare Company at the Royal Shakespeare Theatre, 1989. Hamlet (Mark Rylance) takes a bath (4.2)

case on its hands' (John Gross, *The Sunday Telegraph*, 30 April 1989). But Irving Wardle, referring to its 'courageously imaginative assault on the central relationships', declared this 'a revival no spectator will forget' (*The Times*, 28 April 1989), and John Peter found it 'a deeply shocking production, in the most crucial sense', referring to its 'hard, brutal grandeur' (*The Sunday Times*, 30 April 1989). It was a bold, original, internally consistent interpretation that engaged intimately with its audience's attention, a reading that had something to say about every detail of the text and was impossible to ignore, whether one liked it or not.

Also full of detail and determinedly up-to-date was John Caird's brilliantly clever, consistently post-modern production of *A Midsummer Night's Dream* at the main house in Stratford. Caird declared his hand as the audience were still settling into their seats with a performance of Mendelssohn's overture that began authentically (granted the limitations of a small band and the presence of a couple of synthesizers), progressed through an exhilarating desecration of its central section with rock rhythms and foot-tapping use of side drums, returning to Mendelssohn's cool, calm chords at the end. Caird's direction of the opening scene similarly applied modern techniques to a familiar text, offering a feminist treatment of Hippolyta and Hermia that reflected recent critical thought about the play as expressed in, for example, the opening chapter of Philip McGuire's book *Speechless Dialect: Shakespeare's Open Silences* (Berkeley, CA, 1985): Hippolyta flounced on looking deeply disgruntled and responding with an ironic mock-obeisance to Theseus's 'I wooed thee with my sword, / And won thy love doing thee injuries.' As Theseus delivered judgement on Hermia, Hippolyta moved forwards as if to speak in her defence. She turned scornfully from him as he looked forward to their approaching 'band of fellowship', clearly aligning herself with the wronged Hermia, again turned sulkily away on Theseus's 'Come,

my Hippolyta', and flounced off in the opposite direction.

This interpretation reinforces the now customary doubling of Theseus and Hippolyta with Oberon and Titania in its anticipation of the fairy couple's disharmony, but it was not achieved without a good deal of interpolated business and blatant mugging. It was carried through to the final scene in which (as in Bill Alexander's 1987 production) the Folio's substitution of Egeus for Philostrate was adopted, and Egeus was shown to have submitted wholly to Theseus's will. In 4.1 Hippolyta had seemed resentful of Theseus's uppish claims for the superiority of his hounds to those that she had encountered in Crete and Sparta, but by now they were fully reconciled and ready to end the play in romantic harmony.

The modernity of this production found expression too in much theatrical self-referentiality. Whereas in 1970 Peter Brook had swept away old traditions and substituted something new in their place, John Caird constantly alluded, often mockingly, parodistically, and by antithesis, to the play's performance history. The wood near Athens was a dark metallic conglomeration of junk, a sort of structured rubbish heap of items such as an old bicycle and gramophone, umbrellas and teapots and a battered grand piano held together by three spiral staircases (so providing an upper acting area) and supporting an iron bedstead which could be raised and lowered (as Titania's bower) by Heath Robinsonian devices operated by juvenile fairies. Oberon and Titania each had four attendants, horrible teenagers, the girls with wings and tutus reminiscent of *Swan Lake* (to which Ilona Sekacz's musical score alluded), blowing bubblegum and scratching themselves as if taking part in a fourth-form-at-St-Trinian's skit on the play. Richard McCabe's Puck was a loathsome schoolboy with tufts of sticking-up hair and a habit of mimicking not only Oberon but anyone else within sight or mind, buzzing off like Batman on 'I'll put a girdle round about the earth',

20 *A Midsummer Night's Dream*. Royal Shakespeare Company at the Royal Shakespeare Theatre, 1989.
The Mechanicals: Jimmy Gardner (Snug), Graham Turner (Flute), Paul Webster (Quince), Dhobi Opelai (Starveling),
David Troughton (Bottom), and David Shaw-Parker (Snout)

imitating Olivier's Richard III on 'this their jangling I esteem a sport', then shrugging his shoulders and goggling his eyes at the audience as if to say 'well, why not?', and – in another declaration of directorial intent – reading 'Through the forest have I gone' aloud in mocking tones from a copy of my New Penguin edition of the play, glancing at the cover, and then throwing it derisively aside, sometimes hitting one of the bandsmen.

The young lovers were equally irreverently and inventively treated, constantly subjected to parody and caricature in a manner that you could find hilariously funny if you regarded them as no more than puppets, or wearisomely effortful if you thought of them as human beings. It was all brilliantly, frenetically clever, and one could go on for many more pages

without exhausting the production's fertility of invention, but the cleverness was of the kind that held the play at arm's length except in the performances of John Carlisle and Clare Higgins, who brought a welcome repose to their portrayal of, especially, Oberon and Titania, and of all the mechanicals, played with such respect and sympathy that our laughter was always tinged with affection. They entered looking like members of an Edwardian concert party, each rapidly establishing an entirely credible individuality. David Troughton's Bottom was the ebullient ringleader of the group, ever-anxious to please – he had brought his entire stock of false beards with him, and put them on one on top of another to demonstrate their effect. Paul Webster's Quince was a parody of a neurotic play director, calming his nerves with swigs from a hip-flask in face of Flute's repeated inability to get 'Ninus' right and Snug's total incapacity to remember not only his minimal rôle but even his own name. Delightful above all was Graham Turner's blandly good-natured Flute, unwittingly rubbing salt in his colleagues' wounds as he lingered over his assurances that Bottom would have earned sixpence a day if only he had not disappeared, making numerous efforts to enter followed by rapid withdrawals in the play scene as Theseus interrupted the action and wrangled with Pyramus, and reaching a grand climax in his death scene as Thisbe when, having incorporated the direction 'She stabs herself' in his speech, he made repeated efforts to die falling backwards only to be transfixed at each attempt in a semi-recumbent posture because his dress had got stuck under Pyramus until at last he had the happy inspiration of expiring forwards over Pyramus' heaving chest.

The play's closing episodes were self-indulgently protracted with much comic business as the fairy chorus went all wrong and the delinquents were made to 'rehearse' (in the modern sense) their song by rote, but a touch of the play's romance struggled to the surface as the fairies blessed the three marriage beds, visible on the forest set, to the strains of Mendelssohn's unadulterated nocturne. The final success of this production (which was very popular with audiences) lay in the triumph of geniality and good fellowship over cool reason and critical rigour, so that in the end it seemed to be asserting the values of the text rather than struggling with the technical problems of re-creating it for a modern audience.

Not all of our most interesting directors have worked on Shakespeare in 1989: there have been no new productions from, for instance, Declan Donellan, Nicholas Hytner, or Deborah Warner, and I have had to be selective in my account. Even so, it will I think be obvious that there is an almost anarchic eclecticism in current theatrical approaches to the plays. Yet it may be evident too that theatrically successful productions may be achieved by a variety of means. Audiences differ in quality of attention and degrees of receptivity, and it is perhaps no bad thing that they should be able to choose among productions that are some more, some less demanding in their methods. Comparatively 'straightforward' productions like Richard Eyre's of *Hamlet* or Peter Hall's of *The Merchant of Venice* may satisfy those who seek an uncluttered presentation of the narrative even if they seem lacking in emotional depth to those who know how much these texts can yield; more sophisticated productions, like Ron Daniels's *Hamlet* or John Caird's *A Midsummer Night's Dream*, may seem to require audiences who are already steeped in the plays and who can respond to the intellectual complexities resulting from the superimposition on to Elizabethan texts of modern images and implicit or explicit allusions to the play's critical and theatrical history; yet the warmth of applause with which the productions were regularly greeted suggested that they could speak powerfully even to audiences who might not be able to analyse the nature of the experience they had undergone. The best directors are alert to the problems of bringing Shakespeare's texts to full life for modern audiences, and the variety of their attitudes is exemplified in the debate over styles of verse-speaking.

It has been suggested that the increase in number of Shakespeare productions is not entirely healthy, and there may well be a danger that a demand for continuing productions of a limited number of plays will result in tired work that is either routinely uninventive or eccentric in its search for new ways of brightening up old texts. The increased intellectualism of directors' theatre is not without drawbacks if it results in over-sophistication at the expense of emotional directness; on the other hand, Shakespeare's texts are themselves immensely sophisticated constructs that will not yield up their secrets to unsubtle interpreters. Very few contemporary Shakespeare productions work simply through a direct, unmetaphorical presentation of the text (though Terry Hands's *Romeo and Juliet* – like Deborah Warner's *Titus Andronicus* of 1987 – came close to doing so). Many abbreviate the texts, some considerably adapt them; but before we are too hasty to condemn these procedures, we might do well to remember that this has been true of every stage of the theatrical history of Shakespeare's plays, including those that have given us the most legendary performances by great actors of the past. A four-hour presentation of a virtually complete text, such as Trevor Nunn's of *Othello*, makes great demands on its audiences, even in plushier surroundings than those provided by The Other Place. Every so often one hears calls for a 'moratorium' on Shakespeare productions, presumably in the hope that abstinence would provoke a desire that would at last become transcendently unquenchable, but the only organization in the country that is in any sense compelled to play Shakespeare month in and month out is the Royal Shakespeare Company, which still has a high enough proportion of successes to suggest that, while the search for new talent should be unceasing, it is in no urgent need of foreclosure. Though there have been disappointments, 1989 has been a rewarding year for the playgoer who is interested in seeing how Shakespeare's texts can respond to the 'form and pressure' of the age.

PROFESSIONAL SHAKESPEARE PRODUCTIONS IN THE BRITISH ISLES, JANUARY–DECEMBER 1988

compiled by

N. RATHBONE

Most of the productions listed are by professional companies, but some amateur productions and adaptations are included. Information is taken from programmes, supplemented by reviews, held in the Birmingham Shakespeare Library. Details have been verified wherever possible, but the nature of the material prevents corroboration in every case.

ALL'S WELL THAT ENDS WELL

Flying Colours Theatre Company, Pentameters Theatre Club, Hampstead: 21 Sept.–16 Oct. 1988
Directors: Stewart Gray, Graham Mitchell
Helena: Stephi Hemelryk

ANTONY AND CLEOPATRA

The National Theatre at the Olivier, London: 9 April 1987–6 Feb. 1988
See *Shakespeare Survey 42*, p. 149.

AS YOU LIKE IT

British Actors Touring Company, York Theatre Royal and tour: 1 Mar. 1988–
The company has no director
Rosalind: Kate O'Mara
Jaques: Patrick Marley

Royal Lyceum, Edinburgh: 28 Oct.–19 Nov. 1988
Director: Hamish Glen

Designer: Peter Ling
Rosalind: Siobhan Redmond
Prehistoric standing stones represented Arden. Tartan costumes indicated a Scottish location.

Renaissance Theatre Company, Birmingham Repertory Theatre Studio, Phoenix Theatre London and tour: 8 April 1988–
Director: Geraldine McEwan
Designer: Jenny Tiramani
Rosalind: Tam Hoskyns
Touchstone: Kenneth Branagh
See *Shakespeare Survey 42*, p. 130.

The Duke's Theatre, Lancaster. Promenade production in Williamson Park: 14 June–23 July 1988
Director: Jonathan Petherbridge
Designer: Eve Stewart
Music: Andy Whitfield
Rosalind: Tracie Gillman

COMEDY OF ERRORS

Alarms Off at the Rose Theatre Club, London: 2–27 Feb. 1988
Director/Designer: Maggi Law

CYMBELINE

The National Theatre at the Cottesloe, London, and tour of Russia and Japan: 20 May 1988–
Director: Peter Hall

Designer: Alison Chitty
Music: Harrison Birtwistle
Innogen: Geraldine James
Iachimo: Tim Pigott-Smith
See *Shakespeare Survey 42*, p. 139.

The RSC at the Pit, Barbican, London: 16 March 1988–
Transfer from Stratford. See *Shakespeare Survey 42*, p. 139.

HAMLET

The Everyman Theatre, Liverpool: 4 Feb. 1988–
Director: Glen Walford
Designer: Clair Lyth
Music: Paddy Cunneen
Hamlet: Martin McKellan
Ophelia: Cathy Tyson
Black actors played the Polonius family

Theatrig at Theatr Gwynedd, Bangor and Welsh tour: March–Oct. 1988
Director: Ceri Sherlock
Designer: Simon Banham
Hamlet: Alun Elider
In Welsh.

Hamlet 88. A free adaptation by Hugh Hayes. Cleveland Theatre Company at the Dovecot Arts Centre, Stockton, Half Moon Theatre, London and tour: 12 April 1988–
Director: Alasdair Ramsay
Designer: Ian MacNeil
Hamlet: Nabil Shaban
Music: Stuart Johnson
Adapted for a disabled actor as Hamlet, with a futuristic set dominated by video screens and media gadgetry.

Compass Theatre Company, The New Ensemble (Sheffield) at the Woughton Centre, Milton Keynes and tour (with *The Winter's Tale* and *Volpone*): 18 April 1988–
Director: Neil Sissons

Designer (Costumes): Jenny Neville
Hamlet: Helen Schlesinger
Six actors doubling, and a female Hamlet.

Renaissance Theatre Company at Birmingham Repertory Theatre Studio, the Phoenix Theatre, London and tour: 19 May 1988– Also performed at the Elsinore Festival, Denmark, August 1988
Director: Derek Jacobi
Designer: Jenny Tiramani
Hamlet: Kenneth Branagh
Ophelia: Sophie Thompson

Barnstormers Theatre Company, The Rose Theatre Club, London: 26 July–13 Aug. 1988
Director: Laura Thompson
Hamlet: Vincent Regan
A modern dress production on a matt black stage.

The RSC/Royal Insurance Tour: Wimbledon Theatre and tour: 22 Sept. 1988–
Director: Ron Daniels
Designer: Antony McDonald
Music: Clare von Kampen
Hamlet: Mark Rylance
Later transferred to the Royal Shakespeare Theatre, with some cast and set changes (see pp. 196–200).

The Horseshoe Theatre Company, Central Studio, Basingstoke: 19–29 Oct. 1988
Director: Kit Thacker
Designer: Oliver Johnson
Hamlet: Richard Lumsden
The other players on stage chanted the Ghost's message to Hamlet, while he writhed in the grip of demonic possession. A bare black box set. Simultaneous translation into sign language for the deaf was provided.

Mandrake Theatre Company at the Duke of Wellington, London: 9–26 Oct. 1988
Director: Aaron Mullen
Designer (costumes): Nula Keely

Hamlet: Steven O'Shea
The performance began with the cast circling the Ghost and whispering lines from the play.

Hamlet Improvised, conceived by Alan Marriott and Kevin Carr, Theatresports London at the Canal Café Theatre, Little Venice: 1 Nov.–7 Dec. 1988
Director: Alan Marriott

HENRY IV

English Shakespeare Company, continuation of their British and world tour.
See pp. 171–81; also *Shakespeare Survey 41*, p. 161, *42*, for details of this production.

HENRY V

English Shakespeare Company, continuation of their British and world tour.
See *Shakespeare Survey 41*, p. 161, *42*, for details of this production.

HENRY VI

English Shakespeare Company, continuation of their British and world tour.
See *Shakespeare Survey 41*, p. 161, *42*, for details of this production.

RSC at the Royal Shakespeare Theatre, Stratford: see *The Plantagenets*.

JULIUS CAESAR

RSC at the Barbican, London, in repertory 9 June 1988–
Mark Antony: Linus Roache
Transfer from Stratford, where Nicholas Farrell played Antony
See *Shakespeare Survey 42*, p. 151, for details of this production.

Leicester Haymarket: 9 Sept.–5 Nov. 1988, and tour of India
Director: John Dexter

Designer: Jocelyn Herbert
Music: Stephen Boxer
Mark Antony: Martin McKellan
Brutus: Joseph Marcell
A traditional production, with a simple steel set.

KING JOHN

The RSC at The Other Place, Stratford, in repertory 4 May 1988–
Director: Deborah Warner
Designer: Sue Blane
King John: Nicholas Woodeson
The Bastard: David Morrissey
See *Shakespeare Survey 42*, p. 137, for details of this production.

KING LEAR

Film version, screenplay by Jean-Luc Godard, Cannon Distributors (UK) 29 Jan. 1988–
Director: Jean-Luc Godard
Photography: Sophie Maintigneux
Don Learo: Burgess Meredith
Cordelia: Molly Ringwald
Doctor Professor Pluggy (the Fool) Jean-Luc Godard
William Shakespeare Jnr V: Peter Sellars
An exploration of the themes of performance art, death, and regeneration. The ex-Mafia boss Don Learo has divided his kingdom between his two elder daughters and lives in exile in France with Cordelia.

Lear's Daughters by Elaine Feinstein
The Women's Theatre Group, touring, with cast changes:
Cordelia: Clare Perkins
Goneril: Maureen Hibbert
Regan: Hilary Ellis
Nurse: Jany Chambers
See *Shakespeare Survey 42*, p. 152.

The RSC at The Other Place, Stratford, in rep. 31 Aug. 1988–

Director: Cicely Berry
Designer: Chris Dyer
Lear: Richard Haddon Haines
The Fool: Patrick Miller
Cordelia: Amanda Root

King of England by Barrie Keefe
Theatre Royal, Stratford East: 28 Jan.–27 Feb.
1988
Director: Paul Barber
Designers: Jackie Pinfold and Jenny Tiramani
Mr King: Rudolph Walker
Susan (Cordelia): Claire Benedict
A play about the problems of immigrants from
the Caribbean in the 1950s, loosely based on
King Lear.

LOVE'S LABOUR'S LOST

Living Tissue at the Village Theatre, London:
May 1988
A modern dress adaptation.

MACBETH

Cheek by Jowl, continuation of the 1987 tour.
See *Shakespeare Survey 42*, pp. 136–7.

Pattern 23 Theatre Company at the Belgrade
Studio, Coventry: spring 1988
Director: Gwen Williams
Macbeth: Michael Saffery
Lady Macbeth: Anne Boreland
A cast of five, performing on a minimal set.

Betty and Boaby's Macbeth by John Christopher
Wood
Bristol Express Theatre Company, tour of
Scotland, spring 1988
Elsie and Norm's Macbeth transposed to a
location in downtown Glasgow
See *Shakespeare Survey 41*, p. 186.

The Duke's Playhouse, Lancaster: Jan. 27–Feb.
20 1988
Director: Jonathan Petherbridge
Designer: Pip Nash

Macbeth: Ray Murtagh
Lady Macbeth: Mary McCusher
A production which concentrated on the
bloodier aspects of the play.

Stage Fright by Peter Fieldson
Oldham Coliseum: 8 Feb. 1988–
Director: Paul Elkins
Designer: Nettie Edwards
A comedy whodunnit. The cast re-create a
production of *Macbeth* in which the leading
actor was fatally stabbed ten years previously.

Co-Producers and High Peak Theatre Trust;
Buxton Opera House and tour: 10 Feb. 1988–
Director: Eric Standidge
Designer: Bruno Santini
Macbeth: Ben Robertson
Lady Macbeth: Philomena McDonagh
Set in 1902, with the soldiers in Scottish regi-
mental uniform and the witches as Edwardian
ladies.
Some performances were accompanied by sign
language for the deaf.

Angles Theatre Company, Wisbech: 3 March
1988–
Director: Andy Naylor
Designer: Gordon Gillick
Music: Simon Whitfield
Macbeth: Nick Whitfield
Lady Macbeth: Candida Hall
The ghosts and weird sisters were in modern
evening dress with whited faces.

The Salberg Studio, Salisbury Playhouse: 20
April–14 May 1988
Director: Paul Chamberlain
Designer: Stephen Howell
Macbeth: Paul Blake
Lady Macbeth: Joan Moon
Six actors doubling, and a minimal set.

The RSC at the Royal Shakespeare Theatre,
Stratford, in repertory 28 April 1988– and the
Tyne Theatre, Newcastle on Tyne

Macbeth: Miles Anderson
Lady Macbeth: Amanda Root
A revival of the 1986 production with cast changes.
See *Shakespeare Survey 41*, p. 186.

Webb-Foote Productions (Loughborough)
Alexandra Palace, London: 23 July–7 Aug. 1988
Director: Christopher Pledger
Macbeth: Kevin Burke
Lady Macbeth: Fanny Jones
A traditional production, performed in a scaled-down replica of the Globe as part of the Festival of London.

Towards Macbeth – A Prologue
Zattera di Babele, Sicily, at the Demarco Gallery and on Inchcolm Island, Edinburgh Festival: Aug. 15–18 1988, Sicily: Sept. 1988
Director: Carlo Quartucci
Macbeth: John Bett
Lady Macbeth: Julie Cadzow
A promenade production on Inchcolm Island, to be followed by a production of *Macbeth* on the island during the 1989 Festival.

Orchard Theatre and Plymouth Theatre Royal at the Northcott Theatre, Exeter and tour: 21 Sept.–3 Dec. 1988
Director: Nigel Bryant
Designer: Liz Ascroft
Macbeth: Michael Jenner
Lady Macbeth: Pat Rossiter
A simple set, dominated by a Celtic cross. The witches re-appear to close the play. Banquo was given unusual prominence in this production.

Contact Playday workshops, Contact Theatre, Manchester: 29 Sept.–14 Oct. 1988
Director: Lawrence Till
Designer: Craig Hewitt
With Contact Theatre's Community Drama Team.

St George's Theatre, London: in rep. 1 Nov.–7 Dec. 1988
Director: George Murcell
Macbeth: Nigel Harrison
Lady Macbeth: Carmen Lyn
The witches wore straw masks in a production which was well presented but lacked humour in the Porter scene.

Liverpool Playhouse: 2 Nov.–3 Dec. 1988
Director: Ian Kellgren
Designer: Gillian Daniell
Macbeth: Andrew Byatt
Lady Macbeth: Clare Dow
Set in eleventh century Scotland. One reviewer compared the set to a concrete underpass.

Manchester Royal Exchange: 3 Nov.–17 Dec. 1988
Director: Brabham Murray
Designer: Johanna Bryant
Macbeth: David Threlfall
Lady Macbeth: Frances Barber
Set in a Nazi concentration camp, and played without an interval.

MEASURE FOR MEASURE

The RSC at the Barbican, London: 6 Oct. 1988–
Angelo: John Shrapnel
Transferred from Stratford, with cast changes.
See *Shakespeare Survey 42*, p. 134.

The Boilerhouse Theatre Company, tour: autumn 1988
Isabella: Miriam Cooper
The Duke: Jack Power
Set in the 1930s.

THE MERCHANT OF VENICE

The RSC at the Barbican, London: 21 April 1988–
Transferred from Stratford
See *Shakespeare Survey 42*, p. 154.

A MIDSUMMER NIGHT'S DREAM

The RSC at the Barbican, 13 Aug. 1987–18 Feb. 1988
Continuation of the 1987 production.
See *Shakespeare Survey 42*, p. 154.

Bottom of the Garden and Other Twisted Tales by Nola Rae
A mime based on *A Midsummer Night's Dream*.
Continuation of the 1987 tour.
Music: Peter West
Director/Designer: Matthew Ridout

The Park by Botho Strauss, translated from the German, by Tinch Minter and Anthony Vivis.
The Crucible, Sheffield: British première 29 Jan. 1988–
Directors: Steven Pimlott and Clare Venables
Designer: Tom Cairns
Oberon: John Ramm
Titania: Cecily Hobbs
Cyprian (Puck): Steven Beard
Oberon and Titania return to the soulless modern city.

Bottom's Dream
London Contemporary Dance, Sadler's Wells, London: 11 Feb. 1988 and autumn tour
Choreography: Jonathan Lunn
Designer: Tim Reed
Music: Mozart's 'Dissonance' Quartet, K 465
A new ballet, dealing with the discordant relationships of the lovers and their resolution.

Szkene Szinhaz Theatre Company, University of Budapest, at the Bloomsbury Theatre, London: spring 1988 and tour.
A shortened adaptation of *A Midsummer Night's Dream*, incorporating dance and mime. Puck was played by three acrobats. The performance was in Hungarian except for the play scene and Puck's last speech. The production was first seen at the National Theatre Festival, Hungary, 1986.

Hull Truck, Spring Street Theatre, Hull: 24 May–25 June 1988
Director: Richard Lewis
Designer: Robert Cheesmond
Oberon/Theseus: Robert Sian
Titania/Hippolyta: Kristine Landon-Smith

Bubble Theatre Company, tour of London parks, performing in a tent: 7 June–27 August 1988
Director: Peter Rowe
Designer: Paul Kondras
Oberon/Theseus: Jon Glentoran
Titania/Hippolyta: Liza Spenz
A musical version which presented the lovers as Sloane-rangers.

The New Shakespeare Company, Regent's Park Open Air Theatre, London: 13 June 1988–
Director: Caroline Smith
Designer: Simon Higlett
Music: Stephen Deutsch
Oberon/Theseus: Clive Arrindell
Titania/Hippolyta: Carol Royle
Bottom: Ian Talbot

Lords of Misrule, London, at New College Gardens, Oxford and touring: 4 July 1988–
Director: Alan Leigh

Angles Theatre Company, Wisbech, touring: 15 July–8 Oct. 1988
Director: Andy Naylor
Designer: Gordon Gillick
Oberon/Theseus: Andy Naylor
Titania/Hippolyta: Isobel Smith
A cast of seven performed a fairly full text, with three Pucks, doubling as other characters and the Mechanicals as red-nosed circus clowns, playing circus music.

The Everyman Theatre, Cardiff in the grounds of Dyffren House: 28 July–6 Aug. 1988
Director: Alan Vaughan Williams
Set in the Indian Raj, with Eastern fairies and the Mechanicals as a squad of British soldiers.

The Shakespeare Theatre Company of Diever, Holland; South Warwickshire College of Further Education: August 1988
Performed in Dutch, with a girl punk rocker acting as interpreter of the action.

Oracle Productions; Summer Theatre in Holland Park, Holland Park Open Air Theatre, London: 8–20 Aug. 1988
Director: Peter Benedict
Oberon: Roland Curran
Titania: Fenella Fielding
Bottom: James Powell
Puck: Edward Bryant
Set in an English country garden in the 1940s, with background sounds of air-raid sirens and the Mechanicals as Boy Scouts.

Manchester Royal Exchange at the Assembly Hall, Edinburgh and the Royal Exchange, Manchester, 15 Aug. 1988–
Director: Gregory Hersov
Designer: Lez Brotherston
Music: Mark Vibrans
Oberon: Kenneth Cranham
Titania: Fiona Victory
Modern dress, with the fairies in particularly fantastic costumes of fur and feathers. The wood scenes were set round an abandoned bedstead.

Birmingham Repertory Theatre: 3–24 Sept. 1988
Director: Robin Midgley
Designer: Simon Higlett
Music: Joji Hirota
Oberon/Theseus: Joe Dixon
Titania/Hippolyta: Amelda Brown
Bottom: Tyler Butterworth
Hermia: Toyah Wilcox
Presented as Bottom's dream, on the night before his wedding. Bottom fell asleep after his stag night party, and woke to find a twentieth-century pub had become the Athenian court, which then became a ruined, overgrown palace. Troops of children were used as the fairies.

The National Youth Theatre, the Shaw Theatre, London: 16–30 Sept. 1988
Director: Graham Chinn
Designer: Martin Sutherland
A twenties set, with Busby Berkeley numbers and movie mood music. The male fairies were dressed as pirates.

The RSC/British Telecom tour, with *The Beaux' Stratagem*; Bedford, 19 Sept. 1988–
Director: Bill Buffrey
Designer: Philippe Brandt
Music: Mia Soteriou
Oberon/Theseus: Raad Raw
Titania/Hippolyta: Jennie Stoller
Bottom: Roger Walker

TAG at the Tron Theatre, Glasgow and tour: 21 Sept.–20 Nov. 1988
Director: Ian Brown
Designer: Emma Fowler
Music: Richard Sisson
Oberon/Theseus: Iain Stuart Robertson
Titania/Hippolyta: Lesley Moore
Puck: Stuart McQuarrie
Bottom: Leonard McClure
Eight actors doubling in a fast, slapstick production, set in the modern period. Puck got particularly good reviews.

The Queen's Theatre, Hornchurch: 23 Sept.–22 Oct. 1988
Director: Bob Tomson
Designer: John Lewin
Oberon/Theseus: John Conroy
Titania/Hippolyta: Liz Brailsford
Mendelssohn's music was used, re-scored for a quartet of flute, clarinet, piano and classical guitar. Set in the Edwardian period.

Solent People's Theatre, Broughton Village Hall and tour of local villages: 27 Sept. 1988–
Director/Adaptor: Sue Charman
Designer: Sarah Jane Ash
Titania/Hippolyta/Helena: Jules Davison
Oberon/Theseus/Flute: Kevin Shaw

Lysander (a woman): Julia Findlay
Hermia and Lysander were portrayed as a lesbian couple.

The London Mozart Players and Finchley Children's Music Group at the Barbican, London: 16 Nov. 1988. One performance only.
Director: Julia Hope
Titania/Hippolyta: Maria Aitken
Oberon/Theseus: Peter Eyre
Bottom: Ian Talbot
A semi-staged, cut version, based on Charles Kean's performing edition of 1856, to Mendelssohn's music.

MUCH ADO ABOUT NOTHING

The London Shakespeare Group at Croydon Warehouse and tour of Scotland, followed by a British Council tour of Canada and the Middle East: 9 Feb. 1988–
Director: Delena Kidd
Designer: Mariselena Rossi
Benedick: Gary Raymond
Beatrice: Jill Brassington
Set in Edwardian England

Renaissance Theatre Company, Birmingham Repertory Theatre Studio, Phoenix Theatre, London and tour: 3 March 1988–
Director: Dame Judi Dench
Designer: Jenny Tiramani
Music: Pat Doyle
Benedick: Kenneth Branagh
Beatrice: Samantha Bond
See *Shakespeare Survey 42*, pp. 130–4.

The RSC at the Royal Shakespeare Theatre, Stratford: 7 April 1988–
Director: Di Trevis
Designer: Mark Thompson
Music: Dominic Muldowney
Benedick: Clive Merrison
Beatrice: Maggie Steed
See *Shakespeare Survey 42*, pp. 130–4.

OTHELLO

The University of Essex: 8–13 Dec. 1988
Director: Faynia Williams
Designer: Darian Kelly
Othello: Zahid Tharia
Desdemona: Giovanna Pizzoferno
Iago: Sebastian Mitchell
A modern-dress production, staged by a mixed group of amateurs and professionals.

The Market Theatre, Johannesburg, presented on Channel 4 TV: 27 Dec. 1988
Director: Janet Suzman
Othello: John Kani
Desdemona: Joanna Weinburg
Iago: Richard Haddon-Haines
Janet Suzman believes John Kani to be the first black African to have played Othello in South Africa. Very good reviews.

THE PLANTAGENETS

The Plantagenets: Henry VI, an adaptation of *Henry VI* parts I and II (see pp. 171–81)
The RSC at the Royal Shakespeare Theatre, Stratford, in repertory 29 Sept. 1988– and the Tyne Theatre, Newcastle on Tyne
Director: Adrian Noble
Designer: Bob Crowley
Lighting: Chris Parry
Music: Edward Gregson
Henry VI: Ralph Fiennes
Queen Margaret: Penny Downie

The Plantagenets: The Rise of Edward VI, an adaptation of *Henry VI* parts II and III
The RSC at the Royal Shakespeare Theatre, Stratford, in repertory 6 Oct. 1988–

The Plantagenets: Richard III, His Death
The RSC at the Royal Shakespeare Theatre, Stratford, in rep. 13 Oct. 1988–
Richard III: Anton Lesser

RICHARD II

The English Shakespeare Company tour.
See *Shakespeare Survey 41*, p. 188, *42*, p. 161.

Triumph Theatre Company, Yvonne Arnaud Theatre, Guildford; Phoenix Theatre, London and tour, with *Richard III*; 23 Nov. 1988–9
Director: Clifford Williams
Designer: Carl Toms
Music: Marc Wilkinson
Richard: Derek Jacobi
Bolingbroke: David Rintoul
A traditional, rather static production.

RICHARD III

The English Shakespeare Company, tour.
See *Shakespeare Survey 42*, p. 161.

Mad Dogs and Englishmen devised by John Mowat and John Ladle. A visual comedy, using mime, partly based on *Richard III*. Touring: 4 June 1988–

Glasgow Citizens' Theatre: 30 Sept.–22 Oct. 1988
Director: Jon Pope
Designer: Kathy Strachan (costumes)
Music: Adrian Johnston
Richard III: Ciaran Hinds
A severely cut version, with nine actors, set in Hitler's Germany.

The RSC at the Royal Shakespeare Theatre: see *The Plantagenets*.

ROMEO AND JULIET

Compass Theatre Company, Sheffield touring, with *The Tempest*
See *Shakespeare Survey 42*, p. 157.
1987 tour continued with a largely new cast.

The Young Vic, 1987 tour continued with a largely new cast.
Romeo: Clive Owen

St George's Theatre, London: 3–22 March 1988
Director: George Murcell
Romeo: Louis Hilyer

Juliet: Anastasia Malinoff
A traditional production with workshop sessions.

Temba Theatre Company, Contact Theatre, Manchester and tour: 16 Mar.–30 July 1988
Director: Alby James
Designer: Andrea Montag
Music: John Zaradin
Romeo: David Harewood
Juliet: Georgia Slowe
Set in nineteenth-century Cuba, with a black Romeo and a white Juliet (who went on to play the rôle for the RSC).

The Albany Empire, Deptford: 26 April–28 May 1988
Director: Teddy Kiendl
Designer: Paddy Kamara
Music: Felix Cross
Romeo: Carlton Chance
Juliet: Janet Steel
Set in 1930s Trinidad, among feuding Afro-Caribbean and Indo-Caribbean families.

The London Actors' Theatre Company, Latchmere Theatre, London: 27 April–28 May 1988
Directors: Chris Fisher and Mark Freeland
Director: John Pope
Music: Kjartan Poskitt
Romeo: Kiernan McCrystal
Juliet: Julie Saunders
A multiracial production with the cast in coloured muslin costumes, designed to indicate no particular place or period.

Knife Edge Theatre Company, London, in New College Gardens, Oxford: summer 1988
Director: Tim Price
Romeo: Angus Pope
Juliet: Maria Miles
In period costume

Prem by Jyoti Patel and Jezz Simons, The Young Directors' Festival, Battersea Arts Centre: 8 June 1988–

Director: James Macdonald
Designer: Samantha Griffiths
Rashid (Romeo): Dhirendra
Prem (Juliet): Sudha Bhuchar
A two-hander, relating *Romeo and Juliet* to the difficulties facing relationships between members of the Hindu and Muslim communities.

Traffic of the Stage at Pentameters Theatre Club, London: Aug. 1988
Director: Tom Leatherbarrow
Romeo: Matthew Brenher
Juliet: Lesley Casey
A cut, but otherwise traditional production.

The Shakespeare Alternative at Abbotsford Lodge, Edinburgh Festival: Sept. 1988
Director: Jeffrey Korn
Romeo: Charles Daish
Juliet: Caline Carr
Performed by a cast of seven.

York Theatre Royal and local tour with some workshops: 3 Nov.–26 Nov. 1988
Director: Jonathan Petherbridge
Designer: Pip Nash
Romeo: Sean Gilder
Juliet: Maria Gough
Set in no specific place or period.

Perth Theatre Studio, workshops and schools performances of an adaptation by John Clifford commissioned by TAG in 1984: 12–26 Nov. 1988
Director: Liz Carruthers
Designer: Emma Fowler
Romeo: Liam Brennan
Juliet: Helena Gillies
Set somewhere downtown in the present.

THE TAMING OF THE SHREW

British Actors Theatre Company, continuing the 1987 tour. See *Shakespeare Survey 42*, pp. 157–8.

Kiss Me Kate
The RSC at the Savoy, London, and touring. See *Shakespeare Survey 42*, p. 157.

Brunton Theatre Company, Musselburgh: 27 Jan.–6 Feb. 1988
Director: Charles Nowosielski
Katherine: Emma Currie
Petruchio: Robin Begg
Set in the Wild West.

Kent Repertory Theatre at Hever Castle: June 17–25 and Aug. 5–13 1988
Director: Richard Palmer
Katherine: Elaine Hallam
Petruchio: Peter Sowerbutts
A modern dress production.

The RSC at the Barbican, London, transfer of the 1987 Stratford production: 1 Sept. 1988 – See *Shakespeare Survey 42*, p. 157.

New Triad Theatre Company, touring: Sept. 1988
Director: John Strehlow.

The Mercury Theatre, Colchester: 12 Oct.–29 Oct. 1988
Director: Michael Winter
Designer: Jessica Bowles
Katherine: Belinda Davison
Petruchio: Richard Bonneville
The Sly episodes were played in modern dress, the rest in period, set in a barn.

THE TEMPEST

Compass Theatre Company, Sheffield, continuation of the 1987 tour: spring 1988. See *Shakespeare Survey 42*, p. 158.

Salford Playhouse: 29 Feb. 1988–
Director: Michael Goddard
Prospero: John Watts
Ariel: Freddy Garrity
A modern dress production, with Caliban as a young thug in a leather jacket and Ariel in

glasses, patched trousers and a bow tie, with flippers, wings and carrying a ghetto-blaster.

This Island's Mine by Philip Osment
Gay Sweatshop at the Drill Hall Arts Centre, London and tour: spring 1988
The play revolved around an old London house, and was about refugees, immigrants and personal relationships. Critics felt it made only partially successful use of allusion to *The Tempest*.

The National Theatre at the Olivier, London: in rep. 19 May–25 Nov. 1988. Tour of the USSR and Japan summer 1988
Director: Peter Hall
Designer: Alison Chitty
Music: Harrison Birtwistle
Prospero: Michael Bryant
See *Shakespeare Survey 42*, pp. 144–5.

The RSC at the Royal Shakespeare Theatre, Stratford: in repertory 7 July 1988– and the Tyne Theatre, Newcastle on Tyne
Director: Nicholas Hytner
Designer: David Fielding
Music: Jeremy Sams
Prospero: John Wood
See *Shakespeare Survey 42*, pp. 147–8.

The Ninagawa Theatre Company, Edinburgh Playhouse: 17–21 Aug. 1988
Director: Yukio Ninagawa
Designer: Toshiaki Suzuki
Music: Ryudo Uzaki
Prospero: Haruhiko Jo

The Tempest, adapted from Shakespeare by Simon Stallworthy.
Octopus Studio, Bolton: 24–27 Aug. 1988

Cheek by Jowl, Taunton Brewhouse, tour, with *Philoctetes*: 27 Sept. 1988–Feb. 1989
Director: Declan Donnellan
Designer: Nick Ormerod

Music: Paddy Cunneen
Prospero: Timothy Walker
Like the Ninagawa production, Cheek by Jowl made the play reflect on the nature of theatrical experience, with Prospero playing the director of the action.

Proper Job Theatre Company, Sheffield Polytechnic and tour of West Yorkshire schools and colleges: 2 Nov. 1988–
Director: David Lambert
Designer: Brett Fletcher
Prospero: Nigel Dickenson
Six actors in a production condensed to one hour, but with no speaking parts omitted.

The Old Vic, London: 6 Oct.–26 Nov. 1988
Director: Jonathan Miller
Designer: Richard Hudson
Music: Carl Davis
Prospero: Max von Sydow
Caliban and Ariel were played by black actors.

TIMON OF ATHENS

The Haymarket Studio, Leicester: 11 Feb.–12 March 1988
Director: Simon Usher
Designer: Jocelyn Herbert
Timon: Guy Williams
A modern dress production.

RAT Theatre Company, Hereford, continued: See *Shakespeare Survey 42*, pp. 158–9.

TITUS ANDRONICUS

The RSC at the Pit, Barbican, London: 29 June 1988– Transfer from Stratford, see *Shakespeare Survey 41*, pp. 178–81.

TWELFTH NIGHT

The Renaissance Theatre Company, Riverside Studios, London. See *Shakespeare Survey 42*, p. 160. This production was also televised.

The Coliseum, Oldham: 21 Jan.–13 Feb. 1988
Director: John Retallack
Designer: Kate Burnett
Viola: Carla Mendonca
Malvolio: Malcolm Hebden
Set in the nineteenth century. The production emphasized the slapstick comedy at the expense of the play's lyricism.

Theatre Royal, Stratford East, London: 3–19 Mar. 1988
Director: Jeff Teare
Designer: Fran Thompson
Music: Dave Brown
Viola: Helen Atkinson Wood
Malvolio: Alan Cowan
Set on a tropical island in a backwater of the Empire in the 1930s. Viola and Sebastian were portrayed as blond Anglo-Saxons, the natives were Afro-Caribbean except Malvolio, who was an English sergeant-major.

Channel Theatre Company, tour of small towns in Kent: 18 Mar. 1988–
Director: Philip Dart
Designer: Wiesia Allies
Viola: Kate Marwick
Malvolio/Orsino: David Callister
Modern dress.

The RSC at the Barbican, London: 31 Mar. 1988–
Malvolio: John Carlisle
Transfer from Stratford, with John Carlisle taking over from Antony Sher. See *Shakespeare Survey 41*, pp. 165–9.

The Royal Exchange, Manchester: 12 May–25 June 1988
Director: Brabham Murray
Designer: Johanna Bryant
Music: Chris Monks
Viola: Saskia Reeves
Malvolio: Gary Waldhorn
The production used a mixture of costumes from various periods, including the present.

The Ludlow Festival: 25 June–9 July 1988
Director: Michael Napier Brown
Designer: Ray Lett
Viola: Liz Crowther
Malvolio: Bryan Pringle
A traditional production.

Cambridge Touring Theatre at the Arts Theatre, Cambridge, and regional tour: Aug. 1988
Production team: Julian Murphy and Lisa Goldman
Viola: Annette Fraser
Malvolio: Jack Nightingale
Set in the 1980s.

Metro Theatre Company at the Golden Cross Theatre Club, London: 7–24 Sept. 1988
Set in the present.

The Gateway Theatre, Dublin: autumn 1988
Director: Joe Dowling
Designer: Frank Conway
Music: John Dunne
Viola: Catherine Byrne
Malvolio: John Kavanagh
Feste: Rosaleen Linehan
Set in the jazz age, with black and white sets. The production ended with a fascist salute, which gave Malvolio's final threat a political overtone. Feste was played by a woman. Very good reviews.

THE WINTER'S TALE

RSC at the Barbican, London: 8 Oct. 1987–27 Feb. 1988. See *Shakespeare Survey 40*, pp. 177–8.

The National Theatre at the Olivier, London, and tour of the USSR and Japan; in rep: 18 May–24 Nov. 1988
Director: Peter Hall
Designer: Alison Chitty
Leontes: Tim Pigott-Smith
Hermione: Sally Dexter
See *Shakespeare Survey 42*, pp. 142–4.

The New Shakespeare Company, Regent's Park Open Air Theatre, London: 1 June–10 Sept. 1988
Director: David Gilmore
Designer: Fran Thompson
Music: John de Prez
Leontes: Clive Arrindell
A Victorian setting.

Theatre Set Up, Forty Hall, Enfield and tour: 16 June 1988–
Director/Designer/Paulina: Wendy Macphee
Leontes: Alex Richardson, doubling as Perdita's adoptive father, the old shepherd.

Compass Theatre Company, Sheffield at Rhyl Library Arts Centre and touring, with *Hamlet* and *Volpone*: autumn 1988
Leontes/Autolycus: Nick Chadwin
Hermione/Perdita: Helen Schlesinger
Six performers, using minimal props.

SHAKESPEARE APOCRYPHA

A YORKSHIRE TRAGEDY

Lords of Misrule, London, at the Civic Theatre, Leeds: Nov. 1988
Director: David Ford
Probably a touring production.

Miscellaneous

Acting Shakespeare: excerpts from Shakespeare Ian McKellen one-man show. See *Shakespeare Survey* 41, p. 191, 42, p. 162.

Collage: excerpts from *Richard III*, *The Caucasian Chalk Circle* and *King Lear*. The Rustaveli Theatre Company of Tblisi, Georgia at the Haymarket Studio, Leicester: 24–26 Nov. 1988
Richard III/King Lear: Ramaz Tchkhikvadze
Richard III: Richard plans the murder of Clarence; the ghosts appear to Richard before Bosworth. *King Lear*: the mad scene on the heath; the reunion with Gloucester; the death

of Cordelia. In the mad scene, Lear stabbed the Fool. The acting was rather in the style of the nineteenth century; forceful and dramatic, using very expressive facial and physical gestures. Considerable use was made of music to create atmosphere.

Dark Lady, by Karen Sunde
The Peacock Theatre, Dublin: Dec. 1988
Director: Vincent Dowling
Designer: Carol Betera
Shakespeare: Gerard McSorley
Emilia Lanier: Nuala Hayes
Burbage: Vincent O'Neill

Falstaff, an adaptation from *Henry IV*, *Henry V* and *The Merry Wives of Windsor* by Richard Williams and Andy Rashleigh.
The Oxford Stage company, touring: autumn 1988
Falstaff: Bernard Bresslaw.

Shakespeare, Cole & Co
Alec McCowen one-man show, touring: autumn 1988
Alec McCowen recounted his experiences as an actor, and caricatured acting styles of the 1940s, using extracts from Shakespeare and others.

Venus and Lucrece, a stage adaptation by Bardy Thomas
The Art Depot Theatre Company at the Almeida Theatre, Islington: 26 Jan.–20 Feb. 1988
Director: Bardy Thomas
Designer: David Lewis
Music: Frank Bradley
Lucrece: Sarah Woodward
Tarquin: David Lansbury
Adonis: Jerome Flynn
Venus: Julia Swift
Two complementary pieces. *Venus and Adonis* was first staged at a National Theatre Studio workshop in 1986.

THE YEAR'S CONTRIBUTIONS TO
SHAKESPEARE STUDIES

1. CRITICAL STUDIES
reviewed by R. S. WHITE

DISTINGUISHED SHAKESPEARIANS

Some distinguished Shakespearians who are neither elderly nor particularly stately are none the less moving into the ranks of elder statespersons with the appearance of collections of their essays.

Barbara Everett has reprinted some of her valuable essays in *Young Hamlet: Essays on Shakespeare's Tragedies* (Oxford: Clarendon Press, 1989). Pieces on the four major tragedies are reprinted from the *Times Higher Educational Supplement* and the *London Review of Books*, and the original publishing context has allowed free play to Everett's distinctively lively and intimate tone as she constantly draws the reader into sharing delicately glimpsed moments which unobtrusively lead to firm pictures of the plays as totalities. The other essays have been published before in academic journals, but they retain the qualities of wit and quiet wisdom: *Romeo and Juliet*, *Troilus and Cressida*, *Othello* – and a ring-in comedy, *Twelfth Night*. I hope the inclusion of the last does not mean that we cannot look forward to a volume of Everett on the Comedies.

Ernst Honigmann has published *Myriad-Minded Shakespeare: Essays, Chiefly on the Tragedies and Problem Comedies* (London: Macmillan, Contemporary Interpretations of Shakespeare, 1989). Most of the essays are either reprinted, or interestingly conflate several different pieces. Formerly unpublished pieces include an essay on *Julius Caesar*, and one on *All's Well* (is it a 'feminist play'?). Most of the essays show Honigmann as critic rather than textual scholar, although there is his classic article on stage-directions and a lively amalgam 'Shakespeare at work: preparing, writing, rewriting'. Honigmann bills his book as 'an introduction to several (but not all) important "specialist" approaches' (p. 2), but all scholars will rate the book much more highly than this, respecting the original contributions of a keenly flexible, sometimes provocative and always entertaining critic who demonstrates a special 'myriad-mindedness' of his own.

While Honigmann and Everett, in their very different ways, are both 'European' in approach, Harry Berger Jr is recognizably North American in his capacity to absorb and utilize many scholarly schools from iconography to historicism and metatheatrical criticism. *Second World and Green World: Studies in Renaissance Fiction-Making*, selected and arranged with an introduction by John Patrick Lynch (Berkeley, Los Angeles, London: University of California Press, 1988) gives us as much a map of critical movements as insight into the Renaissance, since Berger demonstrates the methodologically derivative but rigorously thorough approach that marks the profession in

North America. It is a big, handsome book, and the Shakespearian element is represented by 'Theater, Drama, and the Second World: A Prologue to Shakespeare' (1968), '*Troilus and Cressida*: The Observer as Basilisk'' (1968), and 'Miraculous Harp: A Reading of Shakespeare's *Tempest*' (1969).

INTERTEXTUALITY AND RECEPTION

In the world of Shakespearian criticism, the old has a way of returning in new dress. Historical study of Shakespeare in his times has come back with force as new historicism; rhetoric has raised its head again as ideology. Now studies of sources and influences, allusions and imitation are back with us, reshaped as intertextuality and reception. Internal exchanges between authors, whether evidenced by quotation or discursive criticism, are rapidly being opened up as legitimate subjects for analysis. Julia Kristeva sounds a clarion call for the study of such creative transactions: 'tout texte se construit comme mosaïque de citations, tout texte est absorption et transformation d'un autre texte' (*Séméotikè: Recherches pour une sémanalyse* [Paris: Editions du seuil, 1969], p. 146). The ways in which Shakespeare has been received and used are becoming as much subjects for scrutiny as the texts themselves. Such matters tell us as much about the preoccupations and historical imitations and limitations of the borrower as about the apparently infinite potential of the Shakespearian text for being reshaped and reinterpreted from generation to generation.

G. F. Parker's *Johnson's Shakespeare* (Oxford: Clarendon Press, 1989) is an important and thoroughgoing overhaul of many critical assumptions embedded in our traditions. Self-evidently sympathetic to Samuel Johnson's form of criticism which has so long been out of fashion, Parker points to how it raises fundamental questions which have been glossed over by the Romantic critics and their successors up

to the present day. Johnson was courageous enough to be 'shocked' by Shakespeare's violations of audience expectations and of poetic justice, because he presupposed 'natural' conduct as a norm. The Romantics sought to reconcile 'shocking' behaviour to 'nature' by celebrating the aberrant and by psychologizing the more outrageous behaviour of Shakespeare's characters. Parker argues that we have been too inclined to smooth over problems by taking Romantic assumptions for granted. The awkward, honest, and fundamentalist presence of Johnson will need to be confronted again after this book which is rationally and philosophically argued. So many flaws are found in Romantic critics such as Coleridge that we cannot glibly accept their dismissive contempt for Johnson, and a study of his own ideas opens up genuinely new areas for interpretation. His responses may have been exactly right, even if the conclusions he builds upon them were limited.

Goethes Shakespeare-Bild by Kurt Ermann (Tübingen: Studien zur Deutschen Literatur, Band 76, Max Niemeyer, 1983) has been rather slow in finding its way to the *Survey*, but it is worth waiting for. It is a comprehensive and orderly study of an important area of intertextuality not just between writers but between cultures and languages. It deals with Goethe's knowledge of Shakespeare, from his early acquaintance with Dodd's *Beauties of Shakespeare*, and it comprehensively reveals the picture of Shakespeare given to us by the great German writer. As we would expect, the bulk of the book deals with *Hamlet*, and particularly the 'Hamlet-Problem' in *Wilhelm Meisters Lehrjahre* so influential on those interpretations which presuppose a melancholy prince. Ermann's book is a significant contribution to the wider study of the reception and transmission of Shakespearian interpretations.

R. A. Foakes has done us a service in presenting a new selection of *Coleridge's Criticism of Shakespeare* (London: Athlone Press, 1989). The brief Introduction emphasizes Coleridge's seminal belief in the organic unity of each of Shakespeare's plays. The selection of critical statements is distinguished from those by Hawkes and Raysor by drawing heavily on Foakes's own valuable work on the reports made by John Payne Collier of the 1811–12 lectures. If it is undoubtedly true that Coleridge has cast a spell over 150 years of Shakespearian criticism, it is equally clear, from a reading of this selection, that his authority is certain to be challenged in the light of recent theoretical advances. So much of his criticism reveals his own conservative and abstracting preoccupations that questions will be asked, not only about *why* he so judgementally cast Shakespeare in his own preferred image, but also about why so many subsequent generations found it expedient to accept his opinions as truth. In these days of 'cultural materialism' and scrutiny of underlying political ideologies, the assumptions will not remain unexamined. It is a strength of intertextuality that it can interpret the critic's standpoint as largely a product of his own times and not as 'objective' criticism. Foakes's very useful *Selection* will make such a demystifying exercise possible. Of course, for other readers it will reinforce the assessment of Coleridge as one of the most important critics who have lived, which is closer to Foakes's own estimation.

While on the subject of Romantic receptions of Shakespeare, it is worth mentioning Martin Greenberg's *The Hamlet Vocation of Coleridge and Wordsworth* (Iowa City: University of Iowa Press, 1986), although it is of marginal interest to Shakespearians. Greenberg argues that Coleridge's famous statement, 'The prevalence of the abstracting and generalizing habit over the practical ... I have a smack of Hamlet myself, if I may say so', actually determined an area of the poetic movement of Romanticism. It gives an example of the kind of literary colonizing aspect of Shakespeare's texts that Parker seeks to challenge.

My own book, *Furphy's Shakespeare* (Nedlands: Centre for Studies in Australian Litera-ture, University of Western Australia, 1989) demonstrates a different kind of colonization. Joseph Furphy's *Such is Life* (published in 1904) is Australia's most ambitious and significant novel, and deserves to be ranked with *Tristram Shandy* for its innovativeness in structure and narrational stance. Furphy's mouthpiece, Tom Collins, yearns to be a professional Shakespearian critic, and the book loads every rift with Shakespeare, sometimes for humorous effect, sometimes with the overt intention of 'Australianizing' the dramatist, wresting him from his English context which the republican Furphy despises, and sometimes with buried significance for the narrative. The book lists the hundreds of quotations from Shakespeare in Appendices and the sheer bulk of these gives a clear insight into the determination of a 'colonial' writer to appropriate Shakespeare for his own purposes. One unexpected fact that emerged from the research is that the Melbourne Shakespeare Society, founded in 1884, became the largest such association in the world at the time.

The next book is literally about British colonization and Shakespeare's part in it. The general subject of Ania Loomba's *Gender, Race, Renaissance Drama* (Manchester and New York: Manchester University Press, 1989) is the reception in post-colonial India of English Renaissance drama, transmitted through an educational system which is still that of England. The writer emphasizes as of particular importance her own responses, those of a woman, an Indian, and one who is contributing through teaching to education in India. The opening chapter deals with 'Imperialism, patriarchy and post-colonial English studies' and argues that dominant, 'establishment' readings of Shakespeare, and also some western feminist readings, are equally take-over bids of plays in ways that are not necessarily appropriate to different cultural contexts. In dealing with *Othello* Loomba suggests that sexuality and racial difference are equally significant and are completely intertwined through the common nexus of power, patriarchal in the one sphere and colonial in the other but having common cultural roots. Othello is seen initially as an 'honorary white' who is increasingly marginalized and differentiated, and alongside this pattern runs the transference of images of Desdemona from pure white woman to a dangerously duplicitous witch figure. The tragedy is that these changes are wrought within Othello himself, and he becomes fatally divided. In the context of 'Women's division of experience' Cleopatra is also seen as divided between the needs of a sexually active woman and the necessities imposed on her as a political figure. *The Tempest* returns to the connection between the racial plunder of colonial rule and the transfer to patriarchy in relations between men and women. The book concludes with a wider message:

To curse in 'your language' (1.2.362) is not to appropriate the European text on its own terms or to limit ourselves to the spaces allowed by it. Not only will it centre around a disclosure of the similarity and dissimilarity, usefulness and irrelevance of the Western text, but it must extend to the economic, sociopolitical and institutional realities in which our academic practice exists.   (pp. 157–8).

Loomba's book is a lively and timely one, written with personal commitment from a unique context. What is disturbing is that when the Shakespeare industry gets hold of an idea it can become something like a cliché rather than a freshly experienced, personal approach. We have, over the last few years, had an awful lot of essays about colonialism, post-colonialism and *The Tempest* from writers who seem to have seized on the subject as on the latest fashion. *Shakespeare Quarterly* can be voguish. Given the fact that it publishes only about a dozen articles each twelve months, I wonder if it is really representing the spread of genuinely innovative approaches when it gives us two articles on such a similar theme? This is not to disparage the thoroughly workmanlike essays by, respectively, Alden T. Vaughan, 'Shakespeare's Indian: The Americanization of Caliban'

(*Shakespeare Quarterly*, 39 (1988), pp. 137–53) and Meredith Anne Skura, 'Discourse and the Individual: The Case of Colonialism in *The Tempest*' (*Shakespeare Quarterly*, 40 (1989), 42–69). Skura cites ten pieces in the 1980s already, she mentions that the subject was a 'masthead' theme in the Folger Institute's 1988 seminar on new directions in Shakespearian studies, and it would be easy to add another dozen citations to her list. Some things start out as fresh ideas but they can be relentlessly done to death.

Creative reception and intertextuality are at the heart of Michael Scott's modest but stimulating book, *Shakespeare and the Modern Dramatist* (London: Macmillan, 1989). The premise is that a Shakespearian play is never a stable entity and that theatre deals in the re-creation of works. Plays which are based on a Shakespeare text are a stage on the journey of re-creation, and Scott examines some modern examples. Stoppard's *Rosencrantz and Guildenstern are Dead* picks up some of *Hamlet*'s preoccupations (sanity/insanity, players and play-within-play, death), but it does not reshape the material and instead is a 'parasitic comedy', commenting on *Hamlet* with some 'flippancy'. Edward Bond in *Bingo* and *Lear* tries to demythologize Shakespeare with 'A Divergent View of Human Nature' in order to shock modern audiences who may be complacent with 'classics'. Other writers dealt with are Wesker and Marowitz (Shylock), Beckett (whose plays have parallels with several of Shakespeare's), Ionesco, and Pinter. Marowitz is seen as the director rather than the author working and reworking Shakespeare, trying to free the texts from the shackles of narrative, and some RSC productions are examined for what they reveal about directorial assumptions.

Poets also interact with Shakespeare's texts, symbiotically taking from them what is useful while in the process illuminating for us potential significances in Shakespeare. Richard D. E. Burton examines the Shakespearian element in Baudelaire in 'Baudelaire and

Shakespeare: Literary Reference and meaning in "Les Sept Vieillards" and "La Béatrice"', *Comparative Literature Studies*, 26 (1989), 1–27. Burton establishes that Baudelaire almost certainly saw a performance of *Macbeth* in English played by Macready in 1845, and that the play is invoked in the nightmare vision of 'Les Sept Vieillards', the poem written in 1859. Similarly, the influence of *Hamlet* on 'La Béatrice' is clear. Burton does not present these findings simply as 'sources', but instead he suggests that in a poet like Baudelaire intertextuality is a part of the meaning of the host poems and should be analysed as such.

Our distinguished cousin on the continent, *Deutsche Shakespeare-Gesellschaft West Jahrbuch 1988* (Bochum: Verlag Ferdinand Kamp, 1988) under the editorship of Manfred Pfister and Kurt Tetzeli v. Rosador exhibits a general concentration upon reception and intertextuality this year. It opens with the engaging 'How to Rape Shakespeare and Emerge Psychologically in Tact' by Charles Marowitz (pp. 7–24) which stresses that 'Shakespeare is a political issue' and deals with some of the quirkier theatrical versions of some plays, showing that Shakespeare has been 'received' in some odd ways. An intertextual study is Eckhard Heftrich's 'Friedrich Gundolfs Shakespeare-Apotheose' (pp. 85–102), while Theodor Wolpers takes up aspects of reception of Shakespeare in eighteenth-century Germany in 'Die Shakespeare-Sammlung der Göttinger Universitätsbibliothek im 18. Jahrhundert. Erste Vermittlung Shakespeares aus dem Geist "fortschreitender Wissenschaft"' (pp. 58–84). This essay has an appendix listing all eighteenth-century English criticism in the Göttingen University Library. Different kinds of reception and intertextuality are discussed by Michael Wachsmann in 'Die Architektur der Worte. Überlegungen zur Übersetzung Shakespeares ins Deutsche' (pp. 44–57). Frank Günther in 'Sein oder nicht Sein – Was ist hier die Frage? Vom Abbild der Zeiten im Spiegel *Hamlet*' (pp. 25–43) considers among other

versions of *Hamlet* 'einen No-future-Punk-Hamlet'. Finally, two essays neatly parallel each other, although they do not fit in this thematic section. Dale B. J. Randall ponders on the leonine basis for Leontes' name ('A Glimpse of Leontes through an Onomastic Lens', pp. 123–9), and Inge Leimberg examines the mythological dimensions in Hermione's name ('"The Image of Golden Aphrodite": Some Observations on the Name "Hermione"', pp. 130–49).

APPROACHES

It is arguable that the approach which, over the last ten years, has precipitated the most searching and radical reassessment of Shakespeare is the feminist or gender-based one. Dympna Callaghan's *Woman and Gender in Renaissance Tragedy: A Study of 'King Lear', 'Othello', 'The Duchess of Malfi' and 'The White Devil'* (New York and London: Harvester Wheatsheaf, 1989) is pre-eminently a critique of other approaches rather than interpretation of the plays by Shakespeare and Webster. The sophisticated argument is built on the notion of the Renaissance (male) need in the system of social relationships to differentiate relentlessly between the genders. Man is placed at the centre, continually constructing and reclassifying women (passive, angelic, lecherous, transgressive, daughter, wife, and so on), while women are placed in impossible contradictions as both the ultimate cause of tragedy by the mere fact of giving birth, and also marginalized from the prerogative of tragic suffering assumed by the male heroes. Men carry out their constructions, judging as much from female silence and absence as from utterance, driven by patriarchal imperative and often motivated by misogyny. Callaghan does not accuse Shakespeare and Webster of creating such a state of affairs, but instead she examines dramatic situations with a cool eye as problems revealed by the writers. The analysis challenges many of our cherished assumptions about tragedy, and in particular those positing the moral primacy of men such as Lear and Othello. Since the argument is logically deployed and amply illustrated it amounts to a fresh and powerful new set of understandings.

The Shakespearian chapters of Patricia Parker's very readable book, *Literary Fat Ladies: Rhetoric, Gender, Property* (London and New York: Methuen, 1987) links effectively a subject reminiscent of older scholarship, the study of Elizabethan rhetorical figures, with a feminist concentration on the representation of women. The trope of *hysteron proteron* (the Preposterous) has implications for hierarchies based on gender. The logic of *chiasmus* with the related forms of doubling has wider, structural implications for plays like *The Merry Wives of Windsor* and *The Comedy of Errors*. Many other figures are dealt with in ways that show the linguistic level providing a microcosm for larger issues in the plays. Especially memorable are the analyses which link up rhetoric, politics, and gender. Parker points out that rhetoric had traditionally been a male preserve which enables both social control and specifically control over women. 'Proper ordering' of the potentially subversive is its hidden motive. The link between rhetoric and gender-ordering is shown at length in Parker's development of Nancy Vickers' study of the *blazon*. 'The economic motive of itemizing – the dealing of a woman's parts as an inventory of goods' (p. 131) is shown in practice in Henry V's linguistic games with Katherine of Valois and more generally in *Cymbeline*. The book also contains a highly entertaining essay, full of insight, about fat ladies in Shakespeare, from the one in *The Comedy of Errors* through the pregnant gossip and votaress in *A Midsummer Night's Dream* to Falstaff disguised as the fat woman of Brentford. The rhetorical trope behind all these is *dilatio*, a topic on which Parker has published her best-known work.

Isobel Armstrong in an important survey of criticism and theatre in the 1980s, 'Thatcher's Shakespeare?', *Textual Practice*, 3 (1989), 1–14, seems to see feminism as one of the most optimistic and fruitful ways forward in making Shakespeare a progressive rather than reactionary force. This, however, is not her main theme. What she objects to is the kind of approach that has emerged almost as a defeatist response to the radical conservatism of the British Government in the 1980s, the move that would 'trash' (p. 5) Shakespeare as no more than an educationally homogenizing, white, middle-class institution. She points out that this 'plays into conservative hands' at a time when 'a more ruthless conservatism by far than that of patrician liberals like Scarman is *assuming* the redundancy of literary studies and the arts as institutions and practices' (p. 5). Armstrong looks at some 'so-called "radical" Shakespeare productions' (p. 7) such as David Hare's *King Lear* at the National Theatre and finds that they miss the opportunity to explore 'an increasingly devastating critique' (p. 8) of modern institutional failures which could potentially awaken people's conscientious resistance to brutal policies. (Such an approach, incidentally, is presented in my own article, '*King Lear* and Philosophical Anarchism', in *English*, 37 [1988], pp. 181–200.) On the other hand, Michael Bogdanov's work with the English Shakespeare Company (self-evidently 'popular' at the box office in England and Australia) shows successful, radical presentations. At the very least it is significant that political and ideological debate is being carried out in Shakespearian criticism, and academic work is demonstrating a new sense of social responsibility which Armstrong welcomes. She concludes 'We cannot afford not to engage with aesthetics and redefine it for the left' (p. 14).

Alongside feminism, new historicism is the other distinctive approach given to us by the 1980s. There is now a series called 'The New Historicism: Studies in Cultural Politics' published by the University of California under the General Editorship of Stephen Greenblatt. Leah S. Marcus has contributed an impressive volume, *Puzzling Shakespeare: Local Reading* and Its Discontents (Berkeley, Los Angeles, London: University of California Press, 1988). Marcus gives 'topical' readings of Shakespeare, readings that are conducted alongside knowledge of the 'temporarily commonplace' issues being debated in Shakespeare's time. *King Lear* is examined from the perspective offered by King James's use of the royal prerogative and the debate about the Stuart Project for Union between England and Scotland. The liturgical context of the play being performed on St Stephen's Day in 1606 proves another fruitful entry-point, as does comparison between the Folio and Quarto texts. Elizabeth is seen as both a woman and an office, another 'topical' debate of the time, and perhaps less flattering to her, echoes of Elizabeth are detected in Shakespeare's depiction of Joan of Arc. *Cymbeline* is seen as almost sycophantic in its insistence on James's pet policies. Beneath the specific areas of examination runs a critique that marks new historicism, a questioning of the assumptions about Shakespeare's 'universality'.

Claire McEachern seeks to bring into a synthesis feminism, new historicism, and intertextuality, in 'Fathering Herself: A Source Study of Shakespeare's Feminism', *Shakespeare Quarterly*, 39 (1988), pp. 269–90. She makes the useful point that patriarchy (a frame of reference for feminists) and the court (new historicism) have a strong link if we accept assumptions that politics operate in the family as well as in the state. The plays considered in most detail are *Much Ado About Nothing* and *King Lear*. Feminism and patriarchy are the twin subjects of the next article in the same journal, 'Grubbing Up the Stock: Dramatizing Queens in *Henry VIII*' by Kim H. Noling, *Shakespeare Quarterly*, 39 (1988), pp. 291–306.

Meanwhile, Derick R. C. Marsh in '*Othello* Re-Read' in *Sydney Studies in English*, 14 (1988–9), pp. 3–12 sounds a note of caution in assessing the contribution of all new literary theories. His contention is 'that the great critical discovery of our time, the liberating recognition that everyone has an ideology and writes from within its point of view, is neither liberating nor a discovery' (p. 5). He cites Dr Johnson as one who knew full well that he shared the literary suppositions of his time, arguing that Johnson's responses pulled him away from his critical conditioning, a tension which is fruitful. Marsh reads *Othello* in a 'universalist' fashion, arguing that the play shows inescapable confrontations with death rather than exemplifications of social injustice or political victimization.

Graham Holderness, Nick Potter and John Turner, authors of *Shakespeare: The Play of History* (London: Macmillan Press, Contemporary Interpretations of Shakespeare, 1989) distance themselves for different reasons from new historicism which, they say, has a tendency to collapse the cultural artefact into its economic basis to the exclusion of other considerations. They do not, however, give up the terms materialist, ideological, and dialectical, since they see the plays as depicting a history which is 'a dynamic process driven by desires, ambitions and beliefs that operate so powerfully precisely because they spring from the deepest conflicts and contradictions of the societies in which they occur' (p. 3). Holderness returns to his former concentration upon the political struggles of the late Middle Ages between monarchy and nobility as an example of contradictions in the feudal order. Turner interprets Shakespeare's revival of interest in romance as a return to feudal preoccupations upon the accession of James. He sees *King Lear* and *Macbeth* in ways that recall Leah Marcus, as 'tragic romances' depicting the debate between unionism and nationalism. Potter in 'This is Venice' suggests that because of the settings of the plays, *Othello* and *The Merchant of Venice* differ from the histories and tragedies in giving us a social world 'drained of the coherences of the sacred and devoted instead to profit' (p. 159). These plays, he argues, show developing capitalism, the triumph of commercial 'realists' over idealists, rather than the breakdown of feudalism under its own contradictions.

Richard Dutton in his brief *William Shakespeare: A Literary Life* (London: Macmillan, 1989) begins to apply the rigour of new historicism to the notoriously tricky area of biography. Instead of racy anecdotes and romantic speculations, Dutton supplies hard-nosed information and analysis of what we know about the various institutional contexts in which Shakespeare lived and worked. The system of patronage for poets and dramatic companies, commercial arrangements within the companies, the conditions of state censorship, the physical attributes of the Elizabethan stage, and the propagandist intention of historiography at the time are all explained as breeding-grounds for Shakespeare's output. The book is also interesting for its being written by a critic best known for his work on Jonson. Dutton neatly turns the tables on a history of unfair comparisons by returning to the 'silent question ... why did Shakespeare not write, or try to write, like Jonson' (p. xi). This fine book can be recommended to the specialist or that mythical creature the 'general reader'.

THEMES

Shakespeare's Dilemmas by Richard Horwich (New York: Peter Lang, 1988) contributes to a fertile field of criticism which has been developed by writers such as Empson, Rossiter, Rabkin, and most recently Graham Bradshaw. The dilemmas really belong not to Shakespeare himself but to his characters, as they face radical alternatives so wickedly framed that resolution and negotiation are impossible except in death or formal closure of the play. The 'dilemma-play', argues Horwich, 'is a uniquely Shakespearean accomplishment' (p. 207). The chapter headings alone indicate the approach and the scope of the argument: '"A Mingled Yarn, Good and Ill Together": From Dilemma to Riddle in The Problem Comedies'; '"O Well-Divided Disposition!": The Dilemmas of Tragic Love'; '"To Be, or Not to Be": *Hamlet* and The Dilemmas of Existence'; '"Welcome

and Unwelcome Things At Once": *Macbeth* and The Dilemmas of the Psyche'. Sometimes Horwich himself, faced with dilemmas, takes easy ways out. He sees Macduff, for example, as the answer to all Scotland's problems, 'because the polarities, symmetries, and antitheses that lie at the farthest remove from the vagaries of human nature are foreign to him' (p. 202). He is also a little too dependent on the old cliché of Shakespeare's age being a 'divided' one (surely *every* age can be thus described, depending on what evidence we use?). But despite some glibness and a reluctance to drive analysis into harder paths, Horwich's argument is well-sustained and his criticism sensible.

The title of Derek Cohen's book, *Shakespearean Motives* (London: Macmillan, Contemporary Interpretations of Shakespeare, 1988) does not give much away about the contents, and admittedly it would be hard to find a title that would encompass these diverse essays. The writer's central interest lies in characterization, but the concept is deployed flexibly to say the least. The most freshly trenchant essay is the one on *The Merchant of Venice* which argues powerfully that the play can be read as 'a profoundly and crudely anti-Semitic play' (p. 104) where at best Shakespeare betrayed 'for mercenary and artistic purposes' (p. 118) his own innate tolerance. In its assertiveness this essay is an exception in the volume. Through some other essays runs a thread (implicit in the chapter on *The Merchant*) which emphasizes contrasts of world-views in the plays. In *Twelfth Night* Viola is seen as the active to Orsino's passive; Othello is most comfortable in re-creating the past while Iago faces the present and the future; Hal changes while Hotspur does not; Angelo and Isabella through their encounters are both forced to face inward selves which they had respectively tried to deny; in *King Lear* memory and the pre-play past are considered in relation to the play's present action. In examining *Richard II* Cohen develops his own version of response-theory, arguing for the transformative capacities of audiences.

Murray J. Levith in *Shakespeare's Italian Settings and Plays* (London: Contemporary Interpretations of Shakespeare, Macmillan, 1989) reminds us of the apparently hypnotic hold Italy had on Shakespeare's imagination. He examines the accounts of travellers such as Fynes Moryson and also the popular view of Italy, before looking at the particular case of Venice in the Elizabethan imagination and specifically in *The Merchant of Venice* and *Othello*. In dealing with the latter play, Levith is extremely helpful in placing Cyprus. There is briefer analysis of other plays set in Italy, *Romeo and Juliet*, *The Taming of the Shrew*, *The Two Gentlemen of Verona*, *All's Well*, *Much Ado* and (glancing at Italy) *The Tempest*. Levith concludes that it doesn't really matter whether Shakespeare went to Italy or not. The book is short, interesting, and does not claim to be critically penetrating.

Ralph Berry's *Shakespeare and Social Class* (Atlantic Highlands, New Jersey: Humanities Press International, 1989) is entertaining and informed, from a critic who is as concerned about the plays in performance as on the page. Given the expectations raised by the title, however, it is lightweight, reading more like a series of urbane paragraphs on individual plays rather than an argument. Taking as a starting-point the distinctions made by Sir Thomas Smith in 1583 between nobility, gentry, citizens and 'the fourth sort of men which do not rule', Berry aims to demonstrate the existence of these classes among Shakespeare's *dramatis personae*. The point of view is often that of the nobility, assuming that the existence of 'the fourth sort' does little more than add 'realism' to the plays. Treatment of each play is (necessarily, given the breadth of coverage) very brief – a snip and away onto another. We do not get sustained analysis of dynamic interaction between classes, and in a book dealing with such a subject it is surely not adequate to mention Marx only once, and dismissively at that. However, Berry writes with refreshing lucidity and has an acute critical perceptiveness about local effects. As a general introduction to Shakespeare's plays for students it is first-rate.

In composing *Discovering Shakespeare's Meaning* (Totowa, New Jersey: Barnes and Noble Books, 1988), Leah Scragg seems to have been sheltered from the scrutiny of underlying assumptions that marks recent criticism. Even extending the most generous latitude to a book that aims 'not ... to elucidate, but to suggest how an interpretation may be arrived at' (p. ix) it has to be admitted that the enterprise is generally uncritical. It takes us back to a time when trite banalities passed as understated wisdom, and that day has passed. Beginning with the normativeness of blank verse in Shakespeare, the book then displays examples of iterative imagery, looks at how Shakespeare gives information at the beginning of plays in expository passages, passes on to structural matters of plays within plays and parallel actions, then on to character and soliloquy, and ends with an insistence that the plays are artifices rather than reality. Too often very long passages are quoted without leading on to detailed analysis. Despite some interesting 'points' (such as the visual indivisibility of the crown in *Lear* being enacted in the disastrous partition of the kingdom) there is little sustained or satisfactory analysis.

The title of George T. Wright's book, *Shakespeare's Metrical Art* (Berkeley and Los Angeles: University of California Press, 1988), does not promise a very entertaining read, but in fact this is not so. The book is not nearly so statistical as are, for example, the works of Marina Tarlinskaja, and it is written not primarily for the specialist in Elizabethan metrics, but for the reader who is generally knowledgeable in Shakespeare and wants explanations for the poetic effects. Wright, a poet himself, believes in the expressiveness of poetry and in control of metre as contributory factors in the creation of effects. Some critics these days might find some naïvety in the belief in the iambic pentameter's 'speechlike' qualities, and in the general reliance on affective rhetoric which lies behind the conviction that 'much of human feeling' lies behind the structures of metre (p. xiii). The insistent theme of finding 'techniques of expressive variation' within 'a metrical norm' (p. 20) is hardly original. However, the book is appealingly written and the close critical exegesis is convincing if we quell our fundamental doubts. Wright moves through the iambics of Chaucer and Wyatt, discovers that Sidney is the first to use 'metrical expressiveness' comprehensively (a welcome linking of Sidney with Shakespeare which is not often made). After detailed examination of Shakespeare's use of pentameters, paying attention to such variations as short and shared lines, long lines, syllabic ambiguity, and 'the play of phrase and line', Wright concentrates on some passages which he argues exemplify the full weight of Shakespeare's metrical expressiveness. Brief comparisons with Donne and Milton conclude the book.

Most writers who wish to get to grips with poetic features of the Sonnets find themselves frustratingly driven to use very technical terms to explain effects which are usually breathtaking in their subtle simplicity. Sandra L. Bermann finds herself up against this problem in *The Sonnet Over Time: A Study in the Sonnets of Petrarch, Shakespeare and Baudelaire* (Chapel Hill and London: University of North Carolina Press, 1988). Her general theme in the one chapter devoted to Shakespeare is not unlike Wright's idea of variation within a norm. She argues that Shakespeare inherited a normative tradition from Petrarch, and he modified rather than fundamentally altered it. The modifications are crucial, however, with Shakespeare's enriching wit, paradox and wordplay, with his development of the drama of an I and Thou, with his metaphoric rather than metonymic rhetoric. If there is 'repetition with difference', the difference ends up outweighing the repetition in significance. Bermann's account cannot be said to be innovative or heavyweight, but it does make lucid connections between the three sonneteers who are so separated in time.

A Shakespeare Merriment: An Anthology of Humor by Marilyn Schoenbaum (New York and London: Garland Publishing Inc., 1988) is a healthy corrective to those who get too earnest about Shakespeare. It is not the humour *in* Shakespeare that is the subject, but the humour inspired by Shakespeare, and we are given a miscellany of irreverent pieces by such writers as Fielding, Washington Irving, Mark Twain, Bernard Shaw, James Thurber, Tom Stoppard, Woody Allen and many others. Rereading Oscar Wilde's 'The Portrait of Mr W. H.' convinces me afresh that Mr W. H. was Shakespeare's expert boy-actor, but when the fate of poor Erskine, the proponent of this theory, is contemplated, I find it judicious not to follow up the idea as more than an after-dinner amusement, which is precisely the spirit in which Marilyn Schoenbaum's book can be enjoyed.

BOOK-LENGTH STUDIES OF PLAYS

Martin Elliott in *Shakespeare's Invention of Othello: A Study in Early Modern English* (London: Macmillan Press, 1988) provides a very close reading of the play through its language and syntax. It is a sober, and sobering book, which should prevent others making too many vague and general statements about *Othello*. Time after time we are given examples of 'how a small point of lexicon, when closely examined, can enrich or confirm one's interpretation of a character' (p. 87).

Although S. C. Sen Gupta's *'Hamlet' Once More* (Calcutta, Delhi, Bombay, Hyderabad: A. Mukherjee & Co., 1988) is a brief book, its appearance gives an occasion to pay tribute to a scholar who has devoted a lifetime's work to Shakespeare. The book begins with a survey of some influential critical statements on *Hamlet* in which the writer is most severe on Eliot. There follows Sen Gupta's own 'reading' of the text which is based partly on the premise that 'Indian poetics ... holds that poetry is suggestive rather than expressive' (p. 46). Many of the distinctions are suggestive without being pursued in any detail:

> The father is willing to pass over an errant wife's infidelity but he must have his revenge on his murderous brother while for the son it is the mother's shame that is like a festering ulcer which nothing can heal ... It is this difference in attitude between father and son that makes the tragedy complex and baffling, misty and mystical. (p. 64)

The book concludes with an essay on Shakespeare and Keats which is a useful corrective to Middleton Murry's celebrated panegyric on both writers. Sen Gupta argues that many of Keats's quotations from Shakespeare are insensitive to their original dramatic contexts, and that Keats displays a 'fumbling approach to the complexity and depth of Shakespeare's imagination' (p. 86). While not denigrating Keats's poetry, he argues that none of it is 'Shakespearian' either in kind or quality.

Three Harvester New Critical Introductions to Shakespeare have appeared. The series is uniquely generous to its contributors, in allowing each a whole book to develop an argument about one play, without restrictions on length or critical approach. If there is a risk of eclecticism this would seem worth taking in these days of drearily uniform serials. Whether the series is as generous to readers only time will tell, but the volumes that have appeared are much more than 'Introductions' for each is a serious, scholarly work in its own right.

Cedric Watts was offered either a unique opportunity or a thankless task in being consigned the volume on *Hamlet* (New York, London, Toronto, Sydney, Tokyo: Harvester Wheatsheaf, 1988). Although the book is lively and interesting, it would seem that the challenge has not been taken up with a lot of alacrity. Forty-eight pages are devoted to Stage and Critical History, and only two chapters (eighty pages) to the play itself. Furthermore, anxious to demonstrate the theme that 'When we look into *Hamlet*, we tend to see ourselves reflected; and that's because the text has many mirrors built into it' (p. 80), Watts seems reluctant to expose many of his own predilections. The two chapters follow an antithesis/thesis format. The former shows 'problems, gaps, anomalies' in the play and dwells on the uncertainties of dating and text, justifying the critics who can find no consistency in the play. The latter turns to the other end of the spectrum, examining ways in which 'Yet there be method in't', showing that details can be coordinated into one reading or another that will offer 'a remarkably coherent and subtly-organised work' (p. 40). Vengeful sons, realism and subverted stereotypes are offered as the clues to levels of consistency.

In dealing with *King Lear*, Alexander Leggatt adopts a more familiar technique of sticking close to chronology of the text, and not hazarding too much by way of critical theory (New York, London, Toronto, Sydney, Tokyo: Harvester Wheatsheaf, 1988). Some traditional problems are raised such as the Christian element, and the approach is through character essentially rather than ideas. In dealing with character, Leggatt is most illuminating on 'the unfixed and contradictory nature of identity' (p. 38) in the play's presentation. Adrian Poole, in dealing with *Coriolanus* (New York, London, Toronto, Sydney, Tokyo: Harvester Wheatsheaf, 1988) moves through the play Act by Act. After beginning 'with a rush' (like the play itself in Poole's phrase) with the important question of whether the crowd is presented as an unthinking mob or a reasonable group with legitimate political demands, the analysis settles gradually into a more psychological and character-centred approach. I find it a shame that the broader problems of sympathies and political ideologies are not pursued more rigorously, since as the book goes on it becomes more conventionally focused on explaining Coriolanus's responses. There is a lot of very astute and sensitive attention to detail of language in particular, but partly as a result of his chosen level of attention Poole does not fully capture the harsh and intractable nature of the central character or his world. There is also a sense in which the writer is too often looking over his shoulder at other critics, sometimes very conventional ones, rather than committing himself to more personal statements. All three books, however, are rewarding and soundly presented in their own individual ways.

JOURNALS AND COLLECTIONS

Two international journals make their appearances, the first being *Shakespeare in Southern Africa* (Volume 1, 1987). It is launched with an impressive Advisory Board and lectures from M. M. Mahood, M. C. Bradbrook and J. L. Styan specially commissioned for the occasion of the inauguration of the Shakespeare Society of Southern Africa. There are reviews of Janet Suzman's apparently electric production of *Othello* at the Market Theatre in Johannesburg ('a milestone in the history of South African theatre' giving its audience '"a metaphor for South Africa"' (p. 69)). In picking her way through the thorny subject of 'Shakespeare and Race', Hilary Semple concludes that, while the dramatist expressed many of the current attitudes towards race in Elizabethan England, his personal integrity allowed him 'to go beyond the stereotype, where, tragically, most men stick'. He 'acknowledges the value and importance of a shared humanity no matter what the creed or colour' (p. 37). D. G. Damant writes on Shakespeare's 'Anti-Clericalism', and the conclusion is rather similar. Less controversially, Rodney Edgecombe gives some reflections on adaptations of Shakespeare to ballet and Reingard Nethersole writes on the reception of Shakespeare into German Romantic literature.

The second new journal is *Hungarian Studies in Shakespeare* (*Új Magyar Shakespeare-Tár*, 1, Budapest: Modern Filológiai Társaság, 1988). All eighteen articles are in Hungarian, but there are abstracts to help those of us who need them. Some pieces concern the reception of Shakespeare in Hungary, and there is a bibliography

of recent performances which includes a 'Rock Opera in two parts' based on *Hamlet* in 1987. Several essays deal with the current state of Shakespeare criticism in America, while others cover aspects of *Hamlet*, *Love's Labour's Lost*, *Henry IV* ('thou' and 'you'), *Othello*, *King Lear*, *The Tempest*, and one on *The Merry Wives of Windsor* in Hungarian theatres which indicates that the play is alive and well there. We wish the series well, as another manifestation of the internationalism of the Shakespeare industry.

'Bad' Shakespeare: Revaluations of the Shakespeare Canon, edited by Maurice Charney (London and Toronto, Associated University Press, 1988) is salutary in raising the apparently iconoclastic question 'Can any of Shakespeare be bad?' Bardolatry and canonical thinking are treated sceptically, and Shakespeare is brought 'back to the field' by consideration of his plays in the context of those by contemporaries. We find the patriarchy of *The Taming of the Shrew* treated in two essays (Peter Berek, Shirley Nelson Garner). 'Conflicting Images of the Comic Heroine' dwells on *All's Well That Ends Well* (Dolora Cunningham), while the status of farce is examined with reference to *The Comedy of Errors* (Russ McDonald). *Romeo and Juliet* is treated as 'bad tragedy' (Avraham Oz), Horatio's inconsistencies are unpicked (Alex Newell), cuts in the last scene of *King Lear* are regarded as 'The Worst of Shakespeare in the Theater' (John Russell Brown). *Timon of Athens* is still regarded as a 'Problem' (Ninian Mellamphy) and the low critical estimation of *Henry VIII* is seen alongside its theatrical successes, raising the question of whether performance can reform a text which readers find 'bad' (Iska Alter). Steven Urkowitz brings 'Good News about "Bad" Quartos'. The most entertaining essay is Harriett Hawkins' 'From *King Lear* to *King Kong* and Back: Shakespeare and Popular Modern Genres', which reminds us that if we denude Shakespeare's plays of 'popular' appeal then we kill them. The book grew out of a seminar at a meeting of the Shakespeare Association of America in 1986.

Such collections of diverse and loosely connected essays raise fiendish problems for a reviewer. Even more difficult to present in manageable form is a book such as *Images of Shakespeare: Proceedings of the Third Congress of the International Shakespeare Association, 1986* (Newark, University of Delaware Press, 1988). It is impossible to draw into any unity that is not spurious twenty-nine papers delivered by an extremely international set of speakers who seem to have had a festive time in Berlin. Characteristically, Samuel Schoenbaum steals the show with an illustrated essay that spots the potential of the Conference theme reflected in the title of the book. He writes learnedly and wittily on 'Artists' Images of Shakespeare'.

I gather that 'triple play' is a term from baseball, the United States's second greatest cultural export after Coca Cola, and there is something particularly American about the conception of *Shakespeare and the Triple Play: From Study to Stage to Classroom* edited by Sidney Homan (Lewisburg, London and Toronto: Bucknell University Press, 1988). Without a more infectious editor the volume could have been a completely miscellaneous and incoherent set of unrelated essays. It is undoubtedly Homan's personality that makes of it a generous, genial romp, answering the plea by Norman Holland in his Afterword for more personal response, more 'humaneness' in Shakespeare criticism. By linking together study, stage and classroom, and the editor's contacts with Universities in the People's Republic of China, the book's conception could include everything and anything. The only shame is that the Chinese representatives, politely deferential amongst this self-confident company, tend to be cautiously Western in their general approach. Equally disappointing, Homan's own essay (or rather notebook) on directing *The Merry Wives of Windsor* in the People's Republic of China does not show very much awareness of being away from Florida. Others deal with cultural contexts and expectations in various ways. Laura Keys, with only a slight touch of the tongue in cheek, speculates about the critical appropriateness of having an obese Hamlet, and Marvin Rosenberg demonstrates the emergence into acting tradition of a Lady Macbeth who, without the inner resistance of conscience, submits to her aggressively physical and erotic drives. The book as a whole is impossible to summarize except by saying that, for better or worse, it is a mixed bag.

Two other volumes which are equally impossible to review, but should at least be noticed, are Volumes 7 and 8 of *Shakespearean Criticism: Excerpts from the Criticism of William Shakespeare's Plays and Poetry, from the First Published Appraisals to Current Evaluations* edited by Mark W. Scott and Sandra L. Williamson (Detroit, Michigan: Gale Research Company, 1988 and 1989). Volume 7 deals with *All's Well That Ends Well*, *Julius Caesar* and *The Winter's Tale*. Volume 8 covers criticism on *Much Ado About Nothing*, *Richard III*, and *The Tempest*. Although a series with potential usefulness, it should be mentioned that 'Criticism' is defined as literary exegesis. There is no attempt to include theatrical criticism or work of non-interpretative scholarship. These subjects always remain for two more bulky, multi-volume series, if the editors still have the energy. Meanwhile, it looks as though one more volume will complete the present project.

King John: New Perspectives edited by Deborah T. Curren-Aquino (Newark, London and Toronto: University of Delaware Press and Associated University Press, 1989) seems a labour of faith. The Introduction is called '*King John* Resurgent'. Admitting that the play is a 'loner', 'either ignored, tolerated, or forced to assume a theatrical image untrue to itself' (p. 24), the editor hangs on to the critics from the past who have called for a positive revaluation, and invites her team of essay-writers to take up the challenge of a thorough revaluation. The 'modernity' of the play is celebrated in some of the titles, which cover 'Historiographic Methodology', 'Subversion and Containment', 'Patriarchal History and Female Subversion',

'Fraternal Pragmatics: Speech Acts of John and the Bastard' and 'The "Un-End" of *King John*: Shakespeare's Demystification of Closure'. All the essays are new ones, the result of two seminars held in 1986 at the annual conference of the Shakespeare Association of America in Montreal. I certainly wish the campaign well. All the essays are professional and fond, the play is genuinely in need of fresh light, and recent theatrical performances, such as that at the Other Place in Stratford, show the power of the play on stage.

It never seems profitable to review the latest volume of *Shakespeare Survey* since readers of this section will have access to, and will probably already have read, the distinguished journal. It seems to be taking metacriticism to new extremes. All that needs to be said for those who want to know what was in Volume 41, edited by Stanley Wells (Cambridge: Cambridge University Press, 1989) is that the theme is 'Shakespearian Stages and Staging' and there are essays on *The First Part of the Contention*, Charles Calvert's *Henry V*, *Hamlet*, *Twelfth Night*, *Troilus and Cressida*, *Antony and Cleopatra*, *The Tempest* at Blackfriars, the Ovidian element in *Othello*, *King Lear* and *Othello*, and *King Lear* in its own right. My own interests drew me to John Kerrigan's essay on 'Keats and *Lucrece*' (p. 103–18).

Some articles from *Shakespeare Quarterly* have already been mentioned. One more that deserves comment is Robert Weimann's 'Bifold Authority in Shakespeare's Theatre', *Shakespeare Quarterly*, 39 (1988), 401–17. Weimann examines 'that disparate set of relationships between language, power, and authority best exemplified in Shakespearean drama' (p. 401). The 'bifold' nature of authority spawns various distinctions such as that between authority as object and as agency in a stage-play, and that between the authority of order and the authority of misrule.

At the centre of *Shakespeare Studies*, 20 (1988) lies a cluster of essays on *The Merchant of Venice* which emanated from the Bernard Beckerman

Symposium. There are also essays on Shakespeare's staging, on *A Midsummer Night's Dream*, *Richard II*, *Henry V*, *Measure for Measure*, separate Calvinist readings of *King Lear* and *Macbeth*, *Henry VIII*, Shakespeare's knowledge of the Bible, and 'Containment of Female Erotic Power'.

The *Iowa State Journal of Research*, vol. 62, no. 3 (February, 1988) is entirely devoted to Shakespeare. While none of the articles is unworthy, they cannot be said to be in the class of those appearing in either the *Survey*, *Quarterly* or *Studies* and they perhaps reflect the individual academic's career necessity to publish in the United States rather than genuinely new approaches. There are four essays which could be seen as contributions to new historicism, the movement which seems destined to dominate at least the North American critical scene in the near future: W. Nicholas Knight's 'Shakespeare before King James: Betrayal and Revelation' (pp. 387–96); Douglas F. Rutledge's 'The Structural Parallel between Rituals of Reversal, Jacobean Political Theory and *Measure for Measure*'; Bruce W. Young's 'Haste, Consent, and Age at Marriage: Some Implications of Social History for *Romeo and Juliet*' (pp. 459–74); and William S. E. Coleman's study of an early eighteenth-century actor who pointed the way to Garrick's acting styles, 'Anthony Beheme: A Forgotten Tragedian' (pp. 359–76). Two essays deal with plays in terms of their literary contexts: John Edward Price's '"Because I would Followe the Fashion": Rich's *Farewell to the Military Profession* and Shakespeare's *Twelfth Night*' (pp. 397–406); and Brian W. Shaffer's '"To Manage Private and Domestic Quarrels": Shakespeare's *Othello* and the Genre of Elizabethan Domestic Tragedy' (pp. 443–58). Kate Burke gives us 'From Page to Stage: The Use of Shakespeare's Sonnets in Introducing Intimidated Students to His Drama' (pp. 347–58). Sara Eaton writes on the ambiguity of Gertrude as constructed by Hamlet's rhetoric in 'The Rhetoric of (Dis)-praise and Hamlet's Mother' (pp. 377–86), and finally Constance C. Belihan contributes 'Appropriation of the "Thing of Blood": Absence of Self and the Struggle for Ownership in *Coriolanus*' (pp. 407–20).

ARTICLES AND CHAPTERS

Barbara Hardy's F. W. Bateson Memorial Lecture, 'Shakespeare's Narrative: Acts of Memory', published in *Essays in Criticism*, 39 (1989), 93–115 is impressive in its intellectual display. Beginning with an acknowledgement of the powerful sense of rootedness in the present in Shakespeare's Sonnets and plays (where nostalgic characters are, it is argued, usually ridiculed), the Lecture becomes a wide-ranging analysis of Shakespeare's various representations of memory and memory lapses. I am not convinced by all the argument (Shakespeare does not seem so harsh on the fondly recollective characters as he is on those like Iago who live relentlessly in the present alone) but the Lecture is lively and stimulating.

Colin MacCabe in 'Abusing Self and Others: Puritan Accounts of the Shakespearian Stage', *Critical Quarterly*, 30 (1988), pp. 3–17 is an exercise in new historicism. MacCabe regards Gosson's attacks on the stage as evidence 'that major questions of social order and sexual identity were intimately linked to the drama and its forms of performance' (p. 15). 1599 is seen as a watershed, as Kempe's dance to Norwich signifies the death-knell for a popular, participative relationship between stage and spectators, summed up in the sexually charged jig. After this, plays were regarded more as economic commodities, and perhaps the dangers of social and sexual disorders feared by Gosson became less acute.

The title of Paul Dean's article, 'Tudor Humanism and the Roman Past: A Background to Shakespeare', *Renaissance Quarterly*, 41 (1988), 84–111 is accurate to its proportions. It does not deal directly with Shakespeare, but instead details the Renaissance discovery of the Roman past, and how attitudes changed. The

conclusion points to Shakespeare's centrality in such changes, arguing that his Roman plays are not sealed off from his other plays by their imputed 'sense of *Romanitas*' (p. 110), but rather they are linked with the English history plays through a common preoccupation with civil war. Another article which deals with one Roman play is Thomas Pughe's '"What should the wars do with these jigging fools?": The Poets in Shakespeare's *Julius Caesar*', *English Studies*, 69 (1988), 313–22. Both Cinna the Poet in 2.3 and the camp-poet in 4.3 are treated badly by the play's world, and their common fate is seen as representative of the banishment or suppression of imagination and intuition by the prevailing discourse of rationality. 'The poets function as a kind of litmus test within a sick society' (pp. 321–2). The suggestion is appealing, since Shakespeare would have had some vested interest in its thrust.

Several critics have dealt with the Pauline references in *The Comedy of Errors*, but none with the exhaustive detail employed by Arthur Kinney in 'Shakespeare's *Comedy of Errors* and the Nature of Kinds', *Studies in Philology*, 85 (1988), 29–52. Kinney shows Shakespeare mixing farce, classical comedy, and Christian, liturgical elements. One of the most tantalizing details produced is that the play was produced on Holy Innocents' Day, 28 December, in two years, 1594 and again in 1604. The fact chimes with Shakespeare's persistent interest in innocents throughout his career.

The Taming of the Shrew is read by Camille Wells Slights not as a debate on the distribution of power between men and women but as a play 'built on a contrast between civilized and uncivilized behaviour' (p. 169). In her article, 'The Raw and the Cooked in *The Taming of the Shrew*', *Journal of English and Germanic Philology*, 88 (1989), 168–89, Slights argues that the Induction introduces the contrast between the cultivated and the brutish, and that by the end of the play Kate is 'no longer wild but self-assured, self-controlled, and considerate – a civilized woman who understands human relationships as a balance of duties and privileges' (p. 189). I suspect the arguments that rage about whether this outcome is for the better or worse will not be allayed by the article.

Gillian West in 'Falstaff's Punning', *English Studies*, 69 (1988), 541–58, gives a list of fifty unnoticed puns made by Falstaff, showing that the habit is far more pervasive than has been recognized. The general conclusion is that through his puns Falstaff stands against the 'treacherous abuse of language in the political world' (p. 542). He uses language purely as a toy for the intellect and thus satirizes the political world which through perjury, evasion, bombast and tirade persuades men to die for 'honour'.

All's Well That Ends Well seems to have had an *annus mirabilis* with several articles devoted to it. Peggy Muñoz Simonds examines the play in the context of Renaissance texts dealing with matrimony, arguing that such material formed a part of a common cultural map in Shakespeare's England ('Sacred and Sexual Motifs in *All's Well That Ends Well*', *Renaissance Quarterly*, 42 (1989), 33–49). The argument is that 'the play simultaneously discusses both sexual and sacred matters without essential conflict between them...' (p. 34). Another article which attempts to link contemporary thought to *All's Well* is David J. Palmer's 'Comedy and the Protestant Spirit in Shakespeare's *All's Well That Ends Well*' in *Bulletin of the John Rylands University Library of Manchester*, 71 (1989), 95–107. The article shows signs of being pulled out from the bottom-drawer, or rather perfunctorily assembled around a few serendipitously found quotations. Palmer attempts to link the Protestant doctrine of predestination with the play: what is unforeseen and appears as fortuitous chance is actually predetermined and such a strategy creates the structural ironies of *All's Well*. Maurice Hunt, in more challenging vein, draws upon contemporary speech-act theory and upon the Christian emphasis on 'the Word' to unlock some mysteries of the play, in '*All's Well That Ends Well* and the Triumph of

the Word', *Texas Studies in Literature and Language*, 30 (1988), 388–411. Hunt argues that language, 'potentially divine by nature' works 'propitiously, at key moments through riddles, to fashion a toned-down yet nonetheless authentic happiness for the play's main characters' (p. 390). Language is seen as the most important transformational agency.

Cherrell Guilfoyle's '"The Redemption of King Lear"' in *Comparative Drama*, 23 (1989), 50–69 returns us to familiar territory, but with an intense concentration on details. Her careful tracing of Christian analogies and imagery through the play leads to the conclusion that as the play progresses, 'the Old Testament analogies give way to New Testament imagery' (p. 55). 'Shakespeare's characters are not Christians, but as the action of the play intensifies, they find themselves acting in scenic forms from the Christian story, whether or not they are supposed to be living before that time, as they are before Merlin's' (p. 50). There is a discernible promise of redemption, but only just, in the sacrifice of innocents.

Links between Middle English Romance and *The Winter's Tale* are the subject of Julie Burton's 'Folktale, Romance and Shakespeare' in *Studies in Medieval English Romances: Some New Approaches*, edited by Derek Brewer (Suffolk and New Hampshire: Boydell and Brewer, 1988, pp. 176–97). Burton surveys the long line of stories dealing with family separation and reunion, and concludes that Shakespeare shows more inwardness with the mode of romance than does his source material, Greene's *Pandosto*.

NON-DRAMATIC VERSE

William Kennedy surveys the second-hand influence on Shakespeare's Sonnets of Vellutello's Commentary on Petrarch ('Commentary into Narrative: Shakespeare's Sonnets and Vellutello's Commentary on Petrarch' in *Allegorica: A Journal of Medieval and Renaissance Literature*, 10 [1989], 119–33). In 1525 Velutello sought to regroup Petrarch's poems according to probable date of composition, and in doing so he initiated a new form of Renaissance literary exegesis based on historical and archaeological principles rather than moralizing or allegorical ones. Shakespeare did not have direct contact with the Commentary or with Petrarch's poems, but he inherited and extended the possibilities opened up by Vellutello's contribution.

Anthea Hume in 'Love's Martyr, "The Phoenix and the Turtle", and the Aftermath of the Essex Rebellion' (Review of English Studies, NS 40 (1989), pp. 48–71) revives Marie Axton's claim that 'the Phoenix stands for Elizabeth, the Turtle for her loving subjects, and the New Phoenix James Stuart'. She sees the enigmatic poem as an occasional one which deals with mutual love between monarch and subjects. The implications are, first that by 1601 Shakespeare had changed his view of Essex since 1599, simply by agreeing to contribute to the volume Love's Martyr which condemned the false love offered by Essex to the Queen, and secondly that in 1601 Shakespeare had no relationship with his former patron the Earl of Southampton, the most intimate of Essex's companions who was in prison for his part in the rebellion at the time of Love's Martyr.

Many critics have examined notions of value in Shakespeare, sometimes from an economic point of view and sometimes from a humanist one. Nona Fienberg returns to this particular fray in 'Thematics of Value in Venus and Adonis' in Criticism: A Quarterly for Literature and the Arts, 31 (1989), pp. 21–32. Venus, she argues, recognizes that value is 'continuously shifting, changing, dynamic, not fixed, absolute, or subject to predictable natural law' (p. 22), and she uses commercial imagery. The unstated analogy would be the price of potatoes going up and down with market forces operating. Venus is thus able to indulge in 'play, exchange, and risk' (p. 25). However, her conflict is with 'the naïve Adonis, himself a relic of the time before the commercial and humanist revolutions, when value was a given, not a measure of achieved and mutable standing' (pp. 23–4). He is tied to a stable core of selfhood underlined by fear of risk. After Adonis's death, the argument runs, Venus leaves the legacy that in love all fixed and stable values shall be made unpredictable and uncertain. This is convincing, except that there should be at least a qualification that in fact Venus, for all her mercurial changes, is the immortal goddess of love and therefore must represent some kind of ultimate stability, while Adonis is the one trapped in the market forces of mortality.

2. SHAKESPEARE'S LIFE, TIMES, AND STAGE
reviewed by RICHARD DUTTON

In a year in which the remains of the Rose and now, as it seems, of 'the great Globe itself' have been restored to view, and their status in our heritage has exercised the leader writers of the national press, it is appropriate to start with the theatres Shakespeare himself knew and used, and their status in his own day. John Orrell, the author of two distinguished books, The Quest for the Globe and The Theatres of Inigo Jones and John Webb, has now produced The Human Stage: English Theatre Design, 1567–1640[1]. This is not merely a synthesis of his earlier work,

though inevitably it covers some of the same territory. It is, rather, an attempt to find a coherent thread and purpose running through the theatre-design of the whole period. Contemplating a bird's-eye view of London c. 1600, he observes: 'Save for the great churches, no other class of building in the prospect [than the theatres] announces with such certainty that it is shaped by an idea transcending the utilitarian,

---

[1] Respectively Cambridge, 1983; Cambridge, 1985; and Cambridge, 1988.

or bears so closely the imprint of the human spirit' (p. 4). He adroitly undermines the claims for the two most commonly advanced utilitarian 'models' for the Theatre and its successors, the inn-yards (where he looks closely at the Red Lion and the Boar's Head) and the animal-baiting rings, before advancing his own thesis: 'The theatre design in the Second Book [of Serlio's *Architettura*] was enormously influential in England, especially through its readily imitable scenic constructions, but also through its auditorium planning ... It governed the design of many of the Court theatres of Inigo Jones ... and there is ... some reason for believing that it helped to shape even the commercial playhouses, both public and private, of Elizabethan and Jacobean London' (p. 149).

It is the second half of this claim which will raise most eyebrows, possibly evoking memories of Frances Yates's highly imaginative but unscientific claims for the Vitruvian inspiration of Renaissance theatre-design in *Theatre of the World*.[2] Orrell, however, advances a far more careful and compelling case than that. He does not suggest that Serlio, and behind him Vitruvius, were the immediate inspiration for men like Burbage and Brayne, the builders of the Theatre, but rather: 'Their choice of a name for the new building suggests that their thinking was coloured by the idea of the Roman theatre, which in turn led them to model their scheme on the round houses of the festive tradition, the fullest modern expressions to date of the ancient theatrical forms' (p. 60). He cites the Calais banqueting house of 1520 as the best-documented example of these festive 'round-houses' and the 1581 Banqueting House at Whitehall as evidence that the tradition of ornate, emblematic but essentially temporary wood-framed construction for (in part) theatrical purposes continued late into the century. On these grounds he argues that emulation of classical antiquity was a constant factor behind the construction of *all* purpose-built theatres in the Elizabethan and early Stuart period. He cannot,

of course, get around the fact that some of the standard surveying and building practices of the day may in part have determined the striking proportions of the great public amphitheatres. But he does establish that an Elizabethan master carpenter (like Peter Street, who built both the Globe and the Fortune) was more than likely to have been familiar with the principles of festive 'round-house' design and no mere journeyman worker. This is an elegantly argued book, which authoritatively re-draws the map of theatre design in Shakespeare's day. I should also mention here Herbert Berry, whose pioneering work on the inn-yard theatres Orrell very properly acknowledges. In 'The First Public Playhouses, Especially The Red Lion' he has critically examined the claims of various early structures, but particularly the Red Lion (1567), to anticipate The Theatre as the first purpose-built dramatic auditorium in Britain since Roman times. Reviewing all the available data, his conclusion is sceptical 'if a proper playhouse ought to be an imposing structure built to house plays for many years'.[3]

We may be able to determine the architectural principles behind the theatres Shakespeare wrote for, but can we similarly re-discover his own intentions and predilections in writing for them? Much modern critical theory has dispersed the notion of the purposeful, autonomous author to the winds, but Robert Hapgood's *Shakespeare the Theatre Poet* defies that new orthodoxy: 'This book was in part prompted by my neo-conservative desire – in a time of deconstruction – to reassert the primacy of the writer's creative presence' (p. vii).[4] He finds in Shakespeare's plays, if not quite the definitive authority of the dramatist's own voice, at least a finite and specific range of implied options about performance which have necessary consequences in relation to interpretations of the text: 'although no single reading

---

[2] *Theatre of the World* (London and Chicago, 1969).
[3] *Shakespeare Quarterly*, 40 (1989), 135–45; p. 145.
[4] Oxford, 1988.

is definitive, some are downright wrong and the rest are in certain respects to be preferred to others ... When his intention is regarded not as a single line but as a locus or spectrum of options, interpreters may concern themselves not merely with selecting a single 'reading' of a text but with charting and weighing the range of options that he has built into it' (pp. 13–14). He analyses *Henry V* and *A Midsummer Night's Dream* in a way that highlights Shakespeare's apparent preference for an ensemble approach to acting, which in turn reflects the emphasis he sees in those plays on, respectively, social and sexual fellowship: so a conservative critical methodology, unsurprisingly, rediscovers a (politically) conservative theatre poet. These larger issues apart, Hapgood is alert and discriminating about a wide range of theatrical options, particularly in relation to the major tragedies, *Hamlet*, *Othello*, *Macbeth* and *King Lear*, each of which is accorded its own chapter. *Macbeth* also figures prominently in two other chapters, one of which applies insights from narrative theory to questions of viewpoint and point-of-view, while the other considers in minute detail the performance possibilities of a brief passage (1.7.28–82). His analyses are unfailingly illuminating, but not everyone will be convinced that 'Shakespeare', rather than his own predispositions, dictated his readings and the values he attaches to them.

Although Gerald M. Pinciss writes from an entirely different perspective, and one without an obvious performance dimension, his *Literary Creations: Conventional Characters in the Drama of Shakespeare and His Contemporaries* parallels Hapgood's book in its conviction that the relationship between an author's intentions and the modern reception of his works is essentially unproblematic.[5] Pinciss traces the incidence of four stock character-types, and one stock character-pairing, through a range of (on the whole) firmly canonical Renaissance drama texts: the courtier, the over-reacher, the savage man, the shrew, the Machiavel and his tool-villain. His method is to sketch in a range of contemporary attitudes to the traits represented by these characters, homing in on those he deems most appropriate to the immediate case. So, for example, with the over-reacher, he cites Pico, Montaigne, Luther, Calvin, Hooker, and the preacher William Perkins to represent a broad range of Renaissance opinion on human aspiration and its limits, observing that Perkins's 'more limited, narrow and stern view of human potential is probably closer to the mainstream of Elizabethan thought at the turn of the century than is Hooker's more kindly and lyrical opinion' (p. 54). This leads to a survey of 'failed' over-reachers, both tragic (Tamburlaine, Faustus) and comic (Epicure Mammon, Giles Overreach), while even Prospero, seen as a Pico-type aspirant, 'teaches us that man is incapable of enjoying that dream even if he could affirm it' (p. 69). Similarly, for the shrew, Pinciss cites Henry Parrot's 'character' of the type, the homily 'of the State of Matrimony' and the opinions of two Protestant clergy, including 'the widely followed minister Henry Smith' (p. 96). Subsequently he argues: 'the view presented in *The Taming of the Shrew* is far more moderate than that found in [*The Taming of*] *A Shrew*, dramatizing a conception of marriage close to the more liberal Protestantism of Henry Smith ... [who] argues that "husbands must hold their hands and wives their tungs"' (p. 109) – which is essentially what he sees Katherine and Petruchio doing. Clearly the approach is preferable to the proposition of a monolithic 'Elizabethan World Picture', but the relationship of ideas to texts, and the question of how texts themselves either generate meanings or endorse values, are still left resolutely unproblematized in a way that is disturbingly trusting. One does not have to be a card-carrying cultural materialist to feel that such a simplistic correlation of text and context begs as many questions as it answers.

Altogether preferable, from this point of

---

[5] Woodbridge, Suffolk, and Wolfeboro, New Hampshire, 1988.

view, is an anthology which Pinciss has edited with the historian, Roger Lockyer, *Shakespeare's World: Background Readings in The Renaissance*.[6] This contains a useful selection of brief but heavily contextualized extracts from a range of illuminating sixteenth and seventeenth-century documents. Some names are already firmly etched on the map of Renaissance literary studies – Montaigne, Machiavelli, Hooker, Castiglione, Thomas Wilson, Putenham, Elyot, Ascham – but others are much less familiar, at least in the writings represented here: André DuLaurens, a conservative medic; Reginald Scot, the 'discoverer' of witchcraft; the magus, John Dee; the political theorists, Jean Bodin and Philippe Duplessis-Mornay; the political players, Francis Bacon, the Earl of Essex, Queen Elizabeth and King James VI & I; the lawyers, Sir John Fortescue and Sir Edward Coke; the historians, Sir Thomas Smith and William Camden. Of course, no such selection can claim to be exhaustive and it is dangerous even to suggest that it might be representative, but the extracts here do give a broad flavour of the period and many of its principal concerns, with a pronounced political emphasis. The contextualization, which students and general readers will find helpful, is commendably even-handed, though purists may object that some of the extracts themselves are simply lifted from out-of-copyright editions rather than re-edited from the originals. I can envisage this book being widely adopted as a course-reader.

If the works of Pinciss and Lockyer may be said, from their different perspectives, to find common cause as far as the interpretation of Shakespeare is concerned with that of Hapgood, those of Harry Berger Jr and Robert S. Knapp may reasonably be said to represent a common enemy, or even anathema itself. Harry Berger Jr's *Second World and Green World: Studies in Renaissance Fiction-Making* reads as if it has emerged from a time-warp, which in a sense it has, since it has been constructed – and I use the term advisedly – ('Selected and Arranged, with an Introduction,

by John Patrick Lynch') from a range of the author's essays, none later than 1982 and the great majority dating back to the 1960s.[7] They touch on a wide range of Renaissance topics, paintings as well as the history of ideas, Pico, Erasmus and More as well as Marvell and Milton, but also a central section on Shakespeare. In all of these we see a mind engaged in the transition from the prescriptive autotely of New Criticism, the idealism of which is seen as a response to or escape from consumer capitalism, to the post-structuralist dynamic interactions of 'text' and 'context' central to new historicist *agenda*. On the differences between medieval and Renaissance theatre, for example, he observes: 'The morality play is still erected on a medieval scaffold, an esthetic of A + B, pleasure plus profit, ornament plus argument, sensuous image plus allegorical message, play plus seriousness. And this is different from the Renaissance structure of A *in* B, seriousness *in* play, image *as* message; a structure in which pleasure and profit, withdrawal and return, may be dialectically related *within* the rhythm of the make-believe experience' ('Theater, Drama, and the Second World', p. 124). For Shakespearians, his note is most characteristically struck in a multiple reading of Ulysses's degree speech in *Troilus and Cressida* (1.3.82–124), which was of course central to E. M. W. Tillyard's *Elizabethan World Picture*: 'the first and more traditional reading of Ulysses's speech stresses an objective world order whose creatures have place, motion and function in the ambience of a visible hierarchy. But the second meaning stresses the subjective agency of seers as they influence their objects by the way they see. Degree becomes a matter of perspective, and perspective entails an optical situation in which one judges or sees only at a distance and from the outside' ('*Troilus and Cressida*: The Observer as Basilisk', p. 136). The book as a whole is full of such multiple, inconclusive

---

[6] New York, 1989.
[7] Berkeley, 1988.

readings, as though all its essays were drafts towards a major rethinking of the Renaissance which never was, and perhaps never could have been, carried through. But as a record of an acute mind searching for a new vocabulary, and as it now seems of a restless generation frustrated with old orthodoxies, it makes fascinating reading. It should be required reading for anyone wondering how we got from the comfortable certainties of Tillyard to the radical uncertainties of, say, Stephen Greenblatt and Jonathan Dollimore, or even of Robert S. Knapp.

Knapp's *Shakespeare: the Theater and the Book* pursues the metaphors of the Book of Life and the Theatre of the World from an unusual blend of semiotic and post-structuralist perspectives in order to consider Shakespeare's place in history, on the interface between medieval and modern consciousness, and his pre-eminent place in the literary canon, which Knapp sees as all the more remarkable for having been achieved in that least stable of literary forms, the dramatic.[8] He is erudite and playful, no respecter of reputations or conventional categories, but an undeniable enthusiast. What he says of Lyly's *Endimion* does not describe his own book, but might stand as its epigraph: 'It opens a space in which a fertile indeterminacy comes into play, a place where meaning and being need not pretend to coincide, where identities can dissociate and punfully reassemble' (p. 179). He relates Shakespeare's experimentations with the dramatic medium to his particular moment in history: 'Not troubled by a direct tie to patronage, not so bound to the status and profession of letters as to attempt a distinction between true author and betraying puppets, Shakespeare seems determined from the very start to test the limits of different representational modes, taking the interaction of theatrical positioning and narrational displacement as an infinitely interesting yet almost neutral fact of his life and art' (p. 183). (This compares interestingly with Robert Weimann's much less 'playful' and 'neutral'

view of the problematic relationship between mimesis and power in Shakespearian drama: 'The representing and the represented may incongruously clash, but they may also engage in areas of concurrence, so that representation in the Shakespearean theater may or may not involve that homogenization of discursive space which poststructuralist theory assumes. In that case, representing becomes a site of sociolinguistic contradiction, a site of social and cultural struggle whose authority itself is dramatized', p. 179.[9]) Knapp ascribes Shakespeare's latter-day reputation to a mixture of accident and almost mystical necessity: 'The contingency of Shakespeare is an essential fact ... Things that neither he nor his text could have determined – like the success of British imperialism, which gave to a provincial European tongue the world utility which Alexander's conquests procured for Greek – contribute as necessary conditions to his becoming and remaining literary. Yet even in this there seems to be more than accident at work, the sort of veiled necessity that prompts one to give a certain credence to Hegelian stories about the interaction between human self-awareness and the logic of history' (pp. 245–6). Reader, you will either love it or hate it.

Anyone dissatisfied with Hegelian 'stories' about Shakespeare and history, but also suspicious of other post-structuralist and neo-Marxist ones, should look to a recent rash of essays on the subject. Firstly, in 'Plays Antagonistic and Competitive: The Textual Approach to Elsinor', Joseph Loewenstein is concerned to break away from an over-concentration on courts, monarchs, and the collusive/oppositional relationship of plays to those centres of power, insisting that they also belong to a wider marketplace:

---

[8] Princeton, 1989.
[9] 'Shakespeare (De-)Canonized: Conflicting Uses of "Authority" and "Representation"', *New Literary History*, 20 (1988), 65–81.

Recent criticism has inscribed the English theater within a dialectic of tense dependence on the interests of the new monarchy, so that the drama has been represented as oscillating between ideological collusion and ideological resistance; historical criticism needs to correct this model by recognizing the degree to which English theatricality invented and improvised within spheres relatively autonomous from the ideological productivities of the court. The textual approach to Elsinore leads us away from the English court, back to the city, to the bookstall, the printshop, the box office, and the stage.[10]

Annabel Patterson would apparently agree that an understanding of Shakespeare's historical 'location' should not be limited by an over-narrow concentration on a single issue, however important, but would probably resist Loewenstein's aim, in effect, to inscribe it simply within a more broadly-defined but still essentially abstract market-place. Her specific targets in '"The Very Age and Body of the Time Its Form and Pressure": Rehistoricizing Shakespeare's Theater' are Walter Cohen's *Drama of a Nation: Public Theater in Renaissance England and Spain* (Ithaca, 1985), Ann Jennalie Cook's *The Privileged Playgoers of Shakespeare's London* (Princeton, 1981), and Stephen Greenblatt's much-reprinted essay 'Invisible Bullets: Renaissance Authority and Its Subversion, *Henry IV* and *Henry V*'.[11] For all their palpable differences, she links them in a predisposition to configure Renaissance theatre within narrow, faceless, and uniform structures of power, authority, or social hegemony: 'We need to return to a less impersonal, less totalitarian account of how Shakespeare's theater probably functioned, in a network of power in the abstract and in nobody's hands, but rather of local ordinances, unwritten and unstable policies, fads, fashions, pretexts, improvisations, human impulses, and the occasional application of discipline and punishment both to texts and to persons, by other persons whose names and motives are not indecipherable', (p. 95). It is unfortunate, in the light of this last comment, that she unaccountably

relates Edmund Tilney's famous censorship directive to 'leave out the insurrection wholly' to *Henry VIII* (p. 94) when it is actually in the manuscript of *Sir Thomas More*, but the argument for more pluralist and less monolithic explanations of the complex interactions that must always characterize theatrical production is well made.

It would probably find favour with Leeds Barroll who, in 'A New History for Shakespeare and His Time', is concerned with 'the profound problems posed by the notion of the historical "event"' (p. 464).[12] He argues that recent historical readings of Renaissance drama (especially new historicist and cultural materialist ones) may be said to have failed to address the complexities of historical narrative itself as critically as they have attempted to redefine the rôle of the theatre within that narrative. He focuses in particular on two notorious *exempla* in politicized readings of Shakespeare and his times: the performance of the Richard II play on the eve of the Essex rebellion and King James's supposed special interest in drama, so often linked to his views on monarchy and wider questions of the ideology of Stuart theatre. In the case of the former he emphasizes that the authorities at the time seem to have taken far less note of the Chamberlain's Men's performance than have modern commentators, and that they seem to have been more worried by John Hayward's printed account of the reign of Richard II than they were about what was shown in the theatres; he also reopens the case first advanced by David Bergeron for the possibility that the abdication scene missing in the 1597 and 1598 quartos was not actually censored, but specifically written for a revision of the play, as reflected in the 1608 quarto – a case all the more plausible in the light of the recent growing conviction that Shakespeare did on

---

[10] *Renaissance Drama*, NS 19 (1988), 63–96, p. 82.
[11] *New Literary History*, 20 (1988), 83–104.
[12] *Shakespeare Quarterly*, 39 (1988), 441–64.

occasion revise his own plays.[13] In short, the case for *Richard II* demonstrating the subversive potential of theatre and the fears of the authorities about that potential is far from clear cut and should not be taken for granted. Similarly, although there is clear evidence for the court as a greater 'consumer' of drama after James came to the throne, it is far less clear that James himself was particularly interested in it. The rôle of Prince Henry, and even more particularly of Queen Anne and her aristocratic adherents, as patrons of the drama, needs to be weighed against over-easy equations between court theatre and absolutist tendencies in the monarchy. As Barroll provocatively puts it: 'We might, in fact, wish to consider whether it was the earls of that period, not the king, who attempted to use drama to contain subversion of their own financial and political positions by the monarch and his favourites. James's theories of monarchy were not, after all, traditional ones' (p. 463).

It is entirely symptomatic of the kinds of concerns voiced in these essays that so much current writing about *The Tempest* focuses on the question of its relationship to colonialism, which was only debatably a historical 'reality' (as far as the English were concerned) when the play was written. I mentioned in the last issue Alden T. Vaughan's 'Shakespeare's Indians: The Americanization of Caliban', to which we must now add Meredith Anne Skura's 'Discourse and the Individual: The Case of Colonialism in *The Tempest*' and Deborah Willis's '*The Tempest* and Colonialism'.[14] Skura's is basically a psychological study of the issue: 'My point in specifying Shakespeare's precise literal and temporal relation to colonialist discourse – in specifying the unique mind through which the discourse is mediated – is not to deny that the play has *any* relation to its context but to suggest that the relation is problematic ... To argue for Shakespeare's uniqueness is not to argue that as fiction *The Tempest* is above politics, or that as a writer Shakespeare transcended ideology. It does

imply, however, that if the play is "colonialist", it must be seen as "prophetic"' (p. 57–8). Willis, by contrast, identifies the problematization not in the unique mediating mind but in the politics of the Old World: 'Shakespeare locates the origins of Prospero's colonial project in the crisis that besets the political order of "the core", that is in the failure of that order to contain the threats embodied by Antonio' (pp. 286–7), which she sees as far more central to the play and in every sense more serious than the displaced native, Caliban.

These questions of historical 'location' and 'story-telling' will obviously run and run, and they do so even when they are not foregrounded. In the essay cited, Annabel Patterson suggested that 'there are ways of rethinking and relearning the conditions in which Shakespeare reproduced *Hamlet*, in the aftermath of a failed rebellion (for whose leader he had once thought to intercede), on the threshold of a new régime (whose character was not yet imaginable)' (p. 101). Anthea Hume has re-examined another product of precisely those conditions, *Love's Martyr*, with its Shakespearian contribution, 'The Phoenix and the Turtle': 'My argument will be that Chester [the compiler of the volume] ventured to portray the mental state of the Queen in the aftermath of the Essex rebellion'.[15] Much of her argument is devoted to the Essex associations of the volume's dedicatee, Sir John Salusbury, and ought to be set alongside E. A. J. Honigmann's chapter on the subject in his *Shakespeare: The 'Lost Years'* (Manchester, 1985), but what I found most puzzling was her 'interpretation of the New Phoenix in *Love's Martyr* as an image of James Stuart' (p. 55), which she admits is problematic, but only

---

[13] See 'The Deposition Scene in *Richard II*', *Renaissance Papers 1974* (1975), 31–7.

[14] Respectively, *Shakespeare Quarterly*, 39 (1988), 137–53; *Shakespeare Quarterly*, 40 (1989), 42–69; *Studies in English Literature*, 29 (1989), 277–89.

[15] 'Love's Martyr, "The Phoenix and the Turtle", and the Aftermath of the Essex Rebellion', *Review of English Studies*, NS 40 (1989), 48–71; p. 51.

because Chester mixed male and female pronouns in relation to it; she concludes (p. 65) that this is a subterfuge to get around censorship. But far more basic is the question of why anyone in 1601 should begin to presume that James Stuart *would* succeed Elizabeth. Yes, Robert Cecil had opened secret negotiations with him, but there was no knowing how long Elizabeth would live, and other possible claimants like the Spanish Infanta and Arbella Stuart might have been better placed to make a bid when the time actually came. Yes, she can adduce other references to James as a phoenix, but only after the succession had safely taken place. As regards 'The Phoenix and the Turtle', her conclusion that 'it shows ... that Shakespeare could write with considerable intensity on the theme of mutual love between monarchs and subjects when occasion required' (p. 71) is simultaneously bland (in its lack of specificity) and provocative (in its assumption that this *is* the poem's theme, and that it has implications for Shakespeare's view of Essex and discontinued connections with Southampton by this time).

It is similarly difficult to know what to make of all the evidence that Henk Gras assembles about '*Twelfth Night, Every Man out of His Humour* and the Middle Temple Revels of 1597–98'.[16] He certainly establishes what some (though not he) would describe as intertextuality between the two plays, and establishes some interesting analogues with the Prince of Love festive 'playing' at the Middle Temple before either of them was written; more questionable are the assertions that 'of these Temple connexions it seems certain, first, that *Twelfth Night* was written with a Temple performance in mind, presenting the Prince of Love in the character of Orsino; secondly, that somehow Richard Martin [a Temple lawyer, to whom Jonson later dedicated *Poetaster*] is connected with the revels of 1601–2; thirdly, that Martin's connexions with Jonson might explain the relationship between *Every Man Out* and *Twelfth Night*' (p. 55). The equations are

further complicated by invoking the additional context of the anti-Ovidianism associated with Poets' War; Jonson's play is sometimes linked with those theatrical self-promotions, though Shakespeare's play rarely is, except for some verbal echoes of Dekker's *Satiromastix*. In Gras's view: 'The new play, festive and dreamlike, turns inside out important material from the first play. It opposes midnight to noonday, romance to satire, lies to truths, love to hatred, natural human weakness to vice, acceptance and surfeit to wounding lashes and purging pills, disguise to perspicuousness and untrussing ... It is a play emphatically Ovidian even as it mocks Ovidianism' (p. 564). There is surely too much here to ignore, but whether everyone will make the same 'story' of it that the author does is another matter.

Eric Rasmussen is altogether more tentative than Gras in his claims for 'Shakespeare's Hand in *The Second Maiden's Tragedy*'.[17] The play is strictly anonymous, and was only given its title for his own reference purposes by the censor, Sir George Buc, but is widely thought to be by Middleton. There are, however, a number of additions pasted into the surviving manuscript, possibly even after Buc had 'allowed' it. They are particularly interesting because they seem to allude to relations between Arbella Stuart and William Seymour, a matter of some concern to the king, since both had plausible claims to the throne. Rasmussen's modest aim, however, is to establish that, once a script had been submitted to the King's Men, whose play it was, any revisions were as likely to be entrusted to their 'ordinary poet' as to the author, and he concludes: 'We are left ... with the probability that Middleton did not write the additions and the possibility that Shakespeare did' (p. 24) – a modest but intriguing possible extension to the canon. The idea that Shakespeare might have tinkered in this way with another writer's work is all the more plausible in the light of Neil

---

16 *Modern Language Review*, 84 (1989), 545–64.
17 *Shakespeare Quarterly*, 40 (1989), 1–26.

Carson's 'Collaborative Playwriting: The Chettle, Dekker, Heywood Syndicate', based on his recent work on the Henslowe papers, where he suggests

Dramatists appear to have formed loose partnerships or syndicates which worked together for short periods and then broke up and reformed into other alliances. There is relatively little evidence to suggest that one writer acted as the guiding spirit or co-ordinator ... The impression one is left with is of the playwright as a relatively independent agent who seems to have had considerable control over his own methods of work and to have used that freedom to market his skills, alone or in association with others, to his greatest advantage.[18]

This suggests even more fluidity than pertained, for example, in the Hollywood 'writing-factories' of the 1930s and 40s, and underlines just how complex it is for modern scholars to apply terms like 'author' and 'text' to an industry where the models for such concepts seem as various as those implied in these loose syndicates, those implicit in the notion of the retained 'ordinary poet', and those propagated by the likes of Jonson (after he himself left syndicate-writing) who insisted on his own autonomy and somehow retained copyright control over his own plays.

The 'differences' between Shakespeare and Jonson are, of course, so enshrined in the received historical narrative of Renaissance drama that they could be described as part of popular mythology. One might be tempted to say that Russ McDonald's *Shakespeare and Jonson/Jonson and Shakespeare* aims to deconstruct the polarities of the narrative in its most familiar form – classic and romantic, satirist and detached observer, costive and prolix, and so forth (see Henk Gras's comparison of *Twelfth Night* and *Every Man Out of His Humour*, cited above).[19] But any suggestion of 'deconstruction' would seriously belie the traditionally humanist and essentially formalist approach of this book. McDonald is concerned to look behind the 'rivalry' perhaps implicit in some of Jonson's pronouncements, and more certainly

wished on them by generations of critics, to observe some basic similarities:

Obviously Shakespeare and Jonson were fascinated by some of the same topics: imagination, language, self-delusion, obsession, evil, theatricality, power. They were capable of taking similar attitudes towards such topics. Occasionally, they even developed their concerns by means of some of the same dramatic strategies. Both were capable of imagining an ideal, both of scourging its opposite. Their very greatest works proceed from similar antiromantic impulses. The manifest differences should not obscure the areas of genuine mutual interest ... With both Shakespeare and Jonson, there is something of the other in each. (pp. 186–7)

McDonald's thesis is not entirely original, of course. It echoes such works as S. Musgrove's *Shakespeare and Jonson* (Auckland, 1957) and parts of Anne Barton's *Ben Jonson, Dramatist* (Cambridge, 1984), and inevitably draws on the debate generated by such as G. E. Bentley, D. L. Frost and E. A. J. Honigmann about Shakespeare's influence on, and occasional reactions to, the younger man, and the beginnings of their contrastive reputations. But he develops his own argument, which is often perceptive and illuminating in its attention to detail, and his determination not to be constrained by traditional assumptions and categories ought to be applauded even by those to whom it will seem odd to find it expressed in such a self-consciously conservative idiom.

The issue arises quite acutely if we compare McDonald's book with Robert C. Evans's *Ben Jonson and the Poetics of Patronage*.[20] Evans develops the key Renaissance concept of 'patronage', which has been so central to recent historical 'revisions' of the period, extending it beyond limited notions of payment, personal negotiation and factional allegiance to a pervasive condition of consciousness in the social structures of the day:

---

[18] *Theatre Research International*, 14 (1989), 13–23; pp. 22–3.
[19] Lincoln, Nebraska, and London, 1988.
[20] Cranbury, New Jersey, and London, 1989.

Viewing patronage as a *psychological* system suggests that nearly every work written during this time might be, in some sense, a poem of patronage ... since nearly every work presents, implicitly or explicitly, an image of the author who created it, nearly every work has some effect on the author's status in the patronage hierarchy ... From this perspective, a text need not flatter a patron – or, indeed, even be addressed to a patron; it need not explicitly solicit money, protection, or position. An effective patronage approach to Renaissance texts would assume that few texts could help being touched in some way by a social system so pervasive and inescapable.

(pp. 29–30)

In relation to Jonson himself Evans argues: 'Studying Jonson's writings, including his dramas, as patronage poems involves not simply understanding their economic or social "background" but appreciation of the often immense and intricate impact the patronage situation could have on the minute details of particular works' (p. 267). This opens up some extremely suggestive perspectives on the self-images that pepper Jonson's works, the prologues, prefaces and apologias, the poems of praise and dispraise in which he constantly defines (or 'creates') himself by comparison with models from the classical past and the relentlessly competitive present. It is an approach which one could imagine fruitfully applied to Shakespeare's non-dramatic verse, as well as to contemporaries like Spenser, Donne and Herbert: any context, in effect, where the writing is aimed at semi-permanent authorial self-presentation, either in coterie circulation or print, which of course includes Jonson's surviving plays. It does not so obviously recommend itself in relation to Shakespeare's plays, planned for evanescence, where the 'presence' of the 'author' seems so much less tangible, though it may well help to explain why this should be so. In this sense, Evans's book contradicts McDonald's thesis, not in perpetuating supposed rivalries between Shakespeare and Jonson, but in emphasizing that, though their careers overlapped in so many ways, Jonson opted to attach himself (as the older man did not, at least in his plays) to a new, print-led phase of early modern culture in which the very concept of 'authorship' – and with it concepts like 'imagination', 'language', 'theatricality' and 'power', which McDonald treats as stable entities – was in a state of profound flux.

I should also mention here a separate piece by Robert C. Evans, 'Thomas Sutton: Ben Jonson's *Volpone*', in which he investigates in detail the belief widely current in the seventeenth century, but largely ignored by modern commentators, that Volpone is in some sense a portrait of Thomas Sutton, the founder of Charterhouse and reputedly the richest commoner in England.[21] The status of such topical allusions is always difficult to quantify and this one in particular seems to go against the recent tendency to align the play with the cynical and repressive political climate surrounding the Gunpowder Plot, which has given *Volpone* a peculiarly modern edge for some recent audiences. But in the wider contexts we have been surveying in this review it is only proper to re-think the complexities of the historical 'event', of the ways in which an 'author' like Jonson might define himself in relation to them, and of the partiality of our own historical narratives.

Sandra A. Burner's *James Shirley: A Study of Literary Coteries and Patronage in Seventeenth Century England* is much less radical in its approach to 'patronage' and its effects on literature than Evans's book.[22] It is closer in spirit to 'revisionist' works like Kevin Sharpe's *Sir Robert Cotton* (Oxford, 1979) and Michael Brennan's *Literary Patronage in the Renaissance: The Pembroke Family* (London, 1988), telling an unproblematic story of Shirley's career but steadily accumulating details of his education and patrons, his membership of various professional groups and his associations with other English Roman Catholics, especially at court.

---

[21] *Philological Quarterly*, 68 (1989), 295–314.
[22] Lanham, Maryland, 1988.

Burner makes no attempt to synthesize these various connections in ideological, political, or factional terms, but emphasizes rather the complex network of interdependencies within which a Caroline like Shirley was obliged to work. Perhaps in essence this is not so far removed from what Evans says about Jonson a generation earlier, though Burner makes no effort to re-read Shirley's works in the light of the perspectives she uncovers. The book provides, however, a solid and scholarly redefinition of this neglected playwright's place in the society of his day and as such may act as a spur to further study.

So much of the urgency of the re-historicization of Renaissance literature comes from the conviction that it is still very much alive (never more so than in the case of Shakespeare), part of the present we inhabit. Certain forms of scholarship, however, seem rather to remind us that the past is a foreign country and that they do things very differently there. Symbolic numerology and emblem-studies, for example, inevitably confront us with arcane and remote elements of Renaissance thought, accessible only to initiates then and of limited appeal to readers today – unless the scholars immersed in them can find ways of convincing us of a wider significance (as perhaps D. J. Gordon and Stephen Orgel may be said to have done for the Stuart court masque). Thomas P. Roche Jr's *Petrarch and the English Sonnet Sequences* fails by this criterion in the first of these fields.[23] This is partly because this *magnum opus* (600 pages) seems to have been brewing a very long time and in the process perhaps to have missed its moment, but more importantly because it develops two theses simultaneously – the centrality of symbolic numerology to Petrarchan sonnet-sequences and the concept of 'the unreliable narrator' as a characteristic feature of these fictions – but without ever really binding them together. 'The unreliable narrator' derives from the narratalogical- and reader-response criticism of the early 1970s, but the application of such notions to Petrarchan

sonnet-sequences is still sufficiently unusual that it may help readers to find a contemporary point of contact with these literary dinosaurs. So when we find his section on Shakespeare's sonnets briskly asserting that 'the poet-lover's narratives are unreliable, just as in the case of all the poet-lovers we have examined so far' (p. 385) we may feel ourselves on reasonably familiar territory and able to grant Roche the 'one free speculation' which Northrop Frye (see p. 380) allows any writer on the sonnets: 'My one free speculation, the only begetter of my new story [to replace the old quasi-biographical 'story' of the poet-lover, young man, rival poet and dark lady] is that *will*, not Shakespeare, is the poet-lover of the *Sonnets*; *will*, which is part of Shakespeare's given name and which he had the genius to see was also part of his common human nature, became the *I* of *Shake-speares Sonnets*' (p. 387).

The possibility of the 'unreliable narrator', it will be seen, has not led Roche, as it has some post-modernists, to deny altogether the stability of the 'self' and indeed the concept of 'common human nature', but it has led him to see Shakespeare's sonnets (like Sidney's *Astrophil and Stella*, Daniel's *Delia*, and numerous other religious and amatory sequences) as playful fictions, with counterparts in the late twentieth century, and he illuminates these with some zest. But his insistence on the form *Shake-speares Sonnets*, while it fits his name-playing and frequently phallic game-playing themes, also signals his other preoccupation: with numerology. There are frequent references to Alastair Fowler's *Triumphal Forms* (Cambridge, 1970) and at one point he declares 'I hope to be Copernicus to Fowler's Ptolemy' (p. 422). Where Fowler related the 108 sonnets of *Astrophil and Stella* to the 108 suitors of Ulysses' wife, Penelope, Roche includes the songs printed with them to produce 119 poems, just one short of the 120 months Ulysses took to return to her: Astrophil is *structurally*

[23] New York, 1989.

doomed to failure and frustration. In the case of Shakespeare, it is critical for Roche to link *Shake-speares Sonnets* with 'A Lover's Complaint', printed with them in 1609, in order to produce a round figure of 200 poems/stanzas (as opposed to Fowler's count of 203), a computation with a variety of Pythagorean, mystical and hermeneutic consequences – different, naturally, from those adduced by Fowler.

No one can deny, of course, that mystic numerology figured in some traditions of Renaissance thought and had a bearing on some of the writing of the day, where it might even be seen as one dimension of ludic narrative. But Roche does not make this connection or approach matters in this spirit, which might really have opened up the field to a wider readership. Instead he pursues the theme obsessively, arbitrarily, and at great length, in ways that inspire little confidence. To make only the most obvious point: he gives no consideration at all to the question of whether either Sidney's or Shakespeare's sonnets reached print in a form which their authors would have sanctioned. In both cases there is a very real possibility that hands other than their own made the final editorial decisions. In such circumstances it seems positively bizarre to base so much argument on precise numbers of poems, stanzas, lines and their organization, and to deduce from them definitive 'explanations' of these sequences, while the other half of the book is quite eloquently exploring the indeterminacies of unreliable narration. 'O, matter and impertinency mixed'!

The world of emblem-studies seems staid and sober by comparison, though far from moribund, as the trawl of works that have found their way to your reviewer's desk this year testifies. Three of these are the first fruits of a promised series, AMS Studies in the Emblem, paralleling the same publisher's periodical, *Emblematica*: *The English Emblem and the Continental Tradition*, edited by Peter M. Daly, *The Emblems of Thomas Palmer: 'Two Hundred Poosees'*, *Sloane MS 3794*, edited with intro-

duction and notes by John Manning, and *The English Tournament Imprese* by Alan R. Young.[24] It is impossible not to notice that the same names keep recurring and that various projects have criss-crossed in the production of these volumes. An essay by Young, 'The English Tournament Imprese', appears in the Daly volume (pp. 61–81) and covers similar territory to the introduction in his own book, though the substance of the latter is a descriptive list of all known English tournament imprese, pictures, words and dates where known, all thoroughly cross-referenced and indexed. The impresa is not identical with the emblem, though a sister form; in his introduction, Young helpfully quotes Camden on the distinction: 'An Imprese (as the Italians call it) is a devise in picture with his Motte, or Word, borne by noble and learned personages, to notifie some particular conceit of their owne: as Emblemes (that we may omitte other differences) doe propound some general instruction to all' (p. 1). Among the 'other differences' would be the fact that while the impresa consisted only of a picture and a motto, the typical (if not exclusive) form of the emblem was that pregnant combination of motto, picture and epigram first found in Alciatus' *Emblematum Liber* (1531). The central contention of the essays in Daly's volume is that, while only six emblem books were actually published in England in the sixteenth century, knowledge of the form and its continental traditions was far more widespread than this low number would suggest, and its influence was more significant than is often appreciated.

Manning's edition of Palmer's *Two Hundred Poosees* itself furthers this contention, since it is the first ever publication, as well as the first serious study, of the earliest English book (*c.* 1565) in the mode of Alciatus, antedating by some twenty years Whitney's *Choice of Emblemes* (published 1585), which is usually credited with that status. Palmer never had his book

---

[24] All New York, 1988.

printed, but presented the manuscript to the Earl of Leicester; nevertheless his skill as an emblematist, as well as orator, was widely known (by Jonson, Drayton and Camden, among others) and the existence of such a sophisticated and continentally inspired work so early in Elizabeth's reign requires a slight but significant redrawing of the cultural map of the last half of the century. In Daly's volume, Manning also has an essay on a manuscript of Whitney's *Choice of Emblemes*, antedating and different in important ways from the published version, and this too was presented to Leicester.[25] The differences underline how subtly and sensitively emblems could be selected and arranged for different readerships. This compounds a point made most forcefully in Michael Bath's essay in Daly's volume, relating to material from the most unlikely source for emblematic material – the royal household accounts.[26] What he particularly stresses is that emblems were not statically fixed in their meanings, but capable of quite radical transformation and re-application. Hence, for literary scholars, 'the dangers of snatching a random analogue from emblem books or mythologies to serve as a gloss on a literary text. It might seem that what we need for the purposes of literary scholarship and art history in such cases ... is less a motif-index, indispensable though that is, than a transformational grammar' (pp. 234–5).

That sense of a dynamic indeterminacy in emblem iconography is something that, on the whole, I find lacking in a collection of essays that explores this field with particular reference to literature, *Shakespeare and the Emblem: Studies in Renaissance Iconography and Iconology*, edited by Tibor Fabiny.[27] Most of the contributions have a soundly New Critical sense of the stability of words and images (however complex the hermeneutics of rediscovering their meaning), and the relative ease of applying one to the other. With this reservation they do undoubtedly add to a 'motif-index' of Shakespearian iconography – notably Clifford

Davidson on 'The Iconography of Wisdom and Folly in *King Lear*' (pp. 189–214) and Tibor Fabiny himself on both '*Veritas Filia Temporis*. The Iconography of Time and Truth and Shakespeare' (pp. 215–71) and '*Theatrum Mundi* and the Ages of Man' (pp. 273–336). Perhaps the most thought-provoking piece, however, and one which deserves a wider circulation than it is likely to get in this context, is from the familiar name of Peter Daly: 'Shakespeare and the Emblem. The Use of Evidence and Analogy in Establishing Iconographic and Emblematic Effects' (pp. 117–87). He is properly sceptical about a variety of misconceived and amateurish attempts to identify and elucidate emblem-related material in Shakespeare, observing that only too often 'the knowledge of the literary historian is limited, even accidental' and so 'it is unlikely that [he] will ever bring with him a sufficiently broad knowledge of Renaissance art to recognize all the possible iconographic and emblematic dimensions in a given play' (pp. 168–9). On the other hand, a volume like this demonstrates only too clearly that experts in emblem studies and iconography generally, who might bring such expertise to bear, are not always aware of the developments in critical theory and literary history that might provide a properly dynamic context for their insights. An encouraging demonstration of a fruitful union between the two disciplines, however, is provided by Peggy Muñoz Simonds in 'The Marriage Topos in *Cymbeline*: Shakespeare's Variations on a Classical Theme', which examines the complex application of a topos often expressed, as she shows, in emblematic form.[28] She declares her intention 'to demonstrate not only the presence of a familiar marriage topos in *Cymbeline* but to explore as

---

[25] 'Geoffrey Whitney's Unpublished Emblems: Further Evidence of Indebtedness to Continental Traditions', pp. 83–107.

[26] 'Collared Stags and Bridled Lions: Queen Elizabeth's Household Accounts', pp. 225–57.

[27] Szeged, Hungary, 1984.

[28] *English Literary Renaissance*, 19 (1989), 94–117.

well the several ways in which Shakespeare varies its use and its meanings in respect of matrimony, politics, and Protestant theology' (p. 96). The essay is certainly illuminating in all these respects, though vitiated by the curious mistake of associating Jonson's *Hymenaei* with the wedding of the royal favourite, Lord Hay. Hay was one of the *Hymenaei* masquers, but the piece celebrated the ill-fated wedding of the Earl of Essex and Lady Frances Howard. It was Campion who wrote *Lord Hay's Masque* the following year (1607) for Hay's own marriage.

Some pictures with which the Shakespeare family were particularly familiar are the subject of Clifford Davidson's *The Guild Chapel Wall Paintings at Stratford-upon-Avon*.[29] The broader purpose of the book is to explicate the scheme of wall paintings in the Guild Chapel in Stratford (just across the road from New Place), which were intact until 1563–4, when those considered offensive to the new Protestant orthodoxy were covered or defaced under the direction of John Shakespeare, father of William, then the town's Chamberlain. Davidson reproduces the remarkable illustrations made by Thomas Fisher of some of the paintings which were uncovered for a time in the early nineteenth century (though subsequently either covered again or destroyed completely). He also reproduces William Puddephat's drawings of the Dance of Death paintings on the north wall of the nave, which were *not* obliterated in the 1560s, though panelled over in the nineteenth century and only briefly restored to view during the 1950s, when Puddephat made a detailed study of them. We must presume that the Dance of Death sequence was familiar to the young William Shakespeare; John Stow specifically commented on it in 1576, when the boy was twelve. John Shakespeare's hand in defacing and covering the other paintings because of their Roman Catholic associations is a particularly charged matter, given what is suspected of his own faith. This question has been re-opened by F. W. Brownlow in 'John Shakespeare's Recusancy: New Light on an Old Document,' where he concludes: 'if the recusancy return of 1592 is what it claims to be, a list of Catholic recusants, some in debt, some infirm, some excommunicated, some very determined, some non-committal, but all sufficiently obstinate that they were prepared to have their names taken down in a process that cannot have been secret, then the conclusion that John Shakespeare was a Catholic is the economical one, requiring no forcing of the evidence'.[30]

Literature Criticism from 1400 to 1800, Volume 8, a weighty tome in every sense, belongs to an unstoppable juggernaut of a series, which is itself only one adjunct of the even grander design of the whole Gale Literary Criticism Series.[31] My suspicion, however, is that the enterprise is so invisibly huge, and the relationship of the parts to the whole is so haphazard, that it may well be the fate of a work like this to languish neglected on the shelves of major libraries, who are the only institutions that could even contemplate buying them. The remit of this specific series is to cover any writer of substance, British, European or American, active between 1400 and 1800 – except for Shakespeare, who is catered for in a parallel series of his own. Each entry includes a biography and career overview of about *DNB* length and detail, helpful primary and secondary bibliographies, and substantial portions of critical commentary on the author, from contemporary reactions down to the present day – criticism from the 1970s and 80s getting a fair, if not disproportionate, representation. In this respect each entry does for an author what a Macmillan *Casebook* does for an individual work, and at similar length – entries average around sixty pages of double-column folio. The flaw in the series design is that authors are assigned to volumes entirely arbitrarily, presumably as the work on them becomes available, so it is essential to consult the compen-

---

[29] AMS Studies in the Renaissance, no. 22 (New York, 1988).

[30] *Shakespeare Quarterly*, 40 (1989), 186–91; p. 189.

[31] Edited by James E. Person Jr (Detroit, 1988).

dious Cumulative Author Index in each volume to find out where a particular entry appears, or even if it has yet appeared. So Volume 8 happens to contain entries on Drayton, Machiavelli, Montaigne, Nicholas Rowe and G. E. Lessing, who for one reason or another might all be of immediate interest to Shakespearians, but also on six other authors, four of whom this reviewer admits to never having heard of before. In that sense it is not what computer-buffs would call user-friendly. On the other hand, for those who take the trouble to find their way around the series (singular and plural) they will be immensely helpful to writers of American term-papers and similar assignments, at whom one suspects they are really directed. Those who have to mark such assignments ought for this reason to become acquainted with them. They may well be surprised how much useful material they find, not all of it otherwise readily accessible.

By contrast, *The Cambridge Guide to World Theatre*, edited by Martin Banham, is an attractive single volume, with entries accessibly arranged alphabetically.[32] My niggling worry here is that when a book takes its remit of 'World Theatre' as seriously as this does, with entries on almost everything conceivable, from acting unions to pornographic theatre, from hippodrama to Uganda, from shadow puppets to Danny la Rue, even eleven hundred double-column pages do not allow much room for any particular entry. Shakespeare and his texts warrant 1800 words, while 'Shakespeare in Performance' receives a further 1200 – hardly more than a bare factual outline. Within these limitations, the entries on English Renaissance theatre are consistently serviceable, as we might expect since they are credited to Peter Thomson, though I must take issue with him over the entry on the Master of the Revels: Edmund Tilney was never knighted, was not notoriously idle (a confusion with his predecessor, Benger?) and was not the uncle of Sir George Buc. But even where, as was usually the case, the information seemed accurate, I kept wondering exactly who finds information

useful in this minimalist form, even more compressed – because of the almost inexhaustible remit – than most such 'Guides' and 'Companions'.

If *The Cambridge Guide* may tell us a little bit about almost anything theatrical, Manfred Pfister's *The Theory and Analysis of Drama* seeks to provide a comprehensive classification of the elements comprising dramatic texts.[33] Rigorously excluding the sociological, anthropological, and historical dimensions of the theatre, he provides an immensely thorough neo-Aristotelian survey of the ingredients of literature in the dramatic mode: the relationships of plays to stage design, the multimedial transmission of information, the presentation of figure and story, monological and dialogical communication, and structures of time and space, all broken down relentlessly into progressive sub-categorizations. The nearest equivalents I am familiar with are J. L. Styan's *The Elements of Drama* (Cambridge, 1960) and *Drama, Stage and Audience* (Cambridge, 1975), though in places it is much closer in outlook to Keir Elam's *The Semiotics of Theatre and Drama* (London, 1980). The admirably fluent translation by John Halliday coincides with the fifth edition of what has become a standard textbook in German-speaking countries and, while it draws on examples ranging from the ancient Greeks to contemporary European theatre, there is a marked preponderance of illustrations from Shakespeare which will obviously be attractive to the English-speaking market. It remains to be seen, however, whether this kind of neo-formalist approach to dramatic texts will be congenial to notoriously empirical British habits of mind, and so find a regular place in our class-rooms.

Speaking of ingrained attitudes, I am reminded that in my own student days (not much more than twenty years ago) it was thought unusual, even possibly perverse, to regard 'performance' as relevant to the

---

[32] Cambridge, 1988.
[33] Cambridge, 1988.

academic study and appreciation of Shakespeare's texts: they were dramatic poems, full of interesting ideas and characters, and the fact that they also had (had always had) a practical function in the theatre was an awkward side-issue. *Shakespeare and the Sense of Performance*, a collection of essays dedicated to the late Bernard Beckerman, who was a pioneer of the 'performance criticism' of Shakespeare, underlines how far we have come in seeing the practical potential of plays for enactment (whether on the stages for which they were written, or on those that have evolved since) as an integral part of their meaning.[34] The list of contributors is virtually a roll-call of those who have led this revolution in our perception, and if not all their essays count among their most challenging works, the combined force of the volume bears witness to the continuing vitality of this approach. The pieces are too numerous and varied to be mentioned separately, but the following will indicate something of the range covered: Ralph Berry on 'Hamlet and the Audience: the Dynamics of a Relationship' (pp. 24–28), John Russell Brown on 'The Nature of Speech in Shakespeare's Plays' (pp. 48–59), Marvin Rosenberg on 'Subtext in Shakespeare' (pp. 79–80), Michael Goldman on 'Performer and Role in Marlowe and Shakespeare' (pp. 91–102), R. A. Foakes on 'Stage Images in *Troilus and Cressida*' (pp. 150–61), Andrew Gurr on 'The "State" of Shakespeare's Audiences' (pp. 162–79) and J. L. Styan on 'Stage Space and the Shakespeare Experience' (pp. 195–209). On this evidence, the distance between the Green Room and the lecture hall is shorter than it has ever been.

Ralph Berry further demonstrates this in two more essays: 'Casting the Crowd: *Coriolanus* in Performance' considers the implications both of the ways the crowd is presented in Shakespeare's text (sometimes as 'mutinous citizens', sometimes as 'a rabble of Plebeians', but also sometimes 'a Troope of Citizens' or simply 'Citizens', never a mob) and of how it has been presented in production over the years, observing the tangible difference between a hundred Victorian 'extras' and the modern financial imperative not to go above six or seven assorted types, weighing both against political readings of the play; '*Dramatis Personae*' critically reviews recent editorial habits in the listing of *dramatis personae*, noting the often irreconcilable demands of intelligibility for the modern reader, concision and accuracy (how do we describe the head-borough, Verges? Is Toby Belch really Olivia's 'uncle'?) and being particularly astute on questions of social status (lady, heiress, citizen, merchant, gentleman) which were so critical for the Elizabethans but do not register in the same way for modern readers: small matters in one sense, though they can colour a whole reading or performance.[35] That is borne out indirectly in Julie Hankey's *Richard III* in the 'Plays in Performance Series', a second edition of a volume first brought out in 1981.[36] It is revised to take into account in particular two RSC productions, that by Terry Hands in 1980/1 with Alan Howard as Richard, and Bill Alexander's with Antony Sher (1984/5), about which she is markedly less enthusiastic than the press at the time. In a volume such as this one sees that the kind of small details on which Ralph Berry has been concentrating cumulatively contribute to a total reading, and should not be overlooked when we think of broader issues like the social or political climate that supposedly predicates certain performances. It does perhaps say something about the spirit of the times, however, that this particular volume *already* needs a further revision to take account of Michael Bogdanov's English Shakespeare Company complete histories cycle, the RSC's *The Plantagenets*, and Derek Jacobi's back-to-back *Richard II* and *Richard III*. All of this in turn emphasizes the extent to which Lennart

---

[34] *Shakespeare and the Sense of Performance: Essays in the Tradition of Performance Criticism in Honor of Bernard Beckerman*, edited by Marvin and Ruth Thompson (Newark, Delaware, 1989).

[35] *Assaph* 4 (1988), 111–24; *Essays in Theatre*, 7 (1988), 75–82.

[36] Bristol, 1988.

Nyberg's *The Shakespearean Ideal: Shakespeare Production and the Modern Theatre in Britain* is a historical document, in the sense that it offers a record and an interpretation of a moment that has passed, of a set of attitudes and climate of opinion we can no longer call contemporary.[37] This brief and selective, but lucid and suggestive account of Shakespearian production in Britain focuses mainly on the period 1960–80, arguing that a 'Shakespearean Ideal' emerged, 'an application of what was taken as Shakespearean and Elizabethan theatrical standards and values filtered through the practice and exploration of twentieth-century, and especially post-war, drama and theatre' (p. 124). The 'rediscovery' of the Elizabethan stage both contributed to, and was fuelled by, the line of experimentation running through Stanislavski, Brecht, Beckett and Genet, and into the 'angry' and 'absurdist' generations of the 1950s and 60s, the process of historical recovery being charged with the urgency of contemporary application. But that was in another country, and besides the wench is – if not dead – having to re-assess her rôle in the market place.

Shakespearian 'performance' of course increasingly means performance on film, television and video, and the literature on the subject is racing to keep up. It is a sign of how far we have come, for example, that Anthony Davies's *Filming Shakespeare's Plays* makes no pretence to be comprehensive.[38] His sub-title, 'The Adaptations of Laurence Olivier, Orson Welles, Peter Brook and Akira Kurosawa', points to the heart of the book as a discussion of what he proposes as eight 'classic' film productions of Shakespearian plays since the Second World War – classic in that 'Each of the eight films discussed in close detail has managed, to a remarkable degree, to meet the challenge of reconciling theatrical resonance and centripetality with the fluidity, the discontinuity and the centrifugality of cinematic space' (p. 184). So, while he is aware, for example, of the Kozintsev *Hamlet* and *King Lear* and of Polanski's *Macbeth*, he is less interested in

making comparisons than in examining what he regards as certain particularly successful translations of theatrical texts to the technical and aesthetic requirements of cinema. The book is persuasively written, and unfailingly perceptive about the films on which it concentrates (notably, I think, Olivier's *Hamlet*, Welles's *Chimes at Midnight* and Kurosawa's *Throne of Blood*), but it is bound to meet resistance in relation to the value judgements, both explicit and implicit, that it makes about the status of cinema in relation to the other audio-visual media (which are simply ignored) and about what some will see as the very narrow criteria by which Davies judges successful film. Incidentally, given his approach, it is by no means certain that he would have compared Olivier's *Henry V* with the new version by Kenneth Branagh, even had it been available to him; Jill Forbes, however, has provided a brief but suggestive early comparison of the films, concentrating on details like the settings and the fight scenes.[39]

If Davies may be accused of élitism, Bernice W. Kliman runs no such risk. Her *Hamlet: Film, Television and Audio Performance* starts from the premise that there is no definitive performance or realization of a play, and that any version is inherently interesting whether or not it is totally convincing.[40] She is extremely knowledgeable and enthusiastic about all aspects of *Hamlet* on film, including silent film, 'live' TV, video, and sound-only recordings. Moreover she avoids the dangers of a monochrome 'history' of recorded *Hamlets* by dividing the rich stock of material so as to address certain key questions: her first section concentrates on the three most discussed and accessible recordings, the Olivier and Kozintsev films, and the BBC video with Derek Jacobi in the title rôle, exploring the relationship between filmic technique and theatrical traditions

---

[37] Uppsala, 1988.
[38] Cambridge, 1988.
[39] 'Henry V', *Sight and Sound*, 58 (1989), 258–9.
[40] London and Toronto, 1989.

(including the vexed question of the cutting and re-arranging of 'the text'); her second section examines a range of TV productions, many of which will be entirely unknown to British readers (including versions with Maurice Evans, Maximillian Schell, Richard Chamberlain and the Swedish actor Stellan Skarsgaard as Hamlet), concentrating in particular on the nature of the setting in each instance; her third section examines silent-movie *Hamlets*, notably that of Forbes-Robertson, and sound recordings, including those of John Barrymore and Richard Burton. A brief epilogue explores the influence on particular productions of some critical theories, notably those of Dover Wilson and Ernest Jones on the Olivier film, observing how continual '"misreadings" challenge us to shape our own creative revision of the play' (p. 306) – a fitting epigraph to a book which should provide much food for thought.

Shakespeare on Television: An Anthology of Essays and Reviews, edited by J. C. Bulman and H. R. Coursen, is a wide-ranging collection of pieces on televised Shakespeare.[41] Many of its entries decry the limitations of what Marshall McCluhan categorized as a 'cool' medium, one that relies on the deep involvement of the audience rather than its unignorable presence to give its product real life. But the anthology itself gives recognition to the fact that it is the medium through which *most* people today experience Shakespeare, and that in subtle ways it affects how they then read the plays or even respond to them in the theatre; it also emphasizes that permanent video recordings make possible on a wide scale *comparative* judgements of productions and performances with a detail and precision hitherto impossible. The entries are divided into three sections – 'Wide Angles', general and theoretical reflections on the televising of Shakespeare; 'Close-Ups', which consider particular productions, and series of productions, in which the BBC TV Shakespeare naturally predominates as the most comprehensive to date, though far from universally loved; and 'Short Subjects', reviews of more than

seventy productions over forty years, some very brief though others mini-essays. The book is a gold-mine for anyone who already uses video in the teaching of Shakespeare and may well encourage others to take it up, not least because so many of the entries demonstrate that the familiarity of the medium helps to overcome so many of the awe- and incomprehension-factors that inhibit discussions of Shakespeare in other contexts.

Last, but far from least, there is one dimension to all the issues running through this review that I have reserved for a section of its own: the feminist one. This is not in a spirit of ghettoization, but because I wanted to stress the range, variety, and urgency of current feminist writing on Shakespeare, which traditionalists tend to marginalize or to assume has only one thing to say. Take, for example, Dympna Callaghan's *Woman and Gender in Renaissance Tragedy: A Study of 'King Lear', 'Othello', 'The Duchess of Malfi' and 'The White Devil'*.[42] Her vocabulary is a post-structuralist one, not dissimilar to that of Robert Knapp in *Shakespeare: The Theater and the Book*, though her emphases and outlook are far more radical: 'Tragedy is a political space, and the contradictions generated there are produced by the very terms in which orthodox notions are expressed' and within this space 'gender is ... a pivotal and paradigmatic opposition in the structure of antitheses, a condensation of other hierarchies' (pp. 9, 11). In the two Shakespeare plays she relates the tragedy of the central (male) figures to the weaknesses revealed in the double-edged marginalization and subjection of women. But perhaps even more suggestively, in developing the contrasts with Webster's plays, she relates what traditional criticism has often castigated as a lack of dramatic and artistic control on Webster's part to his delineation of the unstable constructions of both power and gender. The kind of precarious centrality accorded the Duchess and Vittoria Corombona in Webster's plays is a key

---

41 Hanover, New Hampshire, and London, 1988.
42 Hemel Hempstead, 1989.

both to their unusual aesthetics and to their radical deconstruction (in both senses) of the social and political structures they represent. Callaghan's thesis parallels at points that of Kathleen McLuskie in 'The patriarchal bard: feminist criticism and Shakespeare: *King Lear* and *Measure for Measure*',[43] who claims *inter alia* that 'we should not look for a sympathetic treatment of "the nature of women"' in Shakespeare's plays because 'they are the products of an entertainment industry which, as far as we know, had no women shareholders, actors, writers, or stage hands'. Richard Levin, never one to leave the stone of a would-be critical orthodoxy unturned, has challenged this in 'Women in the Renaissance Theatre Audience'.[44] Applying the methods of Andrew Gurr in *Playgoing in Shakespeare's London* (Cambridge, 1987), he demonstrates that the plays themselves show awareness of women as a significant and distinctive element in the audience: 'while women were not represented at the production end of [the theatrical] industry, they certainly were at the consumption end, and so probably had an effect on its products,' though he does have to admit that 'men seem to have dominated the audiences and the playwrights' conceptions of these audiences' (p. 174).

Levin himself obviously considers consumers a powerful force in a market economy, but many cultural theorists (and especially feminist ones) would regard them as merely its most sophisticated products. This debate lies behind two contributions to the continuing debate about cross-dressing on the Elizabethan stage, and the extent to which it either reinforces or challenges the suppression of women. Anne Herrmann's 'Travesty and Transgression. Transvestism in Shakespeare, Brecht, and Churchill' takes *As You Like It* as one of three plays which 'use transvestism as a dramatic device to figure historicized forms of social transgression. Such transgression never takes the form of travesty itself; that is, cross-dressing as such is not coded as violation.'[45] She identifies the Epilogue (spoken, of course, by the 'actor' who plays Rosalind) as 'the most trans-

gressive moment in the play because it suggests that the sport, whether athletic or erotic, takes place, both candidly and confidentially, between men. This is the social contradiction *As You Like It* addresses, placing cross-dressed heroines on the stage at the moment they ceased to appear on the streets, thereby reinforcing the fact that its point of address was men, not women' (p. 140). Nevertheless, the very appropriation of the unstable metaphor of cross-dressing 'by the "masculine"' may point to the limits of the unexplored metaphoric structures underpinning society itself and so the more sharply identify 'the female figure as the product of a particular historical moment' (p. 154). Lorraine Helms is less concerned with the particular historical moment that imposed cross-dressing as a conventional norm on Shakespearian drama ('its ideological valence is ambiguous') than on the question of what modern stage practice should do with rôles inescapably created within patriarchal paradigms and perspectives.[46] She is particularly concerned by what she sees as the over-easy optimism of Elaine Showalter, who has argued that 'when Shakespeare's heroines began to be played by women instead of boys, the presence of the female body and female voice, quite apart from details of interpretation, created new meanings and subversive tensions in these roles'.[47] The fact of an actress being female is not, for her, enough. There is a need to explore the physicality of performance itself and the possibility of a mannered foregrounding of key textual moments of stereotyping and repression so that 'feminist Shakespeareans may begin to

---

[43] In *Political Shakespeare*, edited by Jonathan Dollimore and Alan Sinfield (Manchester, 1985), pp. 88–108.

[44] *Shakespeare Quarterly*, 40 (1989), 165–74.

[45] *Theatre Journal*, 41 (1989), 133–54; p. 134.

[46] 'Playing the Woman's Part: Feminist Criticism and Shakespearean Performance', *Theatre Journal*, 41 (1989), 190–200.

[47] Quoted from 'Representing Ophelia: Women, Madness, and the Responsibilities of Feminist Criticism' in *Shakespeare and the Question of Theory* edited by Patricia Parker and Geoffrey Hartman (New York, 1985), pp. 77–94; p. 80.

create a theatre where patriarchal representation of femininity can be transformed into rôles for living women' (p. 200).

In *Clamorous Voices: Shakespeare's Women Today* a group of distinguished actresses consider, from their own professional perspective, the kinds of issues raised so differently by Callaghan, Levin, Herrmann and Helms.[48] It is very much a collaborative venture, the critic and scholar Carol Rutter in conversation with Sinead Cusack, Paola Dionisotti, Fiona Shaw, Juliet Stevenson, and Harriet Walter, and the results edited into book form by Faith Evans. The very form of the product may suggest a particular ('sororal') brand of feminism, while the fact that all the actresses have been associated with the Royal Shakespeare Company in the decade since 1978 (playing between them many of the most contentious female rôles in Shakespeare – notably Kate in *The Taming of the Shrew*, Rosalind and Celia in *As You Like It*, and Isabella in *Measure for Measure*) may suggest that they belong to a specific 'school' or 'movement'. Neither of these propositions is really valid. The collaboration that created the book in this form seems to have been informed by mutual respect, but not exactly by a common purpose, while (in Juliet Stevenson's words) 'each of us has been influenced by the women's movement in varying ways and to different degrees, and we've allowed that influence to inform our choices on the stage' (p. xiv) – which falls some way short of a feminist 'school' of acting (and a long way short of what Helms, for example, is looking for). The voices in the book, in fact, are 'clamorous' as much in the sense of denying that there is a feminist orthodoxy in acting as in insisting on the right to be heard over the predominantly male establishment. Harriet Walter candidly outlines some of the difficulties of being a committed feminist within a collaborative profession: 'My experience with women directors has been that some have a tendency to blur the definitions [between the job of the director and that of the performer]. They depend upon my sisterhood

and sometimes consider it a betrayal if I argue with them ... It's easier to defy a male director' (pp. xx–xxi). On the other hand, all have telling accounts of often less than sympathetic inter-reactions with directors who, in this RSC context, have all been male – a telling fact in itself. '"Barry Kyle wanted a happy ending [to *Measure for Measure*]", says Paola. "Directors often do", rejoins Juliet' (p. 40). Sinead Cusack reveals that 'Adrian [Noble] and I didn't really talk about [*Macbeth*] until the eve of the first rehearsal ... Jonathan Pryce (Macbeth) was allowed to participate but not me. I wanted to talk to the designer, Bob Crowley – but that didn't happen either' (p. 57). Of course, many people will want to read the book simply for what it tells us about the interpretations of particular rôles – the pros and cons of Isabella wearing a nun's wimple, for example, or the challenge of Celia's long on-stage silences while Rosalind and Orlando struggle towards a sexual pairing – than about the feminist politics that lie behind them. And it is, indeed, consistently illuminating about the constraints within which performances are produced, the complex pressures that give rise to particular interpretations. But the unstrident feminist sub-texts are the ones that stayed with me longest. Perhaps here is the place to reveal that two of the four authors dealt with in *Literature Criticism from 1400 to 1800, Volume 8*, whom I admitted I had never heard of before, were English dramatists, who just happened to be female: Mary (Griffith) Pix and Catherine Trotter (Cockburn). Of the other two, one (Sigüenza) was a Mexican chronicler and poet and the other (Pétursson) an Icelandic writer of hymns, and with them perhaps the inevitable limitations of cultural horizons may mitigate my ignorance. But there are no such excuses for Pix and Trotter – unless we allow the 'inevitable' limitations of cultural horizons to include those of gender. To do that is to deny half our humanity.

---

48 London, 1988.

3. EDITIONS AND TEXTUAL STUDIES
reviewed by MacDonald P. Jackson

The experience of watching Deborah Warner's RSC production of *King John* in the Pit at the Barbican two days after having seen the whole *Henry VI–Richard III* cycle, adapted as *The Plantagenets*, in the main theatre convinced me that in *King John* scenes are more subtly and dramatically conceived than in the *Henry VI* plays. They are more apt to be built around conflicts within characters as well as between them, to pose moral dilemmas, to be sharpened by ironies and shaped by tensions, and to develop towards climax and resolution. The progress in Shakespeare's art is apparent both in public scenes in which those motivated by 'commodity' manoeuvre to defend or enhance their power and in more private scenes in which individuals suffer the consequences of these political machinations. And the poetry is more complex, the verse more flexible. A. R. Braunmuller must surely be right in deciding, after a careful consideration of the matter, that the anonymous *The Troublesome Reign of King John* (1591) was not derivative from Shakespeare's play but served as a source for it, and that '*King John* was composed and performed in the mid 1590s, most probably 1595–6' (p. 15).[1]

Braunmuller's introduction and commentary are very full – to the point perhaps of congestion. Thoroughness can shade into a pernickety concern with the peripheral, so that the play's essential nature remains obscure. But Braunmuller's enthusiasm for *King John* is evident enough. He discusses the varieties of 'political language' employed in it, fully explores the intricate questions of inheritance, succession, and legitimacy in family and kingdom that link the dispute between the Faulconbridge brothers with contention over the English crown, makes some interesting remarks on 'patterns of action' in the play, and traces its theatrical reputation and stage history, from 'test play for new actors and trusted vehicle for established ones' (p. 84) in an age of spectacular representation to relative neglect.

King John appears to have been printed in the First Folio from composite copy, probably a late transcript made by two scribes, one taking over from the other within 4.2. There are inconsistencies and ambiguities in the Folio's naming of characters and anomalies in its act and scene divisions. In 2.1, for example, an anonymous 'Citizen' who speaks from the walls of the besieged Angers is in later prefixes identified as 'Hubert' – the name given to the important character enlisted by John in 3.3 to blind and kill Arthur in Act 4. In the *Textual Companion* to the Oxford *Complete Works*, John Jowett comments: 'The transition from a French citizen – unnamed in the dialogue, without personal ties with any other character and conspicuously neutral in his political affiliation – to the trusted confidant of King John remains abrupt, unexplained, and bewildering.' He judges that since any attempt to conflate the characters is incomplete in the Folio, an editor's 'best option is to revert to Shakespeare's original conception, evidently prompted by *Troublesome Reign*, and retain the separate identities of the Citizen and Hubert' (pp. 317–18). This seems sensible, but the merging of Hubert and the Citizen into one person, for which, after a lengthy analysis of the issues (pp. 272–82), Braunmuller eventually opts, can make theatrical sense, as Warner's RSC production demonstrated: there the beret-wearing pragmatist who, on the ramparts of Angers,

---

[1] *The Life and Death of King John*, ed. A. R. Braunmuller (Oxford: Clarendon Press, 1989), in the Oxford Shakespeare series. In 'Dating *King John*: The Implications of the Influence of Edmund Spenser's *Ruins of Rome* on Shakespeare's Text', *Notes and Queries*, 35 (1988), 458–63, Charles W. Hieatt argues that the influence of *Ruins of Rome* on *King John*, *The Rape of Lucrece*, and the *Sonnets* confirms that Shakespeare's play followed *The Troublesome Reign* and suggests a composition date of late 1593 or early 1594.

chewed away at a French roll while, like a spectator at a boxing match, sardonically egging on the armies competing for control of his town, developed naturally into the Hubert prepared to throw in his lot with the man in power and do John's dirty-work – until he discovered his own humanity.

The correct distribution of lines in the exchange between Hubert and the Bastard at the beginning of 5.6 is thoroughly problematical, but Braunmuller's simple solution of moving one of the speech prefixes for the Bastard two lines upwards (5.6.4) is a good one. Less convincing is his argument for having King Philip of France elicit five lines from the Dauphin at 2.1.149–54 by addressing to him the words 'Louis, determine what we shall do straight.' In F Austria addresses this line to '*King Lewis*', and the consequent exchange between 'Lew' and 'Iohn' is clearly between the rival kings. In view of the muddled Folio stage direction that at the beginning of 2.1 calls for the entry of 'Philip King of France, Lewis, Daulphin' and others – implying by its comma that Louis and the Dauphin are separate characters – and the Folio attribution of the first and third speeches of 2.1 to 'Lewis', when they must, as Braunmuller accepts, be intended for King Philip, Jowett is surely right in postulating in F 'a straightforward confusion as to the name of the French king' (*Textual Companion*, p. 319). Capell's claims for 'the dramatic value of Philip's requesting Louis to speak' (Braunmuller, p. 272) are unconvincing.

Jowett's text usually strikes me as preferable to Braunmuller's where the two disagree, and Jowett's textual notes more often get to the heart of the matter. Comparison of the supposed 'u' in F's 'expeditious' at 1.1.49 with other Folio examples of 'u' and 'n' suggests that it is in fact a 'turned n', so that Braunmuller is wrong to resist the normal emendation to 'expedition's'. At 1.1.236–7 Braunmuller's punctuation and his refusal to insert 'a' or 'he' after 'Could' in 'Could get me' leave the passage obscure to me, despite his attempts at expla-

nation. Jowett's punctuation of 2.1.187 also makes better sense of Constance's rhetorical wordplay. I do not see how 'Kings of our fear' can mean 'ruled by our fear' at 2.1.371, though this is certainly the meaning required; Tyrwhitt's 'King'd' seems necessary. At 3.1.259 Braunmuller follows F in having Pandulph say that King Philip might more safely hold 'A casèd lion by the mortal paw' than continue to join hands with King John. He accepts Honigmann's explanation that 'a *cased* lion is one still wearing his *case* (= skin), i.e., a live lion'. But even a stuffed lion would retain its skin, and thoughts of Austria's garb weaken the point; the sense demands Thirlby's and Theobald's 'chafed', or, less probably, some such alternative as Jowett's 'crased'. Braunmuller retains F's metrically unsatisfactory lines at 3.3.8–9. The transposition conjectured by Walker and adopted by Keightley would regularize them both, as would Jowett's placement, as proposed by Taylor, of 'Imprisoned angels set at liberty' after 'The fat ribs ... be fed upon'. And I doubt that in Hubert's 'And I will' at 4.1.40 'And' means 'if' and 'continues Hubert's wavering'.

Braunmuller's defence of 'mercy, lacking uses' at 4.1.120 is unpersuasive; Pope's 'mercy-lacking' is far more pointed. Braunmuller notes that F's 'Was' in 'That we ... Was born' at 5.2.25–6 'existed as an available plural form', but does not say whether Shakespeare ever used 'we ... was' elsewhere; if he did not, a compositorial or scribal slip seems likely. Jowett offers an excellent brief vindication of the emendation 'cresset' for 'crest' in 5.4.34. Braunmuller admits that 'cresset' is 'plausible', but thinks that 'it flattens the image'; to me it makes it more vivid, particular, and Shakespearian. And at 5.7.108 both metre and sense are much improved by Taylor's proposal, adopted by Jowett, to replace F's 'kind', which Braunmuller accepts, with 'kind of' in Prince Henry's 'I have a kind of soul that would give thanks'.

Among other worthwhile emendations that Braunmuller rejects are 'I' for 'It' at 1.1.147, 'arise' for 'rise' at 1.1.161, 'insolence' for 'insolent' at 2.1.122, 'niece' for 'near' at 2.1.425, 'O' for 'of' at 2.1.435, 'it' for 'that' at 3.1.196, 'troth' for 'truth' at 3.1.282, 'swear'st' for 'swears' at 3.1.284 (why should Cardinal Pandulph use 'a northern inflection' that Shakespeare normally reserves for verbs in '-t'?), 'vilely' for 'evilly' at 3.4.149, 'water' for 'matter' at 4.1.64, 'better do' for 'do better' at 4.2.28, 'worser' for 'worse' at 4.2.31, and 'when' for 'then' (than) at 4.2.42; and at 4.3.16–17 'Who's ... love. / 'Tis' makes better sense than 'Whose ... love / Is'. Also, while F's spellings in 'Neere or farre off' at 1.1.174 *may* be used for the comparatives, they are common for the positive forms of the adjectives too; Braunmuller's 'Nea'er or farre off' seems a fussy modernization compared to plain 'near or far'. And, like Dyce, I should be inclined to accept Walker's conjecture 'proffered love' for the redundant 'proffered offer' at 2.1.258.

In short, Braunmuller's editorial conservatism underestimates the amount of error to be expected in a text set by Folio compositors B and C from a scribal transcript. He is, however, the first editor to adopt Mull's plausible conjecture 'dread' for F's 'dead' to read 'now doth Death line his dread chops with steel' at 2.1.352. Despite my cavils, this is a painstaking edition, which all serious students of *King John* will need to consult.

Eugene M. Waith's edition of *The Two Noble Kinsmen* is also welcome.[2] It is perhaps possible to see *All Is True* (or *Henry VIII*) as a perfunctory attempt to treat historical fact in the spirit of the Late Romances and shape it into a similar pattern, in which good providentially emerges from a medley of ills and the birth of the infant Elizabeth redeems old woes. But the other extant result of Shakespeare's collaboration with Fletcher is something quite different. It is not, like *Pericles*, a tale, offered as a 'restorative', about those who, after being 'assailed with fortune fierce and keen', are 'crowned with joy at last'. Gain and loss, wedding and funeral remain interdependent at the end, as at the beginning. If this is 'tragi-comedy', it is not of the kind in which a potentially tragic outcome is diverted towards a blissful comic resolution. And it is Shakespeare's contribution to the play that is largely responsible for the sombre tone. In an age when nothing is so comforting to critics as the discovery of 'disturbing' and 'problematical' content in a work, the 'currents of sadness, harshness, and cynicism in *The Two Noble Kinsmen*' must make it a prime candidate for increased critical attention.[3]

Waith is astute on the play's authorship and the probable division of labour. He admits to doubts over some scenes: 'The first thirty-three lines of Shakespeare's 5.1, for instance, bear some of the signs of Fletcher's style' (p. 23). I think that evidence of Fletcher's hand in 5.1 is limited to the first seventeen lines, and that thereafter, from the exit of Theseus with his train, the verse is Shakespeare's. 'So hoist we / The sails that must these vessels port even where / The heavenly limiter pleases' (5.1.28–30) is decidedly Shakespearian.

In his section on 'The Collaborative Structure' Waith notes that there are several pairs of 'closely comparable scenes, one written by one collaborator and one by the other' (p. 62). These display 'Fletcher's characteristic way of making the most dramatically out of the inherent tensions in a situation and ... Shakespeare's equally characteristic way of combining the exploitation of emotional tension with philosophical reflection' (p. 63). But while the two dramatists often saw different sorts of dramatic potential in their material, Waith regards their collaboration as having been 'close and efficient'. His user-friendly critical account of the play includes a knowledgeable discussion of

---

2 *The Two Noble Kinsmen*, by William Shakespeare and John Fletcher, ed. Eugene M. Waith (Oxford: Clarendon Press, 1989).

3 The phrases are from the introduction to a new collection of essays, *Shakespeare, Fletcher and 'The Two Noble Kinsmen'*, ed. Charles H. Frey (Columbia: University of Missouri Press, 1989), p. 2.

chivalric ideals of love and friendship, and his survey of 'The Play in Performance' further defines its nature and contains the sorts of details that recreate particular stagings. He felt that in Barry Kyle's RSC production at the Swan in 1986 the Japanese theatrical conventions were 'mainly a distraction – a needless complication added to a seventeenth-century version of a medieval elaboration of Greek legend' (p. 39).

The 1634 Quarto – which Waith tentatively judges to have been set by two compositors from a transcript prepared by Edward Knight as prompt copy for a revival in 1625–6 – suffers from a good deal of mislineation. Waith deals with the problem in an appendix (pp. 218–21). I think he is wrong to follow Q in printing the Schoolmaster's speech at the beginning of 3.5 as prose. In editing the passage for the Oxford *Complete Works* William Montgomery prints twenty-one lines of typically Fletcherian verse, most of them regular pentameters with feminine endings, but some with extra, partially elided syllables within the line. Respectable verse is also to be recovered from those other patches of prose that Waith retains from Q in 3.5.

Waith is generally judicious in drawing on the verbal emendations of his predecessors. He adds a convincing one of his own, 'bend' for 'blend' at 5.1.72. Worth accepting would have been 'men's' for 'men' at 1.2.69, 'love her' for 'love' at 2.2.180, 'ere' for 'or' at 2.4.33, 'done enough' for 'enough' at 4.3.35, and 'on me' for 'on' at 5.1.44. 'Yet – pardon me – hard language' would convey the intended meaning at 3.1.106 where 'Yet pardon me hard language' does not. At 5.2.103–4 Waith has the Doctor say, 'Nay, we'll go with you. I will not lose the fight', where other editors have emended the last word to 'sight'. Waith asserts that 'it is perfectly logical for the Doctor to say he does not want to miss the "fight"'. But whereas to declare reluctance to 'lose the sight' is an idiomatic way of saying that one does not intend to miss the spectacle, it is not possible to

speak of 'losing the fight' without seeming to be referring to getting beaten; the phrase would be pointlessly confusing here.[4]

Thomas De Quincey judged, not unreasonably in my view, that 'in point of composition', the first and last two acts of *The Two Noble Kinsmen* were 'perhaps the most superb work in the language, and beyond all doubt from the loom of Shakespeare'.[5] The play proves that as late as 1613 Shakespeare was still a supremely eloquent poet, even though his tortuous syntax, kaleidoscopic imagery, inventive vocabulary, serious wordplay, and vigorous, variable rhythms may at times make for a clotted dialogue that is difficult for modern theatre audiences to understand. What, then, are we to think of Donald W. Foster's argument that *A Funeral Elegy* written in memory of an Exeter gentleman by the name of William Peter and published in 1612 as the work of 'W.S.', is Shakespeare's?[6] Foster is duly cautious in advancing this thesis, and he briefly outlines a case for William Strachey as an alternative author, but his belief that Shakespeare wrote the *Elegy* is clearly the main motivation behind his book, which is largely devoted to presenting the evidence for this conclusion. Peter was murdered 25 January 1612, and the poem – 578 lines of cross-rhymed iambic pentameters – was entered on 13 February of the same year, so the date of composition can be precisely fixed. 'The Peter elegy', writes Foster, 'is superior to most other memorial verse of the age, but ... I find the poetry itself rather disappointing – no

---

[4] Noel R. Blincoe, '"Sex individual" as Used in *The Two Noble Kinsmen*', *Notes and Queries*, 35 (1988), 484–5, argues against the customary emendation, made by Waith, to 'sex dividual' at 1.3.82. Blincoe explains, 'Emilia means by the phrase "sex individual", the union of man and woman in wedlock', and cites Henry Cockeram's *English Dictionary* of 1623: 'Individual, not to be parted as man and wife'.

[5] Quoted by Waith, p. 10.

[6] Donald W. Foster, *Elegy by W.S.: A Study in Attribution* (Newark: University of Delaware Press, London and Toronto: Associated University Presses, 1989).

better, if no worse, than what may be found in *Henry VIII* or *The Two Noble Kinsmen*' (p. 201). This strikes me, as it would have struck De Quincey, as an extraordinary statement, revealing a certain impercipience about the very nature of Shakespeare's distinction as a poet.

Shakespeare's poetic language is concrete, incessantly linking words to things and deeds. It is packed with sensuous content. It is active, dynamic. It caters to the inner ear and eye. It is supercharged with metaphor that constantly stimulates the reader's or auditor's imagination. In mature Shakespearian verse words vitalize one another, drawing out latent images and associations. *A Funeral Elegy*, in contrast, has a predominant air of dull abstraction; forays into the figurative end in muddled cliché. The poem is by no means negligible, but it is the product of a dutifully moralistic mind with none of Shakespeare's linguistic awareness, penchant for the particular, or creative flair. Or so it seems to me.

The parallels that Foster notes between the *Elegy* and *Richard II* are more instructive than he realizes. He compares, for example, 'The grave, that in this ever-empty womb / For ever closes up the unrespected' (*Elegy*, 423–4) with 'a grave, / Whose hollow womb inherits nought but bones' (*Richard II* 2.1.82–3), and 'When the proud height of much affected sin / Shall ripen to a head' (*Elegy*, 175–6) with 'foul sin, gathering head, / Shall break into corruption' (*Richard II* 5.1.58–9). The author of the *Elegy* has caught onto the womb-tomb paradox, but succeeds only in making it seem uninteresting; the 'bones' in *Richard II* bring to the image a vividness that the poem lacks. In the passage from *Richard II*, 5.1, the idea of a suppurating boil is implicit in the combination of words; the *Elegy*'s 'ripen to a head' has the potential for the same metaphorical substance, but the author neutralizes it with 'the proud height' – which makes one wonder whether he envisaged sin as a field of ripening corn, but the context does nothing to support such a notion. Whereas in Shakespeare's verse a whole group of words is animated by a basic image or complex of images, in the *Elegy* ill-assorted poetic clichés are bundled lifelessly together.

The contrast is even clearer in another pair of passages. The *Elegy* says of William Peter that

> his mind and body made an inn,
> The one to lodge the other, both like fram'd
> For fair conditions, guests that soonest win
> Applause   (113–16).

Here the mind and body together constitute an 'inn', while the body is also the conventional inn in which the mind lodges. And both mind and body are 'fram'd / For fair conditions', which are welcome guests – as though there had now been built two inns, to which good qualities repaired. This is not complexity but confusion. The author does not really think in images; for him words are mere counters to be marshalled into rhyming lines. In the parallel that Foster cites from *Richard II* 5.1.13–15, the relation between the different types of inn (representing Richard and Bolingbroke) and their abstract guests is consistently and fully imagined in lines that have real metaphorical life:

> Thou most beauteous inn:
> Why should hard-favoured grief be lodged in thee,
> When triumph is become an alehouse guest?

Foster finds in the *Elegy* a Shakespearian partiality for hendiadys, but the poem offers nothing resembling such vital collocations as 'the rose and expectancy of the fair state', 'the inaudible and noiseless foot of time', or 'the perfume and suppliance of a minute'.

Nevertheless, Foster's book is of considerable interest and value. He reprints *A Funeral Elegy* for the first time, in facsimile and in an edited modern-spelling text, gives a lively account of the circumstances of William Peter's death, and provides statistical data for features of vocabulary, prosody, grammar, syntax, and so on, in the *Elegy*, in the acknowledged works of Shakespeare, and in a 'cross-sample' of memorial verse of the period 1570–1630, consisting of forty poems by almost as many authors. Tables show counts for the *Elegy* repeatedly falling within an expected Shakespearian range when other funeral verses do not. On Foster's criteria the *Elegy* is more 'Shakespearian' than any of the control texts. He seeks also to establish some likelihood of a connection between Shakespeare and the worthy young gentleman whom the poet commemorates. He offers much useful information: his newly calculated table of percentages of 'unstopped lines' in Shakespeare's works is one of the best indicators yet of the chronological order of composition. And the concluding chapter, in which he discusses the theoretical issues of canonical studies, is excellent. He has obviously done a lot of painstaking research. How am I to reconcile the results of his tests with my conviction that the *Elegy* is not the product of Shakespeare's imagination?

It seems probable that there has been a degree of unconscious bias in the selection and application of the tests. On page 133, for example, Foster prints a table in which the *Elegy* is presented as conforming more closely than elegies by Donne, Tourneur, and Webster to Shakespearian expectations for word-length. The proportion of words of one, two, three, four, five, and six or more syllables in the Peter *Elegy* falls within an estimated Shakespearian range, but the poems by Donne and Tourneur are unShakespearian in two of the six categories, as is the Webster poem in one of them. But the proper way of comparing the four elegies to the Shakespearian sample is by means of a chi-square 'goodness of fit' test, using the raw figures. When this is carried out the elegies by Webster, Tourneur, and Donne (with their chi-square values of 18.9, 22.2, and 25.5) can be seen to match the Shakespearian sample much more closely than does the Peter *Elegy* (with its chi-square value of 79.0).[7]

In an interesting section on high-frequency function words Foster declares that of all the words in Shakespeare's collected vocabulary, 'there are nine, and only nine – *and, but, by, in, not, so, that, to, with,* – that never deviate in the plays by more than a third from their respective mean frequencies' (p. 141). He claims that the four prepositions (*by, in, to, with*) have 'little if any value as indices of style', and shows that when *most* and *like* are added to the other five words, the *Elegy* exhibits Shakespearian rates for all seven, whereas none of the poems in the cross-sample shows Shakespearian rates for more than four. But had he not dismissed the prepositions from consideration, he would have obtained results far less favourable to his case. *In* occurs in the *Elegy* with exceptional frequency – 139 times, or at a rate of 32.1 times per one thousand words. The overall rate for Shakespeare's plays is 13.1, and for no play is the rate higher than the 16.5 of *Henry V*.[8] For the non-dramatic works the rate is higher, 17.6 overall,[9] but using the same method that Foster himself uses on pages 142–4 of his book we would obtain 13–16 instances of *in* per thousand words as the range within which the rate for a Shakespeare poem written in 1611 would probably fall, and 13–22 as a possible range. The collocation *in the* is especially common in the *Elegy*, occurring twenty-four times for a rate of 5.5 per thousand words. In Shakespeare's non-dramatic works the rates range from 1.4 for *The Rape of Lucrece*, through 1.7 for the *Sonnets* and 2.0 for *Venus and Adonis*, to 2.3 for *A Lover's Complaint*.[10] In two late plays for which

---

[7] The larger the chi-square value, the greater the difference between the samples. The test is described by Anthony Kenny in *The Computation of Style: An Introduction to Statistics for Students of Literature and Humanities* (Oxford: Pergamon Press, 1982).

[8] My figures, derived from Spevack's concordance, include instances of contracted forms, such as *in't*. The only play excluded from consideration is *Sir Thomas More*.

[9] This figure ignores *The Passionate Pilgrim* (for which the rate is 15.1).

[10] 'The Phoenix and Turtle' is obviously too short to offer meaningful data; my remarks concerning Shakespeare's poems ignore it.

the data are available the rates are similar: 1.8 in *Cymbeline* and 1.9 in *The Winter's Tale*.

The incidence of *with* in the *Elegy* would also be anomalous for Shakespeare. It occurs twenty-six times, which yields a rate of 6.0 instances per thousand words, lower than for any Shakespeare play and for any of the non-dramatic works in pentameters. Again using Foster's own procedures, we would obtain an expected late-Shakespearian frequency of 10–13 and a possible range of 9–15. The *Elegy* uses *by* too often to have been written by Shakespeare – forty times, for a rate per thousand words of 9.2. For Shakespeare's non-dramatic works the range is quite narrow, 5.1 in *Venus and Adonis*, 5.3 in the *Sonnets*, 6.2 in *A Lover's Complaint*, and 6.3 in *The Rape of Lucrece*, while *Cymbeline* and *The Winter's Tale* are typical of the late plays with rates of 4.5 and 5.1. *To*, which occurs 133 times in the *Elegy*, is also used at an unShakespearian rate of 30.7 instances per thousand words. Rates for plays range from 18.6 in *1 Henry IV* to 26.6 in *Measure for Measure*;[11] there is no tendency for the rates to increase towards the end of Shakespeare's career, and those for poems range from 19.4 in *Venus and Adonis*, through 23.2 and 22.4 in the *Sonnets* and *A Lover's Complaint*, to 27.1 in *The Rape of Lucrece*. Foster's assertion that for the four prepositions 'the practice of Shakespeare and W.S., though much the same, is not remarkably different from that of other English poets of the same era' (p. 141) is clearly incorrect; in respect of each one of the four prepositions, Shakespeare and 'W.S.', far from being 'much the same', are utterly dissimilar.

If such solid-looking blocks in the case that Foster constructs can be shown to be hollow, the whole edifice seems in danger of collapsing. Whether or not such suspicions are justified, the natural inference from those passages in the *Elegy* that Foster discusses on pages 171–6 of his book, namely lines 137–56 and 553–78, is that in 1611 'W.S.' had recently suffered disgrace at Oxford and was a young man – certainly very much younger than the forty-seven-year-old Shakespeare.[12]

In order to avoid selectivity in our handling of the objective data discovered in canonical studies, we need procedures that have clearly defined rules, that yield the same results when undertaken by different investigators, and that can correctly pick the writers of control texts whose authorship is known. M. W. A. Smith has evolved just such a set of computerized routines for dealing with Renaissance plays. Once he has a wider range of playtexts in machine readable form, his method – in which separate analyses are made of first words of speeches, all the other words of dialogue, and pairs of consecutive words – seems capable of settling many problems of the Shakespeare canon. He has already given good grounds for thinking that George Wilkins is more likely than Shakespeare to have written the first two acts of *Pericles*.[13]

Eliot Slater's techniques, now explained in a posthumously published book, cannot, as he had hoped, prove that Shakespeare wrote *Edward III* (1596), but they can help determine the date of composition of his undoubted plays.[14] By charting all instances of words that

---

[11] Acts 1–2 of *Pericles* are responsible for the slightly higher overall rate (27.6) for that play.

[12] Foster lists some other almost insuperable obstacles to belief in Shakespeare's authorship of the *Elegy* in the last two paragraphs of his section on 'Contrary Evidence', pp. 197–202.

[13] 'A Procedure to Determine Authorship using Pairs of Consecutive Words: More Evidence for Wilkins's Participation in *Pericles*', *Computers and the Humanities*, 23 (1989), 113–29. Smith outlines his methods in 'Function Words and the Authorship of *Pericles*', *Notes and Queries*, 36 (1989), 333–6.

[14] *The Problem of 'The Reign of King Edward III': A Statistical Approach* (Cambridge University Press, 1988). For the limitations of Slater's techniques, see M. W. A. Smith, 'A Critical Review of Word-Links as a Method for Investigating Shakespearean Chronology and Authorship', *Literary and Linguistic Computing*, 1 (1986), 202–6, and 'Word-Links as a General Indicator of Chronology of Composition', *Notes and Queries*, 36 (1989), 338–41.

occur from two to ten times in more than one Shakespeare play, Slater demonstrated that there tend to be more links in vocabulary between plays written at about the same time. Likeness or unlikeness of subject matter and genre may increase or decrease the degree of linkage, but the chronological factor is dominant. Slater's method was to compare by the use of chi-square tests the actual number of word links between plays with the number to be expected were the distribution purely random and proportional to total vocabulary size. The results are presented in a series of tables. His data do confirm the dual authorship of certain plays: for example, the last three acts of *Pericles* link most strongly with *The Tempest*, whereas in the first two acts the links are haphazardly distributed among early, middle, and late plays, and links with *The Tempest* are well below chance expectation. Slater's valuable book includes a survey of scholarship on *Edward III*.

Also appearing in the series of studies supplementary to the New Cambridge Shakespeare is a collection of essays on *Sir Thomas More*.[15] The volume on *More* edited for Cambridge University Press in 1923 by A. W. Pollard concentrated on strengthening the case for accepting the three 'Hand D' pages as Shakespeare's autograph. The new essays range more widely. William Long considers the occasion of the play's original composition; Scott McMillin, 'setting aside questions of authorship and pursuing questions of the theatre instead', attempts to date the play by identifying the acting company or companies for which it was written; Giorgio Melchiori offers a detailed account of the script's evolution towards 'dramatic unity'; and John W. Velz, in 'Sir *Thomas More* and the Shakespeare Canon', reworks and supplements R. W. Chambers's celebrated contribution to Pollard's symposium. In 1980 Carol Chillington challenged orthodox opinion about *Sir Thomas More*, arguing that Hand D was not Shakespeare's but Webster's, and that the play had been written and revised for Henslowe in the early seventeenth century. Impressive rebuttals of Chillington's claims come from Charles R. Forker and Gary Taylor. Scrutinizing the disputed additions line by line and checking features of style, idiom, vocabulary, and spelling in concordances to the works of Shakespeare and of Webster, Forker establishes that in all respects Hand D and More's soliloquy in Hand C's Addition III are much more Shakespearian than Websterian. Taylor examines all the issues raised by Chillington, exposes the flaws in her logic, and shows that nothing that can reasonably be inferred about the history of the *More* playscript stands in the way of the identification of Hand D as Shakespeare's. In another solid contribution to the volume, John Jowett adduces a wealth of evidence that Chettle participated with Munday in the composition of the original text; comparison of Chettle's *Hoffman* with Munday's *John a Kent* yields various discriminators which, when applied to individual scenes of *More*, are in substantial agreement in indicating which of the two playwrights was mainly responsible. G. Harold Metz offers a comprehensive historical survey of *More* scholarship,[16] and editor T. H. Howard-Hill's preface to the book expertly and tactfully sums up the present state of knowledge and speculation. His contributors agree on an early date, such as Long's 1592–3, for the composition of the original text by Munday and Chettle (and perhaps others), but are divided over the date of the additions: Melchiori thinks that they were made 'not later

---

15 *Shakespeare and 'Sir Thomas More': Essays on the Play and its Shakespearian Interest*, ed. T. H. Howard-Hill (Cambridge University Press, 1989).

16 *Sources of Four Plays Ascribed to Shakespeare*, ed. G. Harold Metz (Columbia: University of Missouri Press, 1989), includes introductory surveys of scholarship on *Edward III*, *Sir Thomas More*, *Cardenio*, and *The Two Noble Kinsmen*, and reprints the main sources for each play.

than 1594' (p. 95),[17] and while McMillin assigns most of them to the seventeenth century he believes that Hand D's belonged to the early 1590s; but Taylor argues strongly that they were all written after 1600, probably in 1603–4.

This book registers an increased interest in *Sir Thomas More* as a theatrical document and as a play of some intrinsic merit. Yet the possibility that the manuscript includes three pages composed by Shakespeare and in his handwriting remains far and away the most interesting thing about it. The stylistic and sub-stylistic evidence associating the Hand D addition with the middle-to-late phase of Shakespeare's playwriting career is so strong that I do not see how it is possible to reject Taylor's dating without also rejecting Shakespeare's authorship.

There is still some doubt whether Hand B of the *More* manuscript is Thomas Heywood's. In *Notes and Queries* Thomas Merriam tackles the question by comparing letter frequencies in three 25,000-letter samples from each of Heywood's autograph plays, *The Captives* and *The Escapes of Jupiter*, and two from Munday's autograph play, *John a Kent*, with the figures for the 4,773 letters in Hand B.[18] Frequencies are assumed to reflect spelling habits. Merriam presents a table of correlation coefficients between the various samples. This shows that correlations for texts by the same author are all higher than correlations for texts by different authors, and that the correlation between Hand B and the six Heywood samples is of the order associated with texts by different authors. Merriam denies that these results can be explained by the relatively small size of the Hand B sample, and asserts that if all the sample blocks were reduced to 4,773 letters the 861 correlations that would then have to be made would still fall into the same pattern.

'Shall I die?' continues to receive attention. Thomas A. Pendleton has undertaken a minute examination of the poem's language that, to his mind, 'clearly establishes that it cannot be Shakespeare's' (p. 323).[19] His method is 'to present occurrences in the poem of words used with at least some frequency in Shakespeare's authentic work, but bearing in "Shall I die?" meanings that they virtually or literally never bear in that authentic work' (p. 328). He has compiled an impressive list, but several items might be challenged. The poet, for example, says that his mistress suffers from 'Noe mishap, noe scape / Inferior to natures perfection'. Gary Taylor's text in the Oxford *Complete Works* modernizes 'mishap' as 'mis-shape'. Pendleton, while arguing that 'mis-shape' is itself unShakespearian in such a context, regards Taylor's 'emendation' as 'a desperate attempt to exculpate the text from saying what Shakespeare would not have said'. But although 'mishap' and 'mis-shape' are, as Pendleton asserts, 'completely distinct words semantically and etymologically' (p. 346), they are less distinct orthographically. Of *OED*'s five citations of the noun 'mis-shape' only the first (1465) and last (1875) have the 'ss' spelling; examples from 1542, 1610, and 1654 employ a single 's', and the rhyme with 'scape' lends support to the modernization of the Bodleian manuscript's word as 'mis-shape'. John Weever's 'mishapt' (1601), for instance, is correctly cited by *OED* under 'mis-shaped'.

Yet another attempt to enlarge the Shakespeare canon is that of Eric Rasmussen, who suggests that the fifty lines of additional material inserted, on five separate slips of paper, into the manuscript of *The Second Maiden's Tragedy* were written not, as has previously been believed, by the author of the original play, who has been identified on internal evidence as Thomas Middleton, but by Shakespeare as he

---

[17] He reaches the same conclusion in 'The Master of the Revels and the Date of the Additions to *The Book of Sir Thomas More*', in *Shakespeare: Text, Language, Criticism: Essays in Honour of Marvin Spevack*, ed. Bernhard Fabian and Kurt Tetzeli von Rosador (Hildesheim: Olms-Weidmann, 1987), pp. 164–79.

[18] 'Was Hand B in *Sir Thomas More* Heywood's Autograph?', *Notes and Queries*, 35 (1988), 455–8.

[19] 'The Non-Shakespearian Language of "Shall I die?"', *Review of English Studies*, 40 (1989), 323–51.

revised the script for the King's Men.[20] My own reasons for thinking Rasmussen mistaken will appear in a forthcoming issue of *Shakespeare Quarterly*.

Investigators of problems of authorship connected with the Shakespeare canon have a new tool in the *Electronic Edition* of the Oxford *Complete Works*, which holds the modern-spelling text on twenty 5.25-inch disks or ten 3.5-inch disks for use with the IBM PC and compatibles.[21] A comprehensive coding scheme distinguishes elements in both the text and the extra-textual material. Micro-OCP, Oxford's easily usable microcomputer concordance programme, can search any portion of this machine-readable Shakespeare text in order to generate lists and counts of words, grammatical forms, phrases, collocates, and so on. These mechanical aids have, for example, enabled me to determine that the first two acts of *Pericles* afford, proportionally to the total number of rhymes, more rhyme-links with George Wilkins's *The Miseries of Enforced Marriage* than does any other part of the Shakespeare corpus. But the *Electronic Edition* of the *Complete Works* will facilitate many other sorts of stylistic, thematic, and lexical analysis. For Shakespeare scholars who are also users of personal computers this form of the Oxford edition is a highly desirable acquisition.

The latest issue of *TEXT* contains several articles of particular interest to editors of Shakespeare.[22] Discussing various ways in which our task is 'to turn triangles into straight lines', Gary Taylor concludes that the 'substance of textual criticism cannot be disentangled from its rhetoric' (p. 53). In an article backed by a great deal of meticulous typographical analysis, Adrian Weiss exposes the limitations of 'Reproductions of Early Dramatic Texts as a Source of Bibliographical Evidence', pp. 237–68. T. H. Howard-Hill's concern in 'Playwrights' Intentions and the Editing of Plays', pp. 269–78, is with the special consequences that follow from the fact that for plays, as distinct from purely literary texts, 'the

ultimate facilitating interpreter of authorial intention is a company of actors in the theatre' (p. 270); he draws attention to the correspondence provoked in the *Times Literary Supplement* of 1935 by some remarks by C. S. Lewis that seem strangely prescient of attitudes taken in, for example, the Oxford Shakespeare. Yet not all plays, even by successful practising dramatists, are most appropriately considered as achieving their fullest realization in performance. Ben Jonson's *Sejanus*, which failed on the stage, was, as John Jowett points out, subjected to an authoritative rewriting 'that systematically repressed the play as theatre' and in the course of its transmission into print 'received the author's persistent and creative invigilance' (p. 279). In this case the Quarto of 1609, with its Latin marginalia and sculpted blocks of dialogue, is a veritable icon to Jonson's untheatrical intentions. The measures that Jonson took 'make the play impressive as a literary artefact' and 'defensively redefine it in relation to its public' (p. 281). We need a photographic facsimile, complete with introduction and commentary. Fredson Bowers's presidential address, 'Unfinished Business', which prefaces this volume of *TEXT*, pp. 1–11, emphasizes the flexibility of 'our developed conventional editorial theory' and defends it against the increasingly popular notion that, the author's former primacy having dwindled, 'the most definitive textual form of a book results from the collaborative work of author, editor, copyreader, compositor, and proofreader' (p. 6).

---

[20] 'Shakespeare's Hand in *The Second Maiden's Tragedy*', *Shakespeare Quarterly*, 40 (1989), 1–26.
[21] William Shakespeare, *The Complete Works: Electronic Edition*, ed. Stanley Wells, Gary Taylor, John Jowett, and William Montgomery (Oxford University Press, 1989); electronic text prepared by William Montgomery and Lou Burnard.
[22] *TEXT: Transactions of the Society for Textual Scholarship* 4, ed. D. C. Greetham and W. Speed Hill (New York: AMS Press, 1988). The following details supplement those in the body of my review: Taylor, 'The Rhetoric of Textual Criticism', 39–57; Jowett, '"Fall before this Booke": The 1605 Quarto of *Sejanus*', 279–95.

The collaboration of performers in the realization of a theatrical script is, however, a different matter. T. H. Howard-Hill's 'Modern Textual Theories and the Editing of Plays' reinforces his article in *TEXT*.[23] Reconsidering the classic theories associated with McKerrow and Greg in the light of accepted facts of theatre history, Howard-Hill ends with 'three main contentions', of which 'the third is the most important': 'authorial intentions relinquished to the theatre by design and custom should be completed by an editor in accordance with his understanding of the author's intentions as reflected in surviving documents, and of the theatrical milieu in which the playwright wrote' (p. 115). This article offers a knowledgeable, bold, and clear-headed discussion of issues relevant to all editors of Shakespeare.[24]

An issue of *Renaissance Drama* is also devoted to essays on texts of Renaissance plays.[25] Paul Werstine is convinced of the futility of our attempts to classify printed texts of Shakespeare's plays as deriving from 'foul papers', 'promptbooks', and 'reports'. He argues that the extant manuscripts dissolve distinctions between these categories, inherited from McKerrow and Greg, since features supposed to identify one kind of text turn up in the others. Werstine raises issues that must concern textual critics and editors of Shakespeare and his fellow dramatists over the next few years. What do we know, and what can we legitimately infer, about the kinds of manuscripts created as Renaissance plays evolved from being mere ideas in a playwright's head to theatrical scripts governing performances? And what characteristics, if any, of printed texts can serve to suggest the likely status of the manuscript copy?[26] Werstine's thoroughgoing scepticism should encourage a methodical attempt to re-answer such questions. His own article is not without its provocative exaggerations. It is, for example, a distortion of the views advanced in the Oxford *Textual Companion* to state that the editors promote such 'bad quartos' as *Henry V* and *Richard III* 'to the top of the hierarchy of

classes of text' (p. 170), considering them the 'best of all' (p. 156) and 'exact records of performance' (p. 162). Their claim is the less extravagant one that, for all their many im-

---

23 *The Library*, 11 (1989), 89–115.
24 Another theoretical paper is Marion Trousdale's 'Diachronic and Synchronic: Critical Bibliography and the Acting of Plays', in *Shakespeare: Text, Language, Criticism* (as in n. 17), pp. 304–14. She perceives contradictions between our desire to assimilate Shakespeare's plays into a literary tradition of 'works which are stable and permanent, and . . . can be held as books in the hand' and the essential nature of those works, which 'are perhaps more accurately seen as texts held not in the hand but in the language, fluid, variable, inconsistent as is any oral discourse, and as, it would seem, were the working methods of the age itself' (p. 313). In 'Bulgakov's Lizard and the Problem of the Playwright's Authority', *TEXT*, 4 (1988), 385–406, John Glavin argues that 'a text's function in and for the theatre inevitably subverts the playwright's authority to circumscribe the limits of his inscription even in the original production' (p. 386).
25 *Renaissance Drama*, 19 (1988). The volume is subtitled *Essays on Texts of Renaissance Plays*, ed. Mary Beth Rose (Evanston: Northwestern University Press and The Newberry Library Center for Renaissance Studies). Full details of contents are as follows: Jonathan Goldberg, 'Rebel Letters: Postal Effects from *Richard II* to *Henry IV*', 3–28; Annabel Patterson, 'Back by Popular Demand: The Two Versions of *Henry V*', 29–62; Joseph Loewenstein, 'Plays Agonistic and Competitive: The Textual Approach to Elsinore', 63–96; Barbara Mowat, 'The Form of *Hamlet*'s Fortunes', 97–126; David Bevington, 'Editing Renaissance Drama in Paperback', 127–47; Paul Werstine, 'McKerrow's "Suggestion" and Twentieth-Century Shakespeare Textual Criticism', 149–73; Leslie Thomson, 'Broken Brackets and 'Mended Texts: Stage Directions in the Oxford Shakespeare', 175–93; Gary Taylor, 'Textual and Sexual Criticism: A Crux in *The Comedy of Errors*', 195–225; C. E. McGee (ed.), 'Cupid's Banishment: A Masque Presented to Her Majesty by Young Gentlewomen of the Ladies Hall, Deptford, May 4, 1617', 227–64. Points similar to Mowat's are made by Grace Ioppolo, '"Old" and "New" Revisionists: Shakespeare's Eighteenth-Century Editors', *Huntington Library Quarterly*, 52 (1989), 347–61.
26 T. H. Howard-Hill's examination of two theatrical manuscripts may be mentioned here: 'Crane's 1619 "Promptbook" of *Barnavelt* and Theatrical Processes', *Modern Philology*, 86 (1988), 146–70; 'The Author as Scribe or Reviser? Middleton's Intentions in *A Game at Chess*', *TEXT*, 3 (1987), 305–18.

perfections, the 'bad quartos' contain some readings that correspond more closely than those of alternative texts to Shakespeare's 'final intentions' for the play on the stage.

On *Henry V* Annabel Patterson, in the same volume of *Renaissance Drama*, would go further: in her view, the theory which 'explains the greatest number of the most significant divergences' between Quarto and Folio *Henry V* is that the Quarto derives from Shakespeare's own abridgement, which represents 'a tactical retreat from one kind of play to another, from a complex historiography that might have been misunderstood to a symbolic enactment of nationalistic fervor' (pp. 40–1). She connects the preparation of the shorter, more jingoistic version with the Essex crisis, but it is uncertain whether she thinks it was done for theatrical performance (as seems to be implied on p. 40) or expressly for publication (as seems to be implied on pp. 46–7). Jonathan Goldberg's dazzling exhibition of pseudo-critical wordplay is less concerned with the text than with 'text', 'textuality', and the 'textualized'; the probabilities are against his one proposal about the text, in the old-fashioned sense of the word – that it should be Hal who at the end of *1 Henry IV*, 2.5, reads aloud Falstaff's tavern bill. Joseph Loewenstein's essay centres on the lines about the 'eyrie of children' that appear in the Folio text of *Hamlet*, and are represented in Q1, but are absent from Q2. Loewenstein does not use the passage to argue for any particular relationship between the texts. His thesis, he says, 'is that in these lines Shakespeare makes *Hamlet* the sign of important authorial and historical emergencies', and his goal 'is to describe, not what happens in *Hamlet*, but what *Hamlet* happens, specifically how these lines locate the play in what can, without terminological strain, be referred to as the cultural *economy* of the English Renaissance' (p. 64). It is unclear to me whether or not he achieves this mysterious goal.

Other articles in the volume are more traditional in their textual concerns. Barbara Mowat writes a carefully researched history of the editing of *Hamlet*, correcting inaccuracies in the current record, and showing that on a long view the radical instability of the text in the 1980s 'is more typical than unusual' (p. 98). David Bevington, fresh from editing the Bantam Shakespeare,[27] discusses the many practical decisions on general policy – concerning layout, spelling, hyphenization, and so on – that must be made by the editor of Renaissance drama in a popular paperback series. Without ever adopting a captious tone, Leslie Thomson draws attention to some difficulties about the treatment of stage directions in the new Oxford *Complete Works*. Remarking on the 'underrepresentation of women in the Shakespearean editorial club' (p. 197), Gary Taylor reasons his way towards a solution of a crux in a speech expressing a woman's point of view, that of the aggrieved Adriana, wife of Antipholus of Ephesus, in *The Comedy of Errors*. And C. E. McGee edits, with introduction, the rediscovered manuscript of Robert White's masque, *Cupid's Banishment*.

While Werstine chips away at the early twentieth-century foundations of Shakespearian textual criticism, Steven Urkowitz concentrates his attack on the hypothesis that the 'bad quartos' were printed from memorially reconstructed texts.[28] He favours the old

---

[27] *Bantam Shakespeare: The Complete Works*, ed. David Bevington, and others (New York: Bantam Books, 1988), 29 vols.

[28] '"If I Mistake Those Foundations Which I Build Upon": Peter Alexander's Textual Analysis of *Henry VI* Parts 2 and 3', *English Literary Renaissance*, 18 (1988), 230–56; 'Good News about "Bad" Quartos', in *"Bad" Shakespeare: Revaluations of the Shakespeare Canon*, ed. Maurice Charney (Rutherford, Madison, Teaneck: Fairleigh Dickinson University Press, London and Toronto: Associated University Presses, 1988), 189–206; in 'Five Women Eleven Ways: Changing Images of Shakespearean Characters in the Earliest Texts', in *Images of Shakespeare*, ed. Werner Habicht, D. J. Palmer, and Roger Pringle (Newark: University of Delaware Press, London and Toronto: Associated University Presses, 1988), pp. 292–304, Urkowitz urges that we should 'read, criticize, and perform ... multiple text plays in their multiplicity' (p. 304). In 'The Original

view that they are based on Shakespeare's earliest drafts. In particular, he seeks to expose flaws in Peter Alexander's influential analysis of the Quarto of *The First Part of the Contention* (*2 Henry VI* in the Folio) and the Octavo of *Richard Duke of York* (*3 Henry VI*), arguing 'that the historical analogues Alexander proposes are invalid, that Alexander's theatrical, literary, and bibliographical interpretations of important textual variants are wrong, that he omits crucial evidence from the chronicle sources, and that the conclusions he draws from the evidence he offers are supportable only by suppressing contradictory examples and by ignoring surrounding contexts' (p. 232). Where Urkowitz and Alexander disagree over the relationship between a passage in the Quarto or Octavo and in the Folio, Alexander's interpretation of the evidence usually seems more plausible to me. But to set forth the grounds of my disagreement with Urkowitz's disagreement with Alexander would be impossible within the scope of this survey. The provenance and nature of the 'bad quartos' are matters that will continue to require reconsideration, and Urkowitz's plea that in our evaluation of these texts we take due account of theatrical values is one that participants in the debate must heed.

One 'bad quarto' to have attracted at least its fair share of respect lately for its supposed 'theatricality' is QI of *Hamlet*. David E. Jones, who believes that in the order of its scenes QI takes us nearer than Q2 or F to 'performance as Shakespeare [eventually] envisaged it' (p. 104), calls for an edition of *Hamlet* 'which rearranges FI and cuts it in accord with QI' (p. 109).[29] This would certainly be of interest.

Urkowitz has a strident ally in Eric Sams, who ridicules the textual theories of the Arden, Cambridge, and Oxford editors of *Hamlet*, especially the notion that QI is based on a memorial reconstruction.[30] John Dover Wilson is accused of using 'Mad Hatter's logic' to produce 'shameless nonsense' (p. 28), G. I. Duthie of having 'no firm grasp of what constitutes evidence or reasoning' (p. 31), Harold

Jenkins of making 'outrageous' claims (p. 30), and so on. Sams's own view is that Shakespeare wrote the *Ur-Hamlet* first mentioned in 1589, that this early play is preserved in QI, that Q2 is Shakespeare's enlarged and improved version, and that F represents a further revision. He quotes samples of QI lines that – as I understand him – he believes to belong to the *Ur-Hamlet*. These include 'Borne before an everlasting judge' (spelling modernized) from QI's rendering of 'To be or not to be', but Sams does not say whether he considers QI's ludicrous text of the whole soliloquy to be authentic. Nor does he explain why the one scrap of dialogue recorded from stagings of the *Ur-Hamlet* – the Ghost's 'Hamlet, revenge!' – is absent from QI. But he does make some worthwhile points. The author of the *Ur-Hamlet* had evidently anglicized Belleforest's Amleth to Hamlet. As an argument for Shakespeare's authorship of the lost play, Sams connects the name-change with the occurrence of Hamlet as a 'Stratford name' (p. 19) – that of Katherine Hamlett, drowned in the Avon in 1579 in circumstances echoed in Ophelia's fate, and of Shakespeare's friend Hamlet (or Hamnet) Sadler, after whom the playwright's own son was christened in

---

Staging of *The First Part of the Contention* (1594), *Shakespeare Survey* 41 (Cambridge University Press, 1989), 13–22, William Montgomery, accepting the theory of memorial reconstruction, demonstrates that 'the text as reported reflects the full staging facilities of a well equipped London amphitheatre or hall playhouse', though it 'may have been put together *for* a provincial tour' (p. 22).

29 'The Theatricality of the First Quarto of *Hamlet*', *Hamlet Studies*, 10 (1988), 104–10. Also worth recording here are two items missed from previous reviews: David Richman, 'The *King Lear* Quarto in Rehearsal and Performance', *Shakespeare Quarterly*, 37 (1986), 374–82; Gerald D. Johnson, '*The Merry Wives of Windsor*, QI: Provincial Touring and Adapted Texts', *Shakespeare Quarterly*, 38 (1987), 154–65.

30 'Taboo or Not Taboo? The Text, Dating and Authorship of *Hamlet*, 1589–1623', *Hamlet Studies*, 10 (1988), 12–46. See also Sams's 'Shakespeare, or Bottom? The Myth of "Memorial Reconstruction"', *Encounter*, January 1989, 41–5.

1585. Were real-life Hamlets really concentrated in Stratford at the period of the *Ur-Hamlet*'s composition, or is Kyd as likely as Shakespeare to have introduced this English form of the hero's name to the stage?

It is, of course, quite possible to reject the notion that the 'bad quartos' are based on Shakespeare's early drafts and yet accept other evidence of revision afforded by the various printed texts. In a paper delivered before the Oxford *Complete Works* appeared, co-editor Stanley Wells gives a characteristically lucid and well organized account of 'the kinds of revision that modern scholarship detects, or suspects, in Shakespeare's plays' and of the attendant problems and possible means of handling them (p. 69).[31] Several such problems are posed by the Folio text of *The Taming of the Shrew*, and they have a bearing on the question of its relation to *The Taming of a Shrew* (the indefinite article distinguishing the anonymous play from Shakespeare's). Wells and Gary Taylor examine them in an article showing that 'there is no need to hypothesize a lost source play' upon which the two extant ones are based, 'and that the only revision that needs to be postulated is such as might be expected to occur in the heat of composition, and so be preserved in foul papers' (p. 353).[32] Even if, as seems to me likely, *The Taming of the Shrew* was not set from autograph, the main conclusions may still stand.

Two more of the Garland Shakespeare Bibliographies have appeared: *Henry VIII*, compiled by Linda McJ. Micheli, and *Two Gentlemen of Verona*, compiled by D'Orsay W. Pearson;[33] and *Shakespeare's 'Othello': A Bibliography*, by John Hazel Smith, has been posthumously published by AMS Press, New York (1988). Pearson, assigned what R. S. White called the 'Cinderella' among Shakespeare's comedies, has worked hard to fill a volume, discovering that commentary on the play exists 'w[h]ere one may least expect to find it' (p. x). The Garland items are all annotated, and the introductions helpfully chart the territory.

Smith's volume contains a useful index to commentary on individual lines.

The two lines with the most entries are Iago's about Cassio being 'damned in a fair wife' and Othello's about the 'base Indian/Judean'. In a brief note I propose that 'Indiaes' in George Peele's *Edward I* should be emended to 'Judea's' (in modern spelling), and that the misprint may throw light on the *Othello* crux.[34] In the same *Notes and Queries* Robert F. Fleissner contends that Folio *Othello*'s 'Iudean' resulted from misreading,[35] and G. Harold Metz prolongs the debate about the sequence in which play, ballad, and prose history on Titus Andronicus were written; he argues for the priority of the prose history, wrongly in my opinion.[36]

Elizabethan printer John Wolfe had no

31 'Revision in Shakespeare's Plays', in *Editing and Editors: A Retrospect*, ed. Richard Landon (New York: AMS Press, 1988), papers from the University of Toronto conference on editorial problems, 1985, pp. 67–97. In 'The Unstable Image of Shakespeare's Text', *Images of Shakespeare* (as in n. 28), pp. 305–13, Wells touches on similar matters; the same book contains Klaus Bartenschlager's 'Editing Shakespeare for "Foreigners": The Case of the English-German *Studienausgabe* of Shakespeare's Plays', pp. 324–34. The implications of the theory that Shakespeare revised *King Lear* are considered by Klaus Bartenschlager and Hans Walter Gabler, 'Die zwei Fassungen von Shakespeares *King Lear*: Zum neuen Verhältnis von Textkritik und Literaturkritik', *Deutsche Shakespeare-Gesellschaft West Jahrbuch 1988*, pp. 163–86.

32 Stanley Wells and Gary Taylor, 'No Shrew, A Shrew, and The Shrew: Internal Revision in *The Taming of the Shrew*', in *Shakespeare: Text, Language, Criticism* (as in n. 17), pp. 351–70. Also in this volume, pp. 57–79, is G. Blakemore Evans's meticulous analysis of '*The Merry Wives of Windsor*: The Folger Manuscript', which is 'literary' and ultimately based on F2 (1632).

33 New York and London: Garland Publishing, 1988.

34 MacD. P. Jackson, 'India and Indian or Judea and Judean? Shakespeare's *Othello* v.ii.356, and Peele's *Edward I* 1.107', *Notes and Queries*, 35 (1988), 479–80.

35 'Base Iúdean' in *Othello* Again: Misprint or, More Likely, Misreading?', *Notes and Queries*, 35 (1988), 475–9.

36 '*Titus Andronicus*: Three Versions of the Story', *Notes and Queries*, 35 (1988), 451–5; compare MacD. P. Jackson, '*Titus Andronicus*: Play, Ballad, and Prose History', *Notes and Queries*, 36 (1989), 315–17.

Shakespearian associations, but he was involved with Gabriel Harvey's Martin Marprelate pamphlets and with Italian-language printing. In *Elizabethan Impressions: John Wolfe and His Press* (New York: AMS Press, 1988), Clifford Chalmers Huffman 'explores the contents of the books Wolfe printed, to identify what appear to have been their intellectual, artistic, cultural, and, in some cases, political interests' (p. x). Other bibliographical studies for the year include W. Craig Ferguson's 'Compositor Identification in *Romeo* Q1 and *Troilus*',[37] in which the spacing of speech prefixes and similar details of typography and spelling serve to refine earlier analyses of these quartos; Paul Werstine's 'More Unrecorded States in the Folger Shakespeare Library's Collection of First Folios',[38] and N. W. Bawcutt's 'A Ghost Press-variant in Folio *Measure for Measure*'.[39]

In 'Repetition, Revision, and Editorial Greed in Shakespeare's Play Texts' Kristian Smidt examines a variety of awkward duplications.[40] He suggests that Shakespeare may have meant, and even marked, for deletion more dramatically redundant material than editors have recognized. In 'Disambiguation in Recent Editions of Shakespeare's *Julius Caesar*: The Silent Tradition' John W. Velz looks at some expressions that editors have always, or nearly always, 'disambiguated' in the same way.[41] But we need not conclude that editors have acted like sheep. In virtually every case the Folio 'ambiguity' seems to me purely theoretical, in that it would disappear in performance: what member of a theatre audience, hearing 'groaning vnderneath this Ages yoake' or 'we can both / Endure the Winters cold, as well as he' or 'the Times Abuse' will understand anything but 'this age's yoke', 'the winter's cold', and 'the time's abuse', regardless of the position of the apostrophe or (in the case of 'winter's/winters cold') its inclusion or exclusion?

A few emendations have been proposed or revived. Ransacking Gerard's *Herbal* and other botanical books for information about the weeds that 'grow / In our sustaining corn',

Kathryn Sprinkle-Jackson supports the old notion that in *King Lear* the Quarto's 'hordocks' and Folio's 'hardokes' are charlocks, which Shakespeare may have known as harlocks, l/t confusion being responsible for the printed readings.[42] J. J. M. Tobin seeks to revive Theobald's suggestion that Hamlet's 'very very pajock' should be a 'puttock'.[43] In 'A Codfish and a Famous Bedside Scene' Francis Celoria cites a reference in John Fletcher's *Bonduca* to a character whose 'brave body' is 'Turn'd to a tail of green-fish without butter', and wonders whether Falstaff's nose was as sharp as a pen 'and a tail of green-fish'.[44] Somehow I rather doubt it.

In a more substantial piece, '"Runnawayes Eyes": A Genuine Crux', Roger Prior argues strongly that the Quarto text of *Romeo and Juliet* is in need of emendation at 3.2.5–7, where Juliet entreats:

> Spread thy close curtaine loue-performing night,
> That runnawayes eyes may wincke, and *Romeo*
> Leape to these arms, vntalkt of and vnseene.[45]

His demonstration that 'runnawayes' is unsatisfactory, however interpreted, is subtle and cogent. His own solution to the crux is suggested by Thomas Moffet's poem *The Silkworms and their Flies*, which has been seen as influencing the Pyramus and Thisbe interlude in *A Midsummer Night's Dream*, and which Prior now claims as an important source for *Romeo and Juliet*. Juliet's encomium to the night certainly appears to echo a passage from Moffet, from which Prior deduces that the

---

[37] *Studies in Bibliography*, 42 (1989), 211–18.

[38] *The Library*, 11 (1989), 47–51.

[39] *Shakespeare Quarterly*, 39 (1988), 360.

[40] *Cahiers Élisabéthains*, 34 (1988), 25–37.

[41] *Analytical and Enumerative Bibliography*, NS 2 (1988), 1–11.

[42] 'King Lear IV.iv.4: A Proposal for Emendation', *English Language Notes*, 26 (1989), 15–23.

[43] 'Kite Flying, Again', *Hamlet Studies*, 8 (1986), 93–6.

[44] *Notes and Queries*, 35 (1988), 470.

[45] *Shakespeare Quarterly*, 40 (1989), 191–5.

original of 'runnawayes' in Q *Romeo and Juliet* was a word meaning 'guards' or 'watchmen'; this word he takes to have been 'turnkeys', spelt 'turnekeyes' or possibly 'turnekayes'. Letter formations in Hand D of *Sir Thomas More* are adduced in support of the misreading of 't' as 'r' and of 'k' as 'w'.

Finally, in 'Textual Double Knots: "make rope's in such a scarre"', Gary Taylor sets forth at considerable length the reasoning that led him to emend this notorious crux in the Folio text of *All's Well That Ends Well* to (in modern spelling) 'make toys e'en such a surance';[46] this gets my vote for the most brilliant discussion of a Shakespearian textual crux that has ever been put into print.[47]

[46] In *Shakespeare: Text, Subtext, and Context*, ed. Ronald Dotterer (Selinsgrove: Susquehanna University Press, London and Toronto: Associated University Presses, 1989), pp. 163–85.

[47] The scope of this survey does not allow more than brief mention of the following items: two scholarly editions in the Revels series, Ben Jonson's *The Staple of News*, ed. Anthony Parr, and George Chapman's *The Conspiracy and Tragedy of Charles Duke of Byron*, ed. John Margeson (Manchester University Press, 1988); *The Plays of John Lyly*, ed. Carter A. Daniel (Lewisburg: Bucknell University Press, London and Toronto: Associated University Presses, 1988) – re-edited, in modern spelling, from microfilm copies of the original quartos, but with a minimum of textual apparatus; Sir William Berkeley's *The Lost Lady*, prepared by D. F. Rowan, G. R. Proudfoot, and Lois Potter for the Malone Society (1987): the transcription is of a Folger manuscript in the hand of a scribe, but containing corrections by the author and bearing evidence of theatrical origin; it deserves careful study by Shakespearian textual scholars. Also received was Peter Corbin and Douglas Sedge, *An Annotated Critical Bibliography of Jacobean and Caroline Comedy (excluding Shakespeare)* (London: Harvester Wheatsheaf, 1988).

EDITOR'S NOTE: Two regrettable errors crept into the review of 'Editions and Textual Studies' in *Shakespeare Survey 42*. On page 206, the last sentence of the second paragraph should read: 'Spevack's use of the possessive for "ancestors" at 1.3.81 is a sensible innovation.' And at the foot of column 2 of page 210 the words '*because* of our virtues – our powers *and* the' should be added.

BOOKS RECEIVED

This list includes all books received between 1 September 1988 and 31 August 1989 which are not reviewed in this volume of *Shakespeare Survey*. The appearance of a book in this list does not preclude its review in a subsequent volume.

Cohen, Michael. *Hamlet in my Mind's Eye.* Athens (G.A.) and London: University of Georgia Press, 1989.

Fabricius, Johannes. *Shakespeare's Hidden World: A Study of his Unconscious.* Copenhagen: Munksguard, 1989.

Iselin, Pierre, and Jean-Pierre Moreau, eds. *Le Songe d'une Nuit d'été et La Duchesse de Malfi. (Texte et représentation).* Actes du colloque Shakespeare-Webster, Limoges. Limoges: University of Limoges, 1988.

Kiernan, Ryan. *Shakespeare.* Harvester New Readings, 1989.

Kullman, Thomas. *Abschied, Reise und Wiedersehen bein Shakespeare: Zu Gestaltung und Funktion epischer und Romanhafter Motive im Drama.* Tübingen: Max Niemeyer Verlag, 1989.

Porter, Joseph A., *Shakespeare's Mercutio: His History and Drama.* Chapel Hill and London: University of North Carolina Press, 1989.

Snyder, Susan, ed. *Othello: Critical Essays. Shakespeare Criticism Vol. 7*, New York and London: Garland, 1988.

Toliver, Harold. *Transported Styles in Shakespeare and Milton.* University Park and London: Penn State University Press, 1989.

Wells, Charles. *The Northern Star: Shakespeare and the Theme of Constancy.* Upton-upon-Severn: Blackthorn Press, 1989.

INDEX

INDEX

INDEX

INDEX

INDEX

INDEX

INDEX

DATE DUE

DEMCO 38-297